Medieval to Renaissance
in English Poetry

Medieval to Renaissance in English Poetry

A. C. SPEARING

*Fellow of Queens' College, Cambridge
and Reader in Medieval
English Literature*

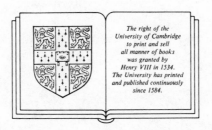

The right of the
University of Cambridge
to print and sell
all manner of books
was granted by
Henry VIII in 1534.
The University has printed
and published continuously
since 1584.

CAMBRIDGE UNIVERSITY PRESS

Cambridge
London   New York   New Rochelle
Melbourne   Sydney

Published by the Press Syndicate of the University of Cambridge
The Pitt Building, Trumpington Street, Cambridge CB2 1RP
32 East 57th Street, New York, NY 10022, USA
10 Stamford Road, Oakleigh, Melbourne 3166, Australia

© Cambridge University Press 1985

First published 1985

Printed in Great Britain at the University Press, Cambridge

Library of Congress catalogue card number: 85–375

British Library Cataloguing in Publication Data
Spearing, A. C.
Medieval to Renaissance in English poetry.
1. English poetry – Middle English, 1100–1500 –
History and criticism   2. English Poetry –
Early Modern, 1500–1700 – History and criticism
I. Title
821'.2PR521
ISBN 0 521 24769 1 hard covers
ISBN 0 521 31533 6 paperback

Contents

Contents

Preface

In some ways this book is a development of trains of thought implicit in earlier work of mine on late-medieval literature – in particular, those of the final section of *Medieval Dream-Poetry* (Cambridge University Press, 1976) and, still further back, of the chapter on *The Testament of Cresseid* in *Criticism and Medieval Poetry* (Edward Arnold, 1964 and 1972) and of my edition of *The Knight's Tale* (Cambridge University Press, 1966). But the present book would certainly not have taken its actual form if I had not had the good fortune of being Visiting Professor of English at the University of Virginia in the academic year 1979–80, and of being asked to teach a graduate course on Medieval Transitions to the Renaissance. I am deeply indebted to the participants in that course (several of them potential scholars of considerable distinction) and to many colleagues in the English department at Charlottsville for the intellectual stimulus I gained from contact with them. I cannot be sure that Mr Jefferson would have approved of the outcome, but he cannot escape a share in the responsibility for the book's existence.

I am also indebted to the Cambridge students on whom various drafts were tried out, over several years, in lectures and supervisions given in connection with a course with the same title as the book; and to colleagues and other participants in the Medieval Graduate Seminar of the Cambridge English Faculty, who have helped and suffered likewise. The book's procedure has been influenced, not for the worse I hope, by its origin in teaching; that is, it aims to engage with large themes through the detailed analysis of specific texts.

Various parts of this book have been published elsewhere in earlier versions, and I wish to express my gratitude to editors and publishers as follows for granting me permission to re-use work which originally appeared under their auspices. Parts of chapters 1 and 2 were published under the titles 'Renaissance Chaucer' and 'Father Chaucer' in *English* 34 (1985).

Part of chapter 3 appeared as 'Lydgate's Canterbury Tale: *The Siege of Thebes* and Fifteenth-Century Chaucerianism' in *Fifteenth*

Preface

Century Studies: Recent Essays, ed. Robert F. Yeager (Archon Books, 1984); and another part of the same chapter as 'Chaucerian Authority and Inheritance' in *Literature in Fourteenth-Century England*, ed. Piero Boitani and Anna Torti (Gunter Narr Verlag, 1983). Part of chapter 4 appeared as '*The Awntyrs off Arthure*' in *The Alliterative Tradition in the Fourteenth Century*, ed. Bernard S. Levy and Paul E. Szarmach (Kent State University Press, 1981). Another portion of chapter 4 and part of chapter 5 appeared as an article, 'Central and Displaced Sovereignty in Three Medieval Poems' in *The Review of English Studies* n. s. 33 (1982), 247–61 (published by Oxford University Press).

I have also benefited greatly from the opportunity to discuss some of the book's ideas in connection with lectures given in universities other than those of Cambridge and Virginia. There have been too many such occasions for me to list them all here; I am grateful to all my hosts, but I would particularly like to mention the hospitality of the State University of New York at Binghamton (1975); the University of California at Davis (1980); the University of Bristol (Tucker-Cruse Lecture 1981); the University of Perugia (J. A. W. Bennett Memorial Lecture 1982); the University of Utrecht (English Medievalists' Research Symposium 1982); and Birkbeck College, University of London (William Matthews Lectures 1983).

In quoting from English texts of the sixteenth century and earlier, I have normalized orthography to the extent of removing ȝ and Þ and regularizing i/j and u/v; I have also modified editorial punctuation and capitalization without specific comment. The Bible is quoted from the Douai version of the Vulgate. Unattributed translations are my own.

A.C.S.

Queens' College,
Cambridge
July 1984

1 · Renaissance and medieval

It was the Renaissance that invented the Middle Ages; and therefore this book, which moves from medieval to Renaissance, must begin with its end. My initial aim is modest: to remind the reader of some ways in which 'Renaissance' has been conceived by recent scholars,[1] as a preliminary to my own task of examining English poetic history in the transition from medieval to Renaissance. I do not suppose that my key terms are capable of exact definitions that would be acceptable to scholars in all fields, still less do I presume to define them afresh myself; on the other hand, whatever their slipperiness, the terms are indispensable. As a scholar wrote in an article forty years ago, 'for the purpose of this paper it is necessary to assume that something happened in the course of history in the fourteenth, fifteenth, and sixteenth centuries which merits consideration'. From this truly minimal assumption he is able to reach his triumphant final sentence, 'I therefore come to the conclusion that there was a Renaissance.'[2] I agree with him; there was a Renaissance; but what was it?

A first difficulty is that, even if there was a Renaissance, and even if we confine ourselves to the fourteenth, fifteenth and sixteenth centuries, setting aside the various Ottonian, Carolingian and Twelfth-Century 'renaissances' that have been discerned in earlier periods, the Renaissance was not a single event or movement. 'The Renaissance' was put into currency in the mid-nineteenth century as the name of a historical period by the French historian Michelet, whose descriptive formula, 'the discovery of the world and the discovery of man' achieved greater fame by being taken up by Burckhardt in his influential *Civilization of the Renaissance in Italy*.[3] But what we have since been in the habit of calling '*the* Renaissance' is not a single phenomenon but an untidy cluster of related phenomena. There are several different Renaissances in the various cultural fields such as literature, the visual arts, architecture, philosophy and political thought, to which the term applies, and they begin at different moments, proceed at different paces, interact differently

I

with earlier cultural traditions, and affect different parts of Europe at different times. Part of the difficulty of definition comes from the persistent and perhaps irresistible attempt to subsume these various though related phenomena under a single heading. This book is concerned with English poetry from Chaucer onwards, and it begins by urging that Chaucer can properly be considered as, in some respects, a Renaissance poet, and by asking what happened after his death to the Renaissance elements that entered English poetry through his work. The Renaissance that interests me is therefore predominantly that which affects literature and thought about literature, and which began in Italy in the fourteenth century in the work of three great writers: Dante, Petrarch, Boccaccio. The work of all three was known to Chaucer, and this was where the medieval English poet encountered the Renaissance. It is necessary to supply a larger context, in order that the very concept of Renaissance may be given some meaning, and it is also helpful from time to time to bring in the Renaissances in other cultural fields for analogy, support, and contrast. Art history proves particularly, and I believe fruitfully, suggestive, if only because great art-historians such as Panofsky and Gombrich have written so penetratingly about their subject. But my primary concern is with the literary Renaissance.

One widely held view of the Renaissance in general sees all its various expressions in different fields of human endeavour as deriving from an enlarged conception of man himself. To generalize very broadly, medieval culture tends to take a somewhat low view of man, seeing the human condition as one of separation from its true source of value in God. Traditional Christianity, for all its focus on original sin as the human blemish that alienates man from his heavenly father, does not necessarily imply this low view of man's nature, for it sees God himself, by the sacrifice of his Son in human form, as having made possible the overcoming of this separation. It has been pointed out, indeed, that a number of writers associated with the revival of learning in the twelfth century insisted on the dignity derived by man from his creation by God in God's own image and likeness,[4] and further that the late-medieval theological movement called nominalism also tends to emphasize the dignity of man as partner in a covenant with God which makes salvation possible.[5] Nevertheless, the characteristic medieval emphasis is on the misery of the human condition, as set out, for example, in the *De miseriis humanae conditionis* of Pope Innocent III, a work so widely

2

read that it survives in over five hundred manuscripts, and one
which Chaucer himself claimed to have translated into English,
though his translation does not survive.[6] Even the more optimistic
medieval literary works tend to represent man as utterly – sometimes comically – dependent on God, and therefore not capable of
heroic stature. In English, the *Gawain*-poet's Jonah, a petulant child
in his absurd wish to live a life free from the constraints of God's will,
perfectly exemplifies this medieval conception at its most humane
and charitable.[7] Jonah is always in a state of metaphysical dependency, never alone; his attempts at rebellion are absurd, and his only
hope of happiness is to endure obediently the commands of his
heavenly father. The poet, with a characteristically homely and
de-heroizing image, joins with God in advising Jonah and the reader,

> Be noght so gryndel, godman, bot go forth thy wayes,
> Be preve and be pacient in payne and in joye;
> For he that is to rakel to renden his clothez
> Mot efte sitte with more unsounde to sewe hem togeder.[8]

A comparable sense of man's smallness is pervasive in the 'realism' of
late-medieval art, especially in northern Europe. The human figure
tends to be represented in unheroic proportions, with a large head in
relation to the trunk and limbs. It has been noted, too, how Gothic
cathedrals characteristically make us conscious of the smallness of
our stature, while Renaissance buildings encourage us imaginatively
to expand our ideal stature to match their own dimensions.[9]

If there was a Renaissance, it began in fourteenth-century Italy,
and it was there that a grander view of man's nature and condition
began to be asserted. This did not (as still seems sometimes to be
supposed) involve any rejection of Christianity, but rather a drawing
on different resources within the whole body of Christian ideas. The
first Renaissance treatise on 'the dignity of man' is probably that by
Petrarch, which appears, in the form of a dialogue between Sorrow
and Reason, as chapter 93 of Book II of his longest work, the *De
remediis utriusque fortunae* (completed in 1366). We know that Petrarch had Innocent III's work in mind when he composed this, and in
it Reason, while not denying that 'the miserie of mankinde is great
and manifolde', goes on to insist on the many gifts and powers that
accompany man's creation in 'the image and likenesse of God'.[10] A
fuller and more confident rebuttal to Innocent's *De miseriis* was
written by Gianozzo Manetti in his *De dignitate et excellentia hominis*;
and subsequently the dignity of man became a recurrent topic in

Renaissance writings, and new themes were developed (or old ones revived) to strengthen the sense of man's worth. Among these, as a recent scholar has stated were

man's creation in order to rule over the rest of creation which was given him by providence; the beauties and utilities of the world at man's disposal; the capacities of the human mind, soul and body, for the work of ruling the sub-human universe; the erectness of man's posture pointing to his heavenly goal; the immortality of the soul; the gift of the Incarnation which divinely honoured man; the consequent beatification of man and the resurrection of the body; man's ascent in dignity beyond the angels.[11]

Perhaps the most famous of these Renaissance treatises on man's dignity is the *Oration* of Pico della Mirandola (1486). Pico still emphasizes man's divine creation, but he adds, referring to pagan as well as Christian authority, that God created man *free*. The human condition is 'that we can become what we will', and he imagines God saying to Adam at the moment of his creation:

Neither a fixed abode nor a form that is thine alone nor any function peculiar to thyself have we given thee, Adam, to the end that according to thy longing and according to thy judgment thou mayest have and possess what abode, what form, and what functions thou thyself shalt desire. The nature of all other beings is limited and constrained within the bounds of laws prescribed by Us. Thou, constrained by no limits, in accordance with thine own free will, in whose hand We have placed thee, shalt ordain for thyself the limits of thy nature. We have set thee at the world's center that thou mayest from thence more easily observe whatever is in the world. We have made thee neither of heaven nor of earth, neither mortal nor immortal, so that with freedom of choice and with honor, as though the maker and molder of thyself, thou mayest fashion thyself in whatever shape thou shalt prefer. Thou shalt have the power to degenerate into the lower forms of life, which are brutish. Thou shalt have the power, out of thy soul's judgment, to be reborn into the higher forms, which are divine.[12]

This God-given freedom may lead man to damnation as well as to salvation, for man may abuse God's generosity, and the ultimate order of the universe is still divinely ordained; but it releases man from the childlike dependency that medieval thought sees as his lot. His best virtue is no longer to be 'pacient in payne and in joye'; it is 'a certain holy ambition, . . . so that, not content with the mediocre, we shall pant after the highest and (since we may if we wish) toil with all our strength the obtain it.'[13]

Connected with this Renaissance emphasis on man's dignity and freedom is a conception of human virtue which differs from that predominant in the Middle Ages. Then it was held that the highest form of human life was that of loving contemplation of God, in withdrawal from the bustle and corruption of the secular world. The two ways of life were exemplified as those of Mary and Martha, and no-one doubted that the contemplative Mary had 'chosen the best part, which shall not be taken away from her'.[14] Petrarch himself still blamed the pagan philosopher Cicero for failing to detach himself from a worldly strife which was bound to be vain,[15] but by the fifteenth century philosophers such as Coluccio Salutati, Leonardo Bruni, Matteo Palmieri and Leon Battista Alberti were arguing that man's duty was not to withdraw from the dangers of the world but to be a good citizen, to practise an active virtue not in *otium* but in *negotium*. There was greater optimism than was usually found in the Middle Ages about the possibility that human virtue (now secularized as *virtus* or *virtù*) could overcome Fortune; and one line of argument of the humanists against the scholastics had to do with the need not just to rely on the academic definition of truth but to use the power of words to persuade men to put it into practice. Thus Petrarch writes of Aristotle (and by implication of the 'Aristotelians', the scholastics), 'He teaches what virtue is, I do not deny that; but his lesson lacks the words that sting and set afire the urge toward love of virtue and hatred of vice.'[16] The new emphasis on the value of the active life was one contributory factor in the eventual rejection of monasticism by the sixteenth-century reformers, while the emphasis on the persuasive power of words may be connected with a general tendency to elevate the dignity of poetry. This latter tendency is my next topic.

In the Middle Ages, typically, poetry, and especially vernacular poetry, is seen at best as a form of craftsmanship, a vehicle for entertainment or instruction. This is true above all of poetry in English, for the continuing prestige of French in England down to Chaucer's time meant that there was little or no writing in English that presumed to claim intrinsic value. (It may have possessed it, but it did not lay claim to it.) Indeed, the very term 'poetry' (or 'literature') is misleading if applied to pre-Chaucerian English writing, for it implies verbal structures of intrinsic beauty and lasting value; and this conception, so far as English is concerned, is itself a product of the Renaissance. Most English verse before the 1360s is anonymous, and the idea of the poet, the man known and famed for his original contribution to an acknowledged art-form with its own history, is as anachronistic as that of poetry. For the origin of the Renaissance idea, we must turn again to Petrarch. In 1341, he was crowned with laurel in Rome, in what was imagined to be a revival of an ancient Roman ceremony, as a 'great poet and historian' – so the coronation diploma put it. This was not the first post-antique laureation of a poet, for Mussato had been crowned at Padua in 1315 on the publication of his tragedy *Ecerinis*, but it was the most influential.[17] Petrarch proceeded to deliver an oration on the poetic vocation, which 'has not unjustly been called "the first manifesto of the Renaissance"', and in the course of which he declared that the poet's highest goal was to make himself 'worthy of glory' and in this way to gain 'immortality for his name'.[18] Petrarch put into circulation a new attitude towards literature itself, both classical and vernacular: it was seen not merely as a vehicle but as a vocation, an autonomous sphere of human activity. The poet was, potentially, an inspired prophet, and his work brought undying fame, a secular immortality, to himself and to his subject-matter. None of these ideas was entirely new, even in the period since classical antiquity, but they were presented in fourteenth-century Italy with new force and coherence.

The existence of Dante's *Commedia* was no doubt a powerful motive force in this revival of the dignity of poetry, for here was a major vernacular poem which really could challenge comparison with the classics, and whose author had the astonishing confidence in his own powers to make precisely such a claim. Dante's work gained widespread prestige very rapidly, and was being expounded in public lectures in Florence before the end of the century. One of the lecturers was Boccaccio, and the poetic ideology which is correlative to Dante's achievement can be found expressed with incomparable persuasiveness in his Latin treatise *De genealogia deorum gentilium*. Most of this is an encyclopaedia of classical mythology, but Books XIV and XV offer a defence of poetry itself. Poets are not 'mere storytellers, but rather . . . men of great learning, endowed with a sort of divine intelligence and skill.' Again, 'This poetry, which ignorant triflers cast aside, is a sort of fervid and exquisite invention, with fervid expression, in speech or writing, of that which the mind has invented. It proceeds from the bosom of God, and few, I find, are the souls in whom this gift is born; indeed so wonderful a gift it is that true poets have always been the rarest of men.' Poetry confers fame: 'if the privilege of long life is not granted to a man in any other way, poetry, at any rate, through fame vouchsafes to her followers the lasting benefit of survival . . . It is perfectly clear that the songs of poets, like the name of the composer, are almost immortal.' This inspired quality belongs as much to the poetry of pagan antiquity as to that of Christian times: indeed, in his *Life of Dante* Boccaccio had written that

the ancient poets have really followed, as far as is possible for the human mind, in the steps of the Holy Spirit, who as we see in Holy Writ, revealed to future generations his deepest secrets through many mouths, causing them to speak in veiled language what he purposed to show unveiled, through works in due time.

This 'veiled' quality is, however, to be found in poetic fictions of all kinds, even old wives' tales; great poets deliberately 'veil the truth with fiction' so as to make it 'the object of strong intellectual effort and various interpretation' and thus more highly valued. The reading of poetry thus becomes a learned and moral discipline, comparable to the interpretation of Scripture. Boccaccio quotes with approval Petrarch's assertion that 'What we acquire with difficulty and keep with care is always the dearer to us', and he goes on to sum up this new conception of poetry as worthy of close and repeated attention:

But I repeat my advice to those who would appreciate poetry, and unwind its difficult involutions. You must read, you must persevere, you must sit up nights, you must inquire, and exert the utmost power of your mind. If one way does not lead to the desired meaning, take another; if obstacles arise, then still another; until, if your strength holds out, you will find that clear which at first looked dark.[19]

In Boccaccio's summation of early Renaissance literary theory, a group of ideas that in the Middle Ages had been applied almost exclusively to scriptural exegesis and devotional writing have been transferred bodily to secular poetry, ancient and modern: it is the product of inspiration, it is difficult and demands many readings, and, in order that it may be studied with the closeness it deserves, it must be available as a written text, not merely (like most medieval poetry) as something to be read aloud to listeners. Clearly such an attitude to poetry could become widespread only when the advent of printing increased the availability and fixed the form of texts; but it began before that, and depended initially on the spread of lay literacy and of the prosperity and the literary interests necessary to support the multiplication of manuscript copies of secular literature.[20]

In surveying two fundamental Renaissance ideas, of the dignity of man and the dignity of poetry, I have still not touched on something crucial to the very concept of 'Renaissance': the emergence of a new theory of and attitude towards history, by means of which the Renaissance itself was defined as a distinct historical period. From about the middle of the fourteenth century onwards, we find a number of Italian writers, and especially Florentines, expressing their sense of living through and participating in a renewal of culture and learning, which felt to them like a 'rebirth' – a rebirth of the culture and learning of classical antiquity. That feeling of theirs is the origin of the concept of the Renaissance, and 'antiquity' and 'Middle Ages' originated at the same time, as part of a threefold scheme of periodization. First came classical antiquity, which for these fourteenth-century thinkers meant chiefly Rome, though later, with the recovery of ancient Greek literature, Athens was added to it. This was a period of paganism, and therefore to fourteenth-century Christians an era of theological darkness; but it was now seen, paradoxically, as one too of cultural and philosophical light. So Petrarch put it, in 1373, calling attention to the brilliance of the pagan poets and thinkers:

amidst the errors there shone forth men of genius, and no less keen were their eyes, although they were surrounded by darkness and dense gloom; therefore they ought not so much to be hated for their erring but pitied for their ill fate.[21]

After the decline of classical antiquity, which was generally seen as having taken place about a thousand years before the fourteenth century, followed the long period of cultural darkness called the 'Middle Ages' (*medium aevum, media aetas*) because it came between antiquity and the fourteenth-century revival. The term 'Dark Ages' is still sometimes used by historians to designate the period between the fall of Rome to the barbarians and the emergence of a more settled medieval civilization; but for this Renaissance view of history 'medieval civilization' would have been a contradiction in terms. In literature, philosophy, architecture and the other arts the whole intermediary millennium was seen as a period of ignorant decline from or perversion of the true standards set by Rome. Third came the Renaissance itself, in which these true standards were recovered, and, by means of the imitation of antiquity, the light of culture began to shine once more. (Dawn is a metaphor more often used than rebirth in the early Renaissance to describe what advanced writers, artists and thinkers felt to be happening around them.)

Petrarch himself seems to have been the first to conceive of this new historical scheme. After he had visited Rome and seen for the first time its impressive physical remains of classical civilization, he began to write in 1338 or 1339 a Latin poem called *Africa*. Its subject-matter was taken from the classical historian Livy, its hero was Scipio Africanus, the Roman general who defeated Carthage, and it was the first medieval attempt at the total re-creation of classical epic poetry, reproducing not just classical subject-matter but the authentic style of Virgil's *Aeneid*. This large pioneering enterprise gave Petrarch great difficulty, and it was never completed; but in an epilogue added in 1343 he expressed his sense of living on the verge of a new age in which such works would be possible and would be more fully valued. Addressing the poem itself, he wrote,

for you, if you should long outlive me, as my soul hopes and wishes, there is perhaps a better age in store; this slumber of forgetfulness will not last for ever. After the darkness has been dispelled, our grandsons will be able to walk back into the pure radiance of the past.[22]

Like many key statements of the doctrine of the Renaissance, these lines have a religious intensity, yet they invert the normal Christian uses of slumber and darkness as metaphors for the obliviousness of sin. Indeed, the very idea of rebirth, implied in the term 'Renaissance', holds a central place in Christian thought, for, as Jesus said to Nicodemus, 'unless a man be born again, he cannot see the kingdom of God.'[23]

Petrarch's great admirer and disciple Boccaccio applied this set of ideas in his *Decameron* to the history of painting. Of Giotto, the great Florentine painter, he wrote,

Hence, by virtue of the fact that he brought back to light an art which had been buried for centuries beneath the blunders of those who, in their paintings, aimed to bring visual delight to the ignorant rather than intellectual satisfaction to the wise, his work may justly be regarded as a shining monument to the glory of Florence.[24]

Despite the actual absence of any important antique models for the art of Renaissance painters, this proved to be a highly influential remark – perhaps indeed the most influential remark ever to have been made about the history of art, for it was still being repeated, with approval though without acknowledgment, by Bernard Berenson in the last edition of his *Italian Painters of the Renaissance* nearly six hundred years later.[25] However crude the specific judgment now seems, we may find here the beginning of art history itself: an individual painter is imagined as having a significant relation to an intelligible past. And another fourteenth-century Florentine, Filippo Villani, in his *Liber de civitatis Florentiae famosis civibus*, applied a similar historical pattern to vernacular poetry, when he implied that there were no important poets between Claudian in the fifth century and Dante in his own. The Catholic church, he suggested, had denied the value of poetic fiction, but Dante had shown how even the fictions of the pagan poets were inspired and could be reconciled with Christian truth.[26]

The ideas put forward in these passages from influential writers of the fourteenth century were to have an enduring life: indeed, they still survive, as the existence of books such as this and many others testifies. A reawakening of art, literature and thought after centuries of darkness and slumber was believed to have begun in fourteenth-century Italy, and the message was repeated again and again, first in Italy itself, then all over Europe. I give a single illustrative example, from the Florentine writer Matteo Palmieri, dating from the 1430s, and applying the idea of revival to painting, sculpture, architecture, and literature:

Where was the painter's art till Giotto tardily restored it? A caricature of the art of human delineation! Sculpture and architecture, for long years sunk to the merest travesty of art, are only today in process of rescue from obscurity; only now are they being brought to a new pitch of perfection by men of genius and erudition. Of letters and liberal studies at large it were best to be silent altogether. For these, the real guides to distinction in all the arts, the solid foundation of all civilization, have been lost to mankind for 800 years and more. It is but in our own day that men dare boast that they see the dawn of better things. For example, we owe it to our Leonardo Bruni that Latin, so long a bye-word for its uncouthness, has begun to shine forth in its ancient purity, its beauty, its majestic rhythm. Now, indeed, may every thoughtful spirit thank God that it has been permitted to him to be born in this new age, so full of hope and promise, which already rejoices in a greater array of nobly-gifted souls than the world has seen in the thousand years that have preceded it.[27]

The theory of history which was invented by the Renaissance and in terms of which the Renaissance defined itself has been much questioned by historians of all kinds during the present century. Other and earlier cultural movements have been called renaissances, and it has been doubted whether what happened in fourteenth- and fifteenth-century Italy was really a change as fundamental and unique as some of its participants believed. Increasing historical knowledge, and especially in recent years more detailed and sympathetic study of late-medieval thought (which the propagandists of the Renaissance and later of the Reformation themselves cast into darkness and neglect) has brought forward more and more evidence of continuities in ideas, attitudes and techniques between 'medieval' and 'Renaissance' culture. Yet if the Renaissance is considered as a psychological phenomenon, it undoubtedly happened, for it consisted of a new *experience* of the relationship of the present to the past. Renaissance means not birth but rebirth, and Renaissance writers and thinkers felt themselves to be grasping and bringing back to life cultural achievements that had died or slept. This experience has two essential components: it involves, first, a recognition of the difference, the alterity, of the culture of classical Rome, as something which possessed its own autonomy but which had not been authentically transmitted through the intervening centuries, the *medium aevum*; and then a sense of the possibility of bringing this culture back to life by means of skilful imitation – imitation which is not merely mechanical but imaginative, an imaginative re-creation of the classical past. And this implies that there is also a third and final stage: a sense of reunion with the past, a new recognition of the universality of a high culture which had been supposed dead.

It is worth pausing to emphasize this point. The Renaissance sense of history is far from involving any attack on the idea of 'human nature', of a human essence that stands above historical difference. From the mid-nineteenth century onwards – perhaps from the time of Herder in the late eighteenth century – and certainly with increasing force in our own time, that idea has been questioned and relegated to its own historical place. As Althusser puts it, in an influential essay on 'Marxism and Humanism', 'The earlier idealist ('bourgeois') philosophy depended in all its domains and arguments ... on a problematic of *human nature* (or the essence of man). For centuries, this problematic had been transparency itself, and no one had thought of questioning it.'[28] But, as Althusser argues, Marx in 1845 rejected this philosophical humanism – the product of the Renaissance – which had hitherto been taken for granted. Again (to choose another example almost at random) a recent theorist remarks that Freud's work has not had the revolutionary effect that might have been expected, because 'it has been thought to depend on – and used to reinforce – the concept of a fixed, unchanging human nature in a world at least as fixed and unchanging as the medieval cosmos. And it is this concept of an essential human nature as the source of action and of history which has been the ally of liberal humanism against proposals for radical change.' It is therefore necessary, in the view of this writer, to call on Lacan's reinterpretation of Freud in order to deal the *coup de grâce* against this obstinately persistent notion of 'human nature'.[29] I quote these passages so as to illustrate how, in this as in other respects, the Renaissance marks the beginning of a great phase of thought that may now be ending. The effect of the emergence of the Renaissance historical sense was not to challenge the universality of human nature, but rather to expand and strengthen the concept of a divinely ordained human nature that was already present within medieval Christianity by giving it a historical dimension. Within that historical human universality, even the fundamental opposition between Christian and pagan might be overcome, or at least alleviated. Thus historical separation could be defeated; but only after it had been recognized for what it was.

If we concern ourselves with the earlier Renaissance, setting aside the later phase in which it was the culture of Athens that was brought back to life, it must not be supposed that the Renaissance was essentially a matter of the rediscovery of a *lost* past. Certainly, some important classical Latin texts were recovered by fourteenth- and fifteenth-century scholars: Petrarch himself found manuscripts of the poems of Propertius and of several works of Cicero. But, as a modern study has pointed out, of all the Latin manuscripts unearthed in the fourteenth and fifteenth centuries, 'their total value remains small in comparison with that great body of Latin literature that was already available in Petrarch's youth'.[30] For all the tendency that existed in the late Middle Ages to substitute contemporary Latin texts for classical ones as the basis for 'grammatical' (i.e. literary) studies, the great poets of classical Rome – Virgil and Ovid above all – had never ceased to be read with respect and delight. Their stories had been retold again and again in vernacular languages; but the retelling had involved a systematic though presumably unconscious process of updating, of medievalization. Erwin Panofsky has noted the existence in the visual arts of a virtually unbreakable 'principle of disjunction' by which 'wherever in the high and later Middle Ages a work of art borrows its theme from classical poetry, legend, history or mythology, this theme is quite invariably presented in a non-classical, normally contemporary, form'.[31] He adds that in literature too, among Latin writings, the same principle is at work with very few exceptions; and it is inevitably still more prevalent in the vernacular writings which are the subject of this book. The subject-matter of the *Aeneid* was more likely to be known to medieval readers and listeners not in the words of Virgil's epic but in those of one of a series of vernacular versions, beginning with the twelfth-century *Roman d'Eneas*, which presented it as a courtly romance with Dido as its heroine. (It should be added that this reinterpretation of the *Aeneid* had already begun in classical times, with Ovid's inclusion of Dido's letter to Aeneas in his *Heroides*.) Again, Ovid's *Metamorphoses* was a favourite work in the Middle Ages, but it was commonly read in Latin or French medievalizations which supplied its stories with a detailed allegorical interpretation.

What is most characteristic of the Renaissance, then, is not a rediscovery of lost material, but a new sense of the historical distance and difference inherent in classical texts, most of which had never been lost, together with a sense of the possibility of overcoming that distance and difference by creative imitation. A new sensitivity to style as well as content both permits the recognition of the difference of the past and provides the means by which it can be overcome. Creative imitation in Latin is found in works such as Petrarch's *Africa* in verse and in a great body of Ciceronian prose. My concern is with such imitation in the vernacular, and that begins, as might be supposed, in Italy. Indeed, despite the lateness with which the vernacular developed in Italy as a written language, the practice of such imitation precedes the theory as we have seen it illustrated in Petrarch and Boccaccio. A key instance, from the opening years of the fourteenth century, may be found in Dante himself, the first and greatest of the three great Italian writers of that century. Dante, in his treatise *De vulgari eloquentia*, boldly defined the vernacular as 'nobler' than Latin,[32] and he chose the Italian vernacular as the vehicle of his greatest creative work, the *Commedia*. Yet at the same time he declared that vernacular poets would write more correctly, the more closely they imitated the *regulares*, the Latin classics; and of these Virgil is the first he mentions.[33] By contrast, then, with the medieval habit of representing Virgil's subject-matter in anachronistically modern styles, we may set Dante's visionary encounter with Virgil himself in the opening canto of the *Commedia*. Virgil identifies himself as one who 'lived at Rome under the good Augustus, in the time of the false and lying gods', and Dante addresses him reverently as follows:

Art thou then that Virgil, that fountain which pours forth so rich a stream of speech? . . . O glory and light of other poets, let the long study and the great love that has made me search thy volume avail me. Thou art my master and my author. Thou art he from whom alone I took the style whose beauty has brought me honour (*lo bello stilo, che m'ha fatto honore*).[34]

Dante's Virgil is not the mere source of narrative material or the legendary sorcerer that he had become in the Middle Ages: he is re-imagined as the poet of the Roman past, cut off from the possibility of salvation by his paganism, yet accessible as a supreme model of literary grandeur. And Dante creates in his own vernacular an authentically Virgilian style, which brings his great predecessor back to life while at the same time bringing fame to his revivifier. The presence of Virgil in Dante's *Commedia* is a supreme example of the link between the ability to grasp the intrinsic nature of a dead culture and that sensitivity to classical literary styles that makes possible the elevation of the vernacular through creative imitation.

2 · Chaucer

1. Medieval and Renaissance

Where does Chaucer stand in the context of which the previous chapter has offered a rough sketch? First, it must be said at once that there is no trace in Chaucer or his England of the sense of rebirth or restored light, of a sharp break with the immediate past and a return to the true standards of classical antiquity. In Chaucer's lifetime England lived through a period of acute stress and even crisis, with the Black Death, the Peasants' Revolt, the prolonged war in France, and the political turmoil which led to the deposition and murder of Richard II in 1399; and, in the Wycliffite movement, it saw the earliest major European foreshadowing of the Reformation. But England was lacking in the social conditions which underlay the Italian Renaissance of the fourteenth century.[1] In particular, urban development had advanced much more rapidly in Italy, which had several city-states more than twice as populous as London, England's only large city; and, while in Italy university studies led towards secular specializations such as law and medicine, in England they culminated in theology. In Italy new ideas of the value of the active life thus took root more rapidly, while in England the most highly educated (however worldly their actual behaviour) were still wedded to a world-denying ideal. England was still deeply feudalized and ecclesiasticized, and it would be long before the parallel and exclusive types of clerk and knight, produced by different systems of education, gave way to the more comprehensive Renaissance ideal of 'The courtier's, soldier's, scholar's, eye, tongue, sword'. Lay literacy, though certainly on the increase in fourteenth-century England, was not at all comparable with that in, say, Florence. In England, the very concept of literature did not yet exist, and writing was seen as being no more than instrumental, a vehicle for instruction or entertainment. A measure of the difference between the two cultures is the impossibility of imagining anything comparable to Florence's public lectures on Dante in fourteenth-century England, or indeed for many centuries thereafter.

Chaucer himself in many ways reflects the culture of his nation. In *The Canterbury Tales* the storytelling competition, with its criterion of 'Tales of best sentence and moost solaas' (I 798),[2] seems to mirror the medieval assumption of the instrumentality of writing and the absence of specifically literary values. Though many of the tales, like the pilgrims who tell them, are products of the 'modern' world of specialized work,[3] Chaucer still takes for granted the division between clerk and knight which the Renaissance was to bridge. As a political historian has noted, 'One of the pilgrims described in the *Prologue* is a young scholar from Oxford, while another is a young squire. The former spends all his time reading Aristotle's philosophy, but the latter is wholly preoccupied with practising the ideals of chivalry and learning the arts of war.'[4] Chaucer's fictional pilgrimage has a rather striking bent towards the secular, which emerges from its opening plan to conclude not with worship at the shrine of St Thomas at Canterbury, but with a supper to honour the winning storyteller at the Tabard Inn at Southwark. Yet the work actually concludes (whether or not this was what Chaucer intended all along) with control being taken by the austere Parson, who rejects both fiction and verse and delivers an entirely traditional treatise on penitence, and finally with the poet himself renouncing his secular works, his 'enditynges of worldly vanitees' (x 1085), and praying for salvation. Chaucer nowhere indicates that he feels himself to be living in a new and enlightened age. When the Monk among Chaucer's pilgrims asserts his modernity and his rejection of the traditional ideal of cloistered celibacy –

> This ilke Monk leet olde thynges pace,
> And heeld after the newe world the space (I 175–6)

– the context makes it clear that for Chaucer this 'new world' was one of corruption, not of enlightenment.

John Lydgate in the early fifteenth century emphasized the novelty of Chaucer's achievement, with his own version of 'Enfin Malherbe vint' – our English was imperfect 'Til that he cam' – and saw him as the English Petrarch, crowned with 'the laurer of oure Englishe tonge' in token that his fame should 'passen in noon age'.[5] But it is not till a century later that we find English writers forming a conception of the cultural history of their own nation and assimilating it to the pattern which we have seen to be typical of Renaissance historiography. Thus in 1532, when William Thynne's great edition of Chaucer's works was published, it included a preface by his friend, the learned courtier Sir Brian Tuke, who observed:

it is moche to be marveyled howe in his tyme, whan doutlesse all good letters were layde a slepe throughout the worlde, as the thynge whiche, either by the disposycion and influence of the bodies above, or by other ordynaunce of God, seemed lyke and was in daunger to have utterly perysshed, suche an excellent poete in our tonge shulde, as it were nature repugnyng, spryng and aryse.[6]

In 1555 Robert Braham can be found repeating, in much the same words, this Renaissance condemnation of the slumber of 'good letters' in the *medium aevum*, and adding an equally Renaissance characterization of Chaucer as a 'divine' poet fallen among Dark Age barbarians:

as it hapned the same Chaucer to lease the prayse of that tyme wherin he wrote, beyng then when in dede all good letters were almost aslepe, so farre was the grosenesse and barbarousnesse of that age from the understandinge of so devyne a wryter.[7]

The assimilation of English literary history, and Chaucer's place in it, to the Italian Renaissance pattern was completed by Sir Philip Sidney. In his *Apologie for Poetrie* (1581), he compared Chaucer's priority with that of the great Italians –

So in the Italian language the first that made it aspire to be a treasure-house of science were the poets Dante, Boccaccio, and Petrarch. So in our English were Gower and Chaucer . . .

– and then went on to declare that

Chaucer, undoubtedly, did excellently in his *Troilus and Criseyde*; of whom, truly, I know not whether to marvel more, either that he in that misty time could see so clearly, or that we in this clear age walk so stumblingly after him.[8]

By Sidney's time, the effect of the Reformation had been to complete the acceptance in England of the new periodization introduced by the Renaissance. The paradox of the Renaissance view of the Middle Ages as a time of cultural darkness but religious light was resolved from the Protestant standpoint by seeing medieval Catholicism as itself dark and corrupt, while the reformed churches claimed to be going back behind that darkness to the pristine religious light of the primitive church. No doubt Sidney had in mind that Chaucer's age was 'misty' because papist; and later English commentators (including even the Catholic Dryden), partly misled by the addition of a large apocrypha to Chaucer's authentic work, sometimes saw him as a Wycliffite, a Protestant in advance of his times.

With the rehabilitation of the Middle Ages by Romantic sentiment and nineteenth-century historical scholarship, views of Chaucer's relation to his time also changed. The evaluative assumptions of the Renaissance sense of history were rejected, and the Middle Ages began to be seen more positively, as a distinct and admirable phase in European civilization. Thus it was no longer necessary for admirers of Chaucer to contrast his brightness with his age's darkness; and as early as 1803 William Godwin (Shelley's father-in-law) noted that Chaucer 'had a right to consider himself as fallen upon no barbarous or inglorious age'.[9] With the rise of serious, historically grounded Chaucer scholarship in the later nineteenth and the twentieth centuries, the tendency has been to see Chaucer as in most ways a typically medieval poet – indeed, for many scholars, the more medieval the better. Yet there is one way in which Chaucer was not typical of the medieval English culture into which he was born. Chaucer had come into contact with the beginnings of the Renaissance by visiting Italy and reading substantial parts of the work of Dante, Petrarch and Boccaccio. It is well known that Chaucer, in his capacity as diplomat and civil servant, was sent on at least two missions to Italy: in 1372–3, when he went to Genoa to negotiate a trade agreement and to Florence on a visit the purpose of which we do not know; and in 1378 to Milan, to negotiate with Bernabò Visconti. There may possibly have been an earlier journey in 1368. The negotiations in which Chaucer was involved would probably have been conducted in French,[10] but it is possible that one reason why he was selected for these missions was that he already knew some Italian; there were 'Lombards' resident in London as bankers and merchants from whom he could have learnt it.[11] It is certainly reasonable to suppose that Chaucer's interest in Italian literature was either initiated or greatly intensified by these visits. Petrarch and Boccaccio were both alive in Florence in 1373; indeed, this was the very year in which Boccaccio lectured publicly on Dante. There is no evidence of the existence of any Italian literary manuscripts in fourteenth-century English libraries; and, since Chaucer was subsequently to produce many English poems which consisted of or contained close translations from these three Italians, it seems highly likely that he brought manuscripts of their works back with him. It is possible that the *Gawain*-poet had read some Dante or Boccaccio or both;[12] but with this uncertain exception, Chaucer is the only Englishman of his time who can be shown to be affected by contact with the Italian Renaissance. It is in keeping with this situation that when he mentions the Italian poets in his work, it is sometimes with the air of introducing them for the first time to an English public who have never even heard of them: as he puts it in *The Monk's Tale*, where he is translating from the penultimate canto of the *Inferno*,

> Whoso wol here it in a lenger wise,
> Redeth the grete poete of Ytaille
> That highte Dant . . .   (VII 2459–61)

The situation I have been outlining makes it natural to suppose that Chaucer's contact with the Italian Renaissance was a factor of great importance in shaping his work – perhaps indeed transforming it – from 1373 onwards. Such a view was certainly taken by some scholars in the recent past. In 1909 J. W. Mackail, drawing an important distinction between Chaucer's personal talent and the effect of the opportunity opened up by his response to his Italian reading, wrote as follows:

The specific greatness of Chaucer as a poet lies in a poetic quality neither inherited nor acquired, but personal and incommunicable. His specific importance in the history of literature, which is a different matter, lies in his having, alone in his age, absorbed this Italian influence, and thus created for English poetry a wholly new type and aim. He brought it – whether with or without some loss of its own native qualities – into relation with the main stream of the world's art.[13]

With a similarly ambitious generalization but greater scholarly precision, W. P. Ker spoke as follows in a Clark Lecture given in 1912:

Chaucer belongs to the Renaissance, is caught by the Renaissance, in so far as he began to think of poetical form with reference to ancient models, especially Latin epic poetry. He could not have thought in that way if he had not read Italian and come into contact with the new Italian ambitions.[14]

The main stream of subsequent twentieth-century writing about Chaucer has taken a different direction from this.[15] It cannot deny that Chaucer knew the work of the great *Trecentisti* and made abundant use of it, which scholars have traced in ever-increasing detail; but it insists that he was essentially a 'medievalizer' of these Renaissance sources. A *locus classicus* of this approach to Chaucer is C. S. Lewis's highly influential study of *Troilus and Criseyde*, 'What

Chaucer really did to *Il Filostrato*'.[16] Here Lewis states his purpose as being to show that in the *Troilus* 'the process which *Il Filostrato* underwent at Chaucer's hands was first and foremost a process of *medievalization*' (p. 27). Chaucer, Lewis tells us, 'had never heard of a renaissance' (p. 28), and in the *Troilus* we see him 'groping back, unknowingly, through the very slightly medieval work of Boccaccio, to the genuinely medieval formula of Chrétien' (p. 29). Chaucer went to the *Filostrato* for 'historial' material about Troy (p. 30); he applied to it a process of 'rhetoricization' (p. 32); he found it deficient in *doctryne* and therefore added, for example, philosophical passages from Boethius regardless of any dramatic purpose (pp. 32–5); above all, 'Chaucer approached his work as the poet of courtly love' (p. 35), and in a representative comparison of his work with Boccaccio's 'it is safe to say that every single alteration by Chaucer is an alteration in the direction of medievalism' (p. 41).

Much is to be learnt from Lewis's essay about the ways in which Chaucer does indeed tend to absorb his reading of Boccaccio into the terms of the medieval English world that was familiar to him. But what Lewis completely fails to do is to explain what it was in Boccaccio and the other Italian poets that attracted Chaucer in the first place. Are we really to suppose that he read them with no interest in or appreciation of the ways in which they were offering a new view of classical antiquity, a new glimpse of the means by which a modern vernacular language could be elevated to the level of the classical poets to whom he commends *Troilus and Criseyde* near its end, a new conception of the nature of poetry itself? The same failure is endemic, though not of course universal, in twentieth-century Chaucer criticism. Two reasons why this should be suggest themselves, one respectable, the other less so. The respectable one is simply the increasing depth and subtlety of our understanding of the transition from medieval to Renaissance, which rightly prevents us from accepting the bold contrast the fourteenth-century Italians themselves drew between their own age and that preceding it. Almost nothing that has been attributed to the Renaissance is entirely new, and it is interesting and important to recognize the many threads of continuity that link Petrarch or Chaucer, even at their most modern, with the medieval past. The other reason is that those who are drawn to the study of medieval literature are themselves often deeply conservative, even reactionary, in temperament; they prefer what they find in medieval culture to what they find in more recent culture; and they are therefore driven to emphasize 'medieval' as opposed to 'Renaissance' or 'modern' elements in the literature they study. In 'What Chaucer really did to *Il Filostrato*', C. S. Lewis frankly admitted his belief that *Troilus and Criseyde* was 'more lively and of deeper human appeal' than Boccaccio's poem precisely because it was more medieval, on the grounds that 'certain medieval things are more universal, in that sense more classical, . . . than certain things of the Renaissance'. He ended by comparing Andreas Capellanus favourably with George Moore, Marie Stopes, and D. H. Lawrence (pp. 43–4)! Similar attitudes, though quite different judgments, can be found in other leading twentieth-century Chaucer scholars. D. W. Robertson is a case in point: his interpretation of Andreas Capellanus and of 'courtly love' is dia-metrically opposed to Lewis's, but he shares Lewis's preference for the medieval (as he interprets it) over the more recent. Robertson shares too Lewis's conception of the Middle Ages – itself, ironically enough, derived from the Renaissance – as a single, static, and harmonious culture from Augustine to the fifteenth century. He denies that any conflict or tension is to be found in medieval literature, and he refers approvingly to 'the medieval world with its quiet hierarchies'.[17] It would be interesting to carry further this analysis of modern interpretations of medieval literature and culture, but the subject of my book is not the psychology and sociology of literary scholarship but a certain period of English poetry, a period which begins with Chaucer.

In my view, earlier scholars such as Mackail and Ker were right to see Chaucer's reading of fourteenth-century Italian writers (and possibly in a more general sense his contact with Italian culture in the 1370s) as having a crucial and transformative effect on his work. What I believe Chaucer gained from this reading, I have already indicated in general terms: a new and more exalted idea of what it was to be a poet, a higher sense of what kind of poetry was possible in a modern European vernacular, a new sense of the past and his own relation to it, and an awareness of the possibility of re-creating in poetic fiction the world of classical paganism. My aim, however, is not to prove that Chaucer gained these insights solely from Italian sources – I do not wish, for example, to discount the possibility of Italian influences in the French literature known to Chaucer. My aim is only to show that a certain body of ideas and attitudes is really present in certain of Chaucer's poems which do have Italian sources.

I am less concerned with specific origins than with the presence in his work of elements which can appropriately be associated with the Renaissance. These elements, of course, frequently coexist with medieval elements, and especially with those which are, in effect, literary reflections of the courtly cult or game of love, a tradition which had its roots in early medieval France and Provence, and which showed an impressive power of survival. I begin with the poem of Chaucer's which appears to show the first impact of his Italian reading, *The House of Fame*.

2. The House of Fame

The House of Fame dates from the middle 1370s, and in it we see the earliest effects of Chaucer's encounter with a Renaissance conception of the vernacular poet as divinely inspired, a conception that he found in Dante. Dante's *Commedia* begins, as we have seen, with a visionary meeting between Dante and Virgil, who is to be his guide through hell and purgatory. Similarly, Book I of *The House of Fame* begins with Chaucer in a dream 'meeting' Virgil – not literally, but in the sense of finding himself in a temple decorated with pictures that tell the story of the *Aeneid*. This book really can be described as a medievalization: Chaucer adapts the subject-matter of the *Aeneid*, retold in the medieval manner as a love-story in which the central, sympathetically treated role is that of Dido rather than Aeneas, but he does not attempt to reproduce a Virgilian style in English. The translation of the story into another medium, from words to pictures, helps to underline the medievalizing 'disjunction' involved. It is true that Chaucer begins by quoting Virgil's opening lines in surprisingly close translation –

> I wol now singen, yif I kan,
> The armes, and also the man,
> That first cam, thurgh his destinee,
> Fugityf of Troy contree,
> In Itayle, with ful moche pyne
> Unto the strondes of Lavyne $\qquad$ (143–8)

– but even there Chaucer revealingly inserts a modest, un-Virgilian qualification. Chaucer is no bard, confident in his inspiration, and his 'yif I kan' tellingly betrays the medieval poet's role as deferential entertainer, his audience's humble servant.[18] In Book I indeed that role is almost exaggerated, as Chaucer shies away from the most emotionally demanding aspects of the subject as he conceives it – illicit love and pagan suicide – and seems more at home with medieval formulas such as the catalogue of *exempla* of men's deceptiveness towards women (388ff). Chaucer's earliest reference to an Italian poet comes when he speaks – or rather (and characteristically) declines to speak – of Aeneas's visit to the underworld:

> And every turment eke in helle
> Saugh he, which is longe to telle;
> Which whoso willeth for to knowe,
> He moste rede many a rowe
> On Virgile or on Claudian,
> Or Daunte that it telle kan.   (445–50)

Here Dante is no more than one *auctoritee* among others on yet another important subject that Chaucer prefers to avoid.

When the dreaming Chaucer has seen his fill of the story in the temple, he decides to go outside to find out

> yf y kan
> See owhere any stiryng man,
> That may me telle where I am.   (477–9)

Outside he finds himself in a terrifying desert, from which he is seized up to the heavens by an eagle which shines as brightly as if it were 'Al newe of gold another sonne' (506). That line is translated from one in the first canto of the *Paradiso*,[19] but the eagle itself has flown into the poem from Canto IX of the *Purgatorio*, where Dante, also in a dream, sees it swooping down from the heavens and feels himself snatched up into the sphere of fire. It is as if Chaucer could already see that the medieval tradition offered him only a choice between homeliness and barrenness,[20] and he needed some 'stiryng man' to show him how his encounter with the classics could become more productive. Dante might be what he needed, but first he had to come to terms with Dante's unfamiliar grandeur. What in fact happens in *The House of Fame* is that Chaucer repeats as uneasy and unfinished comedy Dante's sublime experience of visionary rapture.

Rather than attempting a complete study of *The House of Fame*,[21] I shall now concentrate on the 'proems' (or prologues) to Books II and III, these being the places where above all we can see Chaucer attempting to accommodate Dante's re-creation of the classical conception of the epic poet – the poet inspired and granted superhuman power by a force outside himself (for Virgil the Muses, for

Dante God). The result is a revealing and amusing tension (and it was always an important part of Chaucer's skill to make his difficulties into matter for amusement); for he is fascinated by this new conception of the vernacular poet as prophet, yet he cannot quite adopt the role as wholeheartedly as Dante does.

The proem to Book II, after a call for attention that is comfortably medieval –

> Now herkeneth, every maner man
> That Englissh understonde kan,   510
> And listeneth of my drem to lere.
> For now at erste shul ye here
> So sely an avisyon,
> That Isaye, ne Scipion,
> Ne kyng Nabugodonosor,   515
> Pharoo, Turnus, ne Elcanor
> Ne mette such a drem as this!

– consists of three invocations, to Venus ('O Cipris'), to the Muses ('ye . . . that on Parnaso duelle'), and to Memory ('O Thought'):

> Now faire blisfull, O Cipris,
> So be my favour at this tyme!
> And ye, me to endite and ryme,   520
> Helpeth, that on Parnaso duelle,
> Be Elicon, the clere welle.
> O Thought, that wrot al that I mette,
> And in the tresorye hit shette
> Of my brayn, now shal men se   525
> Yf any vertu in the be,
> To tellen al my drem aryght.
> Now kythe thyn engyn and myght!

Chaucer is now daring to attempt an English equivalent to the *bello stilo* that Dante learnt from Virgil, and his choice of invocation as the appropriate stylistic signature is of great interest. Dante himself (if he rather than one of his contemporaries is the author of the famous *Letter to Can Grande*) had written that *invocatio* (also known as *apostropha* or *apostrophatio* in medieval rhetoric) is a fitting device for poets

inasmuch as they have to petition the superior beings for something beyond the ordinary range of human powers, something almost in the nature of a divine gift.[22]

More recently, in a brilliant essay called 'Apostrophe', Jonathan Culler offers some generalizations that are strikingly apt to Dante and Chaucer. *Apostrophatio* is a rhetorical figure of special interest, because it can be seen as a crucial indicator of the claim to poetic inspiration. Culler writes:

to apostrophize is to will a state of affairs, to attempt to call it into being by asking inanimate objects to bend themselves to your desire. In these terms the function of apostrophe would be to make the objects of the universe potentially responsive forces: forces which can be asked to act or refrain from acting.

In the cases of Dante and Chaucer, the forces whose aid is being invoked are not 'the objects of the universe' but personifications and mythological beings, and the poetic will implied is correspondingly even more ambitious, for it creates the objects whose aid is called for. Culler continues,

One who successfully invokes nature is thus one to whom nature might, in its turn, speak. He makes himself poet, visionary. Thus, invocation is a figure of vocation.

I would add that poetry conceived as vocation – vocation as opposed to the craftsmanship of the minstrel or court entertainer – is precisely what Chaucer is here envisaging, with Dante's help. Culler develops this idea further when he describes apostrophe as

the pure embodiment of poetic pretension: of the subject's claim that in his verse he is not merely an empirical poet, a writer of verse, but the embodiment of poetic tradition and of the spirit of poesy. Apostrophe is perhaps always an indirect invocation of the muse. Devoid of semantic reference, the O of apostrophe refers to other apostrophes and thus to the lineage and conventions of sublime poetry.[23]

The address to the Muses in this proem is the first in English poetry, preceding those in which Chaucer (in *Troilus and Criseyde* II 9 and *Envoy to Scogan* 38) and later Gower (in *Confessio Amantis* VIII 3140) employ the actual word 'Muse'.[24] Chaucer's aim in this proem is precisely to attach himself to 'the lineage and conventions of sublime poetry', which, considered as a possibility for a vernacular language, he encountered for the first time in Dante.

Apostrophatio was a well-known figure in medieval rhetoric, and one illustrated at length by rhetoricians such as Geoffroi de Vinsauf, who even apostrophizes apostrophe – 'apostropha, surge!'.[25] But it was not common in English poetry before the late fourteenth century, except when addressed to a living being who might be thought to be literally present, such as God or the Blessed Virgin. Dante himself, writing in the *Vita nuova* about one of his own lyrics, feels obliged to explain that it is justifiable to use in vernacular poetry those figures that were employed by writers in Latin. He is especially concerned about figures that treat 'inanimate things as if they had sense and reason' and that involve 'making things that do not exist speak', and the Latin examples he gives consist chiefly of *apostrophatio*. They include one addressed to the Muse from Horace's *Ars poetica* ('Dic mihi, Musa, virum . . .', line 141), in which, as Dante says, Horace is quoting from Homer, the true fountainhead of Western conceptions of poetic inspiration.[26] We possess no such theoretical defence of his own poetic style by Chaucer; but, whether or not he knew of the *Vita nuova*, it would be difficult to find any earlier passage in English which uses apostrophe to make a claim to inspiration and sublimity in any way comparable to this passage from *The House of Fame*.

The sources of the three apostrophes in this proem are some key passages from the *Commedia*, one coming early in the *Inferno* as Dante braces himself to undertake his awesome task, one from the beginning of the *Paradiso*, and one from a point in the *Paradiso* at which he sees writing in heaven. They are as follows:[27]

O Muse, o alto ingegno, or m'aiutate;
o mente che scrivesti ciò ch' io vidi,
qui si parrà la tua nobilitate.
(Inferno II 7–9)
Veramente quant' io del regno santo
nella mia mente potei far tesoro,
sarà ora matera del mio canto.
(Paradiso I 10–12)
O diva Pegasea che li 'negni
fai glorïosi e rendili longevi,
ed essi teco le cittadi e' regni,
Illustrami di te, sì ch' io rilevi
le lor figure com' io l' ho concette:
paia tua possa in questi versi brevi!
(Paradiso XVIII 82–7)

O Muses, O lofty genius, aid me now! O memory that noted what I saw, here shall be shown thy worth!

Nevertheless, so much of the holy kingdom as I was able to treasure in my mind shall now be matter of my song.

O divine Pegasean that givest glory and long life to genius, as it does through thee to cities and kingdoms, illumine me with thyself that I may set forth their shapes as I deciphered them. Let thy power appear in these brief lines.

In borrowing from Dante, Chaucer imitates Dante's imitation of the complex and elevated style of classical epic poetry; the resulting stylistic effect is quite unparalleled in earlier English writing, and indeed seems incongruous with the metre used, the jaunty octosyllabics normal for medieval French and English narrative. Many untraditional features of style can be noted, beginning of course with apostrophe itself, and more particularly the apostrophizing of a personified abstraction in 'O Thought' (523). Divinities are addressed in circumlocutory terms: 'O Cipris' (518) for Venus, and 'ye ... that on Parnaso duelle' (520–1) for the Muses. The syntax of lines 523–7 is complex, with the double relative clause inserted between the being invoked and the message conveyed. Syntax is counterpointed against metre to produce enjambement in lines 520–1 and 524–5, and there are corresponding divergences from normal English word-order, with 'Helpeth' coming after 'ryme' instead of before 'me', and 'hyt shette' (itself an inversion) inserted between 'in the tresorye' and 'of my brayn'.[28] Moreover, the lines are full of relatively difficult metaphors which are not traditional in medieval English verse: memory is seen as a 'writing' in the brain which precedes the writing on paper, and the brain is seen as a 'treasury' of mnemonic images.[29] Overall, then, this passage is a remarkable exercise in a poetic style new to English, and a style that claims a standing for the poet and for poetry that was also new. On the other hand, two qualifications must be noted about the passage itself: when Dante's 'alto ingegno' becomes Chaucer's 'engyn' (528), meaning no more than 'skill' or 'cunning', it descends from grandeur to a craftsman's humbleness; and the very fact that Chaucer, unlike Dante, invokes Venus as the presiding deity of his poem indicates that Chaucer does not see himself as having escaped from the relatively constricting role of the medieval courtly poet of love. And, of course, when this proem is replaced in its context, its untypicality becomes manifest, for Chaucer's dream of a journey through the heavens in the claws of a garrulously pedantic eagle is no Dantean vision, and to the dream-Chaucer himself it is no more than a disturbing and unsatisfying holiday from his normal work in the custom-house.

The proem to Book III also begins with an invocation, and is also derived from an apostrophic source in Dante's *Commedia* – this time a single passage from Canto I of the *Paradiso*, which immediately follows the three lines from that canto used in the proem to Book II.

> O God of science and of lyght,
> Appollo, thurgh thy grete myght,
> This lytel laste bok thou gye!
> Nat that I wilne, for maistrye,
> Here art poetical be shewed;   1095
> But for the rym ys lyght and lewed,
> Yit make hyt sumwhat agreable,
> Though som vers fayle in a sillable;
> And that I do no diligence
> To shewe craft, but o sentence.   1100
> And yif, devyne vertu, thow

Wilt helpe me to shewe now
That in myn hed ymarked ys –
Loo, that is for to menen this,
The Hous of Fame for to descryve –   1105
Thou shalt se me go as blyve
Unto the nexte laure y see,
And kysse yt, for hyt is thy tree.
Now entre in my brest anoon!

O buono Apollo, all'ultimo lavoro fammi del tuo valor sì fatto vaso, come dimandi a dar l'amato alloro.	O good Apollo, for the last labour make me such a vessel of thy power as thou requirest for the gift of thy loved laurel.
Infino a qui l'un giogo di Parnaso assai mi fu; ma or con amendue m'è uopo intrar nell'aringo rimaso.	Thus far the one peak of Parnassus has sufficed me, but now I have need of both, entering on the arena that remains.
Entra nel petto mio, e spira tue sì come quando Marsïa traesti della vagina delle membre sue.	Come into my breast and breathe there as when thou drewest Marsyas from the scabbard of his limbs.
O divina virtù, se mi ti presti tanto che l'ombra del beato regno segnata nel mio capo io manifesti, Venir vedra' mi al tuo diletto legno e coronarmi allor di quelle foglie che la matera e tu mi farai degno.	O power divine, if thou grant me so much of thyself that I may show forth the shadow of the blessed kingdom imprinted in my brain, thou shalt see me come to thy chosen tree and crown myself then with those leaves of which the theme and thou will make me worthy.
(Paradiso I 13–27)	

Both poets are introducing the third and last division of their work; but Dante's 'ultimo lavoro' shrinks to become Chaucer's 'lytel laste bok' (1093), and in general this proem shows more signs of unease in the sublime mode than the previous one did. Chaucer, it is true, reproduces the address to Apollo, the god of poetry, the plea to that god not just to assist him but literally to inspire him by entering his breast (1109), the idea of the source of inspiration as 'devyne vertu' (1101), and Apollo's laurel as the symbol of the poet's dignity. On the other hand, he omits much from Dante that must have seemed to him to be excessively difficult in its allusiveness or to make excessively arrogant claims for the poet. He does not ask Apollo to make him his chosen vessel, perhaps because the religious associations of this idea were too strong. He omits Dant's allusion to the two peaks of Parnassus, one of which was said to be sacred only to the Muses, the other to Apollo himself. Dante in fact seems to be mistaken in his classical mythology here, but it is less likely that Chaucer recognized this than that he failed to recognize the allusion, or at least thought his public unlikely to understand it. Chaucer also omits the allusion to the flaying of Marsyas for his presumption in challenging Apollo to a pipe-playing contest. Here there is reason to think that Chaucer did not know who Marsyas was,[30] and in any case I suppose he was reluctant to envisage such painful martyrdom as the price to be paid for what he was doing himself – emulating a godlike precursor. The 'beato regno' which Dante has imprinted by memory in his brain is inevitably reduced by Chaucer to 'The Hous of Fame' (1105), for his theme is of far less ambitious scope than Dante's. Finally, Dante's proud expectation of crowning himself with laurel is re-imagined by Chaucer in humbler terms: he will rush up to the next laurel-tree he sees and kiss it! There is a characteristic-ally Chaucerian literalism about this, and it is conceivable that a similar literalism explains his comment on his own imperfect versifi-cation (1098). His explicit concern with metrical technique is itself rare among medieval English poets (this is the first recorded use of the word 'syllable' in English); but it is just possible, I think, that Chaucer had in mind the phrase 'versi brevi' from the passage in *Paradiso* XVIII used in the previous proem. Dante used that phrase to indicate a sense of the general inferiority of his art to the visionary experience it must strive to express, but Chaucer may have taken it more literally as referring to metrical shortcomings.

Both of these proems, representing Chaucer's first literary response to Dante, are fascinatingly awkward in style. *The House of Fame* is incomplete, and it seems possible that Chaucer's inability at this stage to come fully to terms with a Renaissance sense of the poet's calling was one reason why he did not finish it. Later in his career he achieved a more settled relationship with the ideas and attitudes that came to him from Italy, and was able to express them in a style that was more securely classical – or at least a style of which he might have said, as Petrarch did about one of his own works, that it was 'doppio / tra lo stil de' moderni e 'l sermon prisco' (double between the style of the moderns and ancient speech).[31] I turn now to works of the 1380s in which Chaucer's main Italian source was not Dante but Boccaccio. Dante is of course by far the greater poet, and I do not doubt that Chaucer recognized this: there is plenty of evidence that throughout his career, from *The House of Fame* onwards, his mind continued to be filled with recollections of the *Commedia* and with Dantean turns of phrase.[32] But Boccaccio was a less forbidding and awe-inspiring poet: in some ways one more like

Chaucer himself, and certainly of more use to him as a major narrative source. In particular, Chaucer found in some of Boccaccio's earlier poems models for one of the most characteristic artistic activities of the Renaissance – the reconstruction in a modern vernacular of the world of classical antiquity, imagined in all its difference from the present, yet seen too as part of a universal human world which included pagan as well as Christian. Works by Boccaccio are the sources of two and possibly three of Chaucer's greatest later poems – of *Troilus and Criseyde* and *The Knight's Tale*, and possibly of *The Franklin's Tale*. I do not propose to attempt detailed studies of the stylistic relationships of these poems to their sources,[33] but to consider some of the ways in which they more generally reflect Renaissance perceptions and attitudes.

3. Chaucer's classical romances

In chapter 1 I noted that the Renaissance defined itself in terms of a theory of history and in an important sense consisted of a new experience of the relationship of the present to the past, and especially to the classical past. For a fourteenth-century Englishman, Chaucer possessed an unusually strong sense of history. In part this was probably a matter of personal temperament: Chaucer's historical sense was doubtless a special case of his general relativism, which enabled him to imagine so vividly what the world would look like seen from the heavens, or through the eyes of a woman, or (in a process which has its culmination in the whole structure of *The Canterbury Tales*) through the eyes of people of a wide variety of classes and professions. Again, it has been convincingly argued that the Renaissance sense of history could not have developed earlier, because it was dependent on a sense of the passage of time in individual lives which was only made possible when the mechanical clock came into use in the mid-fourteenth century;[34] and here we may note Chaucer's evident fascination with the measurement of passing time, as shown for example in many of the *Canterbury Tales* link-passages. But these temperamental inclinations of Chaucer's were precisely what enabled him to respond creatively to his contacts with fourteenth-century Italy. Morton Bloomfield is surely right to state that 'Chaucer's sense of chronology and of cultural diversity shows an affinity with certain emphases of the Renaissance' and to suggest that 'it is possible to look to the early Italian Renaissance of which Chaucer had first hand experience' as the source of this affinity.[35]

A familiar but striking example of Chaucer's sense of cultural diversity is to be found in Book II of *Troilus and Criseyde*, in a passage which is not translated from Boccaccio, but which we may reasonably take as Chaucer's reflective generalization of that sense of the alterity of the pagan past that he found in *Il Filostrato*. Like Books II and III of *The House of Fame*, each book of *Troilus and Criseyde* begins with an apostrophic proem that declares the poem's relation to 'the lineage and conventions of sublime poetry'. The Book II proem is addressed to Clio, the muse of history, and after it Chaucer apologizes for his shortcomings in the treatment of love. He does not write from personal experience, he says, and

> Ye knowe ek that in forme of speche is chaunge
> Withinne a thousand yeer, and wordes tho
> That hadden pris, now wonder nyce and straunge
> Us thinketh hem, and yet thei spake hem so,
> And spedde as wel in love as men now do;
> Ek for to wynnen love in sondry ages,
> In sondry londes, sondry ben usages.

Here I omit a stanza, and then Chaucer continues:

> For every wight which that to Rome went
> Halt nat o path, or alwey o manere;
> Ek in som lond were al the game shent,
> If that they ferde in love as men don here,
> As thus, in opyn doyng or in chere,
> In visityng, in forme, or seyde hire sawes;
> Forthi men seyn, ecch contree hath his lawes. (II 22-8, 36-42)

There is no parallel in any earlier English poem to this sequence of thought. The sense of language's diachronic changeability – the necessary basis of the Renaissance revival by imitation of authentic classical literary styles – itself has classical origins, for example in a passage from Horace's *Ars poetica* which Chaucer may well have known:

As woods change in leaf as the seasons slide on, and the first leaves fall, so the old generation of words dies out, and the newly born bloom and are strong like young men.[36]

But a closer parallel with Chaucer's thought can be found in Dante's *De vulgari eloquentia*, where he remarks,

I do not think there should be any doubt that language varies with time, but rather that this should be regarded as certain; for if we examine our other works, we see much more discrepancy between ourselves and our ancient fellow-citizens than between ourselves and our distant contemporaries.[37]

Here there is exactly the same transition as in Chaucer from temporal change to geographical change. For both poets, the past is analogous to a distant country: its inhabitants follow laws and customs that differ greatly from our own, yet beneath the differences they are men and women like ourselves. The educated reader must learn to overcome historical as much as national provincialism.

Very near the end of *Troilus and Criseyde*, Chaucer once more pauses to reflect on the relationship of his work to classical antiquity; but now his thought takes a further leap, as he considers its place in a *literary* history that includes the future as well as the past. It is possible, I think, that Chaucer's reflections here originated in a sense of what he was doing in this most ambitious of his narratives that took shape only as he wrote the poem. As the leaves of manuscript accumulated on his desk, I imagine that it came home to Chaucer with new force that he had created not merely an entertainment for transitory courtly performance, but, in the fullest sense of the word, a book – a book possessing something of that potentiality for permanence that in England had hitherto been associated only with Latin writing, and one that might continue to exist in a future he could only dimly envisage. Boccaccio in his *Teseida* (the source of *The Knight's Tale*, and a work from which Chaucer was just about to borrow for Troilus a passage describing the ascent of the hero's soul to the heavens) had modified a long classical and medieval tradition of poets' farewells to their poems by commending his not only to a human recipient but to its literary precursors (though without naming them).[38] Chaucer here follows his example, but develops still further Boccaccio's Renaissance sense of literary history:

> Go, litel bok, go, litel myn tragedye,
> Ther God thi makere yet, er that he dye,
> So sende mygt to make in som comedye!
> But litel bok, no makyng thou n'envie,
> But subgit be to alle poesye;
> And kisse the steppes, where as thow seest pace
> Virgile, Ovide, Omer, Lucan, and Stace.   (v 1786–92)

Probably no earlier writer in English had referred to his own work by either of the grand titles of *tragedye* or *comedye*; indeed, except for Chaucer's own use of the word *tragedye* a little earlier in his translation of Boethius, perhaps neither word had previously been used in English at all. I suppose too that no earlier writer in English had

related his work to *poesye* as Chaucer does here – *poesye*, by contrast
with the native word *makyng*, evidently meaning all that is represented by the catalogue 'Virgile, Ovide, Omer, Lucan, and Stace':
classical literature, together with those few vernacular works that
were beginning to emulate its dignity and permanence.[39] Chaucer
here is influenced by Dante as well as Boccaccio: in the *Inferno*, when
Dante enters the first circle, he is greeted as sixth in a *bella scola* of
poets of which the other members are Virgil, Ovid, Homer, Lucan,
and Horace.[40] With this Italian help, then, Chaucer is doing something quite new in English in this stanza: he is introducing the
conception of what we now call 'literature', and with it that of a
history of literature in which a work in English may have a place,
however modest, alongside the great writers of antiquity. The
moment at which the idea of 'alle poesye' – literature conceived as a
single continuum of great works – was introduced into English may
have a special interest in our time, when that idea is under attack as
élitist, the imposition by one class on others of what favours itself
under the guise of what is intrinsically and permanently valuable. As
a recent study of literary theory puts it, 'Literature, in the sense of a
set of works of assumed and unalterable value, distinguished by
certain shared inherent properties, does not exist. . . . literature is an
illusion.' The same author ends his book by welcoming 'the death of
literature' as conducive to the transformation of society and 'The
liberation of Shakespeare and Proust'.[41] We may be witnessing the
end of what Chaucer began. His book is 'litel', to be sure,[42] and it is
to be subject to its precursors, to kiss the footsteps of the classics; but
for all that, it can be mentioned in the same breath as Virgil, Ovid,
and the rest.

In one stanza, then, Chaucer relates his book to the past; in the
next he relates it to the future, and once more with a new conception
of the possibilities for writing in English:

> And for ther is so gret diversite
> In Englissh and in writyng of oure tonge,
> So prey I God that non myswrite the,
> Ne the mysmetre for defaute of tonge.
> And red wherso thow be, or elles songe,
> That thow be understonde, God I biseche!　　(VI 793–8)

Unlike Latin, the English language is for Chaucer diverse in its
dialectal forms and in its spelling, so it will be difficult for an English
poem to hold its shape against the errors of scribes. (Chaucer's wish

to fix the verbal form of his works, shown also in the little poem which laments the trouble he has to take in correcting the errors of his scribe Adam, was itself new in English. The more loosely woven native styles of octosyllabic couplets or alliterative verse were less effective in defending the poet's *ipsissima verba* than the syntactically complex style of Chaucer's maturity, borrowed, through Italian, from Latin.) Chaucer does, however, imagine a future in which his book will go on being reproduced, even though miswritten and mismetred; and he was, of course, right about both. Unable to foresee the invention of printing, what he imagines is a continuation of scribal copying and textual corruption; yet to do that was an astonishing act of imagination for a fourteenth-century English writer. What Chaucer does in this stanza is virtually to invent the possibility of a history of English poetry. His fifteenth-century successors looked back to him, as we shall see, as 'maister deere and fadir reverent';[43] and we have learned to discard the cliché, coined by Dryden, of Chaucer as 'the father of English poetry',[44] because we are aware that there was poetry of major importance in English long before his time. But he *was* the father of English poetry in the sense that before him there was no such thing as an *idea* of English poetry; and this is to say that he was the father of English literary history – the first English poet to conceive of his work as an addition, however humble, to the great monuments of the classical past and as continuing to exist in a future over which he would have no control. Sir Ernst Gombrich, in an essay on 'The Renaissance Conception of Artistic Progress and its Consequences', has remarked that 'Without the idea of One Art progressing through the centuries there would be no history of art.'[45] Chaucer has not arrived at the idea of artistic *progress* – he does not dare to think of improving on his great predecessors – but here we can witness him inventing the idea of 'One Poesye', to which his own work would make a modest contribution; and this made possible a history of poetry.

How, then, did Chaucer conceive of his relationship to earlier English poetry? No-one can doubt his indebtedness to it: nearly all his identifiable written sources may be in French, Italian, or Latin, but 'there is every sign that the earlier English romances played an important part in the development of his narrative style.'[46] Derek Brewer[47] and P. M. Kean have shown how much of *The Book of the Duchess*, for example, on the level of style, is virtually made up of phrases from the metrical romances. Nor was it only in Chaucer's earlier works that this was so: a powerful stream of native English idiom flows through his whole oeuvre, including the poems of the 1380s which have most fully assimilated Italian Renaissance sources. Lovers, he writes in *The Knight's Tale*, suffer from frequent changes of mood –

> Now in the crope, now doun in the breres,
> Now up, now doun, as boket in a welle.
> Right as the Friday, soothly for to telle,
> Now it shyneth, now it reyneth faste ...   (I 1532–5)

The lines have a rhythm as jauntily accentual, images as homely, and tags as commonplace, as if Chaucer were the maker of *Sir Degaré* or *Ywain and Gawain*. And in some of Chaucer's latest works, the *fabliaux* of *The Canterbury Tales*, this stream is even strengthened, with long passages of vigorous action conveyed paratactically and in largely monosyllabic diction.[48] Great artistry is of course involved in such cases, but it would surely have been recognized and admired by the popular romance-writers in a way that the proems of *The House of Fame* or *Troilus and Criseyde* would not. Although this aspect of Chaucer's poetry is not my main subject, it is plainly of great importance.

It could rightly be said, then, that if Chaucer despised the romances, 'he was biting the hand that fed him';[49] but despise them he evidently did. The attitude towards this quintessentially 'medieval' genre that emerges from Chaucer's work is analogous to that of the originators of the Renaissance towards all the products of the *medium aevum*. Chaucer was praised in his own lifetime by his admirer Thomas Usk, writing about 1387, for his rejection of 'any maner of nycetè of storiers imaginacion',[50] and Usk was right, I believe, to recognize Chaucer's contempt for what he regarded as the foolish fantasies of romance. The contempt can be seen at its most scathing in the first tale that the pilgrim-Chaucer himself tells in *The Canterbury Tales* – the tale of *Sir Thopas*, a brilliant parody of all that is worst in the popular tailrhyme romances. This is indeed the first certain example of literary parody in English, and the ability to criticize by parody is itself evidence of that sensitivity to style and power of stylistic imitation that characterize the Renaissance. In *Sir Thopas*, the parody is as much a matter of style as of content: it is the combination of impossible marvels with phrasing of grotesquely heightened banality that has the effect not just of biting the hand that fed but snapping it off at the wrist.

35

If the target was tailrhyme romance alone, it must be admitted that that was a form of composition so inept as to defy parody. But I think we must recognize in Chaucer, wherever we look, a contempt for romance of all kinds. How striking it is that his whole, enormously varied oeuvre contains not a single example of the most popular of all medieval matters, Arthurian romance. The nearest approach is in *The Wife of Bath's Tale*, which begins by sketching in a setting 'In th' olde dayes of the Kyng Arthour' (III 857), only to make the point that friars have now taken the place of fairies. By the end of this tale, we have been brought to see that its 'magic', by which an ugly old woman is restored to youth and beauty, is only wish-fulfilment on the part of its ageing teller – an effect not without pathos, but grounded in sceptical detachment. Such 'nycetè of storiers imaginacion' is fit only for women, not for rational beings, as the Nun's Priest implies in his tale:

> Now every wys man, lat him herkne me;
> This storie is also trewe, I undertake,
> As in the book of Launcelot de Lake,
> That wommen holde in ful greet reverence. (VII 3210–13)

The nearest that Chaucer comes to a serious treatment of the more courtly kind of medieval romance is *The Squire's Tale*. Here indeed is plenty of 'storiers imaginacion' – an exotic setting in Tartary; magical devices such as a flying horse of brass, a truth-revealing mirror, and a ring that enables its possessor to converse with the birds (and thus the story of a falcon's unhappy love becomes part of the material); and a plot of astounding complexity. It has been described as 'a typical romance',[51] and indeed if Chaucer had wished to devise a narrative specifically for the purpose of displaying the pleasures and the limits of courtly romance he could scarcely have done better. In fact, given that *The Squire's Tale*, most unusually among Chaucer's poems, has no identified source, it seems highly likely that that *was* what he wished – to construct, in effect, a synthetic romance out of the commonest existing motifs and sentiments. Lavish festivities, *demandes d'amour*, rhetorical elaboration the purpose of which seems to be to construct a style so high that no ordinary man could climb over it (the Squire himself is responsible for that regrettable pun (V 105–6)), definitions of the courtly virtues – nothing is lacking. Some readers have taken *The Squire's Tale* with entire seriousness, and Milton himself seems to have regretted that it should have been 'left half-told',[52] but in my view such readers are more in love with medieval fantasy than Chaucer was. It is in fact left about one-twentieth told, and the manner of its ending is a good pointer to Chaucer's intention. The tale's movement has been extraordinarily slow and leisurely, with full descriptions of inessential matters such as the king of Tartary's birthday feast, the speculations of the courtiers about the magic presents he receives, and the effect of the feast on the participants the morning after. If completed, *The Squire's Tale* would surely have been by far the longest of Chaucer's poems. The complication of its plot and the leisureliness of its narration are themselves typical of courtly romance, as it developed in the thirteenth and fourteenth centuries as a means of conspicuous consumption of its public's ample spare time. At the end of Part II, the narrator says he will leave the heroine nursing an abandoned falcon, and turn to other parts of his material:

> But hennesforth I wol my proces holde
> To speken of aventures and of batailles,
> That nevere yet was herd so grete mervailles.
> First wol I telle yow of Cambyuskan,
> That in his tyme many a citee wan;
> And after wol I speke of Algarsif,
> How that he wan Theodora to his wif,
> For whom ful ofte in greet peril he was,
> Ne hadde he ben holpen by the steede of bras;
> And after wol I speke of Cambalo,
> That faught in lystes with the bretheren two
> For Canacee er that he myghte hire wynne.
> And ther I lefte I wol ayeyn bigynne.   (v 658–70)

The breathless enthusiasm of that 'trailer' of forthcoming episodes is captivating; but do we really want to hear any more? It is surely meant to come as a relief when the tale abruptly ceases after only two lines of Part III:

> Apollo whirleth up his chaar so hye
> Til that the god Mercurius hous, the slye –   (v 671–2)

– to be followed immediately, in the manuscripts of *The Canterbury Tales*, by the Franklin's patronizing praise of the Squire's performance as a storyteller, 'considerynge thy yowthe' (675). *The Squire's Tale* is indeed the poem of a young man, enchanted by excess, and lacking in mature judgment. It is delightfully appropriate that it should be terminated by the shooting down in mid-sentence of Apollo, the god of poetic inspiration, on his way into the mansion of Mercury, the god of eloquence. I do not mean to imply that *The*

Squire's Tale is a parody of courtly romance as sharply satiric as *Sir Thopas* is of popular romance. *The Squire's Tale* has a genuine nobility, it quite lacks the social ineptitude of *Sir Thopas*, and it is a work that can profitably be read from within the limits of its genre. Spenser was not stupid to include a continuation of it in *The Faerie Queene*. But it is best seen as an affectionate and indulgent dismissal of the dreams that beguiled that 'slumber of forgetfulness' which for Petrarch constituted the *medium aevum*. It is an example of the kind of work produced by those who, as Boccaccio put it, 'aimed to bring visual delight to the ignorant rather than intellectual satisfaction to the wise'. The remedy had to be a return to nature analogous to that which Boccaccio saw in the art of Giotto.

As Panofsky has shown, in the thought of the Renaissance the two opposing themes of 'back to nature' and 'back to the classics' could be interwoven and indeed reconciled.[53] The same is true of Chaucer. I have been examining the negative side of Chaucer's attitude towards medieval romance; the positive side may be seen in his renewal of the genre in a group of what may be called 'classical romances' (or equally 'philosophical romances'), in which he both returns to classical antiquity and rejects fantasy in favour of a closer imitation of nature. I am referring to *Troilus and Criseyde, The Knight's Tale*, and *The Franklin's Tale*; and it is significant that in these poems the 'return to the classics' could be carried out only with the help of Boccaccio. *Troilus and Criseyde*, as we have seen, is translated from *Il Filostrato*; *The Knight's Tale* from the *Teseida*; and *The Franklin's Tale* probably derives, though less closely, from a story in *Il Filocolo*.[54] What did Chaucer gain from these Italian sources? (In writing of 'gains' here, I am of course trying to enter into Chaucer's point of view, rather than asserting that the changes involved were objectively improvements.) One kind of gain was undoubtedly in style: Chaucer learned from Boccaccio, as we have seen him learning from Dante in *The House of Fame*, how to compose in his vernacular a poetic idiom that would possess the dignity, the splendour of diction, expressiveness of word-order, and coherence of paragraphing that could be found in Virgil and other poets of classical antiquity. But I set this aside, to be considered later as the aspect of Chaucer's work that most attracted the attention and emulation of his successors. Another kind of gain, which we may well tend to overlook, is of stories simpler, and as we would say more classical, in form than those of the chivalric romances, with their polyphonic interweaving of multiple plots. *Troilus and Criseyde* and *The Knight's Tale*, for all their stylistic elaboration, both tell notably simple stories. Their Boccaccian sources had already selected and shaped the Trojan and Theban material on which they were based, and Chaucer has then pushed them further in the direction of a classical simplicity and rationality of structure. In *Troilus and Criseyde* he has reduced Boccaccio's nine cantos to five books, symmetrically arranged in the form of a great classical pediment, so that Troilus rises from sorrow to joy in Books I to III and sinks from joy to sorrow in Books III to v. In *The Knight's Tale* Chaucer has ruthlessly cut Boccaccio's *Teseida*, reducing twelve cantos to four parts, and leaving no narrative complications, no irrelevancies, none of that procedure by digression that is the typical method of medieval romance.

A third gain was in what we would call realism, or the return to nature. The modern reader, to whom all medieval literature tends to bear the glamour of remoteness, may not notice, as Usk in Chaucer's own time evidently did, the absence from these classical romances of the fantastic devices that are the normal machinery of medieval romance. Here there are no fairy mistresses or lights shining from the hero's head or magical vessels of plenty or green knights or life-preserving girdles. Wonders remain, but they may be reduced to science or illusion, as with the 'disappearance' of the black rocks in *The Franklin's Tale*, which is the outcome of an elaborate and expensive experiment, and may, it is hinted, be simply a matter of predicting and taking advantage of an unusually high tide. (To gain a fuller sense of the difference between Chaucerian classical romance and even the best of medieval romances, the reader may care to imagine *Sir Gawain and the Green Knight* retold in the manner of *The Franklin's Tale*, with the transformation of Sir Bertilak into the Green Knight seen as the consequence of a complicated and fully described experiment in natural magic, while a hint or two is dropped that it might be only the result of a clever disguise.) Or again, wonders may be seen historically, as part of the religion of the classical past. When in *The Knight's Tale* Arcite's horse stumbles and brings him to his death at his moment of apparent triumph, it is a matter not of magic but of the intervention of a callous god who really ruled in the pagan universe – though of course we enlightened men of the fourteenth century know that the 'god' is really a planet that works by means the science of astrology can explain. Above all, the gain was in historicity: these three romances are not set in the exotic never-never land of Arthurian Britain, but in a carefully reconstructed pagan past. (Even in *The Franklin's Tale*, supposedly a Breton lay, the setting is carefully classicized: Brittany, we are told, was then called Armorica, Arveragus and Aurelius are Latin names, and Aurelius prays to Apollo, in a speech which also includes references to Lucina, Neptune, Pluto, and 'Thy temple in Delphos' (v 1077).)[55] Here Chaucer's sense of history, discussed briefly above, displays itself most strongly. Inevitably, his attempt to imagine classical antiquity bears in many ways the stamp of his own age, and his ancient Troy or Athens or Brittany is seen partly in terms of medieval ideas of knighthood and courtliness. But we should not underestimate the effort of imagination involved, for a fourteenth-century English poet, in re-creating a past world with its own customs, its own view of life, and, most important of all, its own pagan religion.

The paganism of this imagined classical antiquity was its most important aspect for Chaucer, and this, we may suppose, for two apparently opposing reasons. It appealed to that adventurous historical sense, that curiosity about the inner beings of worlds other than the familiar Christian world, that is characteristic of the Renaissance; and it meshed into late-medieval developments in Christian thought that saw the virtuous pagan as a test case in issues of grace and salvation. These reasons do not really oppose each other, of course: the 'Renaissance' grew out of the 'Middle Ages', and the same phenomena may seem Renaissance or medieval according to the context in which we consider them. *The Knight's Tale* is the classical romance in which Chaucer's interest in paganism is most fully developed (partly, no doubt, because its source is Boccaccio's closest approach in fiction to the classical past), and it is the one to which closest attention will be given here. It should be made clear that what is at issue is not the accuracy, by our standards, of Chaucer's re-creation of classical paganism, but its imaginative effectiveness in terms of the less critical historical sense of his time. It would never have occurred to Chaucer to aim at a total and sympathetic reconstruction of the past, as we may find it in historical novels of the nineteenth century, such as Flaubert's *Salammbô* or George Eliot's *Romola*, or even in Petrarch's *Africa* in his own century. The very fact of writing in the vernacular, as opposed to Petrarch's Latin, meant that his language had to be pervaded with medieval suggestions; the most he could hope for would be some vivid touches of historical colour in the matters that most interested him and an exclusion of religious incongruities so far as he could attain it. (Thus in *Troilus and Criseyde* he is careful never to let his pagan characters refer to specifically Christian doctrines such as the Incarnation or the Redemption.[56])

A clear example of pagan historical colouring in *The Knight's Tale* is the description of the sacrificial rite performed by Emelye in the temple of Diana in the early hours of the morning preceding the day of the tournament which is to settle her fate in marriage. The tournament itself, chivalry risking death for the sake of a lady, is thoroughly embedded in the prolonged medievalism of northern Europe, as indeed the narrator seems to admit by relating it enthusiastically to the English experience of his own time:

> For if ther fille tomorwe swich a cas,
> Ye knowen wel that every lusty knyght
> That loveth paramours and hath his myght,
> Were it in Engelond or elleswhere,
> They wolde, hir thankes, wilnen to be there, –
> To fighte for a lady, *benedicitee!*
> It were a lusty sighte for to see. (I 2110–16)

But the pagan rites preceding it are a different matter:

> Up roos the sonne, and up roos Emelye,
> And to the temple of Dyane gan hye.
> Hir maydens, that she thider with hire ladde,   2275
> Ful redily with hem the fyr they hadde,
> Th'encens, the clothes, and the remenant al
> That to the sacrifice longen shal;
> The hornes fulle of meeth, as was the gyse:
> Ther lakked noght to doon hir sacrifise.   2280
> Smokynge the temple, ful of clothes faire,
> This Emelye, with herte debonaire,
> Hir body wessh with water of a welle.
> But hou she dide hir ryte I dar nat telle,
> But it be any thing in general;   2285
> And yet it were a game to heeren al.
> To hym that meneth wel it were no charge;
> But it is good a man been at his large.
> Hir brighte heer was kembd, untressed al;
> A coroune of a grene ook cerial   2290
> Upon hir heed was set full faire and meete.
> Two fyres on the auter gan she beete,
> And dide hir thynges, as men may biholde
> In Stace of Thebes and thise bookes olde. (I 2273–94)

Chaucer's main aim in this passage is clearly to give the sense of a religion quite different from that of his own society. Nearly all the detail in his description is taken from Boccaccio (*Teseida* VII, stanzas 70–6); as is usually the case in his handling of Boccaccian sources, he has abbreviated somewhat, and has indeed omitted some of the most alien touches, such as the tearing out of the living hearts of lambs; but the overall effect is still of historical difference. This effect is indeed heightened by the uneasy humour of lines 2284–8: one might suppose this to betray the omission of something scandalous in the source, but in fact Chaucer has left out nothing really significant. Instead he has added this moment of narratorial prurience – almost a giggle at the fantasies set off by the thought of rites involving female nudity – which strongly suggests the distance between the narrator's present and a past that is strange to him. Yet that past is granted the autonomy and dignity of its own customs, just as in Boccaccio: Chaucer's 'as was the gyse' (2279) reflects Boccaccio's 'al modo antico' (referring to the lambs' hearts) and possibly too the phrase 'in usanza appo gli antichi' from Boccaccio's prose gloss on the use of horns in the sacrifice.[57] A Latinate term such as 'cerial' (2290), directly translating Boccaccio's 'cereale', both adds to the elevation of the style and gives a sense of historical authenticity. The same is true of the highly unusual construction 'Smokynge the temple' (2281), imitating the ablative absolute of Latin, but arrived at, so it would seem, by a misreading of Boccaccio's 'Fu mondo il tempio' (the temple was clean) as 'Fumando il tempio'.[58] Thus the 'antique' colouring of the style, as well as the subject matter, comes through Boccaccio, yet Chaucer, referring readers who wish for more information about pagan customs to 'Stace of Thebes [the *Thebaid* of Statius] and thise bookes olde' (2294), makes it appear that he is transcribing his material from genuine classical sources. Here we see in little the use he generally makes of Boccaccio in his 'classical romances'. He wants to give the impression of an authentic account of pagan antiquity (and indeed he does seem to have made some direct use of Statius); but it was only with the help of Boccaccio as intermediary – help that he never mentions – that he could find a way of re-creating antiquity in the vernacular.

In the accounts of such pagan ceremonies (a similar but longer one is that of Arcite's funeral at lines 2853ff), and in the magnificent descriptions of the temples of the pagan gods, Chaucer's interest was persistently literal. One medieval approach to the classical past, as we have seen, involved the allegorization of its myths and legends to produce moral significances that would be edifying for Christian readers; and allegorizing interpretations, sometimes of more sophisticated kinds, continued through the Renaissance, being found, for instance, in some of Boccaccio's own glosses on the *Teseida* and in parts of his *De genealogia deorum gentilium*. Chaucer, however, shows no sign of wishing to allegorize classical material; in *The Legend of Good Women*, for example, while drawing extensively on Ovid for his narratives of suffering classical ladies, he makes no use of the widespread medieval allegorizations of Ovid, and in *The Knight's Tale*, while he borrows material for the temples of the gods from the *Ovidius moralizatus* of Pierre Bersuire, he omits Bersuire's moralizations and retains only literal visual details.[59] His wish was to evoke pagan antiquity as he supposed it to have been, not to re-process it as material for Christian teaching.[60]

At the centre of Chaucer's vision of pagan antiquity is his conception of pagan philosophy. The Boccaccian sources of his classical romances are not seriously philosophical; Chaucer adds to them substantial passages of philosophical thought drawn from Boethius's *De consolatione philosophiae*, which he usually attributes to his pagan characters. Among the more important of such passages are Troilus's song in praise of cosmic love in Book III of *Troilus and Criseyde* and his soliloquy on predestination and freewill in Book IV; Palamon and Arcite's speeches on divine providence in Part I of *The Knight's Tale* and Theseus's speech at the end of Part IV; and Dorigen's speech about the black rocks in *The Franklin's Tale*; but in the first two poems especially there are many other Boethian insertions on a smaller scale. These three romances are pervasively Boethian; they alone would justify Usk's contemporary description of Chaucer as 'the noble philosophical poete in Englissh',[61] and there is certainly nothing else like them in English until the sixteenth century – no other writing that deserves an equal stress on both terms in the phrase 'philosophical poetry'. Indeed, this repeated combination of Boccaccian narrative with Boethian philosophy is unique in medieval literature, to the best of my knowledge, and if we had not come to take it for granted it would surely provoke our astonishment and our question. It will certainly not do to assume with C. S. Lewis that, for example, Troilus's Book IV soliloquy can be seen merely as 'an extra bit of "doctryne"', inserted because it appealed to the medieval taste for sententiousness.[62] The Boethian element in these classical romances has a more specific and more interesting function than that implies. Though Boethius was a late-classical Christian writer, in the *De consolatione philosophiae* he had deliberately confined himself to arguments that would have been available and acceptable to philosophically minded pagans without benefit of the Christian revelation. This work would there-fore have seemed to Chaucer to mark out the area of overlap between Christian truth and rational philosophy – an area that was certainly regarded by him and many of his contemporaries as large and important. From one point of view, the difference between pagan and Christian had traditionally been seen as absolute; but from another point of view, one reason why Christian belief had made its way so rapidly in the world of late antiquity was precisely that enlightened classical paganism was so compatible with Hellenized Christianity. For Boethius, writing at a time when Theodoric the Visigoth had made himself master of Rome,

The distinction between Christian and Pagan can hardly ... have been more vividly present to his emotions than that between Roman and barbarian; especially since the barbarian was also a heretic.[63]

And for Chaucer himself, nearly a thousand years later, when the scholastics had driven 'a wedge between theology and philosophy', as A. J. Minnis has put it in an important recent study of *Chaucer and Pagan Antiquity*, 'the doctrine of *De Consolatione Philosophiae* per-tained to philosophy in the strictest possible sense of the term, a specialist discipline which was grounded on natural reason and in which most of the experts were pagans. The material which he extracted from this source would, therefore, have seemed perfectly germane to his pagan characters.'[64] It is for this reason that Chaucer attributed to these characters both 'Boethius''s questions about the ordering of the universe and Lady Philosophy's answers. To him, and to educated contemporaries such as the 'moral Gower' and 'philosophical Strode' whom he invited to correct the *Troilus* (v 1856–9), this strategy would have appealed not just to a taste for sententiousness but to one for historical accuracy.

This historical interest in pagan philosophy is fully compatible with the Renaissance attitudes that come to Chaucer through his contacts with Italy, but it also plays a prominent part in some late-medieval thought. Minnis shows with great clarity that 'The desire to harmonize Christian and pagan opinions on common intellectual problems is one of the most characteristic features of late-medieval scholastic procedure,'[65] and he illustrates the truth of this with abundant evidence from important scholastic writers such as Bradwardine, Vincent of Beauvais, and above all Thomas Holcot, whose Wisdom commentary was widely read and was certainly known to Chaucer. The role of the virtuous pagan was of crucial importance in the controversies aroused by the nominalists or *moderni* of Chaucer's time, who were concerned to determine on what conditions man could hope for salvation. Was it a minimum condition of being saved that one should know and believe in the revealed truths of Christianity? Was sufficient knowledge of this kind available to certain virtuous heathens through natural philosophy? Might God will, or even bind himself, to save any virtuous man who 'did what was in him' according to his lights, regardless of his knowledge or ignorance of Christian truth?[66] The question of the possible salvation of the righteous heathen was prominently discussed even in vernacular literature – for example by Dante (*Paradiso* XIX–XX), Langland (*Piers Plowman* B X–XII and XV), and the author of *Saint Erkenwald*, all of whom find means by which certain of the heathen can achieve salvation. This question is clearly alluded to, though not settled, in two of Chaucer's classical romances. In *Troilus and Criseyde* Troilus's spirit ascends through the heavenly spheres after his death, finally to be housed 'Ther as Mercurye sorted hym to dwelle' (V 1827) (but we are not told where that was); and in *The Knight's Tale* Arcite on the point of death hopes that Jupiter may have a share in his soul (I 2792), but then all the narrator tells us is that

> His spirit chaunged hous and wente ther,
> As I cam nevere, I kan nat tellen wher.   (2809–10)

At the same time, the early humanists were keenly interested in the many ways in which they felt that the great pagan thinkers anticipated or coincided with Christianity. Sometimes this is a matter of asserting that pagan poetry was to be read allegorically. This was a recurrent theme of Petrarch's, and in his *Invectivae contra medicum*, for example, he defended the pagan poets as divinely inspired, arguing that their polytheistic mythology was a mere veil for monotheism: 'The greatest of these poets have confessed in their works one, omnipotent, all-creating, all-ruling, creator of things, God'.[67] Boccaccio tells us that Petrarch interpreted Virgil's poetry as Christian allegory for the benefit of King Robert of Sicily.[68] A similar case was argued by Boccaccio in *De genealogia deorum genti-lium*, and later Coluccio Salutati went further in his *De laboribus Herculis*, asserting that 'everything which seems fabulous in the poets must necessarily be reduced by due exposition to God or to creatures or to something pertaining to them'.[69] This approach, however, is unlikely to have appealed to Chaucer, with his lack of interest in allegorization. On the other hand, we can also find among the early humanists an awareness that some enlightened pagan thinkers came to the very verge of a Christian understanding of the universe in the literal sense of their works. Thus Petrarch in his treatise *De sui ipsius et multorum ignorantia* writes of Cicero: 'I . . . feel sure that Cicero himself would have been a Christian if he had been able to see Christ and to comprehend His doctrine.' He remarks of Cicero's *De natura deorum*, 'At times you would think you were hearing not a pagan philosopher but an Apostle.' And again, 'You see Cicero describing everywhere in this passage one single God as the governor and maker of all things, not in a merely philosophical but almost in a Catholic manner of phrasing.'[70] Precisely the same might be said of the pagans for whom Chaucer borrows Boethian arguments and terminology in his classical romances, and especially of Theseus in *The Knight's Tale*. I do not, of course, wish to assert that the specific source of Chaucer's conception of pagan philosophi-zing was Petrarch rather than, say, Holcot; only to point out that in this area the distinction between 'late-medieval' and 'Renaissance' can scarcely be made,[71] and that what Chaucer may have derived from Holcot and other late-medieval *moderni* fitted neatly into the historical conception of classical antiquity that he would have gained through his contact with Italy.

I return now to *The Knight's Tale*, to consider the part played in it by pagan philosophizing, culminating in the Boethian speech with which Theseus brings its action to an end. For Chaucer, a major advantage of the pagan setting was that it enabled him to enter imaginatively into questions about the order of the world that would not have been appropriate within a Christian world-view. Many Christians in all ages have, of course, been troubled by doubts about life's meaning and purpose, but nowhere in English literature earlier than Chaucer do we find an imaginative openness towards such doubts which enables them to be given full poetic expression. For this to be possible, the orthodox Christian resolutions to doubt, which close off further question and speculation, had to be at least temporarily suspended: Chaucer had to be able to allow himself to imagine what it would really be like to live inside a world to which the Christian revelation had not been granted.[72]

The world of *The Knight's Tale* is governed not by God but by the gods; and the gods are not merely named in relation to the activities over which they preside – Theseus serving Diana after Mars when he turns from warfare to hunting (1682), and then swearing 'By myghty Mars' as he draws his sword and threatens death to peace-breakers (1706–9), or 'the wynged god Mercurie' (1385) appearing to Arcite with a message in a dream – but they are realized imaginatively with extraordinary power. They are the personifications of forces which are cosmic but also psychological; they are thought of as operating through men as well as on them. The purpose of the descriptions of the three temples and the prayers in them in Part III, a section of the poem sometimes seen as merely decorative or pageant-like, is precisely to give poetic definition to these forces. Mars and Venus *are* the aggressive and sexual instincts, which in medieval courtly literature had been at once expressed and controlled in chivalry and in 'the craft of fyn lovynge' (*Prologue* to *The Legend of Good Women* F 544); and in this way *The Knight's Tale* shows the tradition of courtly romance brought to a higher level of consciousness and generality. The effect is more sombre and disturbing than is common in medieval romances. In the case of Mars, especially, Chaucer evokes a propensity to destructive violence that pervades every aspect of life, in suicide, assassination, tyrannical rule, revolution, and all the horrifying 'accidents' (only they are not accidents, but the expressions of a cosmic bent towards violence) of everyday life:

> The hunte strangled with the wilde beres;
> The sowe freten the child right in the cradel;
> The cook yscalded, for al his longe ladel.
> Noght was foryeten by the infortune of Marte
> The cartere overryden with his carte:
> Under the wheel ful lowe he lay adoun.
> Ther were also, of Martes divisioun,
> The barbour, and the bocher, and the smyth,
> That forgeth sharpe swerdes on his styth.   (2018–26)

The scope of this vision far exceeds that of any earlier romance; and though the description of the temple originates in the *Teseida*, Chaucer has also gone far beyond Boccaccio in imagining daily life, in all its squalor and misery, as shaped by the force that expresses

47

itself with greatest intensity in warfare. Chaucer gained important help from the astrology of his time in giving his vision this comprehensiveness, for it was in medieval and Renaissance astrology, held to be a genuine science, that the pagan gods survived in an active form as the planets that influenced every aspect of life; and a well-known pictorial tradition of the 'children of the gods' showed planets ruling over every activity that was attributed to them. Astrology, then, played a role similar to that of Boethian philosophy in providing Chaucer with a bridge back to the world of paganism. The orthodox view in Chaucer's time, and doubtless the view held by Chaucer himself, was that planetary influences were subordinate to divine providence, and that they were not determining to the extent of negating human freewill. In the pagan world of *The Knight's Tale*, on the other hand, there is no force above the planets.

It is true that the narrator refers to

> The destinee, ministre general,
> That executeth in the world over al
> The purveiaunce that God hath seyn biforn,   (1663–5)

but there he is clearly offering an interpretation from his own world of the pagan world of his story. The pagan characters sometimes refer to Fortune as governing their lives, imagining her, it would seem, as a goddess rather than a mere personification of what happens to happen: thus the widowed ladies who stop Theseus on his way home from defeating the Amazons address him as 'lord, to whom Fortune hath yiven / Victorie' (915–16). Sometimes, as might be expected of philosophically minded pagans groping their way to an understanding of the universe, they seem confused, as Arcite does when speaking of Palamon's arbitrary release from prison at the request of Perotheus. First he exclaims, 'Wel hath Fortune yturned thee the dys!' (1238), but then he asks,

> Allas, why pleynen folk so in commune
> On purveiaunce of God, or of Fortune?   (1251–2)

But already in Part I the chief emphasis is placed on the planetary gods. It is under the banner of Mars that Theseus rides off to destroy Thebes, and when Palamon first sees Emelye he supposes her to be Venus in person. By the end of Part I, the two young knights are in a situation which points to a *demande d'amour* of a kind typical of medieval courtly poetry – whose state is the worse, the one who is released from prison but banished from his lady, or the one who is near his lady but still in prison?

> Yow loveres axe I now this questioun,
> Who hath the worse, Arcite or Palamoun? (1347–8)

But in fact the address to lovers is inappropriate, for the question has not been developed in medieval courtly terms, but in philosophical terms which concern the ordering of the universe by the gods. Arcite laments man's folly in supposing that he knows enough to be able to pray the gods to give him what will be for his good, while Palamon questions bitterly and at length whether the gods have any concern for men at all and whether there is any justice in human sufferings:

> O crueel goddes that governe
> This world with byndyng of youre word eterne,
> And writen in the table of atthamaunt
> Youre parlement and youre eterne graunt,
> What is mankynde moore unto you holde
> Than is the sheep that rouketh in the folde?
> For slayn is man right as another beest,
> And dwelleth eek in prison and arreest,
> And hath siknesse and greet adversitee,
> And ofte tymes giltelees, pardee.
> What governance is in this prescience,
> That giltelees tormenteth innocence?
> And yet encresseth this al my penaunce,
> That man is bounden to his observaunce,
> For Goddes sake, to letten of his wille,
> There as a beest may al his lust fulfille.
> And whan a beest is deed he hath no peyne;
> But man after his deeth moot wepe and pleyne,
> Though in this world he have care and wo.
> Withouten doute it may stonden so.
> The answere of this lete I to dyvynys,
> But wel I woot that in this world greet pyne ys. (1303–24)

The line of argument here is one that must of course have occurred to many Christians; Chaucer, drawing it from Boethius (it is not in the *Teseida*) and attributing it to a pagan, is able to give it fuller and sharper expression than he could easily do in a Christian context.

The callousness that Palamon attributes to the gods is indeed shown by them as the action proceeds. It is Cupid –

> O Cupide, out of alle charitee!
> O regne, that wolt no felawe have with thee! (1623–4)

– that causes Palamon and Arcite each to desire exclusive possession
of Emelye (who does not yet even know of their existence), and to be
prepared to kill each other like wild animals in order to obtain her:

> Thou myghtest wene that this Palamon
> In his fightyng were a wood leon,
> And as a crueel tigre was Arcite;
> As wilde bores gonne they to smyte,
> That frothen whit as foom for ire wood.   (1655–9)

Theseus, finding them in bloody conflict, alludes with an older
man's ironic detachment to Cupid's power over them –

> The god of love, a, *benedicite!*
> How myghty and how greet a lord is he!   (1785–6)

– and then organizes the great tournament which is to settle finally
which of them will marry Emelye. Arcite prays for victory in the
temple of Mars and Palamon for the lady in the temple of Venus.
Each god gives a favourable response, and this inevitably produces
conflict in heaven; on the 'scientific' level of astrology, the two
planets have predicted two apparently incompatible futures. The
benevolent Jupiter attempts to end their strife, but without success;
and then, in one of Chaucer's major non-Boethian additions to the
Teseida, the aged Saturn, god of disasters, intervenes, promising that
each prediction will come true. The solution Saturn finds to the
dilemma is ingenious but utterly callous towards the human beings
through whom it must be worked out. Arcite wins the tournament,
but, at his moment of triumph, Saturn sends a 'furie infernal' (2684),
which causes his horse to stumble and throw him; and thus he dies in
agony, leaving the way open for his rival, who has lost, nevertheless
to gain Emelye.

It should be added that, in speaking of the gods as working
through as well as on human beings, one is in a sense granting to
human beings a share in responsibility for what happens to them.
Cupid *is*, in one sense, human desire; and when Arcite and Palamon
pray, respectively, to Mars and Venus, they are, in one sense,
committing themselves voluntarily to the cosmic forces that bring
about violence and sex. But, in the world of the poem, human beings
are plainly not masters of their fates: the means by which the drives
that work through them eventually shape their individual lives and
deaths are determined elsewhere – and determined, the poem suggests, by Saturn, the outermost of the planets, whose circle includes
all the others:

> My cours, that hath so wide for to turne,
> Hath moore power than woot any man. (2454–5)

Saturn is the master of all types of misfortune, whatever their material causes, from 'the drenchyng in the see so wan' (2456) to plague. The ultimate subjection of human beings to forces outside themselves is confirmed by the case of Emelye. The wish expressed in her prayer to Diana, corresponding to Arcite's wish for victory and Palamon's for Emelye, is 'to ben a mayden al my lyf' (2305); but the answer she gets, accompanied by bloody drops running from the firebrands on the altar (evidently a symbol of the loss of virginity that awaits her) is

> Doghter, stynt thyn hevynesse.
> Among the goddes hye it is affermed,
> And by eterne word written and confermed,
> Thou shalt be wedded unto oon of tho
> That han for thee so muchel care and wo;
> But unto which of hem I may nat telle. (2348–53)

Minnis points out that, 'Unlike Boccaccio's Emilia, Emelye never cries out against her gods: as a virtuous pagan, she accepts their will.' When, however, he goes on to argue that 'Emelye's passivity becomes comprehensible only if it is placed in its historical context and related to her fatalism,'[73] it may be that he draws too sharp a distinction between the pagan and the human. It is really the case in the world in which Emelye lives that, as a representative woman, she is unlikely to have any choice as to whether she is to marry; and, as a princess, she can expect no freedom of choice at all. That would surely have been true, for Chaucer, not just of a pagan princess but of a woman in any world he could imagine; if the race were to continue, even the reluctant formel eagle of *The Parliament of Fowls* would have to accept one of her three suitors one St Valentine's day – and who was to know when Saturn might intervene to reduce her choice? In these circumstances, to think of 'fatalism' as distinctively pagan may be misleading: it is rather that Chaucer's imaginative openness towards a pagan world has enabled him to define a universal human subjection from which Christian piety would tend to deflect his attention.[74]

Saturn's solution to the heavenly dilemma leaves events on the human plane in a deeply unsatisfactory state: Arcite is cut down in his prime, and Emelye is destined to a marriage for which she has no wish. It remains for Theseus, the highest human power, to make

what he can out of this wretched situation; and it will be helpful now
to look back over Theseus's role in the earlier parts of the poem.
Theseus has been presented as the wisest of pagans, and, Minnis has
convincingly shown, as dedicated to a pursuit of justice for which
'Ample precedent may be found ... in stories of virtuous pagan
kings and/or judges' in late-medieval writings.[75] Theseus makes a
series of decisive interventions in the action of *The Knight's Tale*,
each time with the noble purpose of imposing order and justice on a
situation of disorder and injustice. First, when he learns from the
Theban widows of Creon's refusal to allow proper burial to the
corpses of their husbands, he breaks off from his victorious return to
Athens to take vengeance against this tyrant: he 'slough hym manly
as a knyght' (987), and restored the bones of the dead husbands to
their widows for appropriate pagan cremation ceremonies. When
Palamon and Arcite are found living after his battle against Thebes,
he does not have them killed, but takes them prisoner and refuses any
ransom, thus showing himself less mercenary than the Christian
lords who fought in the Hundred Years' War. Next, when he finds
the two Theban knights fighting an illicit and beastlike private duel
'Withouten juge or oother officere' (1712) while he is out hunting, he
interrupts his sport, overcomes his initial anger with them –

> And although that his ire hir gilt accused,
> Yet in his resoun he hem both excused   (1765–6)

– and arranges that their dispute shall be settled, in a properly and
magnificently chivalric fashion, with a tournament in a year's time,
in his own presence, adding

> And God so wisly on my soule rewe,
> As I shal evene juge been and trewe.   (1863–4)

Finally, on the day of the tournament itself, he endeavours to make
its proceedings more orderly and less destructive by commanding
that no mortal weapons shall be used, that those overcome shall not
be slain but forced to retire, and that the tournament shall end as soon
as one of the leaders is defeated.

Each of these interventions is nobly intentioned, and whenever the
response of witnesses to them is mentioned, it is unequivocally
favourable. Yet in each case, the consequence is not simply a transformation of disorder into order. By taking a just vengeance on
Creon, Theseus not only gratifies the ladies, but he also destroys a

whole city,[76] tearing down 'bothe wall and sparre and rafter' (990) and leaving behind a 'taas of bodyes dede' (1005). The *penoun* under which he rides has the Minotaur embroidered on it, an emblem recalling his defeat of this monster, half-man, half-beast, but also capable of suggesting that his own enterprise may be no less ambiguous. By neither killing Palamon and Arcite nor permitting them to be ransomed, he condemns them 'to dwellen in prisoun / Perpetuelly' (1023–4). By converting the private duel into a tournament, he involves two hundred knights instead of two in a potentially highly dangerous conflict; and the danger and animal passions involved are symbolized by the two terrifying champions, Lygurge and Emetreus, living icons of all that is predatory and destructive in chivalry. And last, Theseus's command that there should be 'no destruccion of blood' (2564) at the tournament is rendered invalid by Saturn's interference.

It is in the light of this repeated pattern of nobly intended but partly frustrated interventions by Theseus that his final speech in the poem should, I suggest, be understood. This is his attempt to disclose the benevolent cosmic order that underlies the apparently pointless cruelty of Arcite's sudden death, and it has something of the same self-negating or ambiguous quality, on the level of thought, as his earlier interventions have had on the level of action. In the final speech of the last of the poem's four parts, Theseus gropes towards an understanding of that divine *governance* of the universe that Palamon had questioned in the last speech of its first part. Since he is a pagan, the resources at his command can only be those of Boethian philosophy; but he is a pagan as enlightened as the Cicero described by Petrarch, seeing 'one single God as the governor and maker of all things'[77] and coming to the very brink of a Christian interpretation of life. He begins, then, with the 'Firste Moevere of the cause above' (2987), the Aristotelian *primum movens* and first cause which Aquinas and other theologians had identified with the Christian God. Theseus argues that this First Mover bound all things at the creation of the world with a 'faire cheyne of love' (2988), and it is part of His loving ordinance that human life, like the elements, should not exceed its limits: the apparent imperfection and mutability of the material world is only the expression of His perfection and unchangingness. After giving various examples of the mutability of this world, Theseus proceeds to identify the 'prince and cause of alle thyng' (3036) with Jupiter, and to urge that, since nothing is to be gained by struggling against His decrees, the only wise course is

> To maken vertu of necessitee,
> And take it weel that we may nat eschue.　　　　　(3042–3)

From this turning-point in his argument, he moves on to suggest that it is fortunate for Arcite to have died at the height of his fame; that it is wrong for the survivors to regret that he should have escaped 'Out of this foule prisoun of this lyf' (3061); and that – to 'conclude of this longe serye' (3067) – we should 'thanken Juppiter of al his grace' (3069). He concludes that it would be best now for Emelye to marry Palamon, and thus 'make of sorwes two / O parfit joye' (3071–2). This advice is taken, they are joined in matrimony, and live in love and happiness.

It seems clear that this speech, like Theseus's earlier interventions, is nobly and wisely intended, and its practical effect is to produce both personal happiness for Palamon and Emelye and political concord between the warring states of Athens and Thebes. (A late-fourteenth-century English reader might have seen here a fore-shadowing of the means by which peace could have been made between England and France. Such a peace, cemented by marriage between Richard II and the daughter of Charles VI of France, was, for example, proposed by Philippe de Mézières in his *Epistre au Roi Richart* of 1395, a work which also, as it happens, presents virtuous pagans as offering an example of peace and justice to Christians.[78]) Yet Theseus's argument seems faulty in two respects. One is that it changes course as it proceeds. It begins by arguing that, despite appearances, all is for the best in the world, if only we can recognize the supernatural perfection of which it is the product, but gradually it abandons that undertaking, which would seem to require a sweeping aside of the vividly painful realities of our experience in favour of theoretical and abstract assertion. The conclusion the argument actually reaches is far more modest: this life is a foul prison, but we can do nothing about it and must therefore make the best of it, by patient endurance and by seizing any opportunity that emerges for legitimate happiness. The other fault lies in Theseus's identification of the First Mover of his world with Jupiter. We know more than Theseus does of the ultimate forces of his world, because we have seen, as he has not, the dispute among the gods at the end of Part III. In the cosmology which was generally accepted in Chaucer's time, the term 'first mover' or *primum movens* could be applied with true appropriateness not to any of the planetary spheres, but to the outermost crystalline sphere by which God Himself applied motion to the whole system. Theseus's use of the term may be meant to indicate his aspiration towards a fuller understanding than a pagan could reach; but he applies it wrongly, identifying it with a particular planet-god, and moreover with the wrong one – for in his pagan world not Jupiter but Saturn is the supreme power (and indeed in medieval as in classical cosmology Saturn's sphere directly encloses Jupiter's and applies motion to it). Chaucer, by his own alterations to the *Teseida*, has thereby created a disturbingly paradoxical situation, and we must surely assume that he intended to do so. Theseus, with admirable idealism and piety, sees the universe as controlled by the benevolent Jupiter, and thereby comes as close perhaps as a classical pagan could to a Christian cosmic vision. Allegorizing interpretations of classical mythology frequently identified Jupiter with the Christian God and Dante even addressed God as 'Jove supreme, who wast crucified on earth for us'.[79] But the nearer Theseus comes to an optimistic Christian vision, the more mistaken he is. In his world Saturn indeed possesses 'moore power than woot any man' (2455); and Saturn represents a bent towards disaster or entropy in the whole cosmos. Theseus may frame an arena for battle as a perfect circle, and, like the god of Genesis framing the circular world, he may be pleased with his work: 'Whan it was doon, hym lyked wonder weel' (2092).[80] Yet the perfection symbolized by that circularity is soon shattered by the disorderly forces represented by the gods whose temples are incorporated in the arena, and still more by the force represented by Saturn, to whom Theseus erects no temple, whom he never mentions, and of whose very existence he seems to be unaware.

This paradox suggests to me that, though we must grasp that in *The Knight's Tale* Chaucer was imagining a pagan universe such as would have seemed to him historically possible, it is not enough simply to see his characters, with Minnis, as 'benighted pagans, walking by the best light they have, striving for felicity but not finding it, wasting their devotions on false gods'.[81] I believe that there can be discerned in the tale a Renaissance broadness and daring of vision which, passing through the vitally important historical perspective, recognizes beyond it a universal human nature and situation. The questions and doubts about the cosmic order, given

sharpness and fulness with the aid of a historical sense of the pagan
past, serve ultimately to express a questioning and doubting frame of
mind, and even a scepticism,[82] that were also component parts of
medieval experience. In Chaucer's work, questioning of the
governance of the world is most fully expressed in the three classical
romances: I have in mind passages such as Troilus's

> 'O God,' quod he, 'that oughtest taken heede
> To fortheren trouthe, and wronges to punyce,
> Whi nyltow don a vengeaunce of this vice?'
>
> (*Troilus* v 1706–8)

or Dorigen's

> But, Lord, thise grisly feendly rokkes blake,
> That semen rather a foul confusion
> Of werk than any fair creacion
> Of swich a parfit wys God and a stable,
> Why han ye wrought this werk unresonable?
>
> (*Franklin's Tale* v 868–72)

But this interrogative mood is recurrent in Chaucer, and not only
among pagans. A striking illustration can be found in *The Complaint
of Mars* – admittedly also a poem concerned with the planetary gods,
but one in which the questioning comes not from a pagan but from
the poem's presumably Christian narrator. In the following stanzas
what is questioned is God's purpose in inducing or permitting men
to feel a human love that is often tragic and inevitably, like its object,
fleeting:

> To what fyn made the God that sit so hye,
> Benethen him, love other companye,
> And streyneth folk to love, malgre her hed?
> And then her joy, for oght I can espye,
> Ne lasteth not the twynkelyng of an ye,
> And somme han never joy til they be ded.
> What meneth this? What is this mystihed?
> Wherto constreyneth he his folk so faste
> Thing to desyre, but hit shulde laste?
>
> And thogh he made a lover love a thing,
> And maketh hit seme stedfast and during,
> Yet putteth he in hyt such mysaventure
> That reste nys ther non in his yeving.
> And that is wonder, that so juste a kyng
> Doth such hardnesse to his creature.
> Thus, whether love breke or elles dure,
> Algates he that hath with love to done
> Hath ofter wo then changed ys the mone.

Hit semeth he hath to lovers enmyte,
And lyk a fissher, as men alday may se,
Baiteth hys angle-hok with som plesaunce,
Til many a fissh ys wod til that he be
Sesed therwith; and then at erst hath he
Al his desir, and therwith al myschaunce;
And thogh the lyne breke, he hath penaunce;
For with the hok he wounded is so sore
That he his wages hath for evermore.   (218–44)

God, we know, is good and just; why then does He act in a way that
makes Him seem like man's enemy?

I see no reason to resist the conclusion that Chaucer – doubtless
without wishing to abandon his genuine religious faith – felt a
personal need to ask such unanswerable questions. It was not only
'benighted pagans' such as Palamon and Arcite for whom certain
fundamental aspects of the world provoked irresistible questions yet
were beyond understanding; the same was true of Chaucer himself,
and he needed to imagine pagan worlds in order to gain the impetus
and the courage to interrogate his own God. The possibility of
imagining what it would really be like to live in such worlds was
new: it demanded a daring and a freedom of the imagination that no
earlier English poet had possessed, and that Chaucer could scarcely
have achieved if he had not come into contact with the culture of
early Renaissance Italy. In each of his classical romances the historical perspective is complicated by the fact that the story of pagan
life is represented as being passed on from its supposed classical
sources by a narrator who is naively and even timidly attached to
medieval Christian orthodoxy. The Franklin can speak for all three
narrators when he deplores 'swiche illusiouns and swiche meschaunces / As hethen folk useden in thilke dayes' (v 1292–3). Yet all
three narrators seem torn between admiration and disapproval of
their pagan characters, and in all three poems the narratorial method
was perhaps designed to dramatize and exaggerate the situation of
the orthodox medieval poet reeling under the impact of his encounter with classical pagan life and thought.

The conclusion of *The Knight's Tale*, to return finally to that, is
not, I think, entirely pessimistic. Though Theseus's final speech fails
on the plane of philosophical argument, it succeeds on that of
practical politics, and the poem ends, as it began, with a wedding
that turns enemies into allies. It also achieves another kind of success.
Arcite died horribly, defeated by Saturn; but in his dying speech he

achieved a nobility open only to men, not to the gods: he rose above his pain and his mortality to urge Emelye, with his last words, to marry his friend and rival for her love:

> And if that evere ye shul ben a wyf,
> Foryet nat Palamon, the gentil man. (2796–7)

Like Arcite, Theseus too rises above Saturn and the other gods in the generosity of his imagination, though neither he nor any other mortal can defeat the power of death over the material world. Perhaps it is not too fanciful to suggest that the supreme and gracious Jupiter whom Theseus invokes exists in that generous imagination of man himself – an imagination that is displayed too in the ordering power of art, as in Chaucer's own working of the painful human material of his story into the most nobly symmetrical of all his poems.

3 · The Chaucerian Tradition

1. The praise of Chaucer

I have described Chaucer as the father of English literary history. He was the first English poet to establish a personal tradition of influence, and this is in itself a Renaissance phenomenon, in the emphasis it implies on the fame of the individual poet and on the sensitivity to personal style that makes imitation possible. He died in 1400, and, if we accept Harold Bloom's argument that 'Poetic history ... is ... indistinguishable from poetic influence, since strong poets make that history by misreading one another, so as to clear imaginative space for themselves',[1] the fifteenth century is the first age in which it is possible to speak of the history of English poetry. Before then, as N. F. Blake has noted, texts in English 'seem to appear quite fortuitously, without past or future; they are not part of a native vernacular tradition'. Later writers are not usually aware of the work of earlier writers, the imaginative space they occupy; where they are aware of it, they do not see it as the property of individual precursors; they may incorporate parts of it in their own writing by adaptation or modernization, but without intending to produce recognizable quotation or allusion.[2] Only in the strictly limited field of prose devotional writing can we trace unmistakeable influence; only in Richard Rolle, within that field, can we find an English writer before Chaucer who achieved personal fame. With this exception, general accounts of English writing before Chaucer's time have been, and can be, only annals or chronicles, not histories which establish intelligible relations between one author and another; and those accounts which deserve the name of history have been concerned not strictly with *literary* relations but with literary history as a branch of social or some other type of history.

With Chaucer came a crucial change. He was concerned, as we have seen, with the accurate transmission of his poetry to the future: he was not content that it should simply be absorbed into a body of changing and fading verses. One way in which he took care to establish his fame as an author was by including in his writings several lists of his own works. These are the first such lists by an English author: one is found in the *Prologue* to *The Legend of Good Women*, another in *The Man of Law's Prologue*, and a third, paradoxically enough, in the *Retractions* at the end of *The Canterbury Tales*, where the very words in which he expresses regret at having composed nearly all his poems also act as a final Chaucer checklist. As he envisaged at the end of *Troilus and Criseyde*, his work did go on being read and admired by an increasingly large reading public (and indeed the growth of a lay reading public for works in English was one of the things that made possible the change I am describing). This in turn led to the growth of a Chaucerian apocrypha, which became formally attached to Chaucer's authority when his works were printed, and was not removed again until the late nineteenth century. Admiration for Chaucer was expressed in the form of both praise and imitation by subsequent writers; indeed admiration in both forms was already being displayed in Chaucer's own lifetime. I have quoted Thomas Usk's praise of him as 'the noble philosophical poete in Englissh' – a phrase which implies a true recognition of what he had achieved in his philosophical romances ('the book of Troilus' being specified), and also of the uniqueness of that achievement in the native tongue. The first identifiable imitation of Chaucer is probably *The Boke of Cupide* (also known as *The Cuckoo and the Nightingale*), attributed to Sir John Clanvowe,[3] which begins by quoting the opening lines of Theseus's ironic praise of Cupid in Part II of *The Knight's Tale*. *The Testament of Love* and *The Boke of Cupide* are both works of the 1380s, the same decade in which *Troilus and Criseyde* and *The Knight's Tale* were written; about 1390 John Gower praises Chaucer for having filled the land in his youth 'Of ditees and of songes glade';[4] and praise and imitation of Chaucer continued with renewed intensity after his death.

His younger contemporaries, Thomas Hoccleve and John Lydgate, were among his greatest admirers. Hoccleve, who claims to have known Chaucer and to have received his instruction and encouragement, addresses him apostrophically as 'master' and 'father' –

> O maister deere and fadir reverent,
> My maister Chaucer, flour of eloquence,
> Mirour of fructuous entendement,
> O universal fadir in science . . .[5]

– and compares him with Cicero, as the type of eloquent rhetoric. Lydgate is even more fervent in his praise of Chaucer, expressed in many passages scattered throughout his voluminous works. Chaucer is 'the noble rethor that alle dide excelle', and he is seen very clearly as the originator of a new literary tradition in English, who has 'illuminated' *our* language by causing golden dewdrops of rhetoric to rain down on it:

> Noble Galfride, poete of Bretayne,
> Amonge oure Englisch that made first to reyne
> The gold dewe-dropis of rethorik so fyne,
> Oure rude langage only t'enlwmyne.[6]

The idea of the poet as the refiner and enricher of his native and national language is central to Renaissance thought about poetry. As early as 1364, when the prestige of Latin was still generally unchallenged, we can find Petrarch writing to Boccaccio to protest against the latter's intention to destroy his vernacular writings:

Latin is of course the loftier language, but it has been so developed by ancient geniuses that neither we nor anyone else can add much of anything to it. The vulgar tongue however has only recently been formulated. It has been mishandled by many and tended by only a few; rough as it is, it could be much beautified and enriched.[7]

This idea, along with that of the individual poet's contribution to the process of beautification and enrichment, is repeated again and again as Chaucer continues to be praised down to the early sixteenth century.

In this tradition of praise, Gower and especially Lydgate soon get added to Chaucer as the models to whom later poets declare their allegiance. Thus in *The Kingis Quair*, a poem convincingly attributed to King James I of Scotland, and the earliest work by a Scottish poet in this tradition, the final stanza commends the book to the existing achievements of Gower and Chaucer:

> Unto th'inpnis of my maisteris dere,
> Gowere and Chaucere, that on the steppis satt
> Of rethorike quhill thai were lyvand here,
> Superlative as poetis laureate
> In moralitee and eloquence ornate,
> I recommend my buk in lynis sevin –
> And eke thair saulis unto the blisse of hevin.[8]

Gower and Chaucer are here imagined as having sat on the steps of rhetoric (perhaps envisaged as a temple); they are 'laureate' poets, a term deriving from the laurel crowns of fourteenth-century Italian

poets and implying at once divine inspiration and the mastery of a
body of skilled technique. Their skill is in 'rhetoric', which then
seems to be defined as both edifying content and noble style – 'moralitee and eloquence ornate'. More commonly, however, 'rhetoric' is
seen as a matter of style alone, and indeed as a form of gilding, an
application to the native language of an extraneous brightness and
sweetness. Consider, for example, the stanzas in which William
Dunbar, another Scottish poet, writing in the early sixteenth century,
praised the by now stereotyped trio of Chaucer, Gower and Lydgate:

> O reverend Chaucere, rose of rethoris all,
> As in oure tong ane flour imperiall
> That raise in Britane, evir quho redis rycht,
> Thou beris of makaris the tryumph riall;
> Thy fresch anamalit termes celicall
> This mater coud illumynit have full brycht:
> Was thou noucht of oure Inglisch all the lycht,
> Surmounting eviry tong terrestriall
> Alls fer as Mayes morowe dois mydnycht?
>
> O morall Gower and Ludgate laureate,
> Your sugurit lippis and tongis aureate
> Bene to oure eris cause of grete delyte;
> Your angel mouthis most mellifluate
> Oure rude langage has clere illumynate,
> And fair ourgilt oure spech that imperfyte
> Stude or your goldyn pennis schupe to write;
> This ile before was bare and desolate
> Off rethorike, or lusty fresch endyte.   (Kinsley 10 253–70)[9]

For Dunbar Chaucer's contribution is a question solely of 'fresh
enamelled celestial terms', though there is still some trace of a sense
that such terms would have been appropriate to subject-matter of a
particular kind. It is worth noting that for the Scottish Dunbar, as for
the English Lydgate, Chaucer is the poet not only of England but of
Britain: the literary history of both nations, using different forms of
the same language, is seen as deriving from a single source. I do not
intend a comprehensive survey of fifteenth- and early-sixteenth-
century praise of Chaucer,[10] but a final example from another late
Scottish writer, Gavin Douglas, will serve to illustrate the lengths to
which such praise could be taken:

> . . . venerabill Chauser, principal poet but peir,
> Hevynly trumpat, orlege and reguler,
> In eloquens balmy cundyt and dyall,
> Mylky fontane, cleir strand and roys ryall,
> Of fresch endyte, throu Albion iland braid . . . [11]

Here the very ingenuity of the series of metaphors applied to the great precursor – trumpet, clock, regulator, conduit and sundial of eloquence, clear stream and royal rose – is itself a tribute to the rhetorical embellishment that was seen as his initiating contribution to the poetic tradition.

It is sufficiently clear what were the qualities of Chaucer that his successors imitated and admired. In one sense they admired everything: the universality of this 'universal fader in science', whose achievement seemed to correspond to a Renaissance conception of the poet as a master of wisdom, a 'noble philosophical poete' who confirmed Boccaccio's claim that 'the poets . . . should be reckoned of the very number of the philosophers'.[12] But this picture of Chaucer is obviously drawn from one part of his work in particular: from courtly and historical poems such as the three philosophical romances, and from the four courtly (but also in part philosophical) dream-poems. The broadening of the reading public in the course of the fifteenth century contributed to what is sometimes called a 'bourgeoisification of courtliness', with Chaucer's works being used as a source of wooing poetry or complimentary poetry far beyond courtly circles;[13] but in Chaucer's own work we can already discern an attempt to make courtly values and styles available outside the court (*The Franklin's Tale* is only the most obvious example) and to broaden and deepen courtliness itself by giving it a philosophical scope (thus in *The Parliament of Fowls* a St Valentine's day poem expands to take in general ideas of love and nature drawn from Cicero, Boethius and Alanus de Insulis). This was the Chaucer who had the greatest influence on the 'Chaucerians' – not, for example, the author of the *fabliaux*.

Further, as we have seen, it was the style of this part of Chaucer's work that was judged to be its major achievement. Chaucer was praised for his 'rhetoric', for providing the model of a high style that was seen as giving English poetry for the first time the appropriate dignity for serious subject-matter.[14] Nineteenth- and twentieth-century readers have not normally regarded this elevation of style as a very striking part of Chaucer's achievement; but we should pause before dismissing this view as a mere misconception. The Chaucer seen by these admiring disciples is at least part of the real Chaucer: after all, they are not likely to have been totally wrong about him. We may admire him for qualities such as urbane humour, sympathetic realization of human feeling, mastery of narrative structure and pace, irony; and these qualities are doubtless all present in his work, though one may suspect the importance of irony to be as much exaggerated in our time as that of rhetoric was in the fifteenth century. But we generally fail to notice his elevation of poetic style, precisely because his stylistic innovations were totally successful. Chaucer was really 'the firste that ever enluminede owre langage with flowres of rethorike and of elloquence', as Lydgate put it;[15] it is not too much to speak of a Chaucerian stylistic revolution, the achievements of which have become invisible because they have shaped all that followed, and thus have come to seem merely natural components of literary English. Chaucer's innovations, with much help from the work of his early imitators (which, as we shall see, involved some distortion of what they most admired), have passed into the central current of English poetic style from the Elizabethans to the Victorians and beyond.[16] It may be sufficient to mention some names: Spenser, Marlowe, Shakespeare, Milton, Dryden, Pope, Wordsworth, Keats, Tennyson, Yeats. It is this current that has linked English poetry, as it first did in Chaucer, to that of the classical past and the European present. There have been cross-currents, of course, important rebellions against this stylistic hegemony, most notably (to our eyes) in the present century; but it is far too early to suppose that the stream of which Chaucer is the fountainhead has yet run dry.

I will consider in more detail the stylistic features that mark the Chaucerian tradition when discussing Lydgate as its exemplary representative, but here it will be useful to mention one general feature that is especially likely to fade into unnoticeability. This is the composition of individual lines or couplets in which every word is carefully chosen and ordered to create an effect of beauty of sound and meaning. Since the sixteenth century readers have usually taken for granted that this could be expected of English poets: sometimes indeed it has been the only thing expected of them. Yet before Chaucer it was not so. Pre-Chaucerian English poetry (with the possible exception of some works of the Alliterative Revival which were roughly contemporary with Chaucer) is in general fast-moving and loosely textured, intended for listeners and not demanding close local attention. It is usually at its best in narratives of some length, where the overall, large-scale effect is of more importance than the shaping of the individual line. J. A. Burrow has aptly remarked that 'This strict subordination of the local and concentrated effect to the demands of a larger context marks the style of Ricardian poetry as essentially a long-poem style.'[17] Here the only word I would question is 'Ricardian', which fails to make the distinction between Chaucerian and pre-Chaucerian. Poetry in the Chaucerian tradition, at its best, was composed for leisurely and discriminating readers rather than listeners; it achieved lyrical effects even in narrative or exposition, and often incorporated unfamiliar metaphors and similes demanding sensitive attention if their implications were to be grasped. Here is an example from Lydgate:

> Fresshnesse off floures, off braunchis the beute,
> Have ai on chaung a tremblyng attendaunce.[18]

The springtime flowers and branches have a precarious beauty; they literally tremble in the breeze, but they are also imagined figuratively as attending with timidity on the semi-personified change that is their master and that will all too soon make them bare and dry. In sound and rhythm the lines have a tremulous delicacy that echoes their sense: note for example the hesitant movement associated with the chiastic construction in the first line. Another example, even briefer, this time from Hoccleve: 'Excesse at borde hath leyd his knyf with me.'[19] Hoccleve, as part of a mock-penitential exercise addressed to the god Health, is accusing himself of offending against health by indulging in bodily excesses. He personifies Excess, and says that he has been his table-companion or mess-mate (at medieval feasts, the guests were regularly divided into pairs who were served together). And this relationship of abstractions – excess/myself – is then realized in a single concrete detail: Excess has laid his knife at table with Hoccleve. Innumerable other instances might be given, but the general point has perhaps been adequately indicated. Poetry which is even intermittently like this is quite untypical of the period before Chaucer.

It is now time to assess in more detail the use made of Chaucer in specific works by his admiring successors. Of these the most admired in his own time was John Lydgate, who was also by far the most prolific. He was born about 1370 at Lydgate in Suffolk, entered Bury St Edmund's Abbey as a Benedictine monk about 1385, and died and was buried at Bury in 1449 or 1450, after a long life spent mostly outside the cloister, often employed as a writer by royalty, nobility, or civic bodies. Among Lydgate's works were the *Troy Book*, a poem of about 30,000 lines translated from the Latin of

Guido de Columnis for Henry V, 1412–20; *The Pilgrimage of the Life of Man*, about 25,000 lines translated from the French of Guillaume de Deguileville for the Earl of Salisbury, about 1426–28; and *The Fall of Princes*, some 36,000 lines translated about 1431–9 from Boccaccio's Latin for Humphrey Duke of Gloucester. (Humphrey was the greatest patron of letters of his age and the only one to show any interest in Renaissance learning: he possessed, for example, manuscripts of works by Petrarch, Boccaccio and Salutati.) Discussion of poems of such enormous length would inevitably be unwieldy, and their very existence is an indication of an important way in which Lydgate is quite un-Chaucerian. Chaucer's longest single work, the *Troilus*, is of only 8239 lines; there and elsewhere he persistently abridges his sources; and, for all the diffuseness of his style when judged by the standards of the twentieth-century slim volume, he was rightly praised by Caxton in the 1480s, in terms borrowed from Chaucer's own description of his Clerk of Oxenford, as one who 'wrytteth no voyde wordes, but alle his mater is ful of hye and quycke sentence'.[20] There is, however, another and considerably shorter work of Lydgate's which is particularly apt for our present purpose. This is *The Siege of Thebes*, a poem of more manageable length (a mere 4716 lines), and one consciously and carefully composed as part of the Chaucerian tradition, indeed as an addition to *The Canterbury Tales*. It dates from 1420–2; its source is some version of the French *Roman de Thèbes*; the patronage under which it was written, if any, is not known.[21]

2. Lydgate's Canterbury Tale

A major stimulus offered by Chaucer to his successors was that so much of his work was left incomplete. As we shall see later, they frequently expressed anxiety at the impossibility of matching his achievements, but this might be allayed in specific cases by the sense of invitation offered by a gap left to be filled. Harold Bloom, borrowing a term from Lacan, defines one type of poetic influence as 'the *tessera* or link', in which 'the later poet provides what his imagination tells him would complete the otherwise "truncated" precursor poem and poet'.[22] *The Canterbury Tales* is or appears to be genuinely truncated. The most striking gap, if we can take the Host's proposals in the *General Prologue* as Chaucer's plan for the whole work, is the absence of any tales for the homeward journey. It is this gap that *The Siege of Thebes* is designed to fill, or rather to begin filling, since it is offered only as the first tale of the first day of the work's missing second half. In his prologue Lydgate recalls the tale-telling of *The Canterbury Tales*, following Chaucer in treating the pilgrimage as a real event of which the latter was merely 'Chief registrer'.[23] He explains that, visiting Canterbury

> The holy seynt pleynly to visite,
> Aftere siknesse my vowes to aquyte,   (71–2)

he happened by chance to take lodgings in the very same inn as Chaucer's pilgrims. There he was accosted by 'her governour, the Host' (79), and invited to join them for supper and for the return journey next morning, when he would be obliged to join the tale-telling competition. He agreed, and was called on to tell the first tale, and *The Siege of Thebes* is the outcome.

In attaching to *The Canterbury Tales* a story told by a pilgrim not belonging to the original group that set off from the Tabard, Lydgate is already imitating Chaucer.[24] It will be recalled that 'At Boghtoun under Blee' (*Tales* VIII 556) Chaucer's pilgrims had been overtaken by 'A man that clothed was in clothes blake' (VIII 557), and that his unexpected arrival led to the telling of an additional tale, that of the Canon's Yeoman. It seems clear that Lydgate, also dressed in the black garb appropriate to his religious order (*Siege* 73), is a figure parallel to the Canon. Lydgate says that he was accompanied by 'My man to-forn with a voide male' (76),[25] and he appears to have arrived at this detail by combining two elements from *The Canon's Yeoman's Prologue*: the Canon is also accompanied by 'his yeman' (VIII 562), and we are told, in a couplet that a careless reader might well relate to the servant rather than the master, that

> A male tweyfoold on his croper lay;
> It semed that he caried lite array.   (VIII 566–7)[26]

One further indication that Lydgate may have had *The Canon's Yeoman's Prologue* as his model for attaching *The Siege of Thebes* to *The Canterbury Tales* occurs when he makes the Host assert that none dare refuse to obey his command to tell a tale, 'Knyght nor knave, *chanon*, prest, ne nonne' (*Siege* 137).

A far more important connection of the *Siege* with the *Tales* lies in its relationship with *The Knight's Tale*. This is, of course, the first tale of the outward journey, and immediately follows the *General*

Prologue; *The Siege of Thebes* is presented as the first tale of the homeward journey, and is given a prologue (discussed further below, page 75) manifestly modelled in style on the opening of the *General Prologue*. Appropriately, then, the *Siege* is intimately linked with *The Knight's Tale* in subject-matter. It 'completes' Chaucer's first tale by recounting the earlier stages of the Theban legend, to which there are so many allusions in its predecessor, and it ends by taking us up to the beginning of *The Knight's Tale*, 'as my mayster Chaucer list endite' (*Siege* 4501), with the appeal of the Theban widows to Theseus. In the two hundred or so lines of narrative from the assembly of the widows, whose 'clothes blake' (*Siege* 4417) symmetrically match the teller's 'cope of blak' (73) of the prologue, I count allusions to no fewer than thirty separate lines occurring in *The Knight's Tale* I 878–1010. Lydgate obviously had a manuscript of Chaucer's poem in front of him, and as he constructs a mosaic of his own from Chaucer's words and phrases his part of the Theban story merges into that of his master. Lydgate may have persuaded himself that not only *The Canterbury Tales* as a whole but also *The Knight's Tale* was 'truncated': he would have found some warrant for this in the Knight's sharp abridgment of his story at its very beginning, and his modest excuse that

> I have, God woot, a large feeld to ere,
> And wayke been the oxen in my plough.
> The remenant of the tale is long ynough.   (I 866–8)

At any rate, these lines evidently stuck in Lydgate's mind, for he has a passage near the end of the *Troy Book* imitating them.[27] Yet there is a sense in which Lydgate in *The Siege of Thebes* goes beyond 'completing' Chaucer's work. When he encounters the company of pilgrims at Canterbury, Chaucer himself is apparently not among them. Though we may find this surprising, there is no sign that Lydgate does: if in one sense he as taken over the role of the Canon or his yeoman, in another he has taken over that of the pilgrim-narrator of the whole work – he has become the absent Chaucer. I shall return to this idea later.

My immediate purpose is to examine the nature of Lydgate's Chaucerian imitation in *The Siege of Thebes*. In his prologue he praises Chaucer, in terms that correspond to the norm we can now recognize, as

> ... hym that was, yif I shal not feyne,
> Floure of poetes thorghout al Bretayne,
> Which sothly hadde most of excellence
> In rethorike and in eloquence.   (39–42)

Identifying Chaucer without naming him, this passage illustrates the rhetorical figure of *circumlocutio* and at the same time offers a verbal equivalent to Chaucer's physical absence from the pilgrimage as Lydgate describes it. We have seen that the 'rhetoric' and 'eloquence' of the Chaucerians were largely matters of the elevation of verbal style. It should be noted, though, that for Lydgate genuine eloquence was a matter of high meaning as well as high style, or perhaps it would be better to say that elevated thought and feeling could be seen as one element of high style. Thus he goes on to praise Chaucer for faithfully recording the tales of all his pilgrims in *substaunce* and *sentence* as well as by sweetness of expression:

> Be rehersaile of his sugrid mouth,
> Of eche thyng keping in substaunce
> The sentence hool withoute variaunce,
> Voydyng the chaf, sothly for to seyn,
> Enlumynyng the trewe piked greyn
> Be crafty writinge of his sawes swete. (52–7)

(The primary sense of *sawes swete* is 'sweet sayings', but it seems possible that there is a pun on *sawes* meaning 'sauce'. It is the sweet sauce of Chaucer's *sugrid* eloquence that prevents the substance of the pilgrims' tales from decaying and keeps it 'hool withoute variaunce'.) Lydgate converts narrative into eloquence not just by preserving it in the gold dewdrops of rhetoric but also by extracting from it a fruitful moral doctrine. The actual relationship between narrative and moral generalization in Chaucer is more complex than Lydgate grasped, but we may assume that he saw as quintessentially Chaucerian the union of verbal and moral eloquence in some lines near the end of the *Siege* that derive from a similarly placed stanza in *Troilus and Criseyde*:

> Lo her, the fyn of contek and debat,
> Lo her, the myght of Mars, the froward sterre;
> Lo what it is for–to gynne a werre. (4628–30)[28]

In one of the few substantial published studies of the *Siege*, Robert W. Ayers rightly emphasizes that Lydgate's purpose was 'to teach some moral and political lessons'. However, when he goes on to speak of the 'moral – and thus extraliterary – relevance and application' of the *Siege*, he draws a distinction that would probably have been meaningless to Lydgate.[29] The category of 'literature' or 'poetry', introduced into English by Chaucer's practice and theory, must still have included moral weightiness. On the other hand, it must be admitted that from our point of view the distinction between 'literary' and 'moral' is often demanded by Lydgate's practice in the *Siege*. In genuine Chaucerian eloquence, the literary and the moral harmonize subtly, but in Lydgate, as we shall see, each is developed and indeed exaggerated on its own terms, and the result is sometimes odd or painful discord.

The extent to which Lydgate's verbal eloquence in *The Siege of Thebes* can be considered as authentically Chaucerian is difficult to determine, for two reasons. One I have already mentioned: that the Chaucer imitated may be unrecognizable to us because he is different from the Chaucer we see. The other is that the more Lydgate imitates Chaucer, the less, in one sense, he can be like him, for Chaucer was not imitating any other English poet. Further, it is hard to decide how far Lydgate intended his adaptations of specific Chaucer passages to be recognized as such. Did he hope to *be* the Chaucer of his time, or to practice a recognizably secondary art, one of skilful allusion to familiar sources? There is perhaps no simple answer to this question. N. F. Blake urges that in general 'fifteenth-century writers who ... wanted to imitate Chaucer went in for a Chaucerian style rather than for deliberate echoes of his poems',[30] but in the case of the *Siege*, a poem manifestly designed as a counterpart to *The Knight's Tale*, it seems likely that Lydgate would have expected his audience to recognize at least some specific echoes. At times, no doubt, his aim is, as Blake suggests, no more than to create a generally Chaucerian texture by weaving together fragments from different passages in Chaucer. These might be taken from *The Knight's Tale* itself: thus the description of the army Adrastus gathers to assist Polymytes begins as follows:

> Ther men may see many straunge guyses
> Of armying newe and uncouth devyses,
> Every man after his fantasye ...   (2661–3)

If those lines seem oddly familiar, it is because they almost entirely consist of words and phrases taken from two different arming scenes in *The Knight's Tale*. The first describes the knights gathered by Palamon (I 2118ff), and from this Lydgate borrows *guyses*, *newe*, and *Every ... after his*; the second describes the preparations on the morning of the tournament (I 2491ff), and from this come *Ther ... may see*, *uncouth*, and *devyses*. Elsewhere Lydgate moves freely among the various works that make up the Renaissance side of

Chaucer's achievement and that formed the chief sources of the style of his disciples. For example, Amphiorax, the Greek high priest (or, as both Chaucer and Lydgate call him, 'bishop'), disappears with his chariot into the earth in the final battle at Thebes. This is an incident referred to in *Troilus and Criseyde* (II 104–5), but Lydgate chooses to describe it in lines adapted neither from there nor from *The Knight's Tale*, but from a quite different context in *The Franklin's Tale*. Compare Lydgate's lines –

> For he ful lowe is discendid down
> Into the dirk and blake regyoun
> Wher that Pluto is crownyd and ystallyd
> With his quene, Proserpina i-callyd　　　　　(*Siege* 4041–4)

– with the passage in which Chaucer's Aurelius begs Apollo to intercede with Lucina, the moon-goddess, in her role as Proserpina:

> Prey hire to synken every rok adoun
> Into hir owene dirke regioun
> Under the ground, ther Pluto dwelleth inne.
> 　　　　　　　　　(*Franklin's Tale* v 1073–5)

Here we are not called on to remember the context of the source-lines, yet the mythological *circumlocutio* (for the underworld, or hell) into which Lydgate has reshaped them elevates the level of his style and at the same time has an elegant appropriateness to his pagan subject-matter. (It would be more elegant still if Lydgate had not already asserted, with an unChaucerian pious vehemence, that 'thus the devel for his old outrages, / Lich his decert, paied hym his wages' (4039–40) – a characteristic example of discord between eloquence and moralism.)

At other times, though, Lydgate is clearly challenging comparison with Chaucer passages that he must expect us to remember. The opening lines of the *Siege* are manifestly modelled on, and indeed attempt to outdo, the opening lines of *The Canterbury Tales*, thus providing an introduction to the return journey parallel to that which Chaucer had composed for the outward journey. Again, lines 4565–602 of the *Siege* form an imitation of Chaucer's showpiece *occupatio* on Arcite's funeral (*Knight's Tale* I 2919–66). *The Siege of Thebes* is poised somewhat uneasily between being simply another *Canterbury Tale*, comparable with those Chaucer had already written, and being an acknowledged pastiche of the master's methods.

In moving on now to consider in more detail some of the
characteristics of Lydgate's Chaucerian poetic style, I propose to
take for granted the composition of lines of individual beauty,
discussed above. Pearsall notes how frequently 'it seems that a
particular cadence in Chaucer's verse has stuck in Lydgate's mind, so
that he keeps coming back to it, trying to catch it himself'.[31] *The
Siege of Thebes* is full of lines using the resources of parallelism,
contrast, alliteration, assonance, and so on, in such a way that beauty
of sound matches strength and elegance of thought:

> Thy byrth and blood ar bothe two unwist   (494)
>
> Wrong, wrouht of olde, newly to amende.   (3700)

There would be no end to identifying and analysing such lines; many
will be included in passages quoted in this section, and I can only
invite the reader to be alert to them. Beyond this, there are three
aspects of the Chaucerian poetic style that seem especially worth
comment: the predominance of Latinate diction; the use of complex
syntactical structures, often accompanied by an artificial word-
order, on the model of Latin poetry; and the substitution of figurative for literal and straightforward modes of expression. I will
consider each of the three separately.

The Latinate or, as it is often called, 'aureate' diction of fifteenth-
and early-sixteenth-century poetry has been much discussed by
scholars,[32] and can therefore be dealt with briefly here. It seems
likely that Chaucer himself did not introduce many new words from
Latin sources into the English language, but he was probably the first
to use in verse many words of Romance origin which were already
part of upper-class speech or of technical (e.g. scientific or philosophical) vocabularies. This process was then continued and intensified by his followers, and especially by Lydgate, who saw such
diction as a distinctive feature of Chaucer's poetic style. It has been
pointed out that many such words introduced by Lydgate have now
become 'so much part of the English language that we can hardly
imagine how it managed without them'.[33] Chaucer showed notable
tact in mingling this new range of poetic diction with familiar native
vocabulary: indeed, even at his most learned and eloquent, it may be
said that he continued to rely fundamentally on the common experience of life, expressed in the common tongue. It was probably in the
last decade of his career that he wrote the remarkable series of
fabliaux, in which the settings are those of different kinds of working

life; and the distinctive flavour of these works is given precisely by
the mingling of the gross with the refined and learned. A striking, if
extreme, example is the use in *The Summoner's Tale* of learned Latinate terms such as *ymaginacioun, probleme, ars-metrike, demonstracion,
reverberacioun, demonyak* in connection with the unsavoury task of
dividing a fart into twelve equal parts (*Canterbury Tales* III 2218–42).
There was little imitation of the *fabliaux* among the Chaucerians, and
what there was had little success. Chaucer's successors, in England at
least, did not possess his blending power, and they seem to have been
so dazzled by the innovations in diction that were part of his high
style that they imitated them to excess. It must be said, however, that
'aureate diction' is not an especially noticeable feature of the style of
The Siege of Thebes. Let me give a single example which shows
Lydgate as an authentic Chaucerian, using Chaucer in the way in
which Chaucer had used earlier non-poetic writings. We can see
Chaucer, for instance, transferring the word *orizonte* from scientific
contexts (as in his own *Treatise on the Astrolabe*) to poetic uses, as in
'And whiten gan the orisonte shene' (*Troilus* v 276) or 'For th'orisonte hath reft the sonne his lyght' (*Franklin's Tale* v 1017).[34] Lydgate
accurately continues this Chaucerian process of adaptation. Thus in
Chaucer the word *merydyen* occurs only in scientific prose;[35] Chaucer
had begun to adapt it to verse in the line 'Phebus hath laft the angle
meridional' (*Squire's Tale* v 263); Lydgate completes the adaptation by
using *merydyen* itself in an imitation of the Chaucerian *chronographia*:

> Whan Phebus passyd was merydyen
> And fro the south westward gan hym drawe,
> His gylte tressys to bathen in the wawe ...   (*Siege* 4256–8)

Such fusions of scientific astronomy with classical mythology,
learned by Chaucer from Italian sources which were almost certainly
unknown to his imitators, must have seemed among the most
beautiful devices with which he had elevated English poetic style. In
Troilus and Criseyde Chaucer has 'The gold-ytressed Phebus heighe
on-lofte' (v 8) and

> The laurer-crowned Phebus, with his heete,
> Gan, in his course ay upward as he wente,
> To warmen of the est see the wawes weete,   (v 1107–9)

but Lydgate himself added the charming idea of the sun-god *bathing*
his tresses in the waves. Sea-water is unlikely to have been very good
for Apollo's hair, but the mixture of stylistic levels is pleasant, and

the visual effect implied, of sea mingled in strands with reflected sunlight, is delightful.

Of all Chaucer's stylistic innovations, those in syntax and word-order were the most completely successful and have for that very reason become the least noticeable. As we saw exemplified in some passages from *The House of Fame*, he brought to English, with the help of Italian, a stricter and more elaborate syntactical organization, enabling him to compose lengthy periodic sentences in which the logical relationship of the parts was unambiguous, and the word-order was freed for expressive purposes. A good example is the opening stanza of *Troilus and Criseyde*, where the subject and verb of the first sentence are deferred until the fifth line:

> The double sorwe of Troilus to tellen,
> That was the kyng Priamus sone of Troye,
> In lovynge, how his aventures fellen
> Fro wo to wele, and after out of joie,
> My purpos is, er that I parte fro ye.

The artifice has come to seem natural, yet, as C. S. Lewis observed, 'at no period of the English language would such a sentence have been possible in conversation'.[36] An opening was doubtless felt to be an obvious place for such a display of rhetorical skill, and the first sentence of *The Canterbury Tales* – now perhaps the most famous passage Chaucer ever wrote – offers a still more impressive instance of architectonic power at the syntactical level. There too we scarcely notice the syntactical complexity or the un-English word-order, even though the sentence is extended over 18 lines by a whole series of adverbial clauses of time, each compound in structure, and many containing further subordinate clauses. We have to make our way through these, through *Whan that . . . and / Whan . . . and . . . and*, before we get to *Thanne* and the main verb of the sentence in line 12; and that is followed by further co-ordinate clauses and a final relative clause, to make a single syntactical unit with an intensely dramatic structure, a sentence which, for all its length and complexity, never leaves us in any doubt as to its logic.

Throughout his poetry, Lydgate attempts highly ambitious syntactical structures on the Chaucerian model, but he tends to see them as applied decorative devices lacking in any logical or semantic function, and in any case is often quite unable to control and complete them. His sentences trail on from stanza to stanza or couplet to couplet, full of relative clauses and absolute constructions (absolute constructions based on the present participle being almost a Lydgatean hallmark), and there seems no reason why they should ever end – indeed, quite frequently they simply stop without being completed. (We should remember, of course, that neither Lydgate nor Chaucer used modern punctuation, and the decision where a full stop should be placed remains to be made by the nineteenth- or twentieth-century editor.) It was understandable that in *The Siege of Thebes*, as was noted above, Lydgate should compose an opening sentence paralleling that of *The Canterbury Tales*; and his first sentence is an obvious attempt to *quite* or *overmacche* that of the *General Prologue*.[37] It is another *chronographia*, beginning like Chaucer's with *Whan*, and proceeding through a series of adverbial clauses of time; and the intention is doubtless that we should wait eagerly for the long-deferred main clause. If we do, our wait is a long one, for, in the line in which Chaucer's sentence concludes, Lydgate is only just getting into his lumbering stride, and he takes a further *whan* as a cue to embark on a rambling sketch of Chaucer's poem and a eulogy of Chaucer. This does, it is true, eventually return 40 lines later to 'the tyme that thei deden mete', but the sentence finally expires from exhaustion somewhere around line 65 (the moment of death is difficult to determine), without ever having achieved a main clause at all. I am sorry that this extraordinary 'sentence' is too long to quote. Besides its syntactical interest, it is full of Chaucerian recollections, not only of *The Canterbury Tales* but of *Troilus and Criseyde* and the *Prologue* to *The Legend of Good Women*. Yet these memories are essentially verbal, and are accompanied by a remarkably shaky grasp of the substance of what is being praised. Lydgate supposes that Chaucer's Reeve had 'dronken of the bolle' (31), an idea which would have made that sour but sober old man still sourer, and he manages to confuse the Pardoner's beardless chin with the Yeoman's 'pylled nolle' (32) and the Summoner's 'face of cherubyn' (34). It is as though Chaucer for Lydgate was essentially a world of words, rather than, as for most modern readers, a world of people.

The syntax of *The Siege of Thebes* is by no means always as inept as in this prologue. Indeed, even that is mildly pleasing in its soporific way: Lydgate has learned mellifluousness from Chaucer if not syntactical power, and he jogs gently and vaguely along with an irregularity of metre[38] that seems unobtrusively natural and even appropriate to a slow-moving procession of pilgrims. But there are times when Lydgate puts his meandering diffuseness to expressive purposes with surprising dramatic power. When Tydeus goes to Thebes on Polymytes's behalf to persuade Ethyocles to keep his agreement to share the kingship, he begins with a lengthy profession of brevity which seems inept yet catches well the note of diplomatic negotiation:

> 'Sir,' quod he, 'unto your worthynesse
> My purpoos is breefly to expresse
> Th'effecte only, as in sentement,
> Of the massage why that I am sent.
> It were in veyn longe processe forto make,
> But of my mater the verrey ground to take,
> In eschewyng of prolixité,
> And voyde away al superfluyté,
> Sith youre-self best ought to understond
> The cause fully that we han on hond,
> And ek conceyve th'entent of my menynge
> Of rightwisnesse longgyng to a kynge.'   (1901–12)

When Ethyocles answers, 'Dyssimulyng under colour feyned' (1958), his slow-moving indirection admirably suggests hypocrisy (1965–92), with feigned astonishment gradually revealing the open threat that such a request

> ... were no token as of brotherhede,
> But a signe rather of hatrede,
> To interrupte my possessioun
> Of this litil pore regioun.   (1989–92)

In general, however, when Lydgate aims at Chaucerian grandeur by means of hypotaxis, his style lacks the necessary logical under-pinning that was to be achieved by, for example, Gavin Douglas in his translation of the *Aeneid* a century later.

I turn now to the third feature of the Chaucerian poetic style, which must detain us for longer. One type of figuration that Lydgate learned from Chaucer is substitution of learned metaphor for literal statement. This may be illustrated by the instances of *circumlocutio* quoted above: lines 4042–4 meaning 'into hell' or lines 4256–8 meaning 'when the sun was setting'. Again, one might mention the substitution in the following passage of 'Mercury' and 'Mars' for 'persuasion' and 'force', together with the metonymic use of 'harp' and 'sword' to represent the special powers of the two gods:

> Wherfor me semeth mor is fortunat
> Of Mercurye the soote sugred harpe
> Than Mars swerd, whetted kene and sharpe.   (272–4)

This passage has a special felicity in its context, because it is the means by which Lydgate returns from a digression about persuasion and force to his original topic of Amphion's employment of the literal harp given him by Mercury to raise up the city of Thebes. One more example is the extended metaphor (or small-scale allegory) used to convey the meaning that 'the news reached Ethyocles':

> But wel wote I the newe fame ran
> This mene while with ful swift passage
> Unto Thebes of this mariage;
> And by report trewe and not yfeyned
> The soune therof the eeres hath atteyned,
> Myn auctour writ, of Ethyocles.   (1674–9)

Such figures seem perfectly normal elements of literary English, but before Chaucer they were not so, and they are used far more frequently by Lydgate than by his master.

Another type of figuration is the use of the various types of *mora* (or 'delay') treated by writers on rhetoric as means of amplification. In a sense these are all 'natural' devices of eloquence, which can be found in elementary forms even in speech; but Chaucer's widespread and elaborate use of them marked a new departure in English poetic style, and one that deeply impressed his successors. I mentioned above Lydgate's use of *occupatio* (in theory a means of abbreviation, in practice often used to amplify) at 4565–602 in emulation of *The Knight's Tale* I 2919–66. A similar case is the following passage about the wedding of Adrastus's daughters:

> But to telle all the circumstances
> Of justes, revel, and the dyvers daunces,
> The feestes riche and the gyftes grete,
> The pryvé sighes and the fervent hete
> Of lovys folk brennyng as the glede,
> And devyses of many sondry wede,
> The touches stole and the amerous lookes
> By sotyl craft leyd oute lyne and hokes
> The jalous folk to traysshen and begyle
> In their awayt with many sondry wile –
> Al this in soth descryven I ne can.   (1663–73)

This was probably suggested by a series of parallel refusals to describe the details of Cambyuskan's birthday feast in *The Squire's Tale* v 58–75. Or there is the *apostrophatio*, 'O cruel Mars . . . ' (2553), with which Lydgate begins Part III of the *Siege*, in imitation of many of Chaucer's apostrophic proems.[39] Another *mora* is *circumlocutio*, of which some examples have already been given; another is *digressio*, self-consciously introduced by Lydgate, in the form of *digressio ad aliam partem materiae*,[40] as follows:

> But now most I make a digressioun
> To telle shortly, as in sentement,
> Of thilke knyght that Tydeus hath sent . . .   (2466-8)

Though it would be tedious and unprofitable to attempt an exhaustive survey of Lydgate's employment of the rhetorical devices he found in Chaucer, I must pause over his use of one means of amplification, and that perhaps the commonest in medieval poetry generally – *descriptio*. The strongly pictorial quality of much later medieval poetry is well known, and it is found prominently in *The Knight's Tale*, with its elaborate descriptions of people and places – above all of the two knights' champions and of the temples of the gods. There is nothing in *The Siege of Thebes* that corresponds very closely to these formal *descriptiones*, but on the other hand Lydgate, to a greater extent probably than Chaucer himself, does seem to have had a genuinely pictorial imagination. A typical example of the amplification to which this leads can be found in the scene in which King Adrastus, like the Theseus of *The Knight's Tale* I 1696ff, finds two knights fighting 'Withoute juge her querel to departe' (1382). He orders them to stop and reconciles them; and when they disarm Lydgate's probable source says that they were provided with 'deux manteaulx'.[41] In the *Siege* this is expanded to:

> Tweyne mantels unto hem wer broght,
> Frett with peerle and riche stonys, wroght
> Of cloth of golde and velvyt cremysyn,
> Ful richely furred with hermyn,
> To wrap hem inne ageyn the colde morowe,
> After the rage of her nyghtes sorwe,
> To take her reste til the sonne arise.   (1439-45)

Lydgate imagines not only the luxurious external detail but the comforting warmth of fur in the cold morning that follows on the angry night of their combat. A special piquancy is created by the reversal of the expected association of darkness with cold and light with warmth. Here indeed 'pictorial' is far from covering the full range of sensory suggestion evoked.

A different kind of descriptive effect occurs at the end of the scene mentioned above, in which Tydeus goes as ambassador to Ethyocles. Ethyocles angrily rejects his proposal; Tydeus defies him on

behalf of Polymytes and calls on his lords to accept Polymytes as
their king the following year, and then,

> As he that list no lenger ther sojourne,
> Fro the kyng he gan his face tourne –
> Nat astouned, nor in his hert afferde,
> But ful proudly leyde hond on his swerde,
> And, in despit who that was lief or loth,
> A sterne pas thorgh the halle he goth,
> Thorgh-out the courte, and manly took his stede,
> And out of Thebes faste gan hym spede,
> Enhastyng hym til he was at large,
> And sped hym forth touard the londe of Arge. (2113–22)

At this moment of dramatic public action, Lydgate is perfectly in
control of his syntax, and he creates a scene in which movement,
gesture, facial expression, and even the vague sense of stunned
onlookers – 'in despit who that was lief or loth' – are co-ordinated to
produce a fine spectacle of heroic dignity.

Lydgate's most remarkable and characteristic descriptive skill
depends on the evocation of space, light, and colour, often with
haunting delicacy, to produce picturesque effects of a kind comparable to those found in some of the masterpieces of late-medieval
manuscript illumination.[42] An effect of this kind occurs in the scene
in which Polymytes rides away from Thebes after it has been agreed
that his brother shall reign first. The solitary journey is a common
theme of romance, and its setting here is the wild forest that forms
the usual background to such knightly wanderings. But Lydgate
realizes it in greater detail than would be normal in Chaucer:

> ... a forest joynyng to the see, ...
> Ful of hilles and of hegh mounteyns,
> Craggy roches and but fewe playns,
> Wonder dredful and lothsom of passage,
> And ther-with-al ful of beestis rage ... (1163–8)

As night falls, a great storm blows up, with drenching rain and
roaring both from the sea and from the forest beasts –

> ... the wooful sounes
> Of tygres, beres, boores, and lyounes,
> Which for refut, hem-silve forto save,
> Everich in hast drogh unto his cave. (1179–82)

Polymytes however finds no shelter

> Til it was passed almost mydnyght hour,
> A large space that the sterres clere,
> The clowdes voyde, in hevene did appere, (1186–8)

and then he emerges from the forest, finds the city of King Adrastus, and falls asleep outside the palace. I am not sure of the syntactic function of the phrase 'A large space', and Chaucer would never have permitted such uncertainty; but it does have the poetic effect of evoking the opening up of the heavens as the clouds are blown away, and, beyond that, the removal of oppression and the escape into a new freedom of adventure. The landscape and weather evoked by Lydgate surely have some kind of connection – all the more suggestive for being uncertain – with the inner experience of Polymytes as he passes from the cursed city of Thebes to the welcoming land of Argos.

This scene is in some ways more medieval than anything in Chaucer. Chaucer's poetry is largely urban; its settings include many walled gardens, the symbolism of which is complex yet precise, but very few of those open, forested or desert landscapes which form the setting of chivalric adventure in medieval romances, and which possess a less limited symbolic potential. The forest of *The Book of the Duchess* is so regimented that 'every tree stood by hymselve / Fro other wel ten foot or twelve' (419–20); the desert of *The House of Fame*, lacking any 'maner creature / That ys yformed be Nature' (489–90), is rejected with horror; the black rocks of *The Franklin's Tale*, though their existence is undeniable, remain undescribed, while the crucial event takes place in a garden above them arrayed by 'craft of mannes hand' and 'peynted' by May (v 909, 907). It was precisely Chaucer's rationalism, his inability simply to accept the mysterious, that drove him to ask, with his philosophical pagans, 'Why han ye wroght this werk unresonable?' (v 872) or 'What governance is in this prescience?' (*Knight's Tale* I 1313). W. P. Ker once defined 'romance' in its most general sense as 'the name for the sort of imagination that possesses the mystery and the spell of everything remote and unattainable'; and it must be admitted that the English medieval romances rarely realized that imaginative potential.[43] Yet occasionally they did so, as in *Sir Orfeo* or *Sir Gawain and the Green Knight*; and the price Chaucer had to pay for his rejection of all 'nycetè of storiers imaginacion' was the loss of such glimpses of what lies beyond all rational limits. Lydgate, with his mild incapacity for rationalism, was occasionally able to attain such glimpses, especially through the picturesque. In other poems, Lydgate's love for picturesque detail can be merely confusing; so it is in allegorical narratives such as *The Temple of Glass*, where we seek in

vain for the larger significance of moonlight or passing clouds.[44] But
a romance-like historical narrative such as *The Siege of Thebes*, being
exemplary rather than allegorical, can sustain almost any amount of
such descriptive elaboration, for there is no generic expectation that
every detail must convey some further meaning.

The most powerful of all the *descriptiones* in the *Siege* again begins
at night. After Tydeus's departure described above, Ethyocles sends
a party to ambush him. His first suspicion of them comes when he

> Thoght he saugh ageyn the mone shyne
> Sheldes fressh and plates borned bright,
> The which environ casten a gret lyght.   (2168–70)

They attack; Tydeus kills all but one, but is left

> Hym-silf yhurt and ywounded kene,
> Thurgh his harneys bledyng on the grene.   (2221–2)

The implied contrast between blood and grass, red and green,
becomes a leitmotiv in what follows. He rides away, weak with loss
of blood, till he comes to a great castle, once more glimpsed by
moonlight –

> Conveyed thider be clernesse of the ston,
> That be nyght ageyn the moone shon,
> On heghe toures with crestes marcyal.   (2271–3)

The castle has a garden 'joyneaunt almost to the wal' (2274) – a
configuration which juxtaposes two opposite aspects of aristocratic
civilization, the castle and the garden, and which is exactly repeated
from Theseus's prison-tower and garden in *The Knight's Tale*
(1056–61). Within this garden 'lich a paradys' (2280), amid grass
and flowers, the wounded knight lets his horse wander, and lies
asleep, dreaming, on the ground.

> Ther he lay til the larke song
> With notes newe hegh up in the ayr,
> The glade morowe rody and right fayr,
> Phebus also, casting up his bemes,
> The heghe hylles gilte with his stremes,
> The sylver dewe upon the herbes rounde;
> Ther Tydeus lay upon the grounde
> At the uprist of the shene sunne,
> And stoundemele his grene woundes runne
> Round about, that the soyl was depeynt
> Of the grene with the rede meynt.   (2296–306)

In this brilliantly pictorial scene we find not only the pathetic contrast, common enough in heroic poetry, between an idyllic natural setting and human suffering, but an actual mingling of the two in the mingling of green with red on the ground. Lydgate has already mentioned 'grene gras' (2288) and 'herbes grene, whit, and red' (2290); now 'grene' (i.e. fresh) wounds drip with red blood which stains green grass. The material Lydgate is using is supplied by literary tradition rather than by observation of life, but it has undergone an imaginative transformation. For example, his use of *depeynt* in the penultimate line of the last quotation derives from Chaucer's metaphorical use of 'painting' to refer to the spring's adornment of the earth in garden-descriptions such as that in *The Franklin's Tale* v 907–8, referred to on page 80 above; but the line that follows Lydgate's *depeynt* shifts it towards its other metaphorical sense of 'smeared (with blood)'.[45] As the two senses fuse, the Monk of Bury brings us surprisingly close to the horrifying sensory acuteness of Marlowe's 'Besmeared with blood that makes a dainty show.'[46]

Before leaving the subject of Lydgate's poetic style in *The Siege of Thebes*, I must mention briefly two other topics which deserve discussion. First, though Lydgate is aiming at a Chaucerian high style, he rightly recognizes that in Chaucer himself stylistic level is not governed by a rigid decorum. Thus, not only does he attempt in his prologue to match the low style of many of Chaucer's link-passages – Pearsall writes well of Lydgate's 'clumsy playfulness' here.[47] He also imitates successfully in the main body of the poem those sharp turns into dismissive derision which may shock the modern reader of *The Knight's Tale*. Thus

> But lete his brother blowen in an horn
> Wher that hym lyst, or pypen in a red   (*Siege* 1790–1)

clearly derives from

> That oon of you, al be hym looth or lief,
> He moot go pipen in an yvy leef,   (*Knight's Tale* I 1837–8)

daringly fortified by 'Absolon may blowe the bukkes horn' (*Miller's Tale* I 3387). Second, it is difficult to tell how far Lydgate grasped the ironic aspects of Chaucer's narratorial technique, a difficulty redoubled if we feel doubt (as I think we should) as to how securely we grasp them ourselves. At times it would appear that he misses the

shimmer of irony that surrounds Chaucer's use of traditional narratorial devices such as the profession of ignorance. Thus Chaucer's

> But wheither that she children hadde or noon,
> I rede it naught, therfore I late it goon,   (*Troilus* I 132–3)

which shocks us by provoking speculation about Criseyde's earlier
life and responsibilities, reappears as

> And whether that he had a wif or noon,
> I fynde not, and therfor lat it goon,   (*Siege* 465–6)

which refers to Oedipus's foster-father, and apparently has no
special significance. Yet at other times Lydgate's professions of
ignorance are unmistakably intended ironically, as when he concludes his account of how Tydeus and Polymytes fell in love with
Adrastus's daughters by writing:

> Withoute tarying to bedde streght they gon.
> Touchyng her reste, wher that thei slepte or non,
> Demeth ye lovers, that in such maner thing
> B'experience han fully knowlecchyng,
> For it is nat declared in my boke.   (1501–5)

Here of course the situation is more straightforward, and it must
have been an easy step from Chaucer's pose as outsider, inexperienced in love, to the inexperience appropriate to Lydgate's real-life
role as monk. Lydgate's Chaucerianism does extend to narratorial
irony, but, on the whole, only of simple kinds.

I remarked above that it would be an error to draw a sharp
distinction between the literary and the moral, at least so far as
Lydgate's likely intentions in *The Siege of Thebes* are concerned.
Many of the most striking rhetorical devices – *digressio, apostrophatio,
sententia*, and so on – are employed to expound and generalize the
meaning of his story as much as to elevate its style. That meaning is
directed especially to rulers: Ayers has observed that Lydgate's
purpose in the *Siege* was 'to provide an historical "mirror" wherein
kings and governors particularly might observe the social effects of
their actions',[48] and his message to them is that they must rule
mercifully and lovingly, and that resort to warfare is likely to lead to
disastrous consequences for all – 'Lo, what it is for-to gynne a werre
. . . ' (4630). He ends his poem with a passage, possibly reflecting the
Treaty of Troyes, signed between England and France in 1420, in
which he prays to Christ to send peace in this life as well as salvation

in the next. Lydgate may well have seen himself as a true Chaucerian in this moral aspect of his poem. He will have remembered that in *Troilus and Criseyde*, if not in *The Knight's Tale*, a pagan story is given an explicitly Christian ending. He must have noted the importance of kingship in *The Knight's Tale*, as personified in Theseus, the virtuous pagan prince. He may well have thought that the *Tale* implied, if it did not state, that the resort to arms as a means of settling political and personal differences must lead to disaster, as in Theseus's well-meaning destruction of Thebes and his equally well-meaning organization of the tournament which ends in Arcite's death. In these ways Lydgate may well have persuaded himself that he was 'completing' his predecessor's 'truncated' work, not just by supplying the omitted beginnings of the narrative of Thebes, but by making explicit a moral significance that Chaucer had left implicit, and that seemed to demand clarification. Many recent interpreters of *The Knight's Tale* have in fact adopted similar attitudes, though they have not gone so far as to write poems to 'complete' it, and would probably not wish to think of themselves as twentieth-century Lydgates.

In reality, Lydgate has performed upon Chaucer one of those acts of 'misreading or misprision' that Harold Bloom sees as necessary in the relation of poets to their precursors.[49] It is true that the celebration of martial heroism is not central in Chaucer's work, and that *The Knight's Tale* does not gloss over horrors in its depiction of Mars and his influence over men – 'The toun destroyed, ther was no thyng laft' (I 2016). But the *Tale* presents the aggressive instinct as being, like the erotic, an inevitable part of human nature: it produces genuine chivalric splendour, and is capable of being overcome, at least intermittently, by justice, *pitee*, and brotherly love. Thus, for all its sombreness and its questioning philosophical scope, *The Knight's Tale* can still be thought of as a chivalric romance, while *The Siege of Thebes*, despite the generally retrogressive, 'medieval' nature of Lydgate's talent, cannot. Lydgate's opposition to the very substance of romance, the proof of worth by chivalric adventure, is so strong and explicit as to be destructive of the form in which he is writing. When Palamon and Arcite fight together in the grove near Athens, Theseus is humorously critical of their motives – 'Now looketh, is nat that an heigh folye?' (I 1798) – but in the parallel scene of the encounter between Polymytes and Tydeus, the narrator himself is far more absolute in his criticism:

> And thus thies knyghtes, pompous and ellat,
> For litil cause fillen at debat;
> And as they ranne to-gider on horsbak
> Everich on other first his spere brak;
> And after that, ful surquedous of pride,
> With sharpe swerdes they to-gyder ryde,
> Ful yrously, thise myghty champiouns,
> In her fury lik tygres or lyouns. (1349–56)

Although Tydeus is described, apparently admiringly, as 'Lich Mars hym-silf, in stiel y-armed bright' (1882), Jocasta later has a lengthy speech attempting to persuade Ethyocles not to take up arms against Polymytes, in which, in effect, she denounces the part played by Mars in chivalric life:

> And it is foly be short avisement
> To putte a strif in Martys jugement;
> For hard it is, whan a juge is wood,
> To tret aforn hym with-out loos of blood;
> And yif we put our mater hool in Marte,
> Which with the swerd his lawes doth coarte,
> Than may hit happe, wher ye be glad or loth,
> Thow and thy brother shal repente both,
> And many a-nother that is her present,
> Of youre trespas that ben innocent;
> And many thousand in cas shal compleyn
> For the debat only of yow tweyn,
> And for your strif shal fynde ful unsoote. (3661–73)[50]

In part Lydgate, as a monk, is simply ignorant of the details of soldiership and finds them tedious: after the passage quoted above in which he begins to imitate the arming scenes from *The Knight's Tale*, he breaks off abruptly, declining to 'specifie' any further such 'derk' matters (2664, 2668). But above all he strongly disapproves of human aggressiveness.

In this matter and in others, Lydgate resorts quickly and frequently to Christian moralization of his narrative. He opens Part III with an indignant address to 'cruel Mars' (2553), and goes on to trace back the destruction of Thebes to that 'ynfeccioun called Orygynal' (2565) which is the source of all the evils of life. The passage itself is finely eloquent, but, in a very un-Chaucerian way, it uses this utterly comprehensive explanation to close too quickly the issues raised by the story. The rapid resort to moralization is seen at its most destructive in Lydgate's handling of the Oedipus legend. This begins, charmingly enough, by being accommodated to the conventions of romance. Oedipus kills Laius unwittingly in a tournament; the Sphinx is one of many monsters inhabiting 'a wylde and a waast contré' (611), placed there 'I suppose by enchauntement' (626). Then, however, the Sphinx's riddle is posed in such diffusely simple terms as to deprive it of all enigmatic force, and Oedipus's answer is equally tediously drawn-out: in each case one gets the impression that Lydgate was determined not to let his audience's imaginations wander. Finally, the significance of Oedipus's incestuous marriage is reduced to a series of trite moral lessons. Incest 'is neither feire ne good, / Nor acceptable' to God (787–8), and always leads to evil consequences, as is shown by the example of Herod's marriage to his brother's wife and the subsequent slaying of John the Baptist:

> Therfor I rede every man take hede,
> Wherso he be prynce, lorde, or kyng,
> That he be war t'eschewe such weddyng.   (802–4)

After the dreadful conclusion with Oedipus's self-blinding, Lydgate tells us what we are to learn:

> For which shortly to man and child I rede
> To be wel war and to taken hede
> Of kyndely right and of conscience
> To do honur and due reverence
> To fader and moder, of what estat thei be,
> Or certeyn ellis they shul nevere the.   (1019–24)

He continues in this strain for another 19 lines. It would be difficult to imagine a more inept explanation of one of the most haunting myths of Western man; indeed, Lydgate's only tribute to its power is to be found in his apparent determination to defuse it.

Lydgate's treatment of the Oedipus story is an extreme but not untypical example of his 'misreading' of Chaucer's greatest imaginative achievement in *The Knight's Tale*. As we have seen, in this poem even more than in his other classical romances, Chaucer, guided by his reading of Boccaccio, attempted with remarkable success to re-imagine a classical pagan culture in its own terms – a culture interesting for its difference from his own, and yet imaginable as part of a universal human culture, in which pagan and Christian are at one. It was precisely this achievement of the historical imagination, so surprising in an English poet of the fourteenth century, that Lydgate, like most of Chaucer's followers, was least able to grasp and develop. We have seen the special importance of the part played by Boethius in Chaucer's attempt to interpret the philosophical common ground between paganism and Christianity. Boethius, so effective a mediator in *The Knight's Tale* between pagan narrative and Christian narrator, is absent from *The Siege of Thebes*,[51] and there pagan and Christian grind jarringly against each other. Lydgate's only way of avoiding friction between them is an un-Chaucerian resort to allegory: pagan myth is reinterpreted to produce religious or moral meaning, by contrast with Chaucer's wish to allow classical myth and legend a historical autonomy. I noted above, for instance, how Lydgate allegorizes the story of Amphion, a 'derke poysye' (214) interpreted in accordance with Boccaccio's *De genealogia* to mean that Amphion built Thebes by means of the persuasive power of 'rethorik' (219). And later Lydgate explains that Martianus Capella's *De nuptiis Philologiae et Mercurii* treats symbolically of the union of wisdom with learning – an allegorical interpretation which is undoubtedly correct, but which is omitted by Chaucer in the passage from *The Merchant's Tale* (IV 1732–5) from which Lydgate is borrowing.

Lydgate, however, does not attempt to allegorize his whole story, but only to make it point a Christian moral; and here serious problems arise. He has learnt something from Chaucer's willingness to imagine a pagan past on its own terms,[52] but he lacks either the imagination or the courage to follow him all the way, especially in the crucial matter of pagan religion. The result is a tendency to hover between the normal medieval modernization of classical antiquity and a fascinated horror at what he imagines it to have been in itself. Terdymus, chosen by the Greeks to succeed Amphiorax as high priest, can be described as 'a bisshop mytred in his stalle' (4186) when he is 'confermed and stallyd in his se' (4189), though the rites are performed before him 'in many uncouth wyse' (4187). Horror is expressed most vehemently in relation to the death of his predecessor Amphiorax –

> Lo here, the mede of ydolatrie,
> Of rytys old and of fals mawmetrye!
> Lo, what avayllen incantaciouns
> Of exorsismes and conjurisouns?
> What stood hym stede his nigromancye,
> Calculacioun or astronomye?
> What vaylled hym the hevenly manciouns,
> Diverse aspectis or constellaciouns?
> The ende is nat bot sorowe and meschaunce
> Of hem that setten her outre affiaunce
> In swiche werkes supersticious
> Or trist on hem: he is ungracious!   (4047–58)

– and earlier in relation to Oedipus's resort to the oracle of Apollo:

> And with-in a spirit full unclene,
> Be fraude only and fals collusioun,
> Answere gaf to every questioun,
> Bryngyng the puple in ful gret errour
> Such as to hym dyden fals honour
> Be rytys used in the olde dawes
> Aftere custome of paganysmes lawes.   (538–44)[53]

Lydgate doubtless thought he saw good precedent in Chaucer for such condemnation of paganism as fraudulent and vain. The passage about Amphiorax recalls

> Lo here, of payens corsed olde rites,
> Lo here, what alle hire goddes may availle ...   (*Troilus* v 1849–50)

while that about the oracle is generally reminiscent of the attitude expressed in *The Franklin's Tale* towards 'swiche illusiouns and swiche meschaunces / As hethen folk useden in thilke dayes' (v 1292–3). But the *Troilus* passage is briefer, comes from a narrator shocked into repugnance by the end of his tale, and modulates at once into a gentler, more wistful attitude towards 'the sad story that human history tells'[54] –

> Lo here, the forme of olde clerkis speche
> In poetrie, if ye hire bokes seche.   (*Troilus* v 1854–5)

And the nervous attitude of *The Franklin's Tale* seems to be associated with its socially and intellectually insecure narrator: we are meant to be amused by his anxious insistence. Chaucer was not really worried that his audience might think (or think he thought) that there was some truth in pagan religion; Lydgate, I believe, really was, and there is no possibility of detaching the gratuitous denunciation from the poet himself – its vehemence appears to have had no equivalent in his sources. For all its reverent imitation of Chaucer, *The Siege of Thebes* is fundamentally un-Chaucerian in its lack of imaginative openness towards the classical past.[55]

3. Father Chaucer

The Siege of Thebes is one of the most studiedly Chaucerian of fifteenth-century poems, but in important ways it is a retrogressive work, more medieval than *The Knight's Tale*, its point of origin. The same is true of much of the poetry of Chaucer's followers, especially in England (as opposed to Scotland); measured by the doctrine of artistic progress which the Renaissance invented, they move back rather than forwards. It would be quite wrong to suppose that the transition from medieval to Renaissance in English poetry could be seen simply in evolutionary terms: on the contrary, there is a major push towards Renaissance values by Chaucer, followed by a great variety of movements in different directions, some of them (as we shall see) uninfluenced by Chaucer, others attempting to advance from his work yet actually retreating from some of the positions he had established. As. J. W. Mackail put it, 'whatever might have happened without Chaucer, what Chaucer did was decisive. It was even too decisive. He brought the Renaissance into England before the time. We have to wait a hundred and fifty years for the English Petrarch.'[56]

If we ask why those who admired Chaucer so greatly and imitated him so diligently did not usually succeed in building on his work, the answer will no doubt have something to do with their individual capacities: none of them had Chaucer's genius. It would appear, too, that none of them had the opportunities to which Chaucer's genius enabled him to respond: there is no evidence that any of his successors before Wyatt had visited Italy or read Italian.[57] Then again, their contact with Chaucer himself was inevitably indirect. Chaucer undoubtedly wrote for readers as well as listeners, but the speaking voice was of central importance in his poetry, and his work seems to imply the existence of an intimate social circle which could respond intelligently to changing tones of voice. After his death, his work was of course known only in written form, and it seems clear that his tonal as much as his metrical intentions were often misjudged by his successors. But the attenuation of Chaucer's achievement among these successors must also have something to do with more general barriers in the culture of fifteenth-century England. The retreat from Chaucer's intellectual curiosity and courage must have been in part a consequence of the more restricted and repressive intellectual climate in which his successors lived; and here one may hypothesize that the fears aroused by the initial success of the Wycliffite heresy were of considerable importance. One indication in Chaucer's life of the speculative freedom that marks his literary attitude towards classical paganism may be found in his close association with the group of 'Lollard knights',[58] men of position and influence who seem to have sympathized with Wyclif's critical and questioning stance and protected his followers, without necessarily sharing his doctrinal heresies such as the denial of the real presence of Christ in the sacrament. The Sir John Clanvowe whom we have met as author of *The Boke of Cupide*, the earliest Chaucerian imitation, belonged to this group, and even the apparently innocuous love-allegory of this little work may be shaped by his experience as a Lollard sympathizer. The nightingale, the proponent of courtly orthodoxy in love-matters, sounds uncommonly like a spokesperson for repressive religious orthodoxy too, for she wishes that all who reject the true religion of Cupid should be burned. That kind of joke at the expense of religious intolerance was all very well in the fourteenth century, when no-one in England had been burned for heresy; but with the accession of the narrowly orthodox Lancastrians and the passing of the anti-Lollard act of 1401 which permitted the burning of heretics 'that such punishment may strike fear to the minds of others',[59] and still more after Oldcastle had associated heresy with sedition, the atmosphere was different.

The widespread fear of heresy after the opening years of the fifteenth century seems to have been shared by the English Chaucerian poets. Both Hoccleve and Lydgate in their early works had been prepared to express attitudes of the questioning kind that Chaucer had attributed to pagans or had expressed himself in *The Complaint of Mars*. The woeful lover of Lydgate's *Complaynt of a Loveres Lyf* (before 1412), echoing the betrayed pagan Troilus, demands,

> O ryghtful God, that first the trouthe fonde,
> How may thou suffre such oppressyon,
> That Falshed shuld have jurysdixion
> In Trouthes ryght, to sle him gilteles?[60]

And in *The Temple of Glass* (also before 1412) Lydgate echoes the reproaches addressed to God in *The Complaint of Mars*: how lamentable that God and Nature should

> So mych beaute, passing bi mesure,
> Set on a woman, to yeve occasioun
> A man to love to his confusioun.

And once more the question is asked,

> Whi wil God don so gret a cruelte
> To eny man or to his creature
> To maken him so mych wo endure
> For hir purcaas whom he shal in no wise
> Rejoise never, but so forth in jewise
> Ledin his life til that he be grave?[61]

Again, Hoccleve's *Complaint of the Virgin* (before 1405), closely translated from the French of Deguileville, begins, sensationally enough,

> O fadir God, how fers and how cruel
> In whom thee list or wilt canst thou thee make!
> Whom wilt thou spare, ne wot I nevere a deel,
> Syn thow thy sone hast to the deeth betake ... [62]

But later both poets wrote vehement attacks on heresy, urging that it should be ruthlessly extirpated. Lydgate, in his *Defence of Holy Church* (probably 1413–14), reminds the young Henry V that heresy means treason:

> For who is blynde or haltith in the feith
> For any doctryne of these sectys newe
> And Cristes techyng therfor aside laith,
> Unto thy corone may he nat be trewe.

Henry should boldly have God's enemies killed, disregarding any feigned repentance, and let severity hold the scales of justice:

> And Goddys foon manly make to sterve,
> For any fals feynyd repentaunce:
> Of right lat rigour holden the ballaunce. [63]

Hoccleve's works are full of attacks on heresy, and in his case there is some evidence of the influence of the act *De haereticos comburendo*, for in the prologue to *The Regement of Princes* (c. 1412) an account is given of the burning of the heretic Badby in 1410. Hoccleve is urged by a beggar to take this as a warning of the danger of religious speculation, and he readily complies:

> Of oure feith wol I not despute at all;
> But, at a word, I in the sacrament
> Of the auter fully bileve, and schal,
> With Goddes helpe, while life is to me lent;
> And, in despyt of the fendes talent,
> In al other articles of the feith
> Byleve, as fer as that Holy Writ seith.   (379–85)

At the end of the *Regement* he even pauses to defend his inclusion of a portrait of 'my fadir ... , / My worthi maister Chaucer' against those who

> holden oppynyoun and sey
> That none ymages schuld i-maked be:
> Thei erren foule, and goon out of the wey. [64]

91

He addresses balades to Henry V in 1413 and 1414 urging him to support the Church 'in chacyng away / Th'errour which sones of iniquitee / Han sowe ageyn the feith', and asserting that 'This yle or this had been but hethenesse' if Henry had not acted against the heretics.[65] But his most violent assault on Lollardy is the almost hysterical *Remonstrance Against Oldcastle* (1415), a poem of over five hundred lines attacking the dangerous heretic from every angle and wishing that if he does not renounce his errors, 'in the fyr yee feele may the sore'.[66]

There is much evidence, then, after the opening decade of the fifteenth century, of a growth in fear and intolerance. The determination to take shelter within a more rigidly defined orthodoxy against what were perceived as terrifying dangers to Church and state seems likely to have discouraged any further development of Chaucer's questioning attitudes. Those who fear that the country may return to heathendom if heretics are not persecuted will naturally shy away from imaginative sympathy with even virtuous heathens.

There was a further difficulty in the relationship of Chaucer's successors to their master, of which the source is to be found in Chaucer himself and his attitudes towards authority. We have seen Hoccleve addressing Chaucer as 'mayster dere and fadir reverent', and from then down to Dryden's definitive formulation, 'the father of English poetry', the fatherhood of Chaucer was in effect the constitutive idea of the English poetic tradition. There is ample precedent for seeing the authority of the literary precursor over his successors as analogous to the authority of the father over his sons. Lucretius refers to Epicurus as father; Horace and Propertius both refer to Ennius as father; Cicero calls Isocrates the father of eloquence and Herodotus the father of history; and so on.[67] As Dryden was to put it later, 'we [that is, the poets] have our lineal descents and clans as well as other families', so that Milton could be seen as 'the poetical son of Spenser', and Spenser in turn as a son 'begotten' by Chaucer 'two hundred years after his decease'.[68] Descent and inheritance from father to son provide a basic explanatory model for literary history, and the model retains its power, for example in Harold Bloom's conception of the tensely Oedipal relation of son to father as characterizing the whole of English poetic history from Milton to the present.

But what kind of father was Chaucer, and what was it like for fifteenth-century poets to have Chaucer as their father? To answer these questions, we must return to Chaucer himself, and consider the role of fathers in his work and his attitude towards paternal (and thus authorial) authority. It will be helpful to begin with some thought-provoking remarks by Derek Brewer. He has noted that 'Chaucer's poetry shows no sign of an imagination bothered by a dominating father-figure', and he comments especially on *Troilus and Criseyde* that Troilus 'is not in the least hampered by his father, King Priam, who is barely mentioned' and that in Criseyde's case it is indeed 'the absence, the *loss*, of a father-figure, of protective authority, which is so disturbing.'[69] If we look more widely, over the whole range of Chaucer's poetry, we shall find cases in which the 'father-figure', the figure of 'protective authority', is disturbingly absent; and other cases again in which the father-figure is present, but is presented in a distinctly unfavourable light. What is rare indeed in Chaucer is the father who is present and good, possessor of the wisdom and benevolence that a patriarchal age might have expected. One of the few Chaucerian fathers who seem unequivocally benevolent is the 'noble doughty kyng' Cambyuskan of *The Squire's Tale* (v 338); but before the tale is broken off we learn nothing of the relationship between him and his children. Jill Mann has recently analysed the equivocal portrayals of fathers in *The Man of Law's Tale*, in *The Physician's Tale*, and in the section of *The Monk's Tale* concerning Ugolino da Pisa – fathers who are kind and yet cruel, or authoritative and yet subservient, and whose equivocality she sees as a means by which Chaucer explores the mystery of divine providence.[70] A less serious example of an unfavourably portrayed father in *The Canterbury Tales* is Symkyn the miller in *The Reeve's Tale*. He is a ludicrously arrogant and boastful image of husbandly and paternal authority, bristling with phallic weapons –

> Ay by his belt he baar a long panade,
> And of a swerd ful trenchant was the blade.
> A joly poppere baar he in his pouche;
> Ther was no man, for peril, dorste hym touche.
> A Sheffeld thwitel baar he in his hose   (I 3929–33)

– and always ready to counter any threat to his womenfolk 'With panade, or with knyf, or boidekyn' (3960). All his daughter inherits from him is his 'camus' nose (3934, 3974), yet he is determined to protect her virginity and marry her in accordance with his own notions of social dignity. In the end he proves incapable of asserting his own authority or of preserving his daughter's maidenhood or indeed his wife's fidelity; tyrannous paternal authority is reduced to impotence by the two young men from Cambridge.

These are literal fathers; an interesting example of the father-figure is the authoritative informant who is encountered in the type of poetic dream called the *oraculum*. This is the kind of dream defined in Macrobius's commentary on the *Somnium Scipionis* as one in which 'a parent, or a pious or revered man, or a priest, or even a god' appears and gives information or advice.[71] The *Somnium Scipionis* itself belongs to this category; in it, the father-figure is Scipio Africanus the elder, who appears to his grandson in a dream and tells him of his future and of the other world. In *The Parliament of Fowls* Chaucer tells of how he read the *Somnium Scipionis*, and then had a dream influenced by it in which Africanus appeared to him. Africanus promises him a reward for his labour, shows him a gate which leads, according to the inscriptions above it, both to fulfilment and to frustration, pushes him firmly through it, comforts him in his indecision and fear by taking his hand – and then apparently vanishes, since he is mentioned no more in the whole poem. Paternal authority disappears, and Chaucer is left to deal with the uncertainties of the dream by himself. Another of Chaucer's dream-poems that evidently belongs to the same category is *The House of Fame*. Here the eagle who carries Chaucer through the heavens and instructs him in the physics of sound might be seen as a kind of comic father-figure; but at the end of Book II he too abandons him: he says he will wait for Chaucer, but he is never seen again. In Book III, just as the dreamer seems to be on the verge of obtaining the 'love-tydynges' (2143) that he has been promised from one who 'semed for to be / A man of gret auctorite' (2157–8) – the authoritative informant expected in the *oraculum* – the poem breaks off. We do not of course know for certain why *The House of Fame* was not continued beyond this point (a possible reason for its incompleteness was suggested in chapter 2), or why it was put into circulation in an unfinished form, but it is surely revealing about Chaucer's attitude towards paternal or quasi-paternal authority that it should break off at this precise moment. I have suggested elsewhere that the dream in *The House of Fame* might best be seen not as an *oraculum*, but rather as an 'anti-*oraculum*'.[72] As such, it might be seen as representative of a general tendency in Chaucer's age to question the patriarchal, authoritarian bent of the culture that it inherited: the Wycliffite movement and the Peasants' Revolt are only the most extreme examples in public life. In literature, we might consider the case of *Piers Plowman*, with its tearing of the pardon from Truth and its reduction of Holy Church from an awe-inspiring mother-figure to a crumbling barn; or that of *Pearl*, with its reversal of expectation that makes the father the pupil and the child the teacher. But Chaucer goes further than most of his contemporaries in the persistence with which he presents paternal authority as absent or cruel.

Among the Canterbury pilgrims there are two whom we know to be fathers in the literal sense. One is the Knight, the father of the Squire; he may, for all we know, be a most benevolent parent, and certainly he exercises a quasi-paternal authority among the other pilgrims with benevolent and tactful firmness, as when he brings the Monk's dreary series of 'tragedies' to an end, or when he calls on the Pardoner and the Host to kiss and make up. But, surprisingly perhaps, we see nothing of his relations with his real son, and all we are told about them is that the son acted towards him in a way appropriate for a squire in the household of his lord: he 'carf biforn his fader at the table' (*General Prologue* I 100). This act symbolizes the hierarchy of the social estates, without telling us anything about the warmth or otherwise of the family relationship between the two men. The other literal father is the Franklin, and he is evidently sharply at odds with his son, whom he compares most disadvantageously with the Squire. The son cares for nothing but gaming, he loses all his money (meaning, no doubt, his father's money) at dice, and he prefers low company to that which his father thinks suitable to his rank.

> I have my sone snybbed, and yet shal,
> For he to vertu listeth nat entende,   (v 688–9)

says the Franklin. The blame might seem to be differently distributed if seen from the son's point of view, but there can be no doubt that, with whatever justification, the Franklin judges and speaks harshly in relation to his son.

In the company of pilgrims there is another who is a father, not literally but metaphorically – the Parson. The portrait of him in *The General Prologue* is unmistakably favourable, but it is also unmistakably negative. He is defined largely in terms of what he does *not* do – he does not 'cursen for his tithes' (I 486), or give up visiting his parishioners because of bad weather, or leave his flock to gain greater material rewards elsewhere, and so on. Towards any obstinate sinner in his flock he engages like the Franklin in the characteristic fatherly activity of 'snybbyng' or rebuke: 'Hym wolde he snybben sharply for the nonys' (I 523). His Christian virtue and his noble purpose remain unquestionable, but his role on the pilgrimage gives far less emphasis to attractive paternal qualities such as protectiveness, kindness, generosity, than to the negative aspects of fatherhood: his task is to forbid, to inhibit spontaneity and playfulness. In the floating link-passage which Robinson prints as the epilogue to *The Man of Law's Tale*, when the Host calls on him to tell the next tale, the Parson's response is to rebuke the Host for swearing, and thus to be classed as a 'Lollere' (II 1173), a Wycliffite. But his main appearance is of course in the prologue to his own tale, the last of the collection as we have it. Here the Host once more calls on the Parson to tell a 'fable' and thus 'knytte up well a greet mateere' (x 28–9); and once more his answer has the effect of a rebuke – 'Thou getest fable noon ytoold for me!' (31). He rejects fiction itself as mere *wrecchednesse*, mere *draf* (34–5), and he proceeds to offer instead the only tale of the collection that is not a tale, that has no element of narrative or fiction in it. It is indeed 'Moralitee and vertuous mateere' (38), and it makes an end, as he says, to the feast of tales (47), not just by being the last course, but by negating all that has gone before, substituting a systematic treatise on human sinfulness for the unpredictable and various life of the tales, reducing verse to prose, human voices to written discourse.[73] I do not imply that Chaucer means us to criticize the Parson for doing this, only that when the time at last comes for him to exercise his paternal authority over the other pilgrims, he does so – he must do so – with an austerity that dampens the spirits, telling us that the way to eternal life is not through a tale-telling competition which ends with a jolly supper at the Tabard Inn, but 'by deeth and mortificacion of synne' (x 1080).

Fear of God as father is a normal part of medieval Christianity, which we have seen exemplified in an extreme form in the lines from Hoccleve's *Complaint of the Virgin* quoted just now. The typical strategy by which the Blessed Virgin as mother is asked to shield the human supplicant from the wrath of the Father may also be found in Chaucer's *An ABC* (translated, like Hoccleve's poem, from Deguileville):

Glorious mayde and mooder, which that nevere
Were bitter, neither in erthe nor in see,
But ful of swetnesse and of merci evere,
Help that my Fader be not wroth with me,
Spek thou, for I ne dar not him ysee,
So have I doon in erthe, allas the while!
That certes, but if thou my socour bee,
To stink eterne he wole my gost exile.

Redresse me, mooder, and me chastise,
For certeynly my Faderes chastisinge,
That dar I nouht abiden in no wise,
So hidous is his rightful rekenynge.   (49–56, 129–32)

But we have also seen that substantial passages in Chaucer's classical
romances and in *The Complaint of Mars* question the combination of
benevolent wisdom with supreme power that is also attributed to the
heavenly Father in the traditional Christian scheme of things. To
these cases can be added others. Jill Mann notes that in *The Man of
Law's Tale* we are confronted with 'an astonishing vision of the
cosmos which presents an unnatural cruelty as fundamental to its
structure and operation' – the only instance, she suggests, of a
medieval writer calling the *primum mobile* 'crueel'.[74] In the story of
Philomela in *The Legend of Good Women*, a question is put to God
about the birth of the cruel rapist Tereus similar to that put by
Dorigen about the black rocks in *The Franklin's Tale*. God here is
dator formarum, the 'yevere of the formes' (2228), the masculine
principle that imposes shape on the shapeless feminine matter; and
why, he is asked, having borne the whole created world in his
thought before giving it substance, did he make or allow to be made
such a poisonously evil man? If we now return for a moment to *The
Knight's Tale*, and especially to Theseus's final speech, I think we
shall see more clearly a major source of that poem's lasting power. In
that speech Theseus envisages a different heavenly father from the
one we have seen exercising authority in the situation to which the
speech is designed to respond. Jupiter, the benevolent and gracious
father of all things, is a mere idea in Theseus's noble mind; the
reality, with whom he shadowily coexists in Chaucer's poem, is
Saturn, the cruel father who does not hesitate to destroy his own
children. Part of the greatness of *The Knight's Tale* surely derives
from the fact that in it Chaucer has ingeniously combined his two
most compelling images of paternal authority, the cruel father and
the absent father.

I turn now from fathers to inheritance from the father. I suggest that Chaucer's questioning of the role of the father should be associated with his questioning of the father's power to bequeath virtue to the son and the son's power to inherit virtue from the father. It is well known that this is a theme on which Chaucer touches rather prominently in several of his poems, though it is not of course original with him: he could have found it in Boethius, in Jean de Meun, in Dante, and doubtless in other sources too.[75] Nevertheless, it was obviously a theme that greatly interested him, as is shown by the fact that he sometimes gives it an emphasis that seems disproportionate to its contextual relevance. In *The Wife of Bath's Tale*, for example, the Loathly Lady's lecture in bed to her reluctant husband includes a section of seventy-eight lines on the nature of true *gentillesse* (III 1109–76). (It may be worth recalling that the word *gentil* is etymologically connected with family, birth, fatherhood.) This seems an altogether excessive response to the husband's one-line complaint that she is of low birth; but Chaucer was obviously determined to set out in full the argument that our forefathers cannot 'biquethe . . . / To noon of us hir vertuous lyvyng' (1121–2); that if *gentillesse* were a natural inheritance, then those of *gentil* birth could 'nevere fyne / To doon of gentillesse the faire office' (1136–7); and that 'men may wel often fynde / A lordes sone do shame and vileynye' (1150–1); so that the true definition of *gentillesse* is that 'he is gentil that dooth gentil dedis' (1170). Regardless of its relevance to the tale, it is an argument appropriate to a self-made woman like the Wife of Bath, and perhaps equally appropriate to a man like Chaucer, of prosperous bourgeois family, who made his way by his own abilities into high courtly and administrative circles.

We have already seen how the Franklin, before beginning his tale, complains that his son does not possess the *vertu* that marks true *gentillesse*. We may surmise that the Franklin inwardly believes that he himself does possess that *vertu*, and that it is an understandable human weakness that leads him to feel aggrieved at his son's failure to inherit what cannot be inherited; but the burden of his tale is precisely that *gentillesse* is not derived from birth. By his deeds a squire can be as *gentil* as a knight, and a clerk as *gentil* as a squire; where moral virtue is concerned, inheritance from the father is of no significance. A very similar point is made in the ballade *Gentilesse*, but now in a way that contrasts God as father with human fathers. The 'fader of gentilesse' (1) is God alone, and the man who wishes to be *gentil* must address himself 'Vertu to sewe, and vyces for to flee' (4). The true heir to virtue is the man who loves virtue, whatever rank he may have inherited, for

> Vyce may wel be heir to old richesse;
> But ther may no man, as men may wel see,
> Bequethe his heir his vertuous noblesse. (15–17)

Oddly enough, Chaucer's unfavourable attitude towards the power of the father goes so far that, while denying that good qualities can be bequeathed and inherited, he occasionally asserts that evil qualities can. An example that may spring to mind is that of Criseyde, the betrayer of Troilus whose father is a traitor to Troy – though that is not a point that Chaucer ever makes quite explicitly. Unmistakably explicit is the statement at the beginning of the story of Phyllis in *The Legend of Good Women*, that the false lover Demophon was unmatched for falseness by any save 'his fader Theseus' (2400), a fact which demonstrates

> By preve as wel as by autorite
> That wiked fruit cometh of a wiked tre. (2394–5)

The same proverb is quoted by the Host, more jocularly, in *The Monk's Prologue*, with respect to the inheritance of sexual feebleness:

> Of fieble trees ther comen wrecched ympes.
> This maketh that oure heires been so sklendre
> And feble that they may nat wel engendre. (VII 1956–8)

The proverb of course derives from Scripture – 'Sic omnis arbor bona fructus bonos facit: mala autem arbor malos fructus facit' (Matthew 7:17) – and it is surely significant that Chaucer alludes twice to the second clause, which is unfavourable to inheritance, but never to the first, which is favourable to it.

To take this discussion a stage further, it is now necessary to reintroduce a different, metaphorical rather than literal, version of paternal authority: the authority of the literary precursor over his successors. We have seen that there is a long tradition of regarding this authority as paternal; yet Chaucer, though by far the larger part of his work is derived from existing literary sources (chiefly in Latin, French and Italian), never refers to any of his predecessors as father. Indeed, there is something peculiar about Chaucer's attitude to literary authority. He has no objection at all to disclosing that he is indebted to other writers. Sometimes this is a matter of vague

references to distant predecessors from whom a story as a whole is
taken – 'Whilom, as olde stories tellen us . . . ' (*Knight's Tale* I 1859), or

> Thise olde gentil Britouns in hir dayes
> Of diverse aventures maden layes   (*Franklin's Tale* V 709–10)

– while at other times it is a matter of giving references to specific
sources for specific parts of a work:

> The remenant of the tale if ye wol heere,
> Redeth Ovyde, and ther ye may it leere
> > (*Wife of Bath's Tale* III 981–2)

or

> In Omer, or in Dares, or in Dite,
> Whoso that kan may rede hem as they write. (*Troilus* I 146–7)

Like other medieval writers, Chaucer doubtless felt that his work
gained prestige if it could claim to possess an ancestry, and that he
himself gained authority from references to authorities which would
suggest that he was as much a scholar as a poet.[76] Yet Chaucer's
critical attitude towards paternal authority is also reflected in his
approach to the authority of those precursors to whom he might refer
(as in *Troilus and Criseyde* II 18) as 'myn auctour'. It is rare for him to
name a specific *auctour* as the authority for a complete work, as
opposed to referring us to scholarly authorities for further information. One case where he does so, very straightforwardly, is *The
Physician's Tale*:

> Ther was, as telleth Titus Livius,
> A knyght that called was Virginius,   (VI 1–2)

and he proceeds to tell a story which does appear to have Livy as its
ultimate source, though it is uncertain whether Chaucer's immediate
source was that or the French version in the *Roman de la Rose*. But in
two other cases his attitude is less straightforward. The story of Dido
in *The Legend of Good Women* begins with a laudatory reference to
Virgil (itself probably modelled on Dante's greeting of Virgil in the
first canto of the *Inferno* and on Statius's praise of Virgil in the *Purgatorio* as the giver of light to those who follow[77]); and this is accompanied by a passing acknowledgment to Ovid too:

> Glorye and honour, Virgil Mantoan,
> Be to thy name! and I shal, as I can,
> Folwe thy lanterne, as thow gost byforn,
> How Eneas to Dido was forsworn.
> In Naso and Eneydos wol I take
> The tenor, and the grete effectes make.   (924–9)

But the insistence that Chaucer will confine himself to the *tenor* or the *grete effectes*, the essential points, of Virgil's and Ovid's story is later developed into a sceptical and critical attitude towards his classical *auctours*. He will not repeat Virgil's explanation of how Dido came to *Libie* – 'It nedeth nat, it were but los of tyme' (997), and

> I coude folwe, word for word, Virgile,
> But it wolde lasten al to longe while. (1002–3)

When Aeneas visits the temple where Dido is praying, Chaucer adds,

> I can nat seyn if that it be possible,
> But Venus hadde hym maked invysible –
> Thus seyth the bok, withouten any les. (1020–2)

That phrase 'withouten any les' has an interesting function: it is no lie to say that Virgil asserts that Venus had made Aeneas invisible, but Chaucer evidently means to imply the possibility that Virgil is lying in making the assertion. Again, later, 'oure autour telleth us' (1139) that Cupid had taken on the form of Ascanius, 'but, as of that scripture, / Be as be may, I take of it no cure' (1144–5). The initial reverence for Virgil's paternal authority has been corroded by scepticism.

My other example of a questioning attitude towards a revered *auctour* is found in *The Clerk's Tale*. The Clerk begins with high praise of the 'worthy clerk' (IV 27) from whom he has taken his story of the patient Grisilde:

> Fraunceys Petrak, the lauriat poete,
> Highte this clerk, whos rethorike sweete
> Enlumyned al Ytaille of poetrie. (31–3)

Yet, just as in the legend of Dido, the narrator immediately proceeds to a declaration of independence from his *auctour*. Petrarch begins, he says, with a descriptive prologue,

> The which a long thyng were to devyse.
> And trewely, as to my juggement,
> Me thynketh it a thyng impertinent,
> Save that he wole conveyen his mateere. (52–5)

And he therefore omits it. Throughout the tale, the Clerk continues to apply his own *juggement* to his *auctour*'s work, and to protest vigorously against the cruelty of the tale, and especially against Walter's inexplicably harsh treatment of Grisilde.[78] In this case, for reasons indicated earlier in this book, Chaucer is likely to have had the most genuine admiration for Petrarch as *auctour*, and he has not even the excuse, as he has with Virgil, that the *auctour* is pagan and therefore open to doubt. *The Clerk's Tale* indeed provides a particularly interesting example of the parallel questioning of two kinds of authority – the authorial authority of Petrarch and the husbandly and paternal authority of Walter.

Chaucer, then, seems concerned to be, or at least to present himself as being, something other than a passive inheritor of material bequeathed by his literary forefathers. It is in keeping with this that he should sometimes mystify us about his sources. The most notorious case is that of *Troilus and Criseyde*. There indeed Chaucer claims no more than to be a translator (and that is the defence of *Troilus and Criseyde* proposed in the *Prologue* to *The Legend of Good Women* against the God of Love's objection to it as heresy); but his claim is to be translating 'out of Latyn' (II 14) from 'myn auctour called Lollius' (I 394), not, as was in fact the case, from the Italian of Boccaccio. There are perhaps two reasons why Chaucer should attempt to deceive us in this way. One is that the claim to have a Latin source adds to the work's appearance of historical authenticity; for Chaucer, as I have argued, is really aiming to create the sense of a classical past, while at the same time indicating the scholarly effort involved in any such reconstruction of antiquity. The other reason I wish to suggest – admittedly a more speculative one – is that the supposed Lollius, like other classical authors, belongs to a remote past and constitutes no threat to Chaucer's independence; whereas Boccaccio, a vernacular author of his own century, whom, as we have seen, he could even have met, and from whose work he learned of the very possibility of reconstructing the pagan past in a modern language, is dangerously close, a father rather than a remote ancestor. Nowhere in his work does Chaucer name Boccaccio, the *auctour* from whom he derives the three classical romances that constitute his own highest claim to poetic dignity, and, of all his sources, the one who might best be called his literary father. The name of the father, it would seem, is too dangerous to be mentioned. The other two great Italian writers of the *trecento* were less dangerous because Chaucer gained less from them in the way of specific source-material. Petrarch could be mentioned as a Latin author, as the source of *The Clerk's Tale*, but there his death is so strongly emphasized that it is as if Chaucer, Oedipus-like, had killed him himself. 'He is now deed and nayled in his cheste' (IV 29): the death is much to be regretted, and we shall all die in our turn, but how reassuring those nails are that keep Petrarch in his coffin! On the other hand, when Chaucer borrows from Petrarch's vernacular work, for Troilus's song in Book I of *Troilus and Criseyde*, his name must be suppressed and that of Lollius substituted. The influence of Dante on Chaucer is almost beyond assessment, but he was not the father of any single one of Chaucer's works (not even *The House of Fame*), and his name could therefore be mentioned several times without danger.

The present discussion has been somewhat rambling, and it may be helpful to summarize my findings so far. First, Chaucer in his work nearly always presents the father unfavourably, either as absent or as cruel. Second, he does not allow that good qualities can be inherited by sons from their fathers, though he occasionally gramts that bad qualities can. Third, he is unwilling to concede authority to his major poetic ancestors, and especially to the most important of all – Boccaccio, who was of the right generation really to have been Chaucer's father,[79] and who was truly his poetic father as writer of vernacular narratives which aimed at an imaginative reconstruction of pagan antiquity. I now turn to the authority of Chaucer as author and father of his own work. Chaucer is the first secular writer in English to be known by name as the author of a body of work; yet within his work he is most unwilling to assume paternal authority. It has often been noted how modest are the roles he plays as narrator throughout his career: first a mere dreamer, a channel through which fantasy or truth is conveyed, perpetually surprised and puzzled by the events of his dreams; then a clerkly but incompetent historian, who is constantly finding that his sources (on which he is totally dependent for his knowledge of love) fail to tell him crucial things such as his heroine's age, and whether she had any children, and whether or not she really gave her heart to Diomede; last the naïve reporter of the Canterbury pilgrimage, whose own powers of poetic composition are confined to 'rym dogerel' (VII 925). And it surely cannot be quite by chance that two of his most important unfinished works break off just *before* some authoritative pronouncement of meaning is to be made: *The House of Fame*, as we have seen, at the very moment when the dreamer glimpses the 'man of gret auctorite', and *The Legend of Good Women*, almost at the end of the account of Hypermnestra, with the tantalizing line, 'This tale is seyd for this conclusioun –' (2723). Robinson comments that 'It is a little surprising that the legend should have been left incomplete, when the story was finished and a very few lines would have sufficed to make the application.'[80] It is not surprising when we take into account Chaucer's pervasive unwillingness to state definitively the meaning and purpose of his writing.

It is in *The Canterbury Tales* that that unwillingness, that rejection of fatherhood, reaches its culmination. There every tale but two (the two told by the pilgrim Chaucer, one in 'rym dogerel' and the other an exceptionally long 'litel thyng in prose' (VII 937)), is attributed to someone other than Chaucer himself; and the mere fact of its attribution to a specific pilgrim-teller guarantees that Chaucer has no responsibility for it. The principle is stated explicitly in *The Miller's Prologue*: the 'cherles tale' (I 3169) that follows is included only because the drunken Miller insisted on thrusting himself forward to tell it, much to Chaucer's regret:

> And therfore every gentil wight I preye,
> For Goddes love, demeth nat that I seye
> Of yvel entente, but for I moot reherce
> Hir tales alle, be they bettre or werse,
> Or elles falsen som of my mateere. (I 3171–5)

The responsibility for the selection of tales then becomes not Chaucer's but the reader's: 'Blameth nat me if that ye chese amys!' (3181). The same applies to the establishment of a tale's meaning. The teller may have a particular meaning in mind (though even that is not necessarily Chaucer's), and may direct us to it by some such remark as 'Therfore I rede yow this conseil take' (*Physician's Tale* VI 285) or 'Taketh the moralite, goode men' (*Nun's Priest's Tale* VII 3440) or 'Lordynges, by this ensample I yow preye, / Beth war ...' (*Manciple's Tale* IX 309–10), but it is for us to decide whether that is what the tale *really* means. The pilgrim-Chaucer's second tale, the tale of Melibeus, is a prose allegory which for him is evidently meant to show how a ruler can gain good counsel and learn to be merciful. But when it is finished the Host's comments make it clear that for him it was about marriage and how wives ought to behave; he wishes his own virago of a wife could be as patient as the allegorical figure of Prudence in the tale. There is no-one to tell us authoritatively which is the right way to interpret the tale: Harry Bailly is not a very subtle literary critic, but then the tale is not a very coherent moral allegory, and the pilgrim-Chaucer is not a very intelligent tale-teller. We are left with a variety of possible interpretations, a variety summed up in a line which in differing forms is repeated several times in *The Canterbury Tales*: 'Diverse folk diversely they seyde' (I 3857); 'Diverse men diverse thynges seyden' (II 211); 'Diverse men diversely hym tolde' (IV 1469); 'Diverse folk diversely they demed' (V 202). Different people judge differently; and Chaucer's acknowledgment of that fact, his withdrawal of authority both from the tales and from their interpretations, amounts to what might be called a de-authorization of the whole work, or, in the terms used by some more recent theorists, to the conscious trans- formation of the *Tales* from a 'work' to a 'text'.

What I have in mind may be exemplified by two of the most penetrating essays of Roland Barthes, 'The Death of the Author' (1968) and 'From Work to Text' (1971). Here we may find the 'work' defined as writing governed and limited by the purposes of its author, while the 'text' is an anonymous, fatherless space in which an irreducible plurality of meanings play against each other. 'The author,' writes Barthes, 'is reputed the father and the owner of his work', while 'As for the Text, it reads without the inscription of the Father.' Again, 'The Author is thought to *nourish* the book, which is to say that he exists before it, thinks, suffers, lives for it, is in the same relation of antecedence to his work as a father to his child.' Thus it may be said that 'a text is not a line of words releasing a single "theological" meaning (the "message" of the Author-God) but a multi-dimensional space in which a variety of writings, none of them original, blend and clash'. To quote Barthes once more, 'It is not that the Author may not "come back" in the Text, in his text, but then he does so as a "guest". If he is a novelist, he is inscribed in the novel like one of his characters, figured in the carpet; no longer privileged, paternal.'[81] The phrases that I have been quoting offer an extraordinarily accurate description of what Chaucer would seem to have been consciously trying to do in *The Canterbury Tales*: to relinquish his own paternal authority, and to enter the text thereby produced, that 'tissue of quotations',[82] only as a guest. Certainly the Host is someone else; and each tale is literally a 'quotation', set in quotation-marks, not as the message of the Author-God, but as the potentially prejudiced statement of one of a large and various group of all-too-human pilgrims. We, looking back on Chaucer, thus confront an acute paradox. He is the first English poet to exist as an 'author', the first to be known by name as the father of a body of work; and yet throughout his career he seems to be striving towards the culmination achieved in *The Canterbury Tales*, the relinquishment of his own fatherhood, the transformation of his work into a text.

That paradox was already, I believe, a source of embarrassment to Chaucer's immediate successors, and may be part of the reason for their failure to build effectively on some of the most 'advanced' elements in his work. The difficulty involved in being the sons of such a father was already felt by those who were the first to call him 'father'. Let me quote once more Hoccleve's eulogy, this time adding two lines omitted before:

> O maister deere and fadir reverent,
> My maister Chaucer, flour of eloquence,
> Mirrour of fructuous entendement,
> O universal fadir in science,
> Allas, that thou thyn excellent prudence
> In thy bed mortel mightist naght byqwethe![83]

In the following stanza of *The Regement of Princes* Hoccleve refers to Chaucer's 'hy vertu'; and the impossibility of the father's bequeathing his virtue to the son is undoubtedly a theme borrowed by Hoccleve from one of the Chaucer passages quoted above.[84] The son wishes to inherit the authority of a father who has denied that any such inheritance is possible, and has in any case denied his own fatherhood. Chaucer seemed already to have done everything: he was truly a 'universal father', whose achievement was coextensive with the whole range of imaginable possibilities for poetry in English, and whose death, as Hoccleve went on to write, 'Despoiled hath this land of the swetnesse / Of rethorik.'[85] What territory, what imaginative space, did this leave for would-be sons? As father, he made possible their very existence as English poets, yet, as his successors, they inevitably came too late. Like Dryden looking back at the great dramatists of the age of Shakespeare, they must have felt, 'We acknowledge them our fathers in wit; but they have ruined their estates themselves before they came to their children's hands.'[86] As late as the 1470s a point similar to this was being made in the anonymous *Book of Curtesye* about Chaucer, the 'fader and founder of ornate eloquence', and Gower, the 'auncyent fader of memorye', seen as joint originators of the English poetic tradition:

> Loo, my childe, these faders auncyente
> Repen the feldes fresshe of fulsomnes.
> The flours fresh they gadred up, and hente
> Of silver langage the grete riches.

Who wil it have, my lityl childe, doutles
Muste of hem begge – ther is no more to saye –
For of oure tunge they were both lok and kaye.[87]

And even this acknowledgment of indebtedness could not be made without incurring a further debt, for the image of precursors as reapers who have already gathered the harvest of poetry, derived originally from chapter 2 of the Book of Ruth, is itself borrowed from Chaucer's *Prologue* to *The Legend of Good Women*.[88]

A consequence of this attitude towards Chaucer seems to have been a widespread anxiety among his poetic descendants about the impossibility of the task they were undertaking. In many passages scattered throughout his voluminous works Lydgate expresses his sense of inferiority as a mere star beside the sun, 'compared ageyn the bemys briht / Off this poete.'[89] He sees himself and other descendants of Chaucer as mere imitators, who cannot hope to match their model:

Whan we wolde his stile counterfet,
We may al day oure colour grynde and bete,
Tempre our azour and vermyloun:
But al I holde but presumpcioun –
It folweth nat, therfore I lette be.[90]

That is from Lydgate's *Troy Book*; earlier, using the same terminology of 'counterfeiting' Chaucer's style, he had written in *The Flour of Curtesye*:

We may assaye for to counterfete
His gaye style, but it wil not be.[91]

A less well-known disciple of Chaucer is John Walton, composer of a verse translation of Boethius, in the preface to which he expresses a similar anxiety:

To Chaucer, that is floure of rethoryk
In Englisshe tong and excellent poete,
This wot I wel, no thing may I do lyk,
Though so that I of makynge entyrmete.[92]

Such passages are of course examples of the rhetorical *topos* of modesty, but that is no reason to dismiss them as meaningless. They support Harold Bloom's argument that poetic influence is accompanied by anxiety, though not his assumption that Shakespeare and his predecessors belonged to 'the giant age before the flood, before the anxiety of influence became central to poetic consciousness'.[93]

The beginnings of English poetic history in the fifteenth century really do seem to be marked by the anxiety of influence.

For a poet to make use of a great precursor is never easy, but it was perhaps especially difficult for the fifteenth-century poets to make profitable use of Chaucer, because there had never before been such a father-figure in English. It was doubtless impossible for Lydgate, never a thinker of great resource, to envisage any form of use other than what he calls counterfeiting his master's style. There is a passage, however, in a letter of Petrarch's to Boccaccio in which he takes up this characteristically Renaissance issue of stylistic imitation, and distinguishes between two kinds of similarity. He reports what advice he gave 'in a kind paternal manner' to a young man much given to imitating Virgil:

A proper imitator should take care that what he writes resembles the original without reproducing it. The resemblance should not be that of a portrait to the sitter – in that case the closer the likeness is the better – but it should be the resemblance of a son to his father ... Thus we may use another man's conceptions and the color of his style, but not use his words. In the first case the resemblance is hidden deep; in the second it is glaring. The first procedure makes poets, the second makes apes.[94]

Lydgate's use of the language of painting in the lines quoted above from the *Troy Book* (lines incorporating a familiar pun on 'colour' as a rhetorical term, which is also present in Petrarch's letter) strongly suggests that for him the ideal goal of Chaucerian imitation was identicality, literal counterfeiting. He may have seen Chaucer as father, but he did not really want to be his son; he simply wanted to be Chaucer. This may enable us to return to *The Siege of Thebes*, and see it in a new light. We saw that when Lydgate described himself as meeting the Canterbury pilgrims, there was no Chaucer among them. It is as if Lydgate, in his wishes at least, has succeeded in *becoming* Chaucer; and, as we observed, the nearer *The Siege of Thebes* gets to *The Knight's Tale*, the more of Chaucer's actual words Lydgate takes over. The reader begins to suspect that an ideal culmination of Lydgate's enterprise might be simply a recomposition of *The Canterbury Tales* analogous to the recomposition of *Don Quixote* imagined by Borges as the goal of his Pierre Menard.

Harold Bloom sees the poetic influence which constitutes poetic history in Oedipal terms. The literary son feels that his authority is lessened by the imaginative area already occupied by the literary father, and he must, if he is himself a 'strong poet' or 'major aesthetic consciousness',[95] adopt one or more of a variety of modes of misreading in order to gain for himself the already occupied space. It is difficult, no doubt, to see Lydgate, whose strength is a matter of mild persistence rather than of heroic courage, as a 'major aesthetic consciousness' engaged in a life-or-death struggle to win authority from his powerful ancestor, but it is worth bearing in mind that *The Siege of Thebes* includes a retelling of the story of Oedipus. It is tempting to suppose that in the early part of the *Siege* Lydgate was unconsciously dramatizing precisely the innocent destructiveness he had to engage in himself in order to survive a father as powerful yet benevolent as Chaucer. In order to live as a poet, he had to kill Chaucer – unknowingly, of course, but then Oedipus did not know that it was Laius whom he had killed at the crossroads. First, he had to remove Chaucer silently from his own Canterbury pilgrimage, then, casting him as Laius, he had to conceal from himself what he was doing by ensuring that the Oedipus legend should be deprived of all mythic power. This is no more than a fantasy, of course; but even fifteenth-century monks had unconscious minds.

In a way, it might have been easier for Chaucer's poetic descendants to follow him if he had been more willing to play the role of father that they thrust upon him. Lydgate in particular, when he is striving hardest to be Chaucerian, tends to impose on his work a didacticism – 'the "message" of the Author-God' – very different from Chaucer's indeterminacy of ultimate meaning. D. H. Lawrence wrote in a letter to Edward Garnett, 'We have to hate our immediate predecessors, to get free from their authority.'[96] Who could possibly have hated the Chaucer who appears only as a guest in his own work, the Chaucer rightly described by Lydgate as 'gronde of wel-seying'? –

> Hym liste nat pinche nor gruche at every blot,
> Nor meve hym silf to parturbe his reste
> (I have herde telle), but seide alweie the best,
> Suffring goodly of his gentilnes
> Ful many thing enbracid with rudnes.[97]

A Chaucer who had insisted more sternly on his parental authority might have provoked a healthy rebelliousness in his sons. Whatever the reason, it was not until nearly a century after his death that Chaucer's descendants were able to free themselves from the gentle bond of their universal father, his 'repressive tolerance'. Then, as we shall see, John Skelton was able to make radically new use of the

Chaucerian inheritance, for example by his comparative assessment of Chaucer and of Lydgate in *Phyllyp Sparowe*, and later by suggesting in *The Garland of Laurel* that the true purpose of the English poetic tradition that sprang from Chaucer was that it should culminate in the laureation of John Skelton. The 'strong' way out of the son's relation to the father is the kind of respectful repudiation practised, from the safe distance of Scotland, by Robert Henryson: even while praising 'worthie Chaucer glorious', he dared to ask, 'Quha wait gif all that Chauceir wrait was trew?',[98] and proceeded to write an alternative ending to *Troilus and Criseyde*. A little later Gavin Douglas was to judge, boldly but justly, that Chaucer 'standis beneth Virgill in gre' and that his legend of Dido quite misrepresents the account given by that 'prynce of poetis' in the *Aeneid*.[99] Skelton, Henryson and Douglas were truly the sons of Chaucer in daring to be themselves, to adopt a sceptical independence of judgment that is genuinely Chaucerian but that could not be passively inherited from father Chaucer.

4. Hoccleve's Misrule

I end this investigation of the Chaucerian tradition with a brief study of a poem which shows, in a modest way, how it was possible for one of Chaucer's immediate successors to learn from him without either repudiating him or being overwhelmed by his authority – possible, provided that he had matter of his own that he wanted to express, and was not simply applying the master's style, as he perceived it, to material assigned by a patron. The poem is *La Male Regle*, by Thomas Hoccleve, and it was written in 1405 or 1406, within a few years of Chaucer's death. Hoccleve was born in 1366 or 1367,[100] probably at Hockliffe in Bedfordshire. In 1387 he became a clerk in the Privy Seal office, and in his role as a middle-ranking civil servant and scribe he is a living instance of the way that the values and styles of courtly literature penetrated down the social scale in the fifteenth century. Hoccleve implies that he knew Chaucer personally and received literary encouragement from him –

> Mi dere maistir – God his soule quyte! –
> And fadir, Chaucer, fayn wolde han me taght,
> But I was dul, and lerned lite or naght[101]

– and it seems likely enough that the one superior royal servant should have met the other, somewhat less important one. Among Hoccleve's earliest works is *The Letter of Cupid* (1402), a free translation from the French of Christine de Pisan, which manages to reverse her defence of women. (It may even be that Hoccleve did not understand the drift or tone of Christine's poem; in any event, he 'medievalizes' it by making it revert to the clerical anti-feminism against which she was protesting.) In 1411–12 he wrote *The Regement of Princes* for the Prince of Wales (later Henry V), a work of the same type as Lydgate's *Fall of Princes*, though mercifully far briefer, in using English verse to offer advice on the morality of princely rule. It survives in over forty manuscripts. In 1416, Hoccleve suffered a severe mental breakdown. In 1421–2 he wrote for Humphrey, Duke of Gloucester, the work known as the *Series*, an interesting experiment in linking together varied types of writing in verse and prose. It includes the *Complaint*, in which he describes his earlier breakdown and its aftermath in an unusually personal way. He died in 1426; his reputation, despite the popularity of *The Regement of Princes*, was then and subsequently outshone by that of his more prolific contemporary Lydgate.

The immediate purpose of *La Male Regle* is to request Thomas Nevill, Lord Fournival, the sub-treasurer, to pay Hoccleve an instalment of the annuity of £10, which was in effect his salary as a Privy Seal clerk, but which was held up in 1405 by a restriction on the payment of recent annuities enacted by King Henry IV. It is thus in effect a begging-poem, belonging to a kind established in French in the fourteenth century and in English from the time of Chaucer onwards. The existence of this genre reminds us of the subordinate status of poets in northern Europe, dependent as they were on royal or noble support, and support that was usually given for services other than poetry itself.[102] (Before the invention of printing and of copyright there was of course no way in which a writer could make a living directly from the market.) The author of a begging-poem will naturally wish to make it as ingenious a display of literary skill as possible, in the hope that it will catch its recipient's attention. Chaucer, in the delightful *Complaint to his Purse*, directed in the last year of the poet's life to King Henry IV in the first year of his reign, addresses his purse as if it were his mistress. She is his 'lady dere' (2), his 'hertes stere, / Quene of comfort and of good companye' (12–13), and her lightness (the emptiness of the purse and the fickleness of the lady) has brought him to the verge of death. Chaucer was careful, in an envoy, to refer to all three grounds on which Henry IV claimed the throne in succession to Richard II – conquest, descent, and the choice of the people – and his plea was evidently successful, for he was granted an additional stipend of 40 marks a year. A later example, the verse-letter which Lydgate addressed to Gloucester in the 1430s asking for payment for his translation of *The Fall of Princes*, is based on a different but equally ingenious fiction: the purse is sick of consumption, 'Botme of his stomak tournyd up-so-doun' (13); the poet is wearing black in mourning for it (an allusion to Lydgate's Benedictine habit); and the only remedy is 'Nat sugre-plaat maad by th'appotecarye' (41) but 'silver plate' (48) or else *aurum potabile* (46).[103]

Hoccleve's *Male Regle* is longer and more autobiographical than either of these examples, but it too is built on a witty fiction. Like Lydgate a quarter of a century later, he writes in terms of sickness, but for him it is not merely an allegory or sustained metaphor. He composes the whole poem in the form of an address to the imagined god Health, adapting for the purpose the penitential lyric addressed to the Christian God.[104] He has offended against Health by his riotous way of life, his 'male regle' or *misreule*, which he describes in detail. In penitential terms, his full confession and promise of amendment are the necessary preliminary to his plea for the god's mercy:

> From hennes foorth wole I do reverence
> Unto thy name, and holde of thee in cheef,
> And werre make and sharp resistence
> Ageyn thy fo and myn, that cruel theef
> That undir foote me halt in mescheef,
> So thow me to thy grace reconcyle.
> O now thyn help, thy socour and releef! –
> And I for ay misreule wole exyle.   (49–56)

His contrition having been established, the mercy for which he begs is that the god should send 'a tokne or tweye' (419) to Lord Fournival to pay him what is due, and thus he will be able to purchase medicaments to restore himself to Health's service:

> By coyn I gete may swich medecyne
> As may myn hurtes alle that me greeve
> Exyle cleene, and voide me of pyne.   (446–8)

As an example of the sort of verbal play that belongs to the begging-poem in this tradition, we may note that the 'tokens' begged for are heavenly signs or demonstrations of Health's divine authority, but that the word could also mean coins or cash.[105]

La Male Regle begins with a display of Chaucerian high style: a sustained *apostrophatio* incorporating a double *interrogatio* and a good deal of metaphor or *translatio*, all couched in Latinate diction:

> O precious tresor inconparable!
> O ground and roote of prosperitee!
> O excellent richesse commendable
> Aboven alle that in eerthe be!
> Who may susteene thyn adversitee?
> What wight may him avante of worldly welthe
> But if he fully stande in grace of thee,
> Eerthely god, piler of lyf, thow Helthe? (1–8)

The *apostrophatio* constitutes a continued periphrasis or *circumlocutio*: just as in the proem to Book III of *Troilus and Criseyde* Chaucer apostrophizes Venus for seven stanzas without mentioning her name until the seventh (and then only by implication), so here, on a much smaller scale but with more genuine uncertainty, we have to wait for the last word of the stanza to tell us who is being invoked. But the poem as a whole does not engage in a Lydgatean pastiche of Chaucerian rhetoric. Hoccleve's account of his ill-health and of the undignified self-indulgences by which he brought it on is conveyed in simpler diction and a seemingly more natural and spontaneous style. Autobiography did not in fact come 'naturally' to medieval writers, for what seems natural depends on readily available conventions of expression, and for autobiography no such conventions existed in the later Middle Ages (except those of the confessional, which Hoccleve utilizes as best he can). Yet this was certainly a period in England in which we can recognize certain writers struggling to find means of centring their works in their personal histories rather than in abstract intellectual schemes. William Langland is one such,[106] and Margery Kempe is another.[107] Inevitably, those who were driven to find ways of writing their individual life-histories tended to be the eccentric, even the unbalanced, who felt their inner selves to be different from those of their neighbours. Hoccleve evidently felt strongly this sense of difference and of consequent alienation: in his *Complaint* he tells how, after his breakdown, men pretended not to know him and discussed him behind his back, and how he would stare at his reflection in a mirror,

> To loke how that me of my chere thowghte,
> If any other were it than it owghte. (158–9)

In 1406 things were not yet so bad, but in *La Male Regle* he writes about his mild alcoholism, his laziness, his pursuit of prostitutes and his cowardice, all with the fascination of a man observing someone other than himself.

This is confessional poetry in both the medieval and the modern sense. In the poem's fiction, confession is a necessary part of the penitential process, and the fuller the more effective; but the choice of that fiction – and no-one could mistake it for anything but a fiction – seems dictated by a drive towards self-exposure comparable to that found, for example, in some of the later work of Robert Lowell: *Life Studies* or *Notebook*. Of Lowell it has been written that 'The privacies which he betrays are for the most part not those of the bedroom, but of the living room, the telephone booth, the mailbox',[108] and something analogous might be said of Hoccleve. In his case the means by which this drive can be given literary expression have been learned, in important ways, from Chaucer, and not only from Chaucer as 'father and founder of ornate eloquence'. Nor is it a matter simply of Hoccleve's learning from Chaucer's self-portrayal in his work; for whereas the Chaucerian 'I' is always protected by an elusive irony that suggests that it may be only a mask or an act, Hoccleve's 'I' is more wholeheartedly autobiographical and vulnerable. I wrote that Hoccleve recounts his past life with the fascination of a man observing someone else; and I think that in *La Male Regle* Hoccleve's main debt to Chaucer may be to the way in which he allows his Canterbury pilgrims to reveal and expose themselves unguardedly, both in the *General Prologue* and in their tales.

For example, in *The Nun's Priest's Tale* the teller asserts with bold irony, in some lines quoted in chapter 2 to illustrate Chaucer's sceptical attitude towards Arthurian romance, that his story of talking animals

> ... is also trewe, I undertake,
> As is the book of Launcelot de Lake,
> That wommen holde in ful greet reverence.   (VIII 3211–13)

And then, realizing that he has inadvertently let slip his celibate male's real view of women (just as he did earlier, when he blamed woman for man's Fall, and then denied that this clerical commonplace was his own opinion), he hastily adds, 'Now wol I turne agayn to my sentence!' (3214). That very line, so unremarkable in itself, is quoted by Hoccleve in *La Male Regle*. He confesses that, for all his fascination with tavern-ladies, he is actually very shy about going further than a kiss – indeed he even blushes when the sexual act is mentioned in his presence – and then, with that recollected blush merging into one at what he has revealed about himself, he adds, 'Now wole I torne ageyn to my sentence':

> I dar nat telle how that the fresshe repeir
> Of Venus femel lusty children deere,
> That so goodly, so shaply were, and feir,
> And so plesant of port and of maneere,
> And feede cowden al a world with cheere,
> And of atyr passyngly wel byseye,
> At Poules Heed me maden ofte appeere,
> To talke of mirthe and to disporte and pleye.
>
> Ther was sweet wyn ynow thurgh-out the hous,
> And wafres thikke, for this conpaignie
> That I spak of been sumwhat likerous
> Where as they mowe a draght of wyn espie,
> Sweete and, in wirkynge, hoot for the maistrie
> To warme a stomak with. Ther-of they dranke:
> To suffre hem paie had been no courtesie;
> That charge I tooke, to wynne love and thanke.
>
> Of loves aart yit touchid I no deel –
> I cowde nat, and eek it was no neede.
> Had I a kus, I was content ful weel,
> Bettre than I wolde han be with the deede.
> Ther-on can I but smal, it is no dreede:
> Whan that men speke of it in my presence,
> For shame I wexe as reed as is the gleede.
> Now wole I torne ageyn to my sentence.   (137–60)

In this passage there also seems to me to be an intangible Chaucerian recollection in the line 'To suffre hem paie had been no courtesie.' It exemplifies the technique used so often in the *General Prologue*, of allowing a pilgrim to expose his own folly simply by repeating his opinion in his own words – but here, as elsewhere, Hoccleve has turned the technique of poker-faced quotation upon himself. How silly, and yet, in its vulnerability, how touching is the conception of *courtesie* that impelled this younger 'I' to insist on buying drinks for such manifestly predatory ladies!

At times, in his self-absorbed chattiness, Hoccleve sounds rather like the Wife of Bath, forgetting where she has got to in her exhaustive account of her marital history:

> But now, sire, lat me se, what shal I seyn?
> Aha! by God, I have my tale ageyn.   (III 585–6)

Similarly Hoccleve first argues step by step that excess is equivalent
to the devil in its power to destroy man's soul; then dismisses his
own argument impatiently, in favour of an account of staying up late
drinking (imagined so vividly that it is as though it were happening
now – 'go we *now* to wacche'); then passes on to the morning after,
and, having said that he can think of no one as reluctant as he to rise
from bed after such a late night, adds, 'Abyde, let me see!', and
comes up with the names of two of his colleagues who are equally
late risers:

> The feend and excesse been convertible,
> As enditeth to me my fantasie.
> This is my skile, if it be admittible:
> Excesse of mete and drynke is glotonye;
> Glotonye awakith malencolie;
> Malencolie engendrith werre and stryfe;
> Stryfe causith mortel hurt thurgh hir folie;
> Thus may excesse reve a soule hir lyfe.
>
> No force of al this! – go we now to wacche
> By nightirtale out of al mesure,
> For as in that fynde kowde I no macche
> In al the Privee Seel with me to endure;
> And to the cuppe ay took I heede and cure,
> For that the drynke apalle sholde noght.
> But whan the pot emptid was of moisture,
> To wake aftirward cam nat in my thoght.
>
> But whan the cuppe had thus my neede sped
> (And sumdeel more than necessitee),
> With repleet spirit wente I to my bed,
> And bathid there in superfluitee.
> But on the morn was wight of no degree
> So looth as I to twynne fro my cowche,
> By aght I woot. Abyde, let me see!
> Of two as looth I am seur kowde I towche.
>
> I dar nat seyn Prentys and Arondel
> Me countrefete, and in swich wach go ny me,
> But often they hir bed loven so wel
> That of the day it drawith ny the pryme
> Or they ryse up – nat tell I can the tyme
> Whan they to bedde goon, it is so late!   (297–326)

The first line of this extract also goes to a Chaucerian tune: it is
reminiscent of 'For thefte and riot, they been convertible' (1 4395)
from *The Cook's Tale*, a fragment which gives a lively and squalid
glimpse of low life in London. The Cook's Perkyn, that rotten apple

of an apprentice, who 'loved bet the taverne than the shoppe' (1 4376), may well have been one model for Hoccleve's self-portrayal in *La Male Regle*. Another Wife of Bath touch can perhaps be detected when Hoccleve, coming to the end of his confession, mutters

> Ey, what is me, that to myself thus longe
> Clappid have I? – I trowe that I rave! (393–4)

Such an attempt to naturalize the device of the confessional soliloquy, in its very transparency, amounts to a kind of Shklovskian 'baring of the device', and Hoccleve was doubtless well aware of this. *La Male Regle* is not a self-authenticating dramatic monologue. Just as with the Nun's Priest or the Wife of Bath, the apparently spontaneous movement and interjections are carefully calculated, and in Hoccleve's case there remains the framing fiction of the penitential plea to Health, and then, framed by that, the plea to the sub-treasurer to release some part of his annuity. If the poem is intended to intrigue Fournival by its ingenuity, it is also to move him by showing how much Hoccleve needs the money. He needs it to buy medicine; he therefore has to show in detail the sickness from which he is suffering and how it arose; and the fact that it arose from his own youthful excesses (of which he now repents), and that his account of it shows him in such an undignified light, is part of the posture of humility that will, he hopes, induce Fournival's pity.

It has recently been suggested that the final stanzas appealing for payment of the annuity may have been 'a late addition, prompted by news of the lord Furnivall's appointment, to a poem already complete'.[109] This, however, seems highly unlikely, because it disregards the close-knit structure that underlies the poem's apparently loose progression. From the very beginning, the crucial themes of sickness and poverty have been interwoven. In the first stanza Hoccleve addresses Health as 'excellent richesse' (3), and in the second he speaks of his body as being 'Al poore of ese and ryche of evel fare' (16) – that is, poor in well-being and rich in illness. Clearly these metaphors of wealth and poverty are intended to lead up to a plea for payment. Later Hoccleve shows how his excesses have impoverished him as well as undermining his health –

> For riot paieth largely everemo:
> He styntith nevere til his purs be bare (199–200)

– so that he ends by suffering from a 'seeknesse / As wel of purs as body' (337–8), a disease which forcibly prevents him in two ways from continuing his life of *excesse*. The literal sickness of body and metaphorical sickness of purse are intricately interwoven from beginning to end.

La Male Regle does in fact include digressions, but they are carefully planned, and inserted with the skill with which Chaucer incorporates digressions in many of the *Canterbury Tales*. The first digression (lines 65–88) is on the subject of Youth, and especially of Youth's unwillingness to listen to the voices of reason and of *conseil* (76, 86), or good advice. The second and longer digression (lines 209–88) develops this theme of *conseil* in relation to flattery. Hoccleve has explained how he himself succumbed to the flattery of being called *maistir* (201) by Thames boatmen who overcharged him; he goes on to generalize about the danger implicit in all servants who flatter their lords and fail to give them the true advice, even if unpleasant, that they really need. This theme of good and bad counsel is an important one in English poetry from Chaucer's time onwards. Chaucer himself inserts it (in a sense gratuitously) into the story of Januarie and May in *The Merchant's Tale*, in the form of the dispute between Januarie's two advisers, the flattering Placebo and the reliable if cynical Justinus; and Hoccleve may be influenced by *The Merchant's Tale* in *La Male Regle*, though there are few verbal parallels beyond the use of *pestilence* in both poems as a metaphor to refer to the household flatterer.[110] Another poem almost contemporary with *La Male Regle* of which this is a main theme is the alliterative *Mum and the Sothsegger*.[111] The theme reflects not a theoretical moral problem but a practical political concern: where government depends on kings and lords whose personal power is great, and who are not answerable to those below them, a crucial issue is how to ensure that such rulers will be well advised. The temptation will always be for the counsellor to say what he thinks will please his lord, for

> ... whan the sobre, treewe, and weel avysid
> With sad visage his lord enfourmeth pleyn
> How that his governance is despysid
> Among the peple, and seith him as they seyn,
> As man treewe oghte un-to his sovereyn,
> Conseillynge him amende his governance,
> The lordes herte swellith for desdeyn,
> And bit him voide blyve with meschance.   (273–80)

The lord may have power of life and death over his counsellors, but in the last resort his security, as well as the good government of his domains, will depend on their willingness to tell him the truth and risk his displeasure. What is significant for our purposes about the emergence of this theme into English poetry is that it indicates a new, public importance for vernacular poetry itself. In the past, English verse had instructed and it had complained, but it had chiefly instructed individuals about private moral issues (above all, about the sins), and it had complained for the benefit of subjects, not rulers. But, from Chaucer's time onwards, poets writing in English presumed to offer political instruction to royal and noble patrons; and many of the most substantial fifteenth-century poems in the Chaucerian tradition take up historical themes in order to advise rulers what they could learn from them about the art and morality of government. Hoccleve's own longest poem, *The Regement of Princes*, is precisely of this kind; so, in many ways, are Lydgate's *Siege of Thebes* and his much longer *Troy Book* and *Fall of Princes*. English poetry was beginning to have a public ambition and a public significance that it had not previously possessed; and it is particularly striking that this should also emerge in a poem so apparently private and confessional as Hoccleve's *Male Regle*. There is perhaps an unstated analogy between *misreule* in the private life of a clerk in the Privy Seal office and *misreule* in the administration he serves.

The poetry of Hoccleve represents a path alternative to that of Lydgate which Chaucerian influence might have taken. Hoccleve's style is less showy and elaborate than Lydgate's, and its plainness may show some sign of influence from Gower, whom Hoccleve was the first to set alongside Chaucer as master of the new English poetry.[112] Also un-Chaucerian is Hoccleve's persistent use of small-scale personification, as in 'And now my smert accusith my folie' (40) or 'Excesse at borde hath leyd his knyf with me' (112), or 'For riot paieth largely everemo' (198). This is one of the hallmarks of his style throughout his work, and may conceivably indicate the influence of *Piers Plowman*, a poem that was certainly widely read in the London area in the early fifteenth century. Hoccleve, then, was capable of learning intelligently from Chaucer without being overwhelmed by his influence; but, despite the great popularity of *The Regement of Princes*, there is little sign that he had any influence in his turn, though it is possible that closer investigation would reveal Hocclevian strains in the plainer kinds of fifteenth-century courtly verse, such as that of Charles of Orleans or the anonymous *Assembly of Ladies*. There are moments, as we shall see, when even Stephen Hawes sounds not unlike Hoccleve.[113] On the whole, though, it seems likely that the very eccentricity that is now so intriguing counted against him. It was through Lydgate that the main stream of Chaucerianism flowed, and continued to flow right down to the early sixteenth century, when Hawes is reputed to have known much of Lydgate's work by heart. Indeed, much late-fifteenth- and early-sixteenth-century poetry that is generally classified as Chaucerian might be better called Lydgatean.[114] The persistent distortion of Chaucer's achievement that is represented by the poetry of most of his disciples meant that the work of the literary Renaissance, which Chaucer had begun single-handed, had to be done all over again in the sixteenth century.

4 · Outside the Chaucerian tradition

It is not my intention to continue tracing the influence of Chaucer as the central theme of the rest of this book. His presence in later poetry will frequently be noted and discussed, but along with other elements of no less importance. In the present chapter my aim is to give some sense of the achievements of English poets who in the fifteenth century remained entirely medieval, untouched by Chaucer's work even if they were aware of its existence. Two of the most important and successful bodies of English verse in the fifteenth century consist of alliterative poetry and religious drama. (There is some overlap between the two, in that the York cycle underwent a large-scale alliterative revision in the course of the century, with 13 of its episodes being rewritten in alliterative stanzas; and alliteration of an unsystematic kind is quite widespread in fifteenth-century poetry generally, especially as a feature of stylistic elevation.) Neither of these traditions of writing had any independent future; both ceased to exist, for different reasons, in the sixteenth century; but that is no reason for us to disregard them now. As I suggested earlier, it would be a mistake to see the movement from medieval to Renaissance as one of straightforward progress. Between Chaucer and, say, Shakespeare there were losses as well as gains, and some of the most interesting and valuable achievements are located on dead-ends rather than on what now looks like the highroad. The point of view I have adopted so far is that of the Renaissance, which believed itself superior to the barbarism of the *medium aevum*; and, though it may have been the Renaissance that made literary history possible, it also made possible literary–historical perspectives other than its own. I shall take one sample of alliterative poetry and one of religious drama.

1. The Awntyrs off Arthure

We rightly associate the Alliterative Revival with the fourteenth century. Its most famous products – *Piers Plowman*, the works of the *Gawain*–poet, the *Morte Arthure* – are roughly contemporary with

121

Chaucer, and are part of that general efflorescence of writing in the vernacular that occurred in England in the second half of the fourteenth century. It is just possible that the *Gawain*-poet had some contact with Italy and that *Pearl* bears traces of his reading in Italian, but in almost every way this body of writing is distinctively medieval. With a very few exceptions, its authors were anonymous, and it is extremely difficult to recognize literary influence from one work to another, or even to date most of the poems with any certainty. The latest alliterative poems seem to belong to the early sixteenth century: they include Dunbar's *Tretis of Tua Mariit Wemen and the Wedo*, written about 1500, and the anonymous *Scotish Ffielde*, a heroic account of the Battle of Flodden (1513) written in Cheshire in the reign of Henry VIII.[1] As with the Gothic style in architecture, it is difficult to be sure whether such works should be considered as survivals or revivals of the medieval tradition;[2] but it is clear that alliterative poetry went on being composed through the fifteenth century, especially in northern England and in Scotland. Given the uncertainties of dating, unrhymed alliterative poems which may be later than 1400 include the two substantial chronicle-romances, *The Wars of Alexander* and *The Destruction of Troy*, both translated from learned medieval Latin sources, but neither showing any of Chaucer's 'Renaissance' interest in imagining the pagan past from its own point of view; and some poems in the *Piers Plowman* tradition such as *Death and Liffe*.

There is also a substantial group of alliterative poems in complicated rhyming stanzas, usually of thirteen lines; these come from northern parts of Britain, and mostly date from the fifteenth century. They include *The Buke of the Howlat* (about 1446), a bird-allegory incorporating a eulogy of the Douglas family; *Gologros and Gawane* (after 1450), a translation of two separate episodes from the First Continuation of *Perceval; Rauf Coilyear* (after 1450), a burlesque romance; Gavin Douglas's prologue to Book VIII of his translation of the *Aeneid* (1513); and the subject of my discussion, *The Awntyrs off Arthure*. Unlike the other works listed, the *Awntyrs* comes from just south of the Anglo-Scottish border, near Carlisle. Its date is uncertain; it survives in four manuscripts (more than most alliterative poems), 'all of the middle or late fifteenth century',[3] and has been assigned by scholars sometimes to the fourteenth century and sometimes to the fifteenth.[4] Its most recent editor places it 'approximately 1400–30', and the most recent survey of the manuscripts of alliterative poems agrees that an earlier date is 'reasonably doubted'.[5] I suspect that the only reason for placing it in the fourteenth century is an erroneous supposition that that was when most Middle English alliterative poems were written, and my assumption is that it is an early-fifteenth-century work, roughly contemporary with the poems of Hoccleve and Lydgate. My argument will be that it has its own structural aesthetic, which in important respects can be thought of as medieval or 'Gothic' rather than classical or Renaissance, but also that in certain ways twentieth-century readers may be better placed to respond to it than readers of earlier periods were.

In style, the *Awntyrs* has a characteristically Gothic spikiness and restlessness. Not an inch of surface is left undecorated: there is far more alliteration than is to be found in unrhymed poems such as *Sir Gawain and the Green Knight* or *Piers Plowman*, and the alliteration gives additional emphasis to the strongly accented rhythm and constantly varying metrical pattern. There are many repetitions of words and phrases, linking the stanzas together and often linking the eight-line first part of each stanza with its five-line second part. The poem is full of adjectives and adjectival phrases, many of them redundant and honorific. The overall effect is of an ostentatious demonstration of skill, admired for its own sake, like that of the late-medieval goldsmith or jeweller, to produce an intricate verbal object as *curiouse* and *proude* as what it often describes:

> Ho was the worthiest wight that eny welde wolde;
> Here gide was glorious and gay, of a gressegrene.
> Here belle was of blunket, with birdes ful bolde,
> Botonede with besantes and bokeled ful bene.
> Here fax in fyne perré was fretted in folde,
> Contrefelet and kelle coloured full clene,
> With a crowne of crystal and of clere golde;
> Here kercheves were curiouse with many proude prene.
> Her enparel was praysed with prise of might;
> Bright birdes and bolde
> Had note ynoghe to beholde
> On that frely to folde
> And on the kene knight.   (365–77)

There is no question here of the classical principle of *ars est artem celare*, no Italianate mellifluousness of sound and rhythm, no elegant simplicity in the solution of difficult problems. We are meant to feel at every point the difficulty of what is being done, and the highly specialized craftsmanship necessary to do it. All this is to say that the

Awntyrs has the usual characteristics of Middle English alliterative poetry, but raised to a higher degree of intensity. In its flamboyant splendour, it is a typical late-medieval work of art.

The structure of the *Awntyrs* presents more problems, and this is an aspect of the poem that has been almost universally abused by the critics and scholars who have discussed it. A. C. Baugh writes without enthusiasm that in it 'an adventure of Gawain is loosely combined with a religious theme better known in the *Trental of St. Gregory*.'[6] J. L. N. O'Loughlin adds that 'The coupling of two such unrelated themes is certainly naïve.'[7] George Kane had earlier been more vehement: 'Its story is weak and meagre, and scarcely begins to move in the first half of the romance'; and he went on to refer contemptuously to the 'thin little thread of narrative'.[8] John Speirs praises the poetic art of the *Awntyrs* as comparable with that of *Sir Gawain and the Green Knight*, but adds that 'It remains a remarkable fragment of the same kind of poetic art, but a fragment only. It consists, as it stands, of two episodes which have not been made into an inclusive whole.'[9] The fullest discussion of *The Awntyrs off Arthure* is that of Ralph Hanna.[10] Hanna also is dissatisfied with the poem's structure, so much so indeed that he returns to the theory put forward by Hermann Lübke in 1883,[11] that the poem we know as *The Awntyrs off Arthure* actually consists of two poems, written by two different poets, and loosely stitched together by a not greatly gifted third compiler. Hanna, partly following Lübke and partly offering the results of his own research, produces various kinds of evidence, especially stylistic and metrical, in favour of disintegrating the *Awntyrs*; but I think it is reasonable to suppose that neither he nor Lübke would have set about looking for such evidence if they had not felt dissatisfied with the poem's structure – dissatisfied, that is, with the way that it is divided into two quite separate adventures.

The first adventure concerns a hunting expeditiion held by King Arthur and his court at the Tarn Wadling, in the course of which Gawain and Guenevere get separated by a sudden storm from the rest of the party, and encounter a hideous apparition of Guenevere's mother, risen from the grave and from purgatory to give them a dire warning. Guenevere is warned that if she does not amend her way of life, she too will be 'a graceles gost' (163), and she is also urged to have masses said for the repose of her mother's soul. Gawain is warned that the glory of the Round Table is based on unjust conquest and that it will be brought to an end by the treachery of

Mordred, who is at present only a child. The apparition then disappears, the weather clears, and Gawain and Guenevere rejoin the court. This adventure (as Baugh noted) is a version of the story known as *The Trental of Saint Gregory*, which exists in several Middle English versions, and which tells of how the saint meets his mother's ghost, which begs him to perform a trental of masses so as to save her soul and his own. In a more general sense, this adventure is related to a theme which is extremely common in the visual arts as well as literature, that of *The Three Living and the Three Dead*.[12] Three men, often while out hunting, meet three skeletons or corpses, who represent themselves as they will be, and act as a reminder of the inescapable mortality of the flesh. (There is a famous mural version of this in the Camposanto at Pisa.) Later medieval culture displays an almost obsessive concern with fleshly decay and mortality, which very frequently takes the form (as in 'double-decker' tombs) of the juxtaposition of two figures, one in the prime of life and prosperity, the other a rotting corpse preyed on by worms and toads; and this is precisely the relation between Guenevere 'Al in gleterand golde' (27) and her mother 'Serkeled with serpentes' (120) in the first part of *The Awntyrs off Arthure*.

In the second adventure the court are at supper in Randalset Hall when a stranger knight enters, accompanied by his lady, and demands the return of his lands which he alleges have been wrongfully seized from him by Arthur and given to Gawain. The stranger, Sir Galeron of Galloway, is courteously feasted, and then next day he fights a duel with Gawain. Each knight does severe damage to the other, but Galeron has the worse; his lady begs Guenevere to intervene, and Guenevere, taking pity, does so, begging Arthur to make peace between them. Galeron resigns his right to the lands, but Arthur bestows further gifts of land on Gawain on condition that he returns to Galeron those over which they have been fighting. Gawain does so, Galeron becomes a member of the Round Table, and, in the final stanza, Guenevere has 'a mylion of masses' (706) performed for the sake of her mother's soul. No specific source is known for this second adventure, but, as Hanna puts it, it 'simply combines some of the most archetypal motifs of medieval romance – the discourteous challenger, the tournament battle, the civilising virtues of Round Table society'.[13]

No-one can doubt that these two episodes are separate, and it is highly likely that the poet's immediate sources for them were different. Nevertheless, *The Awntyrs off Arthure* has come down to us as a single poem: it survives, with many variant readings, in four manuscripts written in four different dialects, but always as a single work. I believe that it is possible virtually to prove that it was composed by a single author, but my chief concern is not with authorship but with the structure of the work itself, a poem which seems to me not, certainly, to possess 'organic unity', but to be strongly cohesive.[14]

One aspect of the poem which should encourage us to look for connections between its two parts is of a kind likely to be unfamiliar, and perhaps unattractive, to modern readers. In order to explain it, I must pause to expound the argument of an important book on Renaissance poetry, Alastair Fowler's *Triumphal Forms*.[15] Fowler's general argument is that what he calls 'numerical and spatial constructivism' is so widely present in Elizabethan literature that it should be seen 'less as an isolated device or *concetto* than as a general level of organization, intermediate between the prosodic and the internal structure'.[16] More specifically, he points to the importance of the central position in much Renaissance pageantry, architecture, and literature:

This position once carried a generally recognized iconological significance: it was the place, if not for an image of sovereignty, at least for a 'central feature' (to use an idiom still current). The sovereign might occupy either the centre of a circle, such as the zodiacal border of an imperial coin, or the mid point of a linear array, as when a throne was placed at the centre of one side of the table. In the linear form, elaborate symmetries often surround the significant middle point.[17]

And he goes on to note that, besides the many Scriptural texts that could be interpreted as placing the 'cosmic ruler' and objects associated with him in a central position, this conception of the 'sovereign mid point' was sustained through the protocol by which, 'when the sovereign appeared in full majesty on any judicial or state occasion, he had to be placed centrally'.[18] In examples ranging from Dante to Pope, Fowler shows how Renaissance poets, with remarkable frequency, organize literary works about central manifestations of sovereignty, or about significant displacements or other 'finesses' of such manifestations.

Few of Fowler's examples are taken from medieval literature, though he notes in passing the 'recessed symmetry' of the metrical organization of Chaucer's *Anelida and Arcite*[19] and points out that the central line of *Troilus and Criseyde* – 'And me bistowed in so heigh a place' (III 1271) – reveals the hero conferring on himself an ironically inappropriate moment of triumph.[20] I believe that a similar organization about a 'sovereign mid point' can be found in *The Awntyrs off Arthure*; and that this should be so need not surprise us. Even if we do not suppose that the poet was familiar with the symmetrically organized triumphal pageants from which Fowler's book takes its title, or that he was influenced by the Scriptural commentators who were concerned to identify the central verses of books of the Bible, we can at least be sure that he knew of the protocol which placed sovereigns at the centre of their courts, judicial benches, or tables. This protocol is of some importance in *Sir Gawain and the Green Knight*, which there is reason to suppose the *Awntyrs*-poet knew,[21] and is widely represented in the visual arts of northern Europe in the later Middle Ages.

The Awntyrs off Arthure consists of 55 thirteen-line stanzas.[22] If we set aside the last two, which tell of the outcome of the two adventures and have a different location (in Carlisle), we are left with fifty-three stanzas. These are divided as equally as is possible between the two main adventures and their two distinct settings (the two basic settings of medieval romance): the story of the apparition, set outdoors in the forest, occupies 26 stanzas, and the story of Sir Galeron, set indoors in the hall, occupies 27.[23] This near-symmetry already suggests that the author of the complete text of the poem, whether or not he is to be thought of as a compiler, was concerned to achieve a measurable balance between his two main episodes. But a more striking and exact symmetry is also to be found in the poem, and this provides further evidence in favour of its integrity and single authorship.

Hanna points out that there is a verbal correspondence between the beginning and the end of the *Awntyrs*, and that in this it resembles three of the four poems attributed to the *Gawain*-poet, and also *Degrevant* and *The Avowing of King Arthur*.[24] Its opening line is 'In the tyme of Arthur an aunter bytydde' and it closes with two short lines, 'In the tyme of Arthore / This anter betide.' This elementary symmetry in fact goes a little further, for as the first stanza begins with Arthur and ends with Guenevere – 'Dame Gaynour he ledes' (13) – so the last stanza begins with Guenevere – 'Waynour gared wightly write into the west' (703) – and ends with Arthur. Each of the two adventures is chiefly concerned with Gawain, Guenevere, and an intruder – the apparition of Guenevere's mother in the first, and Sir Galeron in the second. In both cases the intruder bursts incongruously upon a scene of courtly pleasure. In the first, Gawain and Guenevere are embowered 'in greves so grene' and canopied 'undur a lefesale' (69–70), evidently enjoying a little private dalliance, when suddenly the sky darkens and the hideous figure comes towards them, howling and moaning. In the second, the king is seated at supper with his court, beneath a silken canopy and surrounded by tapestries embroidered with birds (339–42), when Galeron rides into the hall, heralded by his lady, to demand the restoration of his lands. Yet the entire poem, as we have seen, is framed between references to Arthur, and in both episodes Arthur's role is of some importance. In the first, the apparition warns that 'Your king is to covetous' (265) and that 'Whan he is in his magesté, moost in his might' (267) Arthur will be struck down by Fortune from her wheel, and the fall of the Round Table will follow. In the second, Arthur actually takes part, in a way that seems designed to correspond to and contradict the accusation of covetousness: he grants great tracts of land to Gawain, to compensate him for the lands he is to return to Galeron. Arthur's covetousness is to come later, in the continental conquests described in the *Morte Arthure*. (The *Awntyrs*-poet evidently knew this earlier alliterative poem, and was able to assume either that his audience also knew it or at least that they knew the general outline of Arthurian history.) For the moment, Fortune's wheel has not turned, and the British court is at the height of its glory, with Arthur securely enthroned at its centre.

Appropriately, then, Arthur is also enthroned at the exact centre of the poem. Its central stanza, the twenty-eighth (lines 352–64), is the second stanza of the second adventure. This stanza is devoted entirely to describing the king as he sits at table (presumably in the central position, though this is not mentioned), and to recounting his gracious reply to Galeron's lady:

> The mon in his mantell sittes at his mete,
> In pale pured with pane prodly pight,
> Trefolyte and traverste with trewloves in trete;
> The tasselles were of topas that wer thereto tight.
> He gliffed up with his eighen that grey wer and grete,
> With his beveren berde, on that burde bright.
> He was the soveraynest sir sitting in sete
> That ever segge had sought, or sen was with sight.
> King crowned in kith carpes hir tille:
> 'Welcom, worthely wight!

He shal have reson and right!
Whethen is the comli knight,
If hit be thi wille?'

And the central line of that stanza (which is also, of course, the central line of the whole poem) emphatically enthrones Arthur in his sovereignty: 'He was the soveraynest sir sitting in sete' (358). It would be difficult to imagine a clearer example of the 'sovereign mid point' in any literary text.

We have then an exact symmetry, with the king enthroned in his full majesty as ruler, host, and judge at the precise centre of a poem which also mentions him in its first and last lines. Since it seems scarcely possible that this symmetry should have been arrived at by accident, we must surely assume that *The Awntyrs off Arthure* as it stands is the product of careful planning by a single poet. It remains possible, of course, that that poet was also a compiler, in the sense not just that he was juxtaposing two incidents derived from earlier traditions (as he certainly was), but that those incidents came down to him in more or less finished literary form. This might account for the stylistic differences between the two adventures noted by Hanna; but we are obliged to suppose that the 'compiler' was also a conscious literary artist who imposed on his material a striking and appropriate symmetrical form.

We can now consider in what ways the formal symmetry implies connection in meaning between the two adventures. The bipartite poem seems to offer a literary structure analogous to a favourite pictorial form of the Middle Ages, the diptych.[25] Imagine, for instance, a diptych of which one leaf shows the Virgin and Child, the other the Crucifixion. Each leaf is complete in itself; however, Christ and his mother are leading figures in each, and when the two are put together they generate a meaning and an emotion far greater than either possesses separately. In such a case, the juxtaposition is genuinely creative: the medieval artist is in no way limited by his habit of composing a work in self-contained, discontinuous sections. It is precisely the discontinuity that makes possible a creative gesture in which the spectator or reader himself participates. Sparks leap across the gap between the two parts, and the onlooker's mind is set alight by them.

It may be that in the twentieth century we are better placed to recognize and respond to such structures than people were in earlier post-medieval periods, because we can be familiar with them from the arts of our own time, and especially from the art of the cinema. The technique I have been describing is that of montage. Eisenstein, its greatest exponent, described the origin of this technique as lying in the discovery of the fact that 'two film pieces of any kind, placed together, inevitably combine into a new concept, a new quality, arising out of that juxtaposition'.[26] In his later writings he was inclined to emphasize that the two pieces must be selected so that their juxtaposition would illustrate a chosen theme. It was not enough for them to be unrelated and juxtaposed at random:

> *Representation A* and *representation B* must be selected from all the possible features within the theme that is being developed, must be sought for, that their *juxtaposition* – that is, the juxtaposition of *those very elements* and not of alternative ones – shall evoke in the perception and feelings of the spectator the most complete *image of the theme itself.*[27]

Now of course, in the diptych and (as I shall argue soon) in a bipartite poem such as the *Awntyrs*, the artist or poet does indeed have in mind a theme which the parts of his work are to evoke by their juxtaposition. On the other hand, in the late writing I have just quoted, it seems to me that Eisenstein goes too far in implying that the theme is already *fully* defined in advance. At an earlier stage in his career, his emphasis had been different, and he had written of how he disagreed with his fellow director Pudovkin, whose views then were much the same as those Eisenstein was himself to hold later. He wrote that Pudovkin 'loudly defends an understanding of montage as a *linkage* of pieces. Into a chain. Again, "bricks". Bricks, arranged in series to *expound* an idea. I confronted him with my view on montage as a *collision*. A view that from the collision of two given factors *arises* a concept.'[28] I find more help in this earlier emphasis, which implies that the theme is created or re-created by the act of juxtaposition, and that the meaning thereby produced cannot be defined by any other means. It will be a meaning relating to certain pre-existing concepts, but it will not be defined by these concepts; in fact it will be a potentiality for meaning, to be drawn on by the reader or spectator, rather than a cut-and-dried proposition which the images merely illustrate. The point is worth underlining, if only because of the strong tendency in academic interpretation of medieval literature to a kind of authoritarianism which reduces the reader's freedom of response – for example, in 'readings' of *The Canterbury Tales* which claim to find in the work's combinatory structure a mere illustration of preconceived truths. I do not, of course, mean to imply that a poem with a diptych or montage structure can mean anything the reader chooses to imagine, or that its meaning is beyond rational discussion; but that we should not be surprised or worried to find that the poet's discontinuities leave areas of uncertainty, areas of freedom, in which it is for us to respond to the stimulus the poem provides.

Larry D. Benson has suggested that, within the alliterative tradition especially, structural variation is a common method of conveying – or, as I would prefer to put it, of creating – meaning in medieval poems. He writes of 'the juxtaposition of parallel, opposing elements without an explicit statement of their relation'; he says of *Beowulf* that 'The structure of the narrative is concentrated and appositional, enclosed within the framework of the burials at the beginning and end'; and he even mentions *The Awntyrs off Arthure*, along with the *Morte Arthure* and *Golagros and Gawane*, as examples of medieval alliterative poems where 'one finds the same concern with parallels, contrasts, and variations in the narrative structure.'[29] Before I proceed to a more detailed examination of *The Awntyrs off Arthure*, it will be helpful to consider *Golagros and Gawane* briefly as a structural analogue, because it is another fifteenth-century alliterative poem in rhyming stanzas, in which two apparently quite unconnected adventures are juxtaposed; but it is one in which the semantic implications of the bipartite structure are made more explicit by the poet. In the first adventure of this poem, which is much briefer than the second, Arthur and his knights come upon a castle, and need provisions from it. First Kay is sent to obtain them; he rudely seizes them from a dwarf, but is then knocked down by the lord of the castle and returns ingloriously. Next Gawain is sent; he makes a courteous request, acknowledging that the lord has the right to do what he wishes with his own possessions, and at this the lord offers his hospitality freely. In the second adventure, the Arthurians come to a second castle, a place of great splendour, and Arthur is astonished to learn that its lord, Golagros, owes homage to no king. Gawain, Lancelot, and Ewain are sent to ask politely for the lord's submission, and when he equally politely declines thus to dishonour himself, Arthur makes preparations to besiege him. There follows a series of knightly combats with no decisive result, in one of which Kay makes a great show of being merciful to an opponent who has unexpectedly surrendered just when Kay himself was on the verge of succumbing. At last Gawain fights against Golagros himself, and finally gets him at his mercy. But Golagros says he prefers to die rather than submit to compulsion or even accept mercy: all that he will agree to is that Gawain should return with him to the castle as if defeated, on the promise that 'I sall thi kyndnes quyte / And sauf thyn honoure' (1101–2).[30] Gawain takes the risk, and Golagros, after consulting his people, freely submits and does Gawain homage. Golagros then does homage to Arthur too, and Arthur stays in his castle for nine days, at the end of which he departs, freely releasing Golagros from the submission he freely made.

Even this crude summary suggests, I hope, some of the meanings that are created by the juxtaposition of the two adventures. The poem has to do with knightly courtesy, honour, and generosity – in effect, with the *franchise* of *The Franklin's Tale*, with a generosity that involves committing oneself to trust in the generosity of another man, imposing no compulsion on him, and leaving him genuinely free to act honourably or not. In the first, briefer adventure, this emerges fairly simply from the contrast between Kay's failure and Gawain's success. In the second adventure, Kay has only a minor role, in an episode which provides a comically distorted reflection of the main theme; but the chief burden is again borne by Gawain, in a situation which is far more complicated, and in which honour is shown to be almost painfully complex, for Gawain can preserve Golagros's honour only by relinquishing his own, and yet in submitting himself to apparent shame he is touching the height of honour. This poet did not leave his audience entirely free to interpret the structure of his narrative for themselves; instead he included a *raisonneur* or commentator on the story in the form of Spynagros, who for Arthur's benefit draws a moral from the first adventure – 'It hynderis never for to be heyndly of speche' (358) – and repeatedly warns him that Golagros has an exceptionally high regard for his own reputation and that Arthur will never succeed in *forcing* him to do homage. *The Awntyrs off Arthure* includes no figure equivalent to Spynagros, and it seems to me a purer work of art for the omission, conveying its meaning simply by the balanced relationship of its parts.

The Awntyrs off Arthure, like a number of other poems of the Alliterative Revival, including *Sir Gawain and the Green Knight*, celebrates a noble way of life, which undergoes a serious challenge to its validity; the challenge brings out its limitations, but despite this the noble way of life is able to continue, at least for a time. At the opening of the poem, the noble life is expressed simultaneously on two levels. One is that of the activity described, the Arthurian hunt – hunting conceived as a ritual by means of which the medieval aristocracy demonstrated its exclusive solidarity, while at once expressing and containing its violence. As in *Sir Gawain and the Green Knight*, this is a hunt in the close season, the *fermyson*,[31] and aristocratic violence is therefore circumscribed with special strictness; though, as the combat between Gawain and Galeron in the second part will demonstrate, it is none the less real. The second level of expression is that of the language – the traditionally conventional and pleonastic style which Marie Borroff has shown to correspond to social elevation.[32] Superlative expressions are common; the courtiers are 'wlonkest in wedes' (9) and Gawain is 'graythest on grene' (12). The style is full of semantically empty asseverations: a single stanza contains 'by boke and by belle' (30), 'the trouthe for to telle' (34), and 'ho the trouth trowes' (35). Epithets frequently add nothing to our information, but are merely what is expected: 'bonkes so bare' (41), 'holtes so hare' (43), 'cliffes so colde' (44), 'greves so grene' (61, 69). In such a style, with its conspicuous consumption of words and of time, formalized in the necessarily repetitive stanza-linking, a leisure class confirms its identity; and at the same time an atmosphere of normality is established, on which the abnormal is to intrude with shattering force.

The sudden storm of snow and rain, which makes the day 'als dirke / As hit were mydnight myrke' (75–6), breaks up the hunt, and then the howling apparition terrifies even the greyhounds (126), so that the hunters become the hunted. On the level of language, the very repetitions now become more sharply and individually expressive. Thus one stanza ends with the apparition's first speech, 'I gloppen and I grete' (91); the next stanza repeats the verbs, but with a new subject, transferring the actions mentioned from the ghost to Guenevere, in whom they are less expected: 'Then gloppenet and grete Gaynour the gay' (92). There is a similar transference later, when the ghost ends one stanza with 'Be war be my wo' (195) and Guenevere begins the next with 'Wo is *me* for thi wirde' (196). The traditional phrases are now set in a new context: it profits little to be 'hendest in halle' (131) when one is not in hall, but in a wintry forest confronted with a shrieking thing from the grave; and it profits the apparition little now, that once

> I was radder of rode then rose in the ron,
> My ler as the lelé lonched so light.   (161–2)

The modern reader may have to learn to recognize significant variations within a style which at first seems to be more concerned with overall decorative ingenuity than with specific local meanings. But, somewhat as in *Sir Gawain and the Green Knight*, the arrival of the terrifying intruder stimulates sharp and critical observation of the limitations of the courtly characters. The comforting masculine superiority of Gawain's scientific explanation of the terrifying experience – 'Hit ar the clippes of the son, I herd a clerk say' (94) – is all too clearly threadbare, though the poet's explanation in the following line should prevent us from feeling too superior ourselves towards a knight who is doing his duty as best he can: 'And thus he confortes the quene for his knighthede' (95). Guenevere is observed with a wholeheartedly critical eye: she blames the other knights for abandoning her on what she calls, with hysterical exaggeration, 'my dethday' (98), yet it appears that she had voluntarily stayed in the forest after Arthur had blown the assembly-call, perhaps in order to enjoy a little innocent dalliance with Gawain.

The first of the poem's many instances of parallel with variation occurs with the juxtaposition of Guenevere with the apparition of her mother. John Speirs summed this up well: 'Each is confronted with herself in the other – the daughter as she will be, and the mother as she once was.'[33] But even before the ghost identified itself, it seemed to come as a kind of serious parody of Guenevere's shallowness in lamenting the absence of her usual circle of knights: 'Hit waried, hit waymented, as a woman' (107). We have already seen how the repetitions that link the stanzas are used to transfer activities from one of the pair to the other. Another example occurs when the ghost ends one stanza by telling Gawain, 'I am comen in this cace / To carpe with your quene' (142–3), and then begins the next with 'Quene was *I* somwile' (144), and adds, 'Gretter then Dame Gaynour' (147). Later the ghost explains that her punishment is for 'luf paramour' (213), and thereby suggests another parallel with Guenevere, though it is left to us to decide whether the poet is alluding to her notorious affair with Lancelot, to her seduction by Mordred as recounted in the *Morte Arthure* (if so, it would link the ghost's message to Guenevere with her message to Gawain – both would point forward to the last days of the Round Table), or simply to her predilection for being surrounded with glamorous knights.

Like the two images in a 'double-decker' tomb, the apparition and Guenevere are both like and unlike each other. Guenevere's elaborate dress is described in the poem's second stanza, but of the apparition we are told, 'nauthyr on hide ne on huwe no heling hit hadde' (108); and whereas Guenevere wears a blue hood on her head, the ghost has only a revolting toad. The ghost warns Guenevere that she will come to the same state, 'For al thi fressh foroure' (166). The emphasis on Guenevere's dress might seem to suggest that she is concerned only with externals, mere trimmings; and indeed the wide-spread tendency in medieval literature and art to convey courtly grandeur and luxury through exhaustive representations of costume must always have this as a potential meaning. The same suggestion emerges more strongly from the conversation between Guenevere and her mother. The first action that the ghost urges upon Guenevere is, 'Have pité on the poer while thou art of power' (173), for when Guenevere comes to be as the ghost is now, 'The praier of the poer may purchas the pes' (178). Guenevere asks whether 'matens or mas' (198) can do anything to alleviate her mother's state, and the answer is that 'To menne me with masses grete menske hit were' (230), but her mother goes on to reiterate her plea for practical charity:

> For Him that rest on the rode,
> Gyf fast of thi goode
> To folke that failen the fode
> While thou art here. (231–4)

Guenevere, however, disregards this, and promises the ghost only that she will have her commemorated with 'a myllion of masses' (236). When she asks again how she can aid her mother in the next world, the ghost speaks for a third time of her concern for the poor:

> Mekenesse and mercy, thes arn the moost,
> And have pité on the poer – that pleses Hevenking. (250–1)

In medieval courtly poetry courtly values are rarely tested in this way by the larger social concern that is associated rather with works such as *Piers Plowman* and *Pierce the Ploughman's Crede*; and one possible line of development for the *Awntyrs* would seem to be towards King Lear's recognition that in this world 'Robes and furred gowns hide all', his 'Off, off, you lendings!', and his acknowledgment that he has taken too little care of the sufferings of the poor. But Guenevere is no Lear: she does not respond to the ghost's attempts to turn her attention beyond outward observances to practical charity. On the other hand, she is no Goneril or Regan either: her observ-

135

ances include religious observances, and the poem is not arguing or implying that the masses in themselves will do no good. They will be better than nothing; indeed, they will be a kind of food for the dead soul in its spiritual poverty, and before the apparition departs she couples a last reference to feeding the poor with a striking development of the courtly theme of the rich feast:

> Fede folke for my sake that fauten the fode
> And menne me with matens and masse in melle.
> Masses arn medecynes to us that bale bides;
> Us thenke a masse as swete
> As eny spice that ever ye yete. (319–23)

Just as in this world spices are luxuries that belong to an aristocratic way of life, so in the next masses offer a taste of the heavenly feast to the souls in purgatory.

Before these parting words, the ghost has turned her attention from Guenevere to Gawain. Gawain seems to be more perceptive than the queen about the limitations of the Arthurian way of life, and his very questions to the ghost already imply her answers. He knows that in their warfare the knights 'defoulen the folke on fele kinges londes' (262) and that they invade kingdoms 'withouten eny right' (263), and no more than the audience does he really need to be told what the end will be. They perhaps knew, as the poet probably did, the *Morte Arthure*, or at least they would have been familiar with the Arthurian legend in general; and so the poet is able to make the ghost prophesy the future in a compressed and allusive way which is unusually impressive. It is possible that, in the relation of the *Awntyrs* to the *Morte Arthure*, we can glimpse the growth of a literary tradition analogous to, but independent of, that headed by Chaucer. If so, it was greatly to the advantage of the *Awntyrs*-poet that his tradition did not derive from a single father whose stylistic dominance aroused anxiety in his poetic sons. He seems to have felt no pressure on his imaginative *Lebensraum*, and could simply make use of allusion to already existing works as a means of enriching and condensing his own. Arthur, says the ghost, is 'to covetous' (265); for this moment, while Fortune's wheel stands still, he seems unconquerable, but soon 'That wonderfull whelewright' (271) will bring him low. In this section of the poem, the sense of standing at one particular moment in a predestined history is unusual and moving. France has already been conquered, Italy remains to conquer, but bad news will be brought to Arthur in Tuscany (the news of Mordred's rebellion in Britain), and in the end 'In Dorsetshire shal dy the doughtést of alle' (295) – Gawain himself, fighting for Arthur against Mordred. Mordred is never identified by name, only by his armorial bearings; and, at this very moment, the seeds of the future are growing:

> In riche Arthures halle
> The barne playes at the balle
> That outray shall you alle,
> Derfely that day.   (309–12)

I find this the most poignant moment in the poem: at this point of equilibrium, Mordred is only a child, playing harmlessly and innocently in Arthur's court, yet he is Mordred all the same, and must play the terrible part we know in the coming destruction.

Her errand complete, the apparition disappears; as if by magic the clouds part, the sun shines, and normal life resumes with a blast from Arthur's bugle. The Arthurians all ride off to supper at Randalset Hall, courtly luxury apparently unchanged by the messages from beyond the grave. But the purpose of the diptych structure is to show change as well as repetition. Hanna sees in the poem a simple rather than a complex meaning – simple failure on the part of both Guenevere and Gawain to understand that the way of life they share and represent is superficial and inadequate.[34] But in my view that simple meaning can be read in *The Awntyrs off Arthure* only by separating the first part from the second. The two parts together compose a meaning more complex and less rigidly compelling.

Hardly has the feast at Randalset Hall begun when there is a second intrusion, which at once parallels and contrasts with the first. A scene of aristocratic recreation, but this time of feasting instead of hunting, is disrupted by a challenge from outside, but this time there are two intruders instead of one, and they are not supernatural but human. Indeed, they are themselves courtly, and whereas before luxurious and elaborate clothing were attributes of the court only, now they belong to the intruders as well. The descriptions of the clothing and equipment of Galeron and his lady are developed into full-blown Gothic fantasies (an example is given above, on page 123), with every inch of surface crowded with outlandish detail, culminating in the horse transformed into a unicorn by the thorn-sharp spike on its forehead armour. Such descriptions are intended to be pleasing in themselves, quite apart from any contribution they make to the poem as a whole, and it would be foolish to demand that every detail should have some larger significance. The reader's hypothesis needs to be connectedness – not unity but connectedness – and we shall sense as we read a readjustment of the balance that was struck in the first part. Elegant dress does not necessarily imply shallowness, and the courtly world has a magnificence that is not totally negated by its transience and its imperfection.

The stranger-knight introduces himself as Galeron of Galloway, and his purpose is at once related to the theme of the first part of the poem. Arthur, he claims, has displayed precisely the covetousness and the habit of unjustly seizing others' lands of which the ghost had accused him earlier. He has taken Galeron's lands – 'Thou has wonen hem in werre with a wrange wile' (421) – and bestowed them on Gawain; and Galeron is determined to fight to get them back, either against Gawain himself or against any other knight assigned by Arthur. Arthur explains why this cannot be done immediately, and his explanation provides yet another link between the two parts of the poem – a causal rather than a thematic link. The Arthurian party is out on a hunting expedition, and is therefore unprepared for a duel:

> We ar in the wode went to walke on oure waith,
> To hunte at the herdes with hounde and with horne.
> We ar in oure gamen; we have no gome graithe. (434–6)

But if Galeron will wait until the next day, an opponent will be found. The hospitality shown to Galeron during his overnight stay is described in detail, as an exemplary display; and once more we are made to feel the impressive magnificence of Arthurian courtliness.

Gawain himself volunteers to fight Galeron, and the duel between them is described at length. It is another case of a subject appealing to the audience in its own right, but we should note the special effect created by the poet's double emphasis on luxury and on violence, the peaceful and the warlike aspects of aristocratic life. Frequently the luxurious and the violent are brought together, with a piquant aesthetic quality. There are the carefully burnished swords smeared with blood; or 'Shene sheldes were shred, / Bright brenes bybled' (569–70); or Gawain's splendid and beloved warhorse with its head severed; or the warriors who

> . . . beten downe beriles and bourdures bright.
> Shildes on shildres that shene were to shewe,
> Fretted were in fyne golde, thei failen in fight.
> Stones of iral they strenkel and strewe. (587–90)

The effect is not only aesthetically disturbing and pleasing; it perfectly expresses the nature of the aristocratic life, which consists in a generous willingness to waste those material possessions that seem to be its essence. And, as I suggested earlier, the ample and often redundant style of this description is itself an enactment of such aristocratic waste, a form of conspicuous consumption of the poet's verbal substance and of his listeners' leisure.

The poet's attitude to the combat, at the one point where he directly expresses it, is of interest. Galeron raises his sword to aim devastatingly at Gawain, 'But him lymped the worse, and that me wel likes!' (615). This momentary participation, by its very openness, paradoxically conveys detachment, as though the poet is revealing that his enthusiasm is only for a game. It contrasts strikingly with the earnest commitment of the *Morte Arthure*, a commitment which displays itself at its least likeable early in that poem, in the relations between Arthur and the Roman ambassadors. There is, for example, a kind of bad faith in the scene in which the ambassadors return to their master and praise Arthur to the skies, for the poet is *pretending* to give a Roman view of the British king, without really stepping outside his own partisanship.[35] The *Morte*-poet, typically medieval, lacks precisely the relativistic historical sense that Chaucer possessed and that enabled him, for instance, to give a glimpse of post-Roman Britain as seen through Roman eyes in *The Man of Law's Tale*: 'A maner Latyn corrupt was hir speche' (II 519). The *Awntyrs* conveys a surer poise than the *Morte* in the poet's attitude towards Arthurian civilization. The bloody and extravagant combat is no more than a game, just as the poem itself in its verbal extravagance is a game too. In this unquestioningly Christian culture there are no planetary gods, no interventions by Saturn, no Boethian philosophy: the cosmic and historical dimensions that belong to the Renaissance vision of *The Knight's Tale* are missing. But we do not feel their absence, as we do in the *Morte Arthure*: the admitted playfulness of the *Awntyrs* and the room it leaves for the reader or listener to judge for himself make it possible for it to offer a balanced critique of the civilization it describes, which is a fictional version, we may suppose, of the civilization that produced it.

Gawain seizes Galeron by the collar, and at this point Galeron's lady intervenes with her appeal to Guenevere to have mercy on Galeron. This creates a further unexpected parallel with the first adventure, for the lady now shrieks and groans in a way which reminds us of the earlier apparition's appeal, also directed to Guenevere:

> Then his lemman on loft skrilles and skrikes;
> Ho gretes on Gaynour with gronyng grylle.   (619–20)

The apparition had urged 'Mekenesse and mercy' (150) as the means to salvation, and it seemed as though Guenevere had failed to understand her appeal; but now, within the familiar courtly context, she responds promptly and generously, by kneeling meekly before Arthur and begging him mercifully to 'Make thes knightes accorde' (635). Her appeal at once touches off generosity in others. Galeron abandons his claim to the return of his lands, and offers the king his sword. The king in turn makes Gawain a further huge grant of land, on condition that he will be reconciled with Galeron, and will release his lands to him. And Gawain finally releases them all, on condition that Galeron remains with the Round Table for a while.

This ending, like that of *The Knight's Tale*, implies a political reconciliation between hostile powers. A recent account rightly observes that 'the tale of Galeron shows the reluctance of an independent lord to be assimilated into the scheme of a centralized royal power',[36] but, as *The Knight's Tale* finally adopts an Athenian standpoint, so the *Awntyrs*, while allowing Galeron both justice and courage, seems eventually to adopt a British standpoint. Interpreted in the political terms of the poet's own time, the *Awntyrs*, a poem from the English side of the border, presumably sees Arthur as English and Galeron as Scottish. In the later Middle Ages, the feuds of the great lords of the border areas were often 'a threat to the stability not of the north only, but of the whole kingdom'.[37] The poem's conclusion may imply a wish for a peaceful end to that threat, on the terms that would seem desirable to an Englishman rather than a Scot. Just as the marriage of Emelye to Palamon is a means for Athens 'to have fully of Thebans obeisance' (*Knight's Tale* I 2974), so in the *Awntyrs* peace comes to the borders when the Scottish knight accepts the feudal overlordship of the British/ English king who is enthroned at the centre of the poem.[38]

It is not only Guenevere who seems to have learned something from the first adventure, which she puts into practice in the second. Arthur had been accused by the apparition of being 'to covetous' (265), but he now voluntarily gives up great tracts of land in Wales, Ireland, and Brittany in order to bring peace with honour to the two warring knights. The pattern is formally completed by the admission of Galeron to the Round Table, and Guenevere's arrangement for the 'mylion of masses' (706) that she had promised to her mother's ghost. As at the end of *Sir Gawain and the Green Knight*, however, we are left to decide for ourselves whether the formal completion of the pattern, marked by the ending of the poem with the words with which it began, does or does not correspond to a psychological and spiritual fulfilment. Has Guenevere failed to learn the most important lesson of all, to be charitable to the poor, who lie outside the courtly circle? Does the poem close so neatly in on itself only at the expense of excluding a tract of experience so important as to render its completion trivial? Enigmatically, life continues in the poetic court, as no doubt it did in the court for which the poem was written.

In the poetic court, the continuation is under a shadow, that of the ghost's prophecy of a doom whose seeds lie within the court itself. I think it of great importance – and it is this that makes me most reluctant to believe that *The Awntyrs off Arthure* was not planned as a diptych – that the admiring descriptions of knightly dress and courage and Arthurian hospitality, and the generosity of Guenevere, Arthur, and Gawain, come *after* the prophecy. The poet reverses the flow of time, and in the poem's second part we are made to feel intensely the poignancy of this moment of Arthurian civilization – courage, compassion, generosity – knowing as we do of the destiny that awaits it when the boy Mordred is a man. It was a stroke of genius to make the glorification of what was doomed come after the prophecy of doom. All human achievement is only imperfect and provisional; individuals die and civilizations collapse:

> The grete tounes se we wane and wende.
> Thanne may ye se that al this thyng hath ende.
> *(Knight's Tale* I 3025–6)

But, for this and other medieval poets, that did not make human achievement worthless. They saw in courtly civilization, for all its limitations, an admirable resilience, which enabled it to continue the game even while knowing that it was only a game, and must come to an end. What is most admirable in *The Awntyrs off Arthure* – and this is a quality to which its diptych structure makes a major contribution – is its civilized poise, a feature in which it is superior not only to the better-known alliterative poem *Morte Arthure*, but also to contemporary works in the Chaucerian tradition such as *The Siege of Thebes*. Where Lydgate and other disciples of Chaucer close the imaginative openness of their master's work with anxiously explicit moralism, the *Awntyrs*-poet sets before us a pair of moving images, intriguingly similar and yet dissimilar to each other. The conclusions are left for us to draw.

2. The Wakefield Master

In recent years there has been a strong revival of interest in the drama of late-medieval England, in which a central place has been held by work on its theatrical potentialities. Plays which in many cases have not been performed for centuries have been staged, often with considerable success; and this development is, of course, greatly to be welcomed. It has had one disadvantage, however, and this is that the literary quality of the drama, whether good or bad, has tended to be disregarded. A recent illustration can be found in the volume on medieval drama in *The Revels History of Drama in English*, which in all its 364 pages finds almost no space to say anything at all about the poetry of this drama.[39] I am far from urging that 'poetry' can be separated from 'drama' in this large body of theatrical texts composed entirely in verse; on the contrary, it is precisely because its quality as literary language cannot be separated from its theatrical qualities that the former should not be overlooked in any attempt at overall judgment. The virtual silence of the theatrical historians offers no answer to the unfavourable assessment of a distinguished literary historian:

> of the mystery cycles it must be said that, though they contain some of what is good in the religious verse of the [fifteenth] century, they contain more of what is bad, and that whatever interest these plays have from the point of view of theatre, social history or theology, little of that interest derives from any use of language that might be called effectively poetic.[40]

I do not intend to give much attention here to the bad poetry of medieval drama, but perhaps I may mention in passing that those who have praised and revived, say, the fifteenth-century morality play *Mankind* have usually failed to point out that its poetic language, even in those parts that could be regarded as deliberate parody, is beneath contempt – and this seems an unfortunate omission.[41] The fact that a play can be performed with popular success, as the theatre of our own age (or indeed any other) indicates, tells us nothing about its quality as poetic drama.

In this section I shall be concerned with a contribution made by the religious drama to fifteenth-century English poetry; and I believe it to be a major contribution. The four extant complete cycles of Mystery or Corpus Christi plays make up an enormous body of verse, a large part of which was probably written after 1400; its quality is extremely varied, but at its best it is impressively good (and good in a way which manifestly involved conscious literary choice) in a wide variety of styles. My example is the Wakefield Master, who is rightly the best known and most highly praised of identifiable fifteenth-century dramatists; but I suspect that he is still not sufficiently appreciated as a major fifteenth-century poet. One of his most enthusiastic admirers, A. P. Rossiter, from whom I personally learned to appreciate his work, wrote as follows about the Wakefield Master as a poet:

> But with all his strength and ingenuity, his words are rougher than a Yorkshire tongue, and the crudeness of his Middle English, untempered by Chaucer's French, is like a gag in his mouth. It hurts to think what the man might have done, given a more swift and flexible language: even what he might, given other opportunities, have done in his own age and country.[42]

'Major fifteenth-century poet' may not in fact seem a title of great distinction where the poetry of England is concerned; but one of the purposes of this book is to suggest that a better understanding of the poetic history of the fifteenth century will reveal much that is of intrinsic as well as historical interest.

In the uneven passage from medieval to Renaissance, the Wakefield Master like the equally anonymous author of *The Awntyrs off Arthure*, must be classed as unmistakably medieval. The great cycles of religious drama, four surviving complete and others in fragments, are the most ambitious of all medieval English literary projects, and in most respects they are quite untouched by the work of Chaucer and his followers. They survived in performance right down to the late sixteenth century, and the performances were brought to an end then only when they were deliberately suppressed by the central government on religious grounds. Shakespeare in his boyhood might well have seen one of these cycles staged – perhaps the famous one at Coventry, not too far from Stratford, of which only fragments survive. By a neat coincidence, the last recorded performance of one of the cycles, at Chester in 1575, took place the year before the opening of the first professional playhouse in London, Burbage's Theatre;[43] and the civic authorities at Chester were still attempting to revive their cycle in 1600, after Shakespeare's *Hamlet* would have had its first performance. The continuing vitality of the medieval in England, long after the Reformation had come to reinforce the Renaissance conception of the *medium aevum* as an era of darkness and corruption, is especially striking in the field of drama; and it was a medievalism all the more authentic for being untouched by the Counter-Reformation. To repeat a point made before, it would be an error to suppose that we could trace an evolutionary progress from medieval to Renaissance, either historically or in terms of artistic quality.[44]

The Wakefield Master is the title given to the supposed author of a number of individual pageants in the so-called Towneley cycle, a complete Creation-to-Doomsday cycle which was performed at Wakefield. We have no external evidence at all about the identity of this writer: he is distinguishable in the first place by his use of a specific nine-line stanza in which five of the pageants of the cycle are entirely composed – *Processus Noe, Prima pastorum, Secunda pastorum, Magnus Herodes*, and *Coliphizacio* (Buffeting of Christ). It is like a kind of compressed version of the 13-line stanza of *The Awntyrs off Arthure*, with the first eight lines reduced to half-lines but retaining their rhyme, and the ninth line reduced from four to one or two stresses; the rhyme-scheme is the same, but the Wakefield Master makes no systematic use of alliteration. Little groups of these stanzas are also found in several other pageants in the cycle, and the probability is that the Wakefield Master was commissioned to undertake at least a sporadic revision of the cycle as a whole. Five pageants in the Towneley cycle are versions of the corresponding pageants at York; and it seems a plausible hypothesis that, as Wakefield gained in prosperity from the woollen industry in the fifteenth century, the civic authorities decided that they could afford to have a cycle of their own instead of relying on the York cycle.[45] One of the pageants in which some of the distinctive stanzas are found is the *Mactatio Abel*; and it is generally thought that that whole pageant is also by the Wakefield Master, because it is marked by certain qualities which identify him even more strikingly than his use of a certain metrical form. He is a dramatic poet of extraordinary vitality and skill, with a particular boldness in making profane and even blasphemous humour serve religious purposes. Some have seen a touch of the diabolic in his work, or at least a touch of *Schadenfreude*;[46] there is certainly a disturbingly full recognition and

dramatic realization of the comic yet terrifying energies that oppose
the sense of divine purpose and order on which the cyclic structure is
founded. A medieval dramatist who could allow Cain to respond to
God's rebuke for quarrelling with his brother with

> Whi, who is that hob-over-the-wall?
> We! who was that that piped so small?
> Com, go we hens, for parels all –
> God is out of hys wit! (1 297–300)[47]

is certainly no obvious spokesman of the 'quiet hierarchies' that
some have seen as characteristic of the medieval world-picture. On
the other hand, though the Wakefield Master may have something
in common with Chaucer in his willingness to give voice to challenges to the orthodox order, there is certainly nothing of the
Renaissance, and nothing Chaucerian, in this harsh and jagged
derision.

This dramatic poet is justly, in my view, called a master; he is
called the Wakefield Master because, as I have said, the whole cycle is
associated with Wakefield, and because there are several allusions in
his pageants to Wakefield and places nearby. Their dialect too is
consistent with the Wakefield area. There is no telling who he was
or, very exactly, when he wrote, except that it was some time in the
first half of the fifteenth century. He is one of those anonymous
figures who were the norm before Chaucer, and who remain
common in English literature through the century after Chaucer's
death. We have to assume, without doubt, that he was a cleric. The
Mystery cycles are probably the only form of medieval writing in
verse intended to appeal to the community as a whole (and they
evidently did so, for they achieved great popularity); but their basis
is theological, and the Wakefield Master is manifestly a learned
author, who made use in his work of intricate Scriptural and
theological topics and procedures. In the two Shepherds' plays
particularly he also brings a good deal of secular life into his religious
theme of the angels' proclamation of Christ's birth to the shepherds
and their bringing of gifts to the infant in the stable at Bethlehem.
The relation between the religious and the secular is a central issue in
the interpretation of much fifteenth-century literature and art, and
that is one reason for my choice of these two pageants as samples of
the Master's work. Another reason is that the poet himself seems to
have taken a special interest in these two. It is otherwise unknown
for a cycle to contain two alternative versions of the same episode:

they could clearly not both be performed as part of the complete Towneley cycle.[48] The second might be regarded as a revision of the first, an indication that the poet wanted to have another attempt at a theme and structure that specially attracted him. The second is certainly much longer than any of his other pageants: the other five have around five hundred lines each, but the *Secunda pastorum* has 754. It may of course have been commissioned for performance, perhaps by itself, on some special occasion of which we know nothing;[49] there is no certain evidence that it was ever performed at all; but, whatever the reason for its unusual length, it is manifestly a work in which the poet has invested an unusual degree of skill and creative energy.

I propose to consider the Wakefield Master's two Shepherds' plays under three headings, which will relate them to some of the themes traced out in this book as a whole. The three are: the conception of the past; literary style; and structure. I begin with the conception of the past.

In this respect the Wakefield Master is at the opposite extreme from Chaucer. We have seen that Chaucer in some of his most 'advanced' poems was attempting an imaginative reconstruction of the pre-Christian past in its difference from the medieval Christian present. In the Mystery cycles the equivalent difference would be that between Old Testament times and the era since the birth of Christ; but the whole conception of the Creation-to-Doomsday cycle pushes against any imaginative realization of that difference. It is well known, especially since the publication of V. A. Kolve's seminal study, *The Play Called Corpus Christi*,[50] that the underlying conception of the cycle, as it is realized in each of the surviving examples, derives from the medieval typological or figural reading of the bible.[51] The dramatists' selection of episodes from the Bible, and in some cases from apocryphal or legendary sources, is not based primarily on a consideration of the dramatic potential of each episode considered individually, but on the significance of each as part of the great structure of prophecy and fulfilment which demonstrates God's purpose in history. Some prophecy is in the form of words spoken by human beings under divine inspiration; and in both the Wakefield Master's Shepherds' plays, the shepherds recall these verbal foretellings of Christ's birth.

> That same childe is he that prophetys of told,
> Shuld make them fre that Adam had sold,   (3 332–3)

says 1 Pastor in *Prima pastorum*. He and his fellows go on to recall those alleged prophecies of the coming of Christ which early Christians found scattered throughout the sacred book of the Jews, together with prophecies by enlightened pagans such as the Erythraean Sybil and Virgil himself in Eclogue IV, the so-called Messianic Eclogue. There is a similar section in *Secunda pastorum*: 'We fynde by the prophecy – let be youre dyn!' (the shepherd is addressing one of his fellows, who is attempting to imitate the angels' song) –

> Of David and Isay and mo then I myn –
> Thay prophecyed by clergy – that in a vyrgyn
> Shuld he lyght and ly, to sloken oure syn.　　　　(4 674–7)

These prophecies often form the subject of a separate pageant, the *Processus prophetarum* (which in the Towneley cycle survives only in a damaged form), but the Wakefield Master also incorporates them into his Shepherds' plays.

More important than spoken prophecy is the fact that God, being the author of history, can use not just words but events to prophesy or foreshadow future events. Thus Abraham's intended sacrifice of Isaac is regularly understood in the Middle Ages as a foreshadowing of God's sacrifice of his son, Christ, on the cross. That is why all the cycles that survive include a pageant of Abraham and Isaac; and indeed in the York cycle the figural significance is so dominant that Isaac, instead of being a little boy, as is usually imagined, is a grown man of 'Thyrty yere and more' (X 82)[52] – the age of Jesus at the time of the crucifixion. Similarly both the Old and the New Testament were seen as including events that foreshadowed Christ's Second Coming, at the end of the world. The effect of this reading of sacred history is to discourage interest in the pastness and difference of the past, because it sees the present as already present in the past, and the future as present in the present. The conception of history that is implied by the cycle as a whole is of time as seen by God himself – that is, time collapsed into an eternal present. This was the traditional solution to the problem of predestination and freewill: since past and future are both equally present to God, who exists outside history, we should not think of him as *pre*-destining what (to us) is still to come. St Augustine wrote:

For what is foreknowledge but knowledge of the future? But what is future to God who transcends all time? If God's knowledge contains these things, they are not future to Him but present; therefore it can be termed not foreknowledge, but simply knowledge.[53]

This way of thought was certainly known to Chaucer, for example through Boethius, who presents a similar argument in the *De consolatione philosophiae*.[54] But, significantly, it is not known to the pagan Troilus in his (Boethian) discussion of predestination and freewill in Book IV of *Troilus and Criseyde*; and Chaucer was clearly not influenced by it in his treatment of the pagan past.

Outside the special case of Chaucer, this God's-eye-view of sacred history serves to reinforce the normal medieval lack of historical sense. Each pageant in the Mystery cycles dramatizes an event imagined not as past and re-enacted (or, in the closing sequence which culminates in Doomsday, future and pre-enacted), but simply as present. The present is the one period of history *not* explicitly dealt with in the cycles; but on the other hand, everything they deal with is imagined as present. Man, of course, cannot really imagine the eternal present in which God exists and in terms of which he contemplates history; but the nearest human equivalent to that eternal present may be supposed to be the contemporary present, and that is something that medieval dramatists could easily imagine. The Wakefield Master, like the other dramatists, imagines the first murder, Noah's Flood, the birth of Christ, and everything else, as happening in his own time and place, fifteenth-century Yorkshire. (There is an obvious parallel in the way that most medieval painters, when representing Biblical events, show the characters in costumes and settings of their own time and locality.[55]) One consequence of this in the Shepherd's plays is that the leading characters are late-medieval shepherds from the Wakefield area, and there is not the smallest attempt to provide bits of local colour that would suggest ancient Palestine. We saw above[56] that in *Troilus and Criseyde* Chaucer took care never to let his pagan characters allude to specifically Christian doctrines. The Wakefield Master goes to the opposite extreme, and, even before they know that Christ is born, he makes his shepherds use turns of phrase that belong to the familiar medieval Catholic world. Sometimes this is a matter of swearing 'by Sant Thomas of Kent' (4 458) or of praying to 'Mary and John' (4 443) or (like John the carpenter in Chaucer's *Miller's Tale*, another uneducated medieval craftsman) of muttering garbled bits of ecclesiastical Latin:

> For ferde we be fryght, a crosse lett us kest –
> Cryst-crosse, benedyght eest and west –
> For drede.

Jesus onazorus,
Crucyefixus,
Morcus, Andreus,
God be our spede!   (3 289–95)

Sometimes it is a matter of more specific allusions to Christian
doctrine: in the *Prima pastorum*, when 2 Pastor first enters, he invokes
a blessing from the crucified Christ at a time he has not yet even
heard that Christ has been born:

He save you and me, overtwhart and endlang,
That hang on a tre, I say you no wrang.
Cryst sane us
From all myschefys.   (3 48–51)

We might feel inclined to attribute such practices to *naïveté*
(though the vernacular drama must have been clerical in origin); but
in the case of the Wakefield Master such anachronism cannot be
merely naïve. He incorporates Christian allusion so systematically
immediately before the shepherds see the new-born Christ that it
seems safer to assume that he is deliberately playing typology against
history, and doing so with some wit, for a conscious religious
purpose. Each of the Shepherds' pageants begins with an apparently
gratuitous episode in which the shepherds complain about the
hardship of their working lives. From each episode we gain an
engagingly strong sense of what it must have been like to be a
Yorkshire shepherd in the fifteenth century. They are troubled by
perennial problems such as the weather and the difficulties of
married life, with too many children and not enough money, and
also by more historically localized difficulties such as the arrogance
of 'thyse gentlery-men' (4 18), the bands of hired retainers who were
a product of what historians of this period call 'bastard feudalism'.[57]
But all their troubles, however strong the local colouring, can also be
seen in a larger perspective: they are the consequences of the Fall of
man, an event dramatized at a much earlier stage in the cycle and
shaping all subsequent human history. The fallen world inhabited by
the Wakefield Master and his fifteenth-century characters and audience is fundamentally the same as that before Christ was born; but it
is precisely that fallen world that Christ comes to redeem, and the
redemptive birth too is happening, if at all, in the fifteenth-century
present. At the end of the *Secunda pastorum*, Mary asks the shepherds
to go out into the world and 'Tell furth as ye go' (4 744) what they
have seen. 3 Pastor comments, 'Forsothe, allredy it semys to be told

/ Full oft' (749–50). The coming of Christ has indeed been told many times before, by the performance of pageants like this as well as in other ways; but it is also always a new event. The Wakefield Master knew what he was doing in rejecting any possible historicization of the pre-Christian past.

I turn now to style. We have seen that what Chaucer's fifteenth-century followers most admired in his work was its elevated style. This style was associated with aristocratic values, and that remained the case even when the argument was put, as it is in the *The Franklin's Tale*, that a squire could 'doon a gentil dede' (v 1543) as well as a knight, and a clerk as well as a squire, and even when subsequently the growth of a middle-class reading-public carried the style and the values well beyond courtly settings. The division of literary style into three levels, high, middle, and low, had existed in classical rhetoric,[58] but there it had been a matter of literary choice or appropriateness to forensic occasion; when this division was transmitted to the *ars poetica* of the Middle Ages, the three levels came to be associated with three estates of society, or social classes. Jean de Garlande, for instance, putting the matter as simply as possible, wrote in his *Poetria*,

Thus there are three styles, according to the three estates of men: the low style belongs to the life of shepherds, the middle to that of farmers, and the high to that of high persons who are superior to shepherds and farmers.[59]

The stylistic basis of the religious drama was quite different from this. What lay behind it was the language of Scripture itself; and, as Erich Auerbach has shown, the Fathers of the Church had seen that Scripture would not fit into and could not be judged by the decorum of the rhetoricians. 'The true and distinctive greatness of Holy Scripture' was that 'it had created an entirely new kind of sublimity, in which the everyday and the low were included, not excluded, so that, in style as in content, it directly connected the lowest with the highest.'[60] The English Mystery cycles were sponsored by the craft gilds of the towns where they were performed, and those gilds were organizations of masters, not of labourers. It is impossible to tell whether they had in mind any such sense of the style of Scripture, but in most cases the plays they commissioned were written in styles not associated with the *gentil*. This was not because none of the playwrights knew how to make the gold dewdrops of refined rhetoric rain on their rude language: some of them certainly did, as the *Ludus Coventriae* cycle above all shows. Some indeed were capable of parodying this type of rhetorical eloquence. For example, in the part of the York cycle that was revised by an alliterative poet in the fifteenth century, Pilate and his entourage are treated as parody-versions of medieval courtliness. When a Beadle comes to suggest that Pilate's wife should go home because night is falling, even this servant becomes infected by the atmosphere of exaggerated *gentill-esse*, and he speaks in a way which sharply burlesques courtly rhetoric:

> My seniour, will ye see nowe the sonne in youre sight,
> For his stately strengh he stemmys in his stremys;
> Behalde ovir youre hede how he heldis fro hight,
> And glydis to the grounde with his glitterand glemis.   (xxx 73–6)

As Chaucer's Franklin puts it, after a similar display of the high style at its most extreme, 'This is as muche to seye as "It was nyght"!' (v 1018).

The exclusion of the high style, then, by no means implies lack of sophistication in the Mystery playwrights. In the Wakefield Master's Shepherds' plays there is a conscious and explicit rejection of fancy upper-class ways of putting things; and this has a special appropriateness to plays about shepherds for two reasons. One is that, as we have seen, the low style was associated by the rhetoricians with shepherds; the other is that medieval writing about the Nativity lays emphasis on the fact that not only was the Son of God born in conditions of poverty and humility, but his birth was first made known not to the noble or wealthy, but to poor shepherds. As Langland puts it, in two lines of extraordinary compression and concreteness,

> Riche men rutte tho and in hir reste were,
> Tho hit shon to shepherdes, a shewer of blisse.   (B XII 152–3)[61]

That contrast between the idle rich and hard-working shepherds is precisely what the opening section of the *Secunda pastorum* conveys at greater length.

The episode of the mock-feast in the *Prima pastorum* illustrates well the Wakefield Master's sophisticated awareness of literary style and its contrasting levels. In order to patch up a quarrel among them, the three shepherds unload from their bags a great heap of imaginary (or perhaps largely imaginary) foodstuffs, many of which are aristocratic dishes, or what they suppose aristocratic dishes to be. (We should

no doubt bear in mind the description of the luxurious feast as a
common theme in courtly romance: the delicacies themselves, rare
yet plentiful, and elaborately cooked, and the abundance and elaboration of words used to describe them are equally markers of social
elevation.[62]) 3 Pastor enters thoroughly into the spirit of the occasion, using aristocratic or learned and almost 'aureate' words such
as *restorité* and *appeté*:

> Here is to recorde the leg of a goys,
> With chekyns endorde, pork, partryk to roys,
> A tart for a lorde – how thynk ye this doys? –
> A calf-lyver skorde with the veryose:
> Good sawse,
> This is a restorité
> To make a good appeté. (3 233–9)

Yet this is a feast of words only, and the grand names without the
grand things to accompany them are especially vulnerable to
attack. 3 Pastor's colleagues at once take him down a peg by
mocking the *clergé* (learning) of his language, using similarly recon-
dite terms parodically (*clause, gramery*), and contrasting this elevated but empty diction with the blunt names of real things (*drynk,
ayll, poll*):

> 1 *Pastor*: Yee speke all by clergé,
>   I here by youre clause.
>
>   Couth ye by youre gramery reche us a drynk,
>   I should be more mery – ye wote what I thynk.
> 2 *Pastor*: Have good ayll of Hely! Bewar now, I wynk,
>   For and thou drynk drely, in thy poll wyll it synk. (240–5)

Hely is probably Healey, a village near Wakefield, again a deflat-
ingly familiar reference.

Later in *Prima pastorum* the boot is on the other foot. At the end
of the list of prophecies, Jewish and pagan, of the coming of Christ,
1 Pastor mentions Virgil as a pagan prophet, and he now uses
gramré in all seriousness, alongside *poetré*, a term of a distinctly
elevated kind, as we saw in *Troilus and Criseyde*.[63] (The inconsis-
tency of 'characterization' here should not worry us, for the poet
does not aim to create consistently individualized characters as in
some later drama. As Richard Axton puts it, 'The shepherds of this
play are preeminently role-players; they embody a concept of
acting as improvised buffoonery ...'[64]) 1 Pastor actually quotes
(not quite accurately) two lines from the Messianic Eclogue in
Latin:

Virgill in his poetré sayde in his verse
Even thus by grameré, as I shall reherse:
Iam nova progenies celo demittitur alto;
Iam rediet Virgo, redeunt Saturnia regna.   (3 386–9)

From the rhetorical point of view, this is a perfectly apt quotation, for the *Eclogues* are shepherd-poems, and indeed one common formulation of the three levels of style was to assign Virgil's *Aeneid* to the high style, his *Georgics* to the middle, and his *Eclogues* to the low. Nevertheless, another of the shepherds is quick to abuse 1 Pastor for the pretentiousness of this display of learning: he is preaching, he says, like a friar (a common type of hypocrisy), and he seems to be excessively vain of his knowledge of Cato (the *Disticha Catonis*, an elementary school textbook of Latin). 1 Pastor, however, shows that he really does know what the Latin means, and his quietly impressive explanation convinces the others:

> 2 *Pastor*: Weme! tord! what speke ye here in myn eeres?
>   Tell us no clergé! I hold you of the freres;
>   Ye preche!
>   It semys by youre Laton
>   Ye have lerd youre Caton.
> 1 *Pastor*: Herk, syrs! ye fon.
>   I shall you teche:
>
>   He sayde from heven a new kynde is send,
>   Whom a vyrgyn to neven, oure mys to amend,
>   Shall conceyve full even, thus make I an end;
>   And yit more to neven, that Saturne shall bend
>   Unto us,
>   With peasse and plenté,
>   With ryches and menee,
>   Good luf and charyté
>   Blendyd amanges us.   (388–403)

The effect of this passage is highly characteristic of the Wakefield Master: a cutting derision that seems likely to annihilate the sacred then gives way to a reverence that is all the more secure because mockery has been permitted. At the same time the fiction of shepherd conversation is pushed to conscious absurdity – what real medieval Yorkshire shepherd could quote Virgil in the original, even if it were only the *Eclogues*? – in order to point to larger meanings that lie outside the conversation itself.

One last example of this opposition to stylistic pretension can be taken from the *Secunda pastorum*. Mak, the sheep-stealer, is disguised when he first enters, and he pretends to be a messenger from a great lord (a kind of antitype to the angels who are about to come with a message from another great Lord). To support the pretence, he tries to speak in southern dialect, saying *ich be* for 'I am', *sich* for 'swilk', and *goyth* for 'goys'. The situation is like that of Chaucer's *Reeve's Tale* in reverse – a northern poet imitating southern dialect instead of a southern poet imitating northern dialect – and the Wakefield Master really does possess something of Chaucer's sophistication, in his sense of linguistic relativism and of the way that language can signify social class.[65] The other shepherds are not taken in, however, and 1 Pastor's response has a robustness reminiscent of the Host in *The Canterbury Tales* demolishing the Pardoner's pretensions to grant absolution:[66]

> *2 Pastor*: Mak, where has thou gone? Tell us tythyng.
> *3 Pastor*: Is he commen? Then ylkon take hede to his thyng.
> *Mak*: What! ich be a yoman, I tell you, of the kyng,
> The self and the some, sond from a greatt lordyng,
> And sich.
> Fy on you! Goyth hence
> Out of my presence!
> I must have reverence.
> Why, who be ich?
>
> *1 Pastor*: Why make ye it so qwaynt? Mak, ye do wrang.
> *2 Pastor*: Bot, Mak, lyst ye saynt? I trow that ye lang.
> *3 Pastor*: I trow the shrew can paynt – the dewyll myght hym hang!
> *Mak*: Ich shall make complaynt, and make you all to thwang
> At a worde,
> And tell evyn how ye doth.
> *1 Pastor*: Bot, Mak, is that sothe?
> Now take outt that sothren tothe,
> And sett in a torde! (4 199–216)

There is also a more positive side to the Wakefield Master's stylistic achievement: it is not just a matter of rejecting elevated and pretentious styles, but of developing his own authentic style, which is able to release the full energy and creativeness of colloquial language. In metre, he is entirely unlike Chaucer: whereas Chaucer, in his decasyllabic verse from *The Parliament of Fowls* on, plays a largely syllabic pentameter line against the strong native tendency to compose the line from a pair of two-stress phrases separated by a pause,[67] the Wakefield Master follows that native tendency, and produces heavily stressed lines with no fixed number of syllables, and thus great rhythmic variety. I have noted the similarity of his stanza form to that of *The Awntyrs off Arthure*, but the contraction of the disance between rhymes in the first five lines of the Wakefield Master's stanza means that he requires even greater technical skill. He shows extraordinary ingenuity, both in rhyming and in fitting rapid conversational exchanges into the stanza (occasionally with as many as three different speakers contributing to a single line). His standard of craftsmanship is exceptionally high, and his verse gives a constant sense of delight in difficulties triumphantly overcome.

I cannot hope to offer a full analysis of the Wakefield Master's poetic style, but I may mention two ways in particular in which he makes use of the strengths of the spoken English of his time. One of these has to do with metaphorical and quasi-metaphorical aspects of language. He does not employ the consciously learned and difficult metaphors of Chaucer's high style; but he frequently writes in a way that alludes to well-known sayings, proverbs and stories, and, precisely because they are well known, the allusions do not need to be spelled out in full, but can be compressed and concrete. It will be best to examine a specific extract. In the *Prima pastorum* the first and second shepherds have a quarrel about the pasturing of an entirely imaginary flock of sheep. (Here perhaps I may digress for a moment to note the recurrence of this theatrical device in the two Shepherds' plays. In the Mystery cycles, with their non-realistic and sometimes processional staging, it is normal for the audience to be called on to imagine invisible stage-properties, and no doubt real medieval audiences came to do this very readily. But in the cases of the invisible sheep and invisible feast of the *Prima pastorum*, once we have obediently started imagining them, it is revealed to us that they are not supposed to exist at all, except in the shepherds' own fantasies. The Wakefield Master's theatrical techniques are not the subject here, but it seems characteristic of him to play dangerously with the conventions of his own art, so as to confuse our sense of its relationship to reality; and this applies to his dealings with language as much as with stage-properties.) 3 Pastor brings the quarrel to an end by pointing out, in the following speech, their folly in bickering about sheep that belong only to the realm of wishes:

> Ye fysh before the nett,
> And stryfe on this flett;   140
> Sich folys never I mett,
> Evyn or at morow.

It is wonder to wyt where wytt shuld be fownde.
Here ar old knafys yit standys on this grownde:
These wold be thare wytt make a shyp to be drownde;   145
He were well qwytt had sold for a pownde
Sich two.
They fyght and thay flyte
For that at comys not tyte;
It is far to byd 'hyte'   150
To an eg or it go.

Tytter want ye sowll then sorow, I pray!
Ye brayde of Mowll that went by the way –
Many shepe can she poll, but oone had she ay.
Bot she happynyd full fowll: hyr pycher, I say,   155
Was broken.
'Ho, God!' she sayde;
Bot oone shepe yit she hade.
The mylk-pycher was layde;
The skarthis was the tokyn.   (3 139–60)

Among the metaphorical or other figurative elements in this speech are the following. Line 139 alludes to a proverb about going fishing (in your thoughts) before you have a net to fish with. In line 143 there is a slight verbal play on *wyt* (verb) and *wytt* (noun). In line 144, 'yit standys on this grownde' is a concrete way of saying 'who are still alive' (presumably despite the senile folly implied by *old*). In line 145 there is probably a pun on 'ship' (their wit applied to sailing a ship would undoubtedly wreck it) and 'sheep' (they are more likely to drown one than to create one by their childish imaginings). Lines 146–7 put their worthlessness in a concrete way: someone who managed to sell them both for a pound would have got a good bargain. Line 149 is a colloquial example of litotes: that which 'comys not tyte' is the imaginary sheep, which will not come at all. Lines 150–1 amusingly imply a comparison between those whose wishes leap ahead of reality by producing imaginary sheep and someone who urges an egg to 'hurry up!' before it is even hatched. Line 152 is a roundabout way of wishing 'may sorrow come to you!' by saying, 'May you sooner lack sauce than sorrow' – once more a proverbial and concrete turn of phrase. Finally, lines 153–60 allude more elaborately to the folktale of Moll,[68] who was walking along shearing imaginary sheep in her mind (sheep that she hoped to acquire as a result of a long series of exchanges beginning with her jug): not looking where she was going, she stumbled and broke the real jug through preoccupation with the imaginary sheep. The tale measures fantasy against reality: all that is left at the end is the concrete reality of the bits of broken jug – 'The skarthis was the tokyn.' The whole series of variations on the idea of imaginary sheep is not merely amusing as a display of the resources of the common tongue: ultimately it will be seen to point to the Lamb of God, whose birth is the true fulfilment of the shepherds' wishes.

The other way in which the Wakefield Master makes use of the resources of colloquial English is in his poetic syntax. Again a contrast with Chaucer may be helpful. In *The House of Fame* we saw Chaucer learning to construct complex hypotactic sentences, which would link explicitly a great variety of elements, locking them in place so that there could be no ambiguity in interpreting their relationships. The opening sentence of *The Canterbury Tales* was one masterpiece in this style; another (of many that might be chosen) is the passage in *The Franklin's Tale* which first explains the motives that led Aurelius to feel that he could not force Dorigen to keep her rash promise and then gives the speech in which he reveals his decision to her (v 1514–40). Chaucer in such passages is beautifully clear, admirably tactful, and creates an explicit semantic melody in which no gaps are left to be filled by the reader or listener. It is an achievement that belongs essentially to the written language, however fluently what is written lends itself to speech. The syntax of speech in everyday life is quite different: it is compressed, abrupt, and elliptical, and is in fact difficult to reproduce in writing, because it is hard to understand when seen in written form, and the writer will always tend unconsciously to reduce it (or rather, in most cases, amplify it) to the norms of written English. The Wakefield Master of course composed his work in writing, but he did so in order that it might be spoken, and in such a way as to retain more than usual of this elliptical quality of speech. In the following example,[69] where Mak is grumbling about the idleness, greed, and fertility of his wife, there are real difficulties for any editor in deciding how to punctuate lines in which so much is omitted, and difficulties for the silent reader in making out the sense of some lines; but once the passage is read aloud in the appropriate dialect, the effect is of complete naturalness.

> *1 Pastor*: How farys thi wyff? By thi hoode, how farys she?
> *Mak*: Lyys walteryng, by the roode. By the fyere, lo!
>   And a howse full of brude. She drynks well, to:

Yll spede othere good that she wyll do!
Bot sho
Etys as fast as she can,
And ilk yere that commys to man
She bryngys furth a lakan –
And, som yeres, two.   (4 235–43)

One can never be sure, of course, exactly what the spoken English of
fifteenth-century Wakefield sounded like, and so one can only rely
on one's intuition and one's sense of modern speech to tell one that it
was something like this. What is certain is that the effect of naturalness did not come naturally, but could be achieved only by great
skill.

The Wakefield Master's reliance on the powers of the everyday
language of his locality is the appropriate expression of a certain kind
of realism in his drama; but it is medieval, not nineteenth- or
twentieth-century realism. Medieval realism is not neutral: it tends
towards the comic, the satiric, the grotesque. It does not claim
simply to reflect reality, but selects details so as to show reality in a
distorting mirror. A characteristic result is a set-piece speech, such as
2 Pastor's diatribe on the disadvantages of married life in *Secunda
pastorum*, lines 64–108. (The Chaucerian equivalent, the digression
on marriage near the beginning of *The Merchant's Tale*,[70] is equally
characteristic, in being more explicitly learned and, especially, in
taking the form of a sustained ironic praise of marriage.) No doubt
such passages really do reflect aspects of late-medieval secular life,
and also reflect real feelings that existed in the fifteenth century and
will presumably continue to exist as long as the institution of
marriage itself; but the elements of outer and inner reality are
composed into a comically distorted one-sided argument. The
equally distorted other side has been represented more briefly in the
Processus Noe when Mrs Noah assures the women in the audience
that she is not the only one among them who longs for
widowhood.[71]

For all this, it is certainly true that in the Mystery cycles generally
and especially in the Wakefield Master's work, as in the late-
medieval visual arts of northern Europe, we find an increasing
'density of specification' in the pictures given of daily life in the
secular world. One tendency of this whole body of drama is to build
up large-scale cyclic structures, in which every event's presence is
justified by its function in the whole system of sacred history. But

another tendency, equally religious in its original motivation, is to make every event individually real and immediate to a wide-ranging public, by relating it to their own experience of the world they live in – translating God's eternal present, as I suggested above, into the contemporary present. These two tendencies might seem to be radically opposed; there is indeed an almost constant tension between them, but it is usually a fruitful tension, which challenges us to grasp the way in which apparent contradictions can actually be reconciled. Art-historians have noted in the northern pictorial art of this period – that of the Van Eyck brothers or of masters as anonymous as the Wakefield Master, such as the 'Master of Flémalle' – the growing presence of a kind of symbolism concealed within realism.[72] To mention a single example: pictures of the Blessed Virgin now show her not against a perspectiveless or flat, decorative background, but within a room in a bourgeois or noble household, placed within a three-dimensional space which is full of objects depicted in exquisitely realistic detail. Many of these objects, however – perhaps in extreme cases all of them – will at the same time be symbolic. The glass carafe catching the sun on a window-sill will symbolize Mary's virginity, penetrated yet unbroken by the light of God; or some pieces of fresh fruit will symbolize at once the sin of Eve in eating the forbidden fruit and persuading Adam to do the same, and the fruitfulness of the Virgin's womb which is the means by which that Original Sin is made good and paradise regained.[73]

Something similar seems to take place in the Wakefield Master's work. For instance, at the end of the Shepherds' pageants, the shepherds offer gifts to the infant Christ. In the *Secunda pastorum*, to take that as our example, the gifts are 'a bob of cherys' (4 718), 'A byrd' (722), and 'a ball' (734). These are appropriately humble gifts for shepherds to offer: they belong to the world of shepherd-realism, and they are firmly placed within the comic dimensions of that world by words such as those 3 Pastor addresses to the baby in handing over his gift:

> Hayll, put forth thy dall!
> I bryng the bot a ball:
> Have and play the withall,
> And go to the tenys.   (733–6)

But surely there is also a symbolism concealed within the real material objects.[74] Where would 'a bob of cherys' be obtainable at midwinter in fifteenth-century Yorkshire? It seems likely to symbolize the miracle of midwinter fertility, exemplified by Christ's birth. The bird is perhaps a symbol of the Holy Spirit, though in pictorial art specific types of bird may have more precise significances. (For instance, the goldfinch in pictures of the Virgin and child symbolizes the future crown of thorns, because goldfinches live on thorns.) And the ball to be held in the baby's fist is the globe itself, the *orbis terrarum* over which the infant rules as God. These are straightforward instances: because the real objects are isolated by the quasi-symbolic status they have as gifts, their symbolic dimension is limited and easily recognized, and in the case of the cherries an incongruity further indicates a meaning beyond realism. But there are larger-scale and more complex instances of concealed symbolism, which raise more disturbing questions about the relation of the secular to the religious. These will take us from style to structure.

Here I shall concentrate on the *Secunda pastorum*, where the problem of structure is most acute. In this pageant the crucial Scriptural events, which form the nominal subject (the annunciation to the shepherds by the angels and the shepherds' visit to the stable) are preceded by other, non-Scriptural episodes of far greater length. First come the soliloquies of 1 and 2 Pastor: 1 Pastor laments the hard life lived by shepherds who are *husbandys* by contrast with that of 'thyse gentlery-men' (4 10, 18) who persecute them; and 2 Pastor laments the sufferings of married men. These two complaints occupy the first 108 lines (each of them being of the same length, 54 lines), and each can be seen to be relevant to the pageant's 'official' theme: 1 Pastor is evoking the fallen world which Christ comes to save, while the satire on childbirth which has a prominent place in 2 Pastor's soliloquy is much to the point in a Nativity pageant. Moreover the two soliloquies are linked together by a tacit pun on *husbandys*, meaning first husbandmen and then married men. Then, however, comes the introduction of Mak the sheep-stealer, and the development of a comic plot which is taken from folktale sources[75] and has no previous connection with Scripture. While the other shepherds are sleeping, Mak steals a sheep from them; he takes it home to his cottage, and his wife hides it in the cradle, pretending that it is a baby to which she has just given birth. Mak returns to the other shepherds, and claims to have been asleep and to have dreamt that Gill, his wife, was giving birth to 'a yong lad / For to mend oure flok' (387–8). When the shepherds miss one of their sheep, they at once suspect Mak; when they visit his cottage they are deceived at first by Gill's trick but, having returned to give a present to 'The child . . ., that lytyll day-starne' (577), they discover what is really in the cradle, and punish Mak by tossing him in a blanket. Only at this point, at line 638 of a pageant of 754 lines, do the angels appear so that the proper Nativity sequence can begin.

It would be easy to dismiss the sheep-stealing episode as irrelevant, though intrinsically delightful, comic secularization, having nothing to do with the pageant's real subject – as easy as to say that the two episodes of *The Awntyrs off Arthure* have no connection with each other. In fact, despite the apparent absence of symmetry of organization in the *Secunda pastorum*, it has long been recognized that the Wakefield Master has used the typological principle from which the structure of the cycle derives as a way of linking to the Nativity a secular plot which stands in an antitypical relationship to it. The stolen sheep disguised as a newborn child is a comic parody, or antitype, of the Lamb of God newly born as the Virgin's son. This is the basic idea, which is then developed in daringly blasphemous detail. As the coming of the Lamb is to relieve the misery of fallen man, so Mak tells Gill, 'Now mendys oure chere / From sorow / A fatt shepe, I dar say . . .' (290–2). Later, when the other shepherds are suspicious that Mak may have concealed the sheep in his cottage, Mak piously says, pointing to the cradle where it is,

> As I am true and lele, to God here I pray
> That this be the fyrst mele that I shall ete this day,   (521–2)

and Gill adds (pretending to be suffering from childbirth pains),

> A, my medyll!
> I pray to God so mylde,
> If ever I you begyld,
> That I ete this chylde
> That lygys in this credyll.   (534–8)

Since the body of Christ is indeed eaten as part of the sacrament (which is received fasting), the pointedness of the blasphemy is obvious, especially in a cycle devised to celebrate the feast of Corpus Christi.

Convinced that they have accused Mak falsely, the shepherds leave, but then it occurs to them that they have failed to observe the custom of giving the child a present. They hastily return, much to Mak's embarrassment, and this time they peer into the cradle, and the truth dawns on them. They find that the child 'has a long snowte'

(585) and is 'A hornyd lad' (601) – more like the Devil's son than God's. What is more, they discover how Mak and Gill have persuaded the sheep to stay in the cradle: 'thay swedyll / His foure feytt in the medyll' (598–9) – and it has been pointed out that in late-medieval religious art the lamb with its feet bound together was a recognized emblem of the crucified Christ.[76] Detail after detail, besides playing its part in the *fabliau*-type comedy of the folktale plot, turns out to be capable of functioning as profane parody of the pageant's religious theme. It has even been noted that tossing in a blanket was a means recommended in the Middle Ages to bring on a difficult birth,[77] so that Mak's carnival punishment can also be linked, by contrast, to the Nativity theme, for it was well known that, when Christ was born of the Virgin, the birth was easy, for 'non so clene of such a clos com never er thenne'.[78]

The structural basis of the *Secunda pastorum*, as we have seen, lies in Scriptural typology; but in a more general sense the method is the same as that of *The Awntyrs off Arthure*. The poet sets alongside each other two bodies of superficially disparate material, but the act of juxtaposition provokes recognition of significant similarities and contrasts between them. Just as, on the level of syntax, the *Secunda pastorum* frequently depends upon the reader or listener to complete what is elliptical, so, on the level of plot, it relies on the spectator to put together the sacred and the profane and to 'complete' the meaning thereby generated. Much of the recent scholarly work done on the *Secunda pastorum* has seemed excessively curious in its discovery of religious allusions in the secular material, and that chiefly, I think, because it disregards the freedom which the work itself bestows on the individual spectator to make such connections for himself. Different spectators, having grasped the general principles of typology and juxtaposition, will make different connections, and will rightly take pleasure in doing so for themselves. The dramatic syntax of the *Secunda pastorum*, like the narrative syntax of *The Awntyrs off Arthure*, is paratactic rather than hypotactic. In this, I tentatively suggest, it is medieval rather than Renaissance.

The question remains, why this intricately wrought and infinitely suggestive typological parody should be inserted in a Nativity pageant at all? One kind of answer would speak of the general tendency towards an increase of interest in the secular world in the religious literature and art of the fifteenth century; but it is difficult – perhaps impossible – to distinguish between this and the extension of the religious sphere to incorporate the secular, such as Panofsky finds in late-medieval Netherlandish painting. Every component of everyday reality, from a carafe of water to a stolen sheep, is capable of provoking a religious interpretation; and it can hardly be doubted that, from a religious point of view, every secular object is in principle capable of bearing a religious meaning. More generally, it should be remembered that blasphemous parody is no novelty in medieval literature; indeed, it may be one of the characteristic products of an age of religious faith. In Chaucer's *Pardoner's Tale* the three revellers who set off to kill Death and end by killing each other for a heap of gold coins enact a fourteenth-century blasphemous joke about the Crucifixion.[79] Such blasphemous parody nearly always contributes to a meaning which is ultimately religious, and so it is, I believe, in the Wakefield Master's two Shepherds' pageants. These plays make possible a reverence which is grounded in complete security because the attitudes that oppose reverence have already been allowed the fullest possible expression; the material objects and bodily acts from which religion derives its spiritual meanings have been displayed in their coarsest literality. That is why the typological parody has to come first (just as, for an analogous reason, the critique of Arthurian civilization has to come before its celebration in *The Awntyrs off Arthure*): we are allowed and even encouraged to laugh derisively, we are permitted to see the Lamb of God as a stolen sheep and the Blessed Virgin as a falsely pregnant sheep-stealer's wife, and then we know that the true mysteries of the Nativity and the eucharist are unafraid of entering the secular world. They belong not only in church but on the street, and they do not need to shelter themselves against any possible irony.

5 · Henryson and Dunbar

In this chapter we return to the Chaucerian tradition, but move from England to Scotland and to the late fifteenth and early sixteenth century. We have noted that Chaucer's followers saw their master as the head of a single poetic tradition throughout the whole of Britain; but by the second half of the fifteenth century its Scottish branch is readily distinguishable from its English, not only in technical skill (for example, in its more confident metre, often reinforced by heavy alliteration), but also in the greater independence with which it adapted the Chaucerian inheritance to its own imaginative purposes. There was evidently a real advantage in geographical distance from Chaucer and in the possession of a different national culture as the basis for a different poetic identity. In fact the earliest 'Scottish Chaucerian' work comes from earlier in the fifteenth century – *The Kingis Quair*, a poem convincingly attributed to King James I of Scotland. This is an enthusiastic development of Chaucer's philosophical expansion of the courtly dream-allegory, and one which even attempts to adapt Boethius's thought on divine prescience to practical human purposes. If it is indeed by James I, then its early indebtedness to Chaucer (and also to Lydgate) can be explained by the fact that the king spent many years in England as a prisoner. There is little evidence that *The Kingis Quair* was known to later Scottish poets. There are also some localized signs of Chaucerian influence in the style of the *Wallace* of 'Blind Hary', which dates from the 1470s; but this is a heroic narrative of a fundamentally un-Chaucerian kind. The first Scottish poet whose work can be seen as a major original contribution to 'alle poesye' is Robert Henryson.

Little is known of Henryson's biography.[1] He is likely to have been born in the 1430s, and must have been dead by about 1505, the date of Dunbar's *Lament for the Makaris*, which, listing the Scottish poets who have been carried off by death, says that

> In Dunfermelyne he has done roune
> With Maister Robert Henrisoun.[2]

'Maister' implies that he was a university graduate, and a Robert Henryson who was a master of arts and bachelor of canon law was admitted to Glasgow University in 1462. He may have been a priest, and was stated in 1569 to have been schoolmaster at Dunfermline. This was a burgh of importance in the fifteenth century, and the master of the abbey school is likely to have been a man of learning. Some recent work on Scottish culture in Henryson's age has emphasized the progress of humanism, has mentioned Archibald Whitelaw, secretary of state to King James III, as a classical scholar capable of writing elegant Ciceronian prose, and has asserted that Henryson himself 'must . . . be regarded as in some sense a humanist'.[3] Another scholar, more sceptically, writes that

if there is nothing which clearly shows Henryson was a humanist of the new style, there is a good deal to suggest that he may be related to an older (and wider) tradition marked by an interest in classical antiquity, literature and mythography which is not at all uncharacteristic of the latter Middle Ages. Perhaps we might here compare him with such enthusiasts for the stories of antiquity as Chaucer.[4]

If the case I have made about Chaucer holds good, this second view may be based on an underestimation of the 'Renaissance' quality of Chaucer's interest in antiquity; but in any case little is to be gained by attempting to fit every poet considered into an exclusively 'medieval' or 'Renaissance' category. Robert Henryson is a major poet in whom, as in his age, 'medieval' and 'Renaissance' qualities exist side by side, and at least partially in synthesis.

1. The Testament of Cresseid

Henryson, I believe, shows a deep understanding of Chaucer, an understanding which is not a matter of mere stylistic imitation (or even would-be impersonation, as in Lydgate), but of the creation of work consciously placed in relation to Chaucer's achievement. This is most evident in his greatest poem, *The Testament of Cresseid*, which contains his only explicit references to Chaucer. These will make a good point of entry into his work. At the beginning of the *Testament* the narrator is sitting over his fire on a freezing Scottish night. It is spring, evidently – 'in middis of the Lent' (5) – but a Scottish spring, when

> The froist freisit, the blastis bitterly
> Fra Pole Artick come quhisling loud and schill.   (19–20)

As in much late-medieval Scottish poetry, the real weather intrudes
in opposition to the weather of literary conventions that had their
origin around the Mediterranean, in such a way that the Scottish
climate too becomes one convention played against others. Here
certainly we are made far more aware of a cosmic harshness than in
the winter setting of Chaucer's *House of Fame*, which amounts to no
more than a date – 'Of Decembre the tenthe day' (111) – or the fuller
but still brief glimpse of winter in *The Franklin's Tale*, when

> The bittre frostes, with the sleet and reyn,
> Destroyed hath the grene in every yerd. (v 1250–1)

Henryson's narrator, prevented by the cold from praying to Venus,
resorts instead to 'the fyre outward' (33), takes a drink 'my spreitis to
comfort' (37), and then reaches for a book 'Writtin be worthie
Chaucer glorious' (41). The book is in fact *Troilus and Criseyde* – or
perhaps, since he calls it 'ane quair' (40), it may be only Book v of
Chaucer's poem that Henryson has in mind. He reads it, gives a
summary of Book v, and praises its 'gudelie termis' and 'joly veirs'
(59). This is praise, in accordance with the tradition we have already
studied, of Chaucer's diction and versification; but Henryson then
goes on to show a startling independence. He takes down 'ane uther
quair' (61), in which he finds what Chaucer omitted, the story of
what happened to Criseyde after she had abandoned Troilus –

> the fatall destenie
> Of fair Cresseid, that endit wretchitlie. (62–3)

This makes him ask himself, 'Quha wait gif all that Chauceir wrait
was trew?' (64); and he proceeds to tell the story as it appeared in the
'other book'. This forms the remainder of Henryson's poem.

No convincing identification has ever been offered of a book from
which Henryson could have taken the story he tells, in which
Cresseid, before she dies, becomes a leper and has one last meeting
with Troilus, without either of them recognizing the other. Cresseid's leprosy is unknown in any earlier version; it proved to be an
influential addition to the story, partly perhaps because the *Testament*
gained wide circulation through being printed along with Chaucer's
work in Thynne's edition of 1532 and subsequent editions of
Chaucer. The truth appears to be that Henryson invented his story.
He did not feel able to say so directly, because he was still living in a
culture in which, as in Chaucer's, ancient authority was valued more

than originality, and the 'other book' is presumably his equivalent to Chaucer's Lollius.[5] But Henryson went some way towards claiming or admitting originality by admitting that he did not know whether his supposed source was itself based on earlier authority or whether it was a new creation:

> Quha wait gif all that Chauceir wrait was trew?
> Nor I wait nocht gif this narratioun
> Be authoreist, or fenyeit of the new
> Be sum poeit, throw his inventioun.   (64–7)

This appears to be the earliest use in English of the word 'invention' to mean 'literary creation',[6] and it is interesting to see the dignified term 'poet' used in the same line. Henryson is hovering on the edge of a fully Renaissance outlook, in which the poet is seen as a creator, and originality is one of his great merits.

The *Testament* is clearly intended to parallel Book v of Chaucer's *Troilus*, setting the 'fatall destenie' of Cresseid against the 'fatal destyne' (*Troilus* v 1) of Troilus. Denton Fox has noted how a number of incidents in the *Testament* stand in an ironic relationship to incidents in the *Troilus*. Thus the leper lady's advice to Cresseid not to waste words on lamentation but 'mak vertew of ane neid' (478) is a harsh repayment for Criseyde's advice to Troilus not to lament her forthcoming departure but to make 'vertu of necessite / By pacience' (IV 1586–7); and Cresseid's failure to recognize Troilus when he gives alms to her as a leprous beggar unexpectedly fulfils Troilus's prophecy that

> when ye next upon me se,
> So lost have I myn hele and ek myn hewe,
> Criseyde shal nought konne knowen me   (v 1402–4)

– only it turns out to be Cresseid who has lost both her *hele* and her *hewe*.[7] Cresseid's testament at lines 575–88, which gives Henryson's poem its title and its culmination, is an ironic revision of the briefer testament of Chaucer's Criseyde at IV 785–7. In Chaucer's version (before her betrayal of Troilus), she bequeathes her spirit to 'compleyne / Eternaly' with his in the Elysian fields; in Henryson's (after a whole series of affairs and betrayals) she leaves it to dwell with Diana, the goddess of chastity. But despite these close links, Chaucer's story and Henryson's cannot both be *authoreist*, for they are not compatible with each other. Where Lydgate in his *Siege of Thebes* presumes no more than to write a backward completion of the 'truncated' story of *The Knight's Tale*, Henryson in *The Testament of Cresseid* more boldly offers an antithetical misreading, an alternative ending to *Troilus and Criseyde*, in which Cresseid dies and Troilus remains alive. Thus in Henryson's work the Chaucerian tradition becomes something more than mere repetition of or variation on what the master had already done.

In style, *The Testament of Cresseid* is unmistakeably Chaucerian, but it is less full than Lydgate's *Siege of Thebes* of specific recollections of Chaucer's phrases and rhythms. There are two rhetorical set-pieces in the *Testament* – the description of the seven planetary gods at lines 151–262 and Cresseid's 'complaint' at lines 407–69 – in which Henryson, like Lydgate, is responding to Chaucer as source of the gold dewdrops of rhetoric, but in many other parts of the poem Henryson seems to have grasped and developed aspects of Chaucer's style that Lydgate missed. We have seen that even Lydgate praised Chaucer for 'Voydyng the chaf', and by the later fifteenth century we can find other writers too commending him for his compendiousness or concision. One example is the anonymous *Book of Curtesye*, published by Caxton about 1477:

> Redith his werkis, ful of plesaunce,
> Clere in sentence, in langage excellent.
> Briefly to wryte, suche was his suffysaunce:
> Whatever to saye he toke in his entente,
> His langage was so fayr and pertynente,
> It semeth unto mannys heerynge
> Not only the worde, but verely the thynge.[8]

I noted above that Caxton himself applied to Chaucer Chaucer's praise of the Clerk as one whose speech was 'short and quyk and ful of hy sentence.'[9] John Skelton, in his *Phyllyp Sparowe* (about 1505), contrasts Chaucer's conciseness with Lydgate's diffuse obscurity: in Chaucer's work 'There is no Englysh voyd, . . . Ne worde he wrote in vayne', while

> . . . Johnn Lydgate
> Wryteth after an hyer rate;
> It is dyffuse to fynde
> The sentence of his mynde.   (795, 803–6)[10]

There seems to be a general tendency in late-fifteenth- and early-sixteenth-century discussions of poetic style to place greater emphasis on the interest and value of conciseness than was common among the earliest humanists, who delighted in Ciceronian copiousness.

Erasmus himself, in his *De duplici copia verborum ac rerum* (published 1512), points out that one purpose of rhetorical skill is to achieve brevity, for 'no-one will see more quickly and certainly what can be omitted without disadvantage than the man who sees what can be added and how'.[11] A little later, Vives builds on the *De copia* by asserting the beauty of conciseness and distinguishing among several kinds of concise style.[12] (I shall come back to Vives's distinctions in a moment.) Even in England, when Lawrence Andrew in 1527 printed a third edition of Caxton's *Mirrour of the World*, he added a passage declaring that 'the pryncypall poynt of eloquens restyth ever in the quycke sentence'.[13]

This brief sketch may serve to provide a context for Henryson's ability to respond to Chaucer's power of writing concisely, and thereby to create a Chaucerian style of his own that is very different from what is to be found in Lydgate and other English Chaucer-ians.[14] In *The Testament of Cresseid*, the parliament of the gods summoned by Cupid to punish Cresseid for blaspheming against him and Venus has as its speaker Mercury, the god of eloquence; and Henryson assures us that

> Quha had bene thair and liken for to heir
> His facound toung and termis exquisite,
> Of rethorik the prettick he micht leir –
> In brief sermone ane pregnant sentence wryte.   (267–70)

This conception of eloquence, which sees as its goal weighty meaning in brief speech, is one that Henryson frequently exemplifies in his own poetic practice; and in doing so he is not simply following (or perhaps helping to create) the advanced taste of his time, but is releasing a potential that was really present in Chaucer's poetry. We can find in Chaucer at least two of the types of conciseness that Vives analyses; and it will be helpful now to return to Chaucer so as to set Henryson's style alongside his.

One type of conciseness in Chaucer is that of summary, in which, as Vives puts it, 'nothing whatever is included that could be taken away without loss'. This is apparent, for example, in a long sentence early in *The Wife of Bath's Tale* (III 882–98) which in 17 lines takes us deep into the story, up to the point at which it begins to serve Chaucer's interest in the problem, 'What thyng is it that wommen moost desiren' (905). Another case is the ninth stanza of *Troilus and Criseyde*, the first of actual narrative, which brilliantly compresses the whole course of the Trojan war into just seven lines:

> Yt is wel wist how that the Grekes, stronge
> In armes, with a thousand shippes, wente
> To Troiewardes, and the cite longe
> Assegeden, neigh ten yer er they stente,
> And in diverse wise and oon entente,
> The ravysshyng to wreken of Eleyne,
> By Paris don, they wroughten al hir peyne.   (I 57–63)

In *The Testament of Cresseid* Henryson sometimes employs this summary conciseness, and an instance which is closely comparable to these Chaucerian examples is the passage in which – also to get his story going – he summarizes the events of Book v of *Troilus and Criseyde* in two stanzas:

> And thair I fand, efter that Diomeid
> Ressavit had that lady bricht of hew,
> How Troilus neir out of wit abraid
> And weipit soir with visage paill of hew;
> For quhilk wanhope his teiris can renew,
> Quhill esperance rejoisit him agane:
> Thus quhyle in joy he levit, quhyle in pane.
>
> Of hir behest he had greit comforting,
> Traisting to Troy that scho suld mak retour,
> Quhilk he desyrit maist of eirdly thing,
> For quhy scho was his only paramour.
> Bot quhen he saw passit baith day and hour
> Of hir ganecome, than sorrow can oppres
> His wofull hart in cair and heviness.   (43–56)

More often, though, Henryson's brevity is briefer, and comes closer to another form of conciseness listed by Vives, that in which 'great trouble is taken to bring together much meaning in few words, and as it were to cram or press it together'. This is less a matter of convenience than of gaining specific emotional effects. One such effect (not in itself characteristic of Chaucer, who tends to soften the edges of emotion) is of the cold relentlessness of suffering. This can be found in the lines describing Cresseid's return to her father after Diomede has rejected her –

> This fair lady, in this wyse destitute
> Of all comfort and consolatioun,
> Richt privelie, but fellowschip or refute,
> Disagysit, passit far out of the toun   (92–5)

– or the three-line epitaph that Troilus has carved on Cresseid's tomb, and that sums up her entire career:

> Lo, fair ladyis, Cresseid of Troy the toun,
> Sumtyme countit the flour of womanheid,
> Under this stane, lait lipper, lyis deid.   (607–9)

In such passages not a word is wasted, and each successive phrase or clause has the effect of a hammer-blow. Their ideal form is precisely an epitaph, compressed by the limited space of the tombstone and made durable by the very hardness that resists the chisel. Chaucer's style has important origins in courtly speech, but Henryson's, at least in cases like this, strongly implies writing.

The second kind of conciseness that is to be found in Chaucer is similar to the type defined by Vives as follows: 'less is expressed than is necessary for understanding, but familiarity with this way of speaking supports the sense and supplies what is necessary'. Such conciseness often gives rise to Chaucer's famous irony: 'less is expressed than is necessary for understanding', and the reader or listener is obliged to become an imaginative participant and do some of the creative work himself. Thus, in his account of how Criseyde succumbed to Diomede's attraction, Chaucer concludes a stanza by saying,

> And for to helen hym of his sorwes smerte,
> Men seyn – I not – that she yaf hym hire herte.   (v 1049–50)

It is for us to supply what is necessary for understanding. Similarly Henryson concludes the stanza in which he tells us of the end of this same affair by saying that, after Diomede rejected her,

> Than desolait scho walkit up and doun,
> And sum men sayis, into the court, commoun.   (76–7)

Chaucer is fond of *not* telling us what a character felt in a particular situation, but abridging his account with a 'God knows' that serves to provoke our own powers of imagination. Thus, of May in *The Merchant's Tale*, seeing her new husband Januarie in bed for the first time:

> But God woot what that May thoughte in hir herte,
> Whan she hym saugh up sittynge in his sherte,
> In his nyght-cappe, and with his nekke lene.   (iv 1851–3)

With this might be compared Henryson's terse lines on Cresseid's feelings when she looks in the mirror and sees that she has been struck with leprosy:

> And quhen scho saw hir face sa deformait,
> Gif scho in hart was wa aneuch, God wait!   (349–50)

Another favourite means of abridgment by Chaucer is the helpless 'I kan namore', which again leaves it to the reader to find an adequate expression that escapes the speaker. Near the end of *Troilus and Criseyde*, the usually garrulous Pandarus, confronted with Troilus's grief at the undeniable evidence of Criseyde's infidelity, is reduced to silence:

> And fro this world, almyghty God I preye
> Delivere hire soon! I kan namore seye.   (v 1742–3)

Such resonant silences are more common in *The Testament of Cress-eid*. When Troilus learns that Cresseid was the leprous beggar to whom he felt impelled to give generous alms, he

> Siching full sadlie said, 'I can no moir;
> Scho was untrew, and wo is me thairfoir'.   (601–2)

And the closing words of the whole poem echo the phrase: 'Sen scho is deid, I speik of hir no moir' (616). That sense of utter finality, which yet leaves the reader searching for something beyond 'no more', is strongly characteristic of Henryson. Clearly, he has learnt from one aspect of Chaucer's style, and an aspect that was largely overlooked by Chaucer's immediate successors; but what he has made of it is distinctively his own.

To turn now from style to substance, a further way in which Henryson learned from Chaucer, and indeed from what we have seen as a Renaissance element in Chaucer's work, while at the same time being more than a slavish imitator, is in his treatment of the pagan past. Having its origin in *Troilus and Criseyde*, *The Testament of Cresseid* is set in a classical antiquity which Henryson, like Chaucer, imagines as having a religious outlook of its own that is not to be dismissed as merely erroneous. Whereas Calchas in Chaucer (as in his sources) was a priest of Apollo, Henryson makes him a priest of Venus, so as to complete a pattern in which the narrator is a would-be servant of Venus, 'To quhome sum tyme I hecht obedi-ence' (23), and the heroine, once Venus's servant, repudiates her allegiance to 'the blind goddes' (135) and is severely punished for this 'sclander and defame injurious' (284). As in *Troilus and Criseyde*, the Venus who is a fiction in the literary 'religion of love' is identified both with the planetary Venus whose power survives in the medieval present and with the goddess literally worshipped in an imagined pagan past. That past is evoked, in its own integrity, in phrases such as:

> This auld Calchas, *efter the law was tho*,
> Wes keiper of the tempill as ane preist
> In quhilk Venus and hir sone Cupido
> War honourit,   (106–9)

and (recalling especially the 'olde usage' of Chaucer's pagans in devoutly worshipping in the temples of their gods (*Troilus* I 150))

> *As custome was*, the pepill far and neir
> Befoir the none unto the tempill went
> With sacrifice, devoit *in thair maneir* ...   (113–15)

The specific sources of Henryson's portraits of the pagan gods are various; they may be drawn from memory,[15] and 'He has created them by a boldly imaginative development of details and suggestions from traditional astrological and mythographical lore.'[16] But for his general treatment of the gods he is much indebted to Chaucer, and to *The Knight's Tale* as much as to *Troilus and Criseyde*. He borrows from *The Knight's Tale* both Chaucer's presentation of the gods' callousness towards men and his corresponding presentation of men (whatever their faults and follies) as capable of feelings, and of arousing our feelings, in ways in which the gods are not. Henryson's reading of *The Knight's Tale* appears to me to have been not unlike that proposed in chapter 2 of the present book, but the effect of his writing is to turn what I called just now Chaucer's *presentation* of the gods into a more explicit *emphasis* on the two extremes of divine callousness and human suffering. One way in which these extremes emerge is through Henryson's omission (on the whole) of what Chaucer conveys as to the way the planetary gods work through men. It is true that Henryson appears to have understood leprosy to be a venereal disease,[17] so that when Cresseid is struck with it, it could be interpreted as a natural consequence of the promiscuous way of life into which she fell once her affair with Diomede was over; but what the poem explicitly says is that Cresseid is punished with leprosy for her verbal blasphemy against Venus and Cupid (in blaming them for the unhappiness into which she has fallen). We are given no reason to suppose that she would have become a leper if she had not spoken the blasphemy. Thus the disease is appropriate to her way of life, without being its cosmically

necessary outcome; if we wish to translate Henryson's pagan mythology into a general statement about life, it will have to be that
only gods of extreme cruelty and pride could avenge even the
deplorable moral failing of sexual promiscuity with a punishment as
terrible as leprosy. These touchy and callous gods are those of an
imagined pagan world which, by a remarkable intuition on Henryson's part, is not unlike that of Euripides. In the *Testament* there is
little sense of a natural order, and the Boethian dimension which in
Troilus and Criseyde and *The Knight's Tale* provides the common
philosophical ground between Christian and pagan is largely absent.
What is left is a marked stress on two things: the cruelty of the gods
and pity for their human victims.

I begin with the gods. As in *The Knight's Tale* rather than *Troilus
and Criseyde*, they are beheld directly in a specific section of the
poem. In *The Knight's Tale* this is Part III, in the form of the
descriptions of the temples, the prayers in them and the gods'
responses, the ensuing quarrel between Mars and Venus, and the
self-defining speech in which Saturn settles the quarrel. Events in the
heavens are not seen by any of the poem's characters, but are
revealed directly to us. In *The Testament of Cresseid* the corresponding section is Cresseid's vision. She blames Cupid and Venus for her
misery, and at once falls down 'in an extasie, / Ravischit in spreit'
(141–2). In a vision she sees the seven planetary gods summoned by
Cupid; each is described in turn, they hear Cupid state the case
against Cresseid, and agree to appoint the first and last of their
number, Saturn and Cynthia/Diana, as assessors of her punishment.
Saturn afflicts her with melancholy and poverty, and Cynthia strikes
her with leprosy, and she then wakes and finds that she is indeed a
leper. She has had a pagan equivalent to a Christian mystical vision,
in which, it must be assumed, she sees the truth;[18] and the truth is
horrifying. The gods' chief concern is their own reputation; this
must be defended at any cost against blasphemy such as Cresseid
speaks in blaming them for her misfortunes. Their procedure is in
accordance with legal forms, but (as is often the case too in Henryson's *Moral Fables*) the legal process merely serves the interest of the
powerful. Cupid calls on the planetary gods to 'revenge' (294)
Cresseid's attack on them, and her punishment is described as 'the
vengeance and the wraik / For hir trespas Cupide on hir culd tak'
(370–1). In *The Knight's Tale* we are left to judge for ourselves the
role of Saturn as senior god and final determining force in the poem's

world; in the *Testament* the judgment is made explicitly in the poem, through the narrator's address to him:

> O cruell Saturne, fraward and angrie,
> Hard is thy dome and to malitious!
> On fair Cresseid quhy hes thou na mercie,
> Quhilk was sa sweit, gentil and amorous?
> Withdraw thy sentence and be gracious –
> As thow was never; sa schawis through thy deid,
> Ane wraikful sentence gevin on fair Cresseid. (323–9)

Even if we assume some irony in the praise of Cresseid as *sweit*, *gentil*, *amorous*, and (twice) *fair* – praise that says nothing of her moral worth – the condemnation of Saturn himself, and the description of his sentence as vengeful, only confirm a truth we learn in many other ways. Saturn 'was never' gracious to men; that is the truth that the poem forces us to accept, and, unlike *The Knight's Tale*, it does not even offer us Theseus's vision of the grace of Jupiter as an alternative.

The formal *descriptio* of the seven planetary gods of course includes Jupiter and others who are traditionally seen as favourable to men; but in most cases the power of these beneficent gods is undermined or contradicted. Jupiter himself, carrying a spear 'Of his father the wraith fra us to weir' (182), proves in practice to be as impotent as the Jupiter of *The Knight's Tale*. The normally favourable Venus here smiles deceptively and then reveals her true nature, 'Angrie as ony serpent vennemous' (228). Even the description of the eloquent Mercury as poet and doctor is undermined by the ironic Chaucerian over-insistence of

> Doctour in phisick, cled in ane skarlot goun,
> And furrit weill, *as sic ane aucht to be*;
> Honest and gude, and *not ane word* culd lie. (250–2)

But at least Apollo, the sun-god, is described in unequivocally favourable terms:

> Than fair Phebus, lanterne and lamp of licht,
> Of man and beist, baith frute and flourisching,
> Tender nureis, and banischer of nicht;
> And of the warld causing, be his moving
> And influence, lyfe in all eirdlie thing,
> Without comfort of quhome, of force to nocht
> Must all ga die that in this warld is wrocht. (197–203)

And Apollo is carefully placed at the 'sovereign mid point', with a precise symmetry exactly in accordance with those principles, discovered by Alastair Fowler, that we found exemplified in *The*

Awntyrs of Arthure. I want now to examine this symmetry more closely.

Henryson describes the planets in the order of the distance of their spheres from the earth, and this is why Apollo comes in the middle. The lines describing him are placed exactly in the middle of the overall *descriptio* (lines 151–264); this is clearly deliberate, for Henryson does not give the planets equal numbers of lines or introduce any other kind of symmetrical pattern in their description. First come Saturn with 18 lines, Jupiter with 14, and Mars with 14, making a total of 46 lines. Next, in the middle, comes Apollo, with 21 lines. And last come Venus with 21, Mercury with 14, and Cynthia with 11, once more making a total of 46. The stanzaic pattern underlines this symmetry: Apollo with three complete stanzas is preceded by four lines plus seven stanzas and followed by seven stanzas plus four lines. Moreover, Apollo is the only planet to whom kingship is attributed, and he alone is, as it were, enthroned, riding in the chariot that carries him through the heavens: the first line of the central stanza of the entire *descriptio* is 'As king royall he raid upon his chair' (204). Yet there is clearly a total contradiction between this formal assertion of royalty and the actual events of the 'trial', in which Apollo is not mentioned as taking any specific part; and if we look more closely at the description of Apollo, we shall see that his sovereignty is affirmed only to be undermined. The line that follows 'As king royall he raid upon his chair' is 'The quhilk Phaeton gydit sum tyme unricht' (205) – which reminds us of the potential instability of Apollo's royal throne. The final stanza devoted to Apollo describes the four horses that draw his chariot:

> The first was soyr, with mane als reid as rois,
> Callit Eoye, into the orient;
> The secund steid to name hecht Ethios,
> Quhitlie and paill, and sum deill ascendent;
> The thrid Peros, richt hait and richt fervent;
> The feird was blak, and callit Philogie,
> Quhilk rollis Phebus down into the sey.   (211–17)

The effect of this apparently gratuitously informative stanza is to take us through the day, from dawn to nightfall, and to end with Apollo disappearing from sight; and that is exactly what he is doing, under the name of Titan, at the beginning of the poem, leaving only Venus visible in the wintry sky (lines 8–14). Apollo may be 'banischer of nicht', but his sovereign dominance is only temporary, and night banishes him in turn. This is a poem with a cold night-time setting. Finally, if we look for the central line of the description of Apollo and of all the gods, we find 'Nane micht behald for peirsing of his sicht' (207). When Apollo *is* supreme, his brilliance dazzles men's eyes; and this inability to see is precisely what is exemplified in the final encounter of Troilus and Cresseid. In all other respects, sovereign power among the gods is displaced from the centre to the periphery, from Apollo to the first and the last in the series, Saturn and Cynthia, gods of cold and the night, and unequivocally hostile towards Cresseid. The overall effect of this undermining of the formal symmetry of Henryson's pantheon is to call in question the apparent status of the gods as 'Participant of devyne sapience' (289). One recent critic has written that the blasphemy for which Cresseid is punished signifies 'a refusal to recognise that she is bound to accept the constraints imposed by "devyne sapience" ',[19] but it is open to question on formal as well as substantial grounds whether the gods really do represent divine wisdom in any sense of the phrase that Henryson and his contemporaries would have recognized as valid.

There is one further way in which Henryson heightens the cruelty of the gods, by comparison with Chaucer. Saturn has no place in *Troilus and Criseyde*; in *The Knight's Tale* he defines himself, among other things, as the god of 'The murmure and the cherles rebellyng', of 'vengeance and pleyn correccioun', and of 'the maladyes colde' (I 2459, 2461, 2467). 'Vengeance and pleyn correccioun', as we have seen, are precisely the function in which Saturn participates in the *Testament*, and leprosy is one of 'the maladyes colde'. (Saturn threatens Cresseid that he will turn 'Thy moisture and thy heit in cald and dry' (318), and leprosy was always considered to be 'a disease caused by an excess of melancholy, that is, of cold and dryness.'[20]) But Henryson takes considerably further the association of Saturn with 'the cherles rebellyng'. He himself is represented as 'ane busteous churle' (153), and in this way Henryson follows the increasing tendency in late-medieval art to make Saturn

the leader and representative of the poor and the oppressed, . . . he appears as . . . a ragged peasant, leaning on the tool of his trade . . . He is the representative of the lowest rung of medieval society, to whom all intellectual activity is a closed book, and who spends his life in wresting a meagre subsistence from the soil.[21]

Henryson's Saturn is this himself, but he also reduces Cresseid to the same level, and it is this in particular that gives the *Testament* a scope beyond that of either *Troilus and Criseyde* or *The Knight's Tale*. We have seen how in *The Knight's Tale* Chaucer extended the range of medieval romance by showing the power of the gods over all kinds of human activity. There Saturn demonstrates his destructive power by having Arcite die of a fall from his horse, and the coolly scientific description of the process by which he dies has the effect of removing him from his privileged chivalric position and making him simply a representative of 'men' in 'this world':

> What is this world? what asketh men to have?
> Now with his love, now in his colde grave,
> Allone, withouten any compaignye.   (I 2777–9)

The corresponding medical details in *The Testament of Cresseid*, the 'spottis blak' and 'lumpis haw' (339–40) of leprosy, go further than this. The leper does not die in agony, but endures a kind of living death; it is known that medieval lepers were sometimes treated, in religious and legal terms, as if they were indeed dead while alive.[22] Leprosy really existed in Henryson's Scotland, and what happens to Cresseid appears to be what might really have happened even to a person of high social rank who contracted leprosy. From a life of luxury and privilege, she sinks into the 'mortall neid' and 'greit penuritie' that Saturn threatens – this indeed is the burden of her 'complaint' in lines 407–69 – and, as he predicts, she dies as a beggar (321–2). To become a leper was, in effect, to fall out of the bottom of the medieval class-system.

Courtliness was the matrix of Chaucer's serious poetry, and this was not essentially altered by his encounter with new Italian conceptions of literature. Though wishing to detach *gentillesse* from the aristocracy of birth, he goes no further down the social scale, even in *The Franklin's Tale*, than the clerk, an educated man of considerable wealth, able to command, and to afford to relinquish, fees of a thousand pounds for scientific consultancy. The very poor are absent, except in such a highly idealized form as Grisilde and her father in *The Clerk's Tale*. The underlying assumption of Chaucer's most influential work remains the medieval equivalent to what a modern critic has said of John Galsworthy's novels, that 'there is no sorrow like that of the rich.'[23] In Henryson's *Testament*, however, we get a horrifying glimpse – more than a glimpse indeed – of the lower depths, and see what it is to 'leif efter the law of lipper leid' (480). Utter rejection, utter dependence on the charity of others, 'cauld and hounger sair' (482), and, what in a way is more degrading

than solitude, the constant company of others equally ugly and
degraded – this is the way of life which Cresseid enters as a result of
her punishment by the gods. There is nothing revolutionary about
Henryson's poem, no suggestion that things might be otherwise,
any more than there is in the visions of injustice and tyranny which
form part of his *Moral Fables*: only a hard look at things as they are.
The coexistence of aristocratic splendour and grinding poverty was
just hinted at in *The Awntyrs off Arthure*: here it is a central feature of
the poem's vision, fixed especially in some lines of Cresseid's
complaint which, in effect, transfer the *ubi sunt* theme from the dead
to those living dead, the beggars:

> Thy hie estait is turnit in darknes dour;
> This lipper ludge tak for thy burelie bour,
> And for thy bed tak now ane bunche of stro;
> For waillit wyne and meitis thou had tho
> Tak mowlit breid, peirrie and ceder sour;
> Bot cop and clapper now is all ago. (437–42)

It would be difficult not to feel pity for a woman who had suffered
this reversal of her earthly situation, whatever she might have done
to deserve it, and *The Testament of Cresseid* is a deeply compassionate
poem. Its compassion for a manifestly imperfect woman derives, in
my view, from an intelligent reading of Chaucer's *Troilus and
Criseyde*; and this is a topic that demands another backward glance.
Most treatments of the story of Criseyde, both before and after
Chaucer, adopt what is in effect an antifeminist attitude, treating her
as a type of the fickle and deceptive woman.[24] Even Boccaccio,
Chaucer's chief source, ends by warning men against women:

You young men whose amorous desires keep growing with your years, I beg
you in God's name to restrain your eager steps from this wretched pursuit and
see yourselves mirrored in Troiolo and his love, thus set before you by these
verses of mine. For if you take them to heart as you read, you will not lightly
place your trust in any woman.[25]

The difference in Chaucer's attitude is marked by the changes he
makes to this stanza, which he addresses not to young men only but
to young people of both sexes, warning them of the transience of all
earthly things, yet at the same time going beyond Boccaccio's
surgendo vien (translated above as 'keep growing') to emphasize the
naturalness of human love by the use of terms such as 'fresshe',
'groweth', and 'floures faire' (*Troilus* v 1835–41). Earlier in the
poem, Chaucer added much to the exploration of Criseyde's

consciousness that he found in Boccaccio and his other sources (this is especially noticeable in Book II, as Criseyde falls in love with Troilus), and his whole treatment, while certainly not uncritical, was deeply sympathetic towards Criseyde. His story ended with betrayal by its heroine; it was one he did not invent, and (unlike Henryson) he felt unable to change its outlines. Given this, the question for Chaucer seems to have been, how could a woman who truly deserved the love of Troilus, and who, with him, created a shared experience as near to heavenly bliss as human beings could achieve – how could such a woman end by deceiving him? Chaucer was notorious as a writer who took the part of women wherever possible – 'all womanis frend', as Gavin Douglas put it, excusing thus Chaucer's pro-Dido retelling of the *Aeneid* in *The House of Fame*[26] – but in order to insert his sympathetic treatment of Criseyde into the predominant antifeminist tradition he had to glaze it with an impenetrable irony. Doubtless that irony, constantly calling into play the reader's creative powers of interpretation, and always holding the balance trembling between criticism and defence, was something Chaucer desired, not merely something he was driven to. But it was always open to misinterpretation by readers who saw the irony only as a transparent screen for the antifeminist line they expected, and who mentally inserted a 'Cuius contrarium verum est'[27] at every opportunity. That such misreading was found in Chaucer's own time among the courtly public is indicated in the *Prologue* to *The Legend of Good Women*: there the God of Love himself has evidently managed to read *Troilus and Criseyde* as a work in the antifeminist tradition, and the only defence that Chaucer's dream-patroness can suggest is that it was merely a translation and that Chaucer did not really understand what he was translating. The continuation of this type of misreading, both of *Troilus and Criseyde* and of Chaucer's attitude to women generally, is prominently represented in the work of Lydgate. In *The Siege of Thebes* he added to his source some heavy-handed monkish sarcasm at the expense of Amphiorax's wife, who hid him from the Greeks but then betrayed him when put on oath: 'She was so trewe as wommen ben echon' (2843),

> And yit she was ful sory for his sake,
> Specially whan she saugh hym take;
> Bot I hope that her hevynesse
> Gan asswage ful sone, by processe,
> In short tyme, whan that he was gon. (2871–7)

In his *Troy Book*, Lydgate treats Criseyde herself with an irony
similarly based on a coarse-grained misreading of Chaucer's tone.
He purports to be sympathetic to her and to object to the antifeminism of Guido de Columnis's account of her in the *Historia destruc-
tionis Troiae*; yet, even while criticizing Guido, he greatly expands
the antifeminist detail that he found in his work. Lydgate's own
purpose is initially difficult to interpret, but the likeliest explanation
is surely that suggested by a recent scholar: 'He is playing the earnest
defender of women whose intractable material defeats him. Despite
all his good intentions, he argues a totally damning case. Women, by
nature, are lecherous and deceitful, and no matter how hard he
struggles against that conclusion, the facts return him to it.'[28]
Lydgate undoubtedly believed himself to be faithfully reproducing
Chaucer's real and assumed attitudes towards Criseyde, but it seems
clear that he misunderstood the structure of his master's irony.

In the light of all this, we can now return to Henryson's understanding of Chaucer. There are obvious uncertainties in a twentieth-
century reader's interpretation of the interpretation of a fourteenth-
century poet by fifteenth-century poets, but my judgment is that
Henryson did not share in this misreading of Chaucer. I think he
grasped the paradox of Chaucer's sympathetic portrayal of a notorious female deceiver, and that in his alternative ending to *Troilus and
Criseyde*, just as he heightened the moral degradation of Cresseid, the
arbitrary cruelty of the gods in punishing her, and the misery of her
consequent sufferings, so he also heightened the compassion with
which the poem treats her. The passage about Cresseid which is
most obviously Chaucerian in tone comes early in the *Testament*,
immediately after we have been told of her rejection by Diomede:

> O fair Cresseid, the flour and A per se
> Of Troy and Grece, how was thow fortunait
> To change in filth all thy feminitie,
> And be with fleschelie lust sa maculait,
> And go amang the Greikis air and lait,
> Sa giglotlike takand they foull plesance!
> I have pietie thow suld fall sic mischance.
>
> Yit nevertheles, quhat ever men deme or say
> In scornefull langage of thy brukkilnes,
> I sall excuse als far furth as I may
> Thy womanheid, thy wisdome and fairnes,
> The quilk Fortoun hes put to sic distres
> As hir pleisit, and nathing throw the gilt
> Of the – throw wickit langage to be spilt!   (78–91)

The first of these stanzas, beginning with recollections of Chaucer's praise of Criseyde's beauty as like a flower and as first among women 'Righte as oure firste lettre is now an A' (I 171), describes Cresseid's decline into promiscuity unflinchingly, while still ascribing it to Fortune (which of course plays a major role in the causative scheme of Chaucer's *Troilus*). The second stanza repeats the tactics of Chaucer's Book v, proffering a willingness to excuse yet implying that some conduct may be inexcusable:

> Ne me ne list this sely womman chyde
> Forther than the storye wol devyse.
> Hire name, allas! is punysshed so wide
> That for hire gilt it oughte ynough suffise.
> And if I myghte excuse hire any wise,
> For she so sory was for hire untrouthe,
> Iwis, I wolde excuse hire yet for routhe. (v 1093–9)

It is at these points in both poems that the defence of the heroine against the 'scornefull langage' of antifeminist slander concedes most to her undoubted moral weakness, yet Henryson has rightly grasped the core of generosity in Chaucer's account. Who would *wish* to lead the kind of life into which Criseyde has sunk by the end of Chaucer's poem, by contrast with the happiness she enjoyed with Troilus in Book III? By the beginning of the *Testament*, Cresseid's weakness has led her much deeper into moral defilement – promiscuity, and virtual prostitution – but Henryson's Cresseid is also now only on the brink of a punishment the cause of which has nothing to do with her infidelity. We would be wrong, I think, to interpret the two stanzas quoted above either as expressing only the views of 'a stupid and passionately involved narrator',[29] quite distinct from Henryson himself, or as irony on Henryson's own part intended to mean the opposite of what it says. That the poem's attitude towards Cresseid, in all the wretchedness of her 'fleschelie lust', is fundamentally compassionate is confirmed by Calchas's uncensorious response when she returns to him with her story:

> Douchter, weip thow not thairfoir;
> Peraventure all cummis for the best.
> Welcum to me; thou art full deir ane gest. (103–5)

He cannot of course foresee after what horrors it will indeed prove that Cresseid's degradation has been for the best.

The first stage of her suffering is now complete: it is followed by two further stages, precipitated respectively by her arraignment before the gods and by her final meeting with Troilus. After sunset on the day she has become a leper and joined the other lepers 'at the spittaill hous' (391), she delivers a 'complaint' (lines 407–60) which is the formal expression of her misery. It is set apart from the rhyme royal of the rest of the poem by being composed in nine-line stanzas of a form used by Chaucer for the 'complaint' of Anelida in his unfinished *Anelida and Arcite*. We have already seen that, in its repeated contrast between past happiness and luxury and present wretchedness, it adapts the argument of the *ubi sunt* lyric to the death-in-life of the leprous beggar. Like Henryson himself earlier, it blames Fortune for the reversal of Cresseid's situation (411, 454, 469), and, like Chaucer at the end of *Troilus and Criseyde*, it asserts that 'Nocht is your fairnes bot ane faiding flour' (461) – compare '. . . al nys but a faire / This world, that passeth soone as floures faire' (*Troilus* 1840–1). But (unknowingly doubtless) it completes a transition from Boccaccio's address to 'young men', through Chaucer's address to 'yonge, fresshe folkes, he or she' (v 1835), to an address to 'ladyis fair of Troy and Grece' (452), warning them, as Guenevere's mother warned Guenevere in *The Awntyrs off Arthure*,

> As I am now, peradventure that ye
> For all your micht may cum to that same end,
> Or ellis war, gif ony war may be. (458–60)

In one way there is a close parallel between this set-piece of amplifying rhetoric, with its sombre magnificence, and the earlier set-piece description of the gods. Both consist of seven units – gods in the one case, stanzas in the other – and both are organized about a centre from which the expected meaning is displaced. Alastair Fowler has seen the triumphal pageant as a key example of organization about a sovereign mid point, and has noted various explicit references to triumphs placed at the centre of Renaissance poems.[30] The middle stanza of Cresseid's complaint, the fourth, is the only one that contains any reference to triumph, in its first line – 'Thy greit triumphand fame and hie honour' (434) – but what it goes on to say is that all this is reduced to the leper's 'cop and clapper' (442). The symmetry of the complaint celebrates an inverted triumph, a triumph of Fortune over human splendour.

There is a sense, too, in which the complaint, for all its magnificence, is pointless, or even an evasion of the true nature of Cresseid's situation; and this is yet another way in which Henryson shows himself to have been an intelligent reader of Chaucer. In speaking as she does, it is as though Cresseid wishes to appropriate to herself a rhetorical triumph which is irrelevant to her real situation. In a penetrating study, Lee Patterson has argued that, whereas *ubi sunt* poems are spoken either from the grave or its brink, by a person whose life is finished or nearly finished, Cresseid has more experience to undergo: 'The complaint is thus an attempt to avoid this experience. An enclosed unit set apart from the narrative which flows around it, it is a defensive pause that witnesses to her timid refusal to learn a lesson more painful and more personal than anything she so far knows.'[31] Instead of learning that lesson herself, she wishes simply to be a lesson to others of the fickleness of Fortune. She has seen herself with horror in a mirror once she has become a leper, but now she wishes to be a mirror to others: 'And in your mynd ane mirrour mak of me' (457). Patterson writes, 'By presenting herself as a mirror to be looked at by others Cresseid avoids having to look in a mirror at herself. Turning herself into an object she avoids subjectivity. Her complaint allows her to exemplify her meaning without including it within her consciousness, to embody her truth without understanding it.'[32]

There is a Chaucerian precedent for this oblique and, as it were, disauthenticating use of the complaint, in *The Franklin's Tale*. There, as in *The Testament of Cresseid*, the capacity for copious lamentation is at first taken to be associated with aristocratic origins. The Franklin says of Dorigen that when her husband is away seeking honour in arms,

> For his absence wepeth she and siketh,
> As doon thise noble wyves whan hem liketh,   (v 817–18)

while the reason why the lepers are glad to let Cresseid join them is that

> ... thay presumit, for hir hie regrait
> And still murning, scho was of nobill kin.   (397–8)

In *The Franklin's Tale*, when Dorigen finds herself obliged to keep her rash promise to become Aurelius's mistress if he can remove the rocks from the coast of Brittany, she engages in a *compleynt* of enormous length (v 1355–456), which lasts indeed for 'a day or tweye' (1457). She begins by blaming Fortune for her misery, and then proceeds to urge herself to choose death (by the pagan means of suicide) rather than dishonour. She gives a great list of *exempla* of pagan ladies who have made this choice; but the longer she goes on, the more remote the exemplary cases become from her own, and the clearer it becomes that the rhetorical structure is a form of evasion of reality – not a means of urging herself to action, but a substitute for action. In the ultimately benign world of *The Franklin's Tale*, the evasion turns out for the best, because it gives time for Dorigen's husband to return and to take the burden of decision upon himself. True nobility turns out to be a matter of self-sacrificing generosity, not of the ability to *pleyne*. The world of *The Testament of Cresseid* is altogether harsher, and there the exposure of *compleynt* as mere words is not allowed to emerge gently, but is bluntly stated in the words of the poet, confirmed by those of the 'lipper lady':

> Thus chydand with hir drerie destenye,
> Weiping scho woik the nicht fra end to end;
> Bot all in vane; hir dule, hir cairfull cry,
> Micht not remeid, nor yit hir murning mend.
> Ane lipper lady rais and till hir wend,
> And said, 'Quhy spurnis thow aganis the wall
> To sla thy self and mend nathing at all?
>
> 'Sen thy weiping dowbillis bot thy wo,
> I counsall the mak vertew of ane neid;
> Go leir to clap thy clapper to and fro,
> And leif efter the law of lipper leid.' (470–80)

The strong reductiveness of these lines is characteristic of the *Testament*, the very language of which, as we have seen, is so frequently pared down to the utmost conciseness. But there are Chaucerian echoes here too, at least to the extent that the lady's proverbial sayings are favourites of Chaucer's. 'Quhy spurnis thow aganis the wall?' recalls the advice to 'Be war also to sporne ayeyns an al' (with 'wal' as the rhyme-word to 'al') in *Truth*, one of Chaucer's most concise poems; and 'mak vertew of ane neid' recalls both Theseus's statement in his final speech in *The Knight's Tale*,

> Thanne is it wysdom, as it thynketh me,
> To maken vertu of necessitee,
> And take it weel that we may nat eschue, (I 3041–3)

and also (with some irony) Criseyde's advice to Troilus that he should not meet their forthcoming separation by abducting her: 'Thus maketh vertu of necessite / By pacience . . .' (IV 1586–7).

Once Cresseid has accepted that 'Thair was na buit' (481) but to live as the leprous beggar she is, she is ready to undergo the third and final stage of her suffering, which follows immediately. When Troilus is riding back to Troy with other Trojan knights after a successful expedition against the Greeks, he is halted by the lepers clamouring for alms. He does not recognize Cresseid among them, but something about her hideously disfigured face reminds him of 'fair Cresseid, sumtyme his awin darling' (504). Trembling and sweating with emotion, he throws a 'purs of gold' (521) and other alms to her, 'Than raid away, and not ane word he spak' (523) – a silence more moving than any complaint. Cresseid has also not recognized Troilus, and when she learns who her benefactor was she first swoons and then delivers a speech which shows a more profound moral insight and self-knowledge than she has been capable of before. Its theme is the *trouthe* which is the ultimate value of *Troilus and Criseyde*: the total fidelity which Troilus shows to the end, in his inability to 'unloven' Criseyde (v 1698) even when he knows beyond question that she has betrayed him. Such *trouthe* is the highest virtue known to pagans, and if Troilus ultimately gains salvation, it must surely be through the possession of this virtue – which is also one of the names of the Christian God: 'And trouthe thee shal delivere, it is no drede.'[33] Book v of *Troilus and Criseyde* gives us Troilus's view of things; *The Testament of Cresseid* gives us Cresseid's view. Henryson confines her and his whole story within the bounds of paganism – the question of her possible salvation is not raised – but her highest moral achievement is to admit her own lack of *trouthe* and to recognize that she must blame no-one but herself. Three times she repeats the words: 'O fals Cresseid and trew knicht Troylus!' (546), 'O fals Cresseid and trew knicht Troilus!' (553), 'Fy, fals Cresseid; O trew knicht Troylus!' (560). She accuses herself of fickleness from the beginning, she warns lovers that they will find few whom they may 'traist to have trew lufe agane' (564), but finally she admits that she may be projecting her own inconstancy on to others, and ends simply with 'Nane but my self as now I will accuse' (574). In all her suffering and degradation, she has at last risen higher than her pagan gods,[34] even though we may think it unlikely that her final bequest of her soul 'to Diane, quhair scho dwellis, / To walk with hir in waist woddis and wellis' (587–8) will be acceptable to the goddess. She may not have reached the height of fidelity achieved by Chaucer's Troilus, or that of generosity achieved by the dying

Arcite, but she deserves better gods than pagan antiquity could offer.

2. The Moral Fables

Henryson's other major work is *The Morall Fabillis of Esope the Phrygian*, a collection of thirteen beast-fables, each with a *moralitas*, amounting to nearly three thousand lines in all. The fables are, of course, not original, deriving from 'Aesopic fables, fables associated with the Aesopic collections, and stories from the beast-epic of Reynard the Fox';[35] but Henryson often expands and interprets them in highly original ways. Each fable is a lively, often humorous tale in itself, and is followed by an explicit allegorical interpretation – usually moral, sometimes political, occasionally combining different kinds of meaning. Taken together, the collection offers something like a picture of the whole animal kingdom as a microcosm of the kingdom of Scotland in the fifteenth century and of the life of man as seen by a fifteenth-century Scottish poet. It also offers a study in the varieties and difficulties of allegorical interpretation, for the relationships between *fabula* and *moralitas* are by no means constant, but undergo bewildering shifts and reversals. It would be impossible for me to attempt a study of the whole collection within the limits of this book, so I shall take as samples the Prologue to the whole work followed by the first fable (*The Cok and the Jasp*) and then the seventh fable (*The Lyoun and the Mous*).

The notion that the *Fables* are in some sense about the problems of interpreting narratives is encouraged by the Prologue, which immediately takes up some of these problems, beginning with that of the relation of fiction to truth. We have seen in the *Testament* how cautiously Henryson approaches the idea that his work may be fictional invention rather than 'authoreist' history. Medieval thought about literature did not readily accept that fiction may have an intrinsic value, or that the poet may be justified as the Godlike creator of an independent world. These ideas belong rather to the Renaissance: it has been pointed out that 'the explicit reference of the poet's invention to God's activity in creating the universe appears to have been a product of Florentine writers in the later fifteenth century',[36] and it is from this Neoplatonism, by way of learned texts such as Scaliger's *Poetices*, that there emerge ideas such as Sidney's of the 'golden' world of poetry that improves on the 'brazen' world of material reality.[37] In the Prologue to the *Fables*, Henryson has to

wrestle with the extreme case of beast-fables, writings of which the
literal sense is manifestly and grossly untrue. The theory he produces
to meet such cases is complicated and pluralistic, much expanded
from its source in Gualterus Anglicus, and constructed by running
together several different traditional theories. Since the Prologue is
quite short, and does not form a single connected argument, it will
probably be best to offer some comments on it stanza by stanza.[38]

> Thocht feinyeit fabils of ald poetre
> Be not al grunded upon truth, yit than
> Thair polite termes of sweit rhetore
> Richt plesand ar unto the eir of man;
> And als the caus quhy thay first began
> Wes to repreif the of thi misleving,
> O man, be figure of ane uther thing. (1–7)

Henryson begins by conceding that fictitious fables, though of
ancient classical authority ('ald poetre'), are not entirely based upon
truth – and here already a gap opens between two categories which in
the Middle Ages usually merged together, that which is sanctioned
by ancient sources and that which is true. Fables can be defended,
however, on two grounds: they please men's ears by their elegance
of style (and *poetre*, *polite*, and *rhetore* all suggest the elevated
Chaucerian tradition), and they were originally devised to rebuke
man's evil ways by *figure* (symbol or metaphor).

> In lyke maner as throw a bustious eird,
> Swa it be laubourit with grit diligence,
> Springis the flouris and the corne abreird,
> Hailsum and gude to mannis sustenence,
> Sa springis thair ane morall sweit sentence
> Oute of the subtell dyte of poetry,
> To gude purpois, quha culd it weill apply. (8–14)

Next Henryson offers an apparently clarifying simile: as by culti-
vating rough earth you can make both flowers and nourishing grain
spring up, so a sweet moral meaning can spring out of poetic fiction
if you know how to interpret it correctly. But there are already
problems in interpreting this homely agricultural simile: is the
person who cultivates the earth the writer or the reader of the fable?[39]
and is sweetness to be attributed to the moral significance thereby
elicited or (as the previous stanza suggests) to the verbal expression?

> The nuttis schell, thocht it be hard and teuch,
> Haldis the kirnell, sueit and delectabill;
> Sa lyis thair ane doctrine wyse aneuch
> And full of frute, under ane fenyeit fabill;

And clerkis sayis, it is richt profitabill
Amangis ernist to ming ane merie sport,
To blyth the spreit and gar the tyme be schort.   (15–21)

The third stanza, like the first, offers two parallel defences of fables.
The first is in the form of a metaphor or contracted allegory: thus a
fruitful kernel of wise (and sweet) doctrine lies inside the tough shell
of the nut. This image is traditional, but its familiarity should not
prevent us from noting that it is an instance of something odd yet
extremely common in defences of allegory, namely that it is itself
allegorical. If we were unable to penetrate beyond the literal senses of
kernel and shell, we would fail to grasp Henryson's meaning: the
need to interpret allegorically is stated in a form which already
demands allegorical interpretation if we are to understand it. The
second defence is simple: it is a good thing to enjoy oneself with
game as well as earnest.

For as we se, ane bow that ay is bent
Worthis unsmart and dullis on the string;
Sa dois the mynd that is ay diligent
In ernistfull thochtis and in studying.
With sad materis sum merines to ming
Accordis weill; thus Esope said, I wis,
Dulcius arrident seria picta iocis.   (22–8)

Here the second defence in the previous stanza is amplified with a
proverbial image that once more requires (and then is given) interpretation: if you never cease to study and be serious, your mind
becomes dull and inflexible like a bow that is always bent. Thus, as
Aesop says, serious things please more sweetly when painted with
jests.

Of this poete, my maisteris, with your leif,
Submitting me to your correctioun,
In mother toung, of Latyng, I wald preif
To mak ane maner of translatioun –
Nocht of my self, for vane presumptioun,
Bot be requeist and precept of ane lord,
Of quhome the name it neidis not record.   (29–35)

In this stanza Henryson turns away from the defence of fable to a
modest apologia for his own work: he is only a translator, he has
undertaken it not out of pride but at a superior's command, and he
submits his work to his readers' correctioñ. These are conventional
themes, and we need not believe that the anonymous lord really

existed, any more than the 'other book' alleged to be the source of
the *Testament*: these are both means by which poetic individuality
can cautiously detach itself from medieval dependence. Similarly,
'ane maner of translatioun', like the uncertainty whether the 'other
book' was 'authoreist or fenyeit of the new', allows for the possibility of originality. There is a marked tension in this stanza between
masculine and feminine: on the one hand is the vernacular, learned
from the mother, and normally associated with women; on the other
are the masculine figures of 'this poete' (father Aesop), the 'maisteris'
to whom Henryson submits his work, the 'lord' who is allegedly its
only begetter, and Latin itself, taught, learnt and written by men. It
is perhaps not too fanciful to suggest that the possibility of 'translating' the stern father into the yielding mother was one way out of
the anxiety of influence.[40]

> In hamelie language and in termes rude
> Me neidis wryte, for quhy of eloquence
> Nor rethorike, I never understude.
> Thairfoir meiklie I pray your reverence,
> Gif ye find ocht that throw my negligence
> Be deminute, or yit superfluous,
> Correct it at your willis gratious. (36–42)

This stanza continues the modesty argument of the one before, with
Henryson attributing to himself 'hamelie language' and 'termis rude'
which are the very opposite of the 'polite termes of sweit rhetore'
that are supposed to make fables pleasing. However, the claim to
lack eloquence is itself eloquent, and there is a well-known Chaucerian precedent in the Franklin's request,

> Have me excused of my rude speche.
> I lerned nevere rethorik, certeyn;
> Thyng that I speke, it moot be bare and pleyn. (v 718–20)

The request to the readers to correct the work if they find it too brief
or too lengthy is also a rhetorical device, dependent indeed on the
fundamental distinction in medieval rhetoric between *abbreviatio* and
amplificatio. There is an obvious parallel here too with a Chaucerian
passage from Book III of *Troilus and Criseyde*:

> For myne wordes, heere and every part,
> I speke hem alle under correccioun
> Of yow that felyng han in loves art,
> And put it al in youre discrecioun
> To encresse or maken dymynucioun
> Of my langage. (III 1331–6)

The *Troilus* passage also includes the idea of *correctio*, found in the previous as well as the present stanza of the Prologue; but it is likely enough that passages from Lydgate acted as intermediaries between Chaucer and Henryson.[41]

> My author in his fabillis tellis how
> That brutal beistis spak and understude,
> And to gude purpois dispute and argow,
> Ane sillogisme propone, and eik conclude;
> Putting exempill and similitude
> How mony men in operatioun
> Ar like to beistis in conditioun.
>
> Na mervell is, ane man be lyke ane beist,
> Quhilk lufis ay carnall and foull delyte,
> That schame can not him renye nor arreist,
> Bot takis all the lust and appetyte,
> Quhilk throw custum and the daylie ryte
> Syne in the mynd sa fast is radicate
> That he in brutal beist is transformate.   (43–56)

Henryson now returns, in these two stanzas, to the justification of fiction, and more specifically of beast fables, with a new argument, developed from the end of the first stanza, and suggesting that there is after all a kind of truth in this type of fiction. Aesop's attribution to beasts of human powers of speech and reasoning is intended to show by analogy how many men behave like beasts. Indeed, men who give themselves up to fleshly pleasures, unbridled by shame, do become like beasts in mind, and therefore are appropriately represented as beasts in fables. Thus what seems like fiction is really only a truth that we tend to conceal from ourselves.

> This nobill clerk, Esope, as I haif tauld,
> In gay metir, and in facound purpurate,
> Be figure wrait his buke, for he nocht wald
> Tak the disdane off hie nor low estate;
> And to begin, first of ane cok he wrate,
> Seikand his meit, quhilk fand ane jolie stone,
> Of quhome the fabill ye sall heir anone.   (57–63)

Finally, praising once more the high literary style of his source, Henryson offers yet another justification of fiction, of a quite different kind: Aesop concealed his true meaning in order to avoid offence to all classes. Here Henryson no doubt has in mind the political implications of some of the fables as well as their more general moral implications. It is noteworthy that he does not make

Boccaccio's claim that the poet's concealment of his meaning is justifiable as a means of demanding the reader's fullest attention and thus making him value the work more highly: his conception of poetry is still more modest than that of the Italian Renaissance.

If we look back over the Prologue, we recognize in its easy eclecticism some major uncertainties. Is the 'sweetness' of poetic fiction its rhetorical outside or its doctrinal inside? who is the interpreting ploughman of the field of poetry, the writer or the reader? why is the true meaning concealed beneath the fiction? does the fiction of beast-fable indeed conceal its meaning, or does it rather express a truth that reality often hides from us? The Prologue seems to take now one view, now another, and in doing so it conveys some of the paradoxes that are inherent in the relation between narrative and meaning. Such paradoxes confront us immediately in the first fable of the collection, brief though it is.

The story of *The Cok and the Jasp* is simple. A cock, looking for his dinner on a dunghill, finds a precious stone, swept there by accident out of the house. He addresses it reverently – 'O gentill Jasp, O riche and nobill thing' (79) – and regrets that an object of such value should lie in so dirty a place, but acknowledges that it is of no use to him. What he needs is corn that will nourish him: he cannot sustain his life by the mere outward 'cullour' (86, 100) of a jewel, which would be better suited to a king than a cock. And so he leaves it where it lies.

What do we expect the *moralitas* to be? The assumption that arises naturally from the story as Henryson tells it, and especially from the many additions that he makes to the source-version by Gualterus Anglicus,[42] is probably that the cock has acted rightly, in a way that exemplifies knowing one's own place and avoiding pride and vanity. And in the version of this fable by Lydgate, 'the cock illustrates the morals that one should be diligent, and should take gratefully whatever God sends, instead of hunting for riches.'[43] Our tendency to interpret in this way is strengthened by the fable's proximity to the Prologue, where *corne*, a word used three times in *The Cok and the Jasp* (91, 94, 99), was employed as an image for the nourishing moral truth to be derived from the rough soil of fiction (10); and again the rejected *cullour* of the jewel may remind us of the colours of 'sweit rhetore' which form the mere outer attractions of fiction. Surely the cock is right to prefer wholesome corn to a beautiful but useless jewel? In fact, Henryson's *moralitas* is quite different from this, for it interprets the jewel as prudence, which guides men's actions to virtue and leads men to heaven: 'To mannis saull it is eternall meit' (140). And the cock is a fool, paralleled by the *moralitas* to the swine who care more for swill than for pearls.

The brief fable and the almost shockingly arbitrary-seeming *moralitas* form a paradigm for the whole collection: engaging though the stories and their animal characters may be in themselves, we cannot deduce their inner significance by following and refining our natural responses to them. Clearly this is not just a matter of carelessness or even impudence on Henryson's part: rather it teaches us a valuable lesson. If beast-fables are designed to show how men, by following their natural instincts or appetites, become like beasts, it is appropriate that we should learn that this rebuke applies to us too, when we fall into the trap of following a natural interpretation of the fable, only to be told that the true interpretation is radically different.

The arbitrariness of the relation between fable and *moralitas* may in fact be more acceptable to late-twentieth-century readers than it would have been to their predecessors, for it is analogous to that now-famous axiom stated by Saussure for language, of the arbitrariness of the relation between signifier and signified, which has subsequently become one of the basic principles of structuralism.[44] For example, one recent theorist, Fredric Jameson, distinguishes between two kinds of interpretation. The first is that of the traditional or 'intrinsic' type of literary criticism, in which the second reading of a text remains faithful to one's first impression of it, which it seeks merely 'to articulate and bring to more precise consciousness'. The second is that of structuralism, 'in which a first naive reading is replaced by a second, analytic one, and where there is foreseen, and indeed prescribed, some basic discontinuity between the two from the very outset'. *The Cok and the Jasp*, by its *moralitas*, clearly imposes this second kind of interpretation. The *moralitas* is in effect a second and more analytic reading of the narrative text, which focuses on what Jameson calls 'just those non-functioning and apparently insignificant elements which had been disregarded during the "natural" reading of the text'.[45] (Examples would be the statement about the cock that 'To get his dennar set was al his cure' (67), or his double use of the phrase 'draf or corne' (91, 94), which fails to make a necessary and traditional distinction between the two.) There is a tendency towards arbitrariness in all medieval allegory, for, as Hugh of Saint-Victor wrote, this whole sensory world is as a book written by the finger of God, ... and individual creatures are as symbols (*figurae*) not devised by human will but established by divine authority (*divino arbitrio*).[46]

It may be justifiable, however, to associate the bold and witty arbitrariness of Henryson's *Fables* especially with the strong emphasis on the arbitrariness of this 'divine authority' that is one feature of late-medieval nominalism. From Ockham onwards, the unity of reason and revelation was denied, and it was asserted that God in his *potentia absoluta* could have established a quite different order of things. Thus the world, the book which God has chosen to write, becomes radically contingent, and faith must take the place of a rational metaphysic. Equally contingent are the means by which God governs the world and the meanings he assigns to creatures and events – including the crucial meanings which God assigns to men, of 'saved' or 'damned'. In this way the book of the *Moral Fables* might be seen as a true reflection of God's book, the world.

At the same time, *The Cok and the Jasp* proves to be an allegory of allegorical interpretation. (The same may be true of other fables too: thus in *The Scheip and the Doig* the sheep disguised in a dog's skin is a living and comic image of the meaning hidden within the deceptive outer form of fiction, while in the last of the collection, *The Paddok and the Mous*, the frog and mouse are interpreted in the *moralitas* as man's body and soul, bound together to cross the water of the world, but it is tempting also to see them as the literal and the allegorical, 'Standand distynit in thair opinioun' (2958), yet unbreakably linked.) The cock misreads the text of his world, failing to recognize that in it 'corne' is not 'eternall meit'. Indeed, by far the commonest traditional analogies used to explain allegory have to do with food and drink – wheat and chaff, the kernel and the shell, or the water and wine of the marriage at Cana which, according to the *Glossa ordinaria*, stand for literal and spiritual interpretation.[47] Beast-fables, like their animal characters, are inevitably much concerned with the pursuit of food; and equally inevitably, in a Christian context, one of the lessons they have to teach is that literal food is not spiritual food – in other words, that food is not really food.

What cannot be learned from examining a single, paradigmatic fable is that the arbitrariness of the relation between fable and *moralitas* is itself constantly shifting in arbitrary ways as the collection proceeds. It is not always the case that the allegorical interpretation given will be different from or opposite to our natural response to the story: sometimes the two turn out to be in accordance with each other, while sometimes the reading demanded by the *moralitas* combines the natural with the 'unnatural' or unexpected. Again, if we attempt to predict what the *moralitas* of a particular fable will be, we are likely to be defeated by the fact that in some cases it concerns salvation and in others prudence in earthly matters. Henryson never allows us to become lazy readers, governed by habit; there is no single attitude towards the text that will enable us to be sure of interpreting it correctly, no hermeneutical guarantee or insurance policy. We have to be flexible and wary, sometimes accepting the attitudes of the beast-characters, sometimes rejecting them. Above all, we can never be sure of being right.

Scholarly views have differed as to the overall structure of the *Moral Fables*. It is perhaps most often read simply as a collection of narratives, which might in principle be arranged in a different order;[48] and indeed the manuscripts and early printed texts on which modern editions are based do not all have them in the same order. The basis of the most recent editions is the Bassandyne print of 1571, which contains all 13 of the Aesopic narratives by Henryson which are extant. Here, as in *The Awntyrs off Arthure*, and as in the two rhetorical set-pieces in Henryson's *Testament*, we find evidence of consciously planned symmetry, focused in the centre. The central fable of the Bassandyne collection is the seventh, *The Taill of the Lyoun and the Mous*, and the narrative part of this fable occupies the middle twenty-four stanzas of the 424 of which the complete collection consists.[49] It is also the only fable of the thirteen in which the narrative is framed in a dream. The others are all narrated directly by Henryson himself, and in some he is even present as an eyewitness,[50] but in the introduction to the seventh he dreams of an encounter with the supposed authority for all beast-fables, Aesop. Aesop here is not the deformed slave of legend, but 'The fairest man that ever befoir I saw' (1348) – the idealized poetic ancestor, a man of impressive paternal authority, who addresses Henryson as 'my sone' (1363, etc.) and is addressed by him as 'father' (1366) and even as 'your fatherheid' (1399). Henryson leaves his house, walks alone into a wood, and there falls asleep. He dreams that he meets this distinguished antique figure, the very personification of literary authority; but Henryson clearly feels no anxiety at the encounter, only reverence, and he presses Aesop to tell him 'ane prettie fabill /

Concludand with ane gude moralitie' (1386–7). Then follows the fable itself; last comes a concluding section in which Aesop expounds its moral (or rather hints at a cluster of morals), and Henryson wakes and returns home. The symmetry of the framing device is normal enough in medieval dream-poems; what is striking is that it should here mark only the central fable, rather than framing the whole work, or acting as prologue to the collection, as in Chaucer's *Legend of Good Women* or the Scottish dream-prologues influenced by it, such as those to *Lancelot of the Laik* or Book XIII of Douglas's translation of the *Aeneid*.[51] There are further indications of an interest in centrality in the opening stanza of this seventh fable, for its opening words place the poet's dream 'In middis of June' (1321) and 'In ane mornyng betuix mid day and nicht' (1325).

We are to be aware, then, of the special place held by the middle fable of the collection; what of its content? *The Taill of the Lyoun and the Mous* is obviously appropriate for the 'sovereign mid point' in view of the traditional identification of the lion as the king of beasts. The lion himself asks the offending mouse, whom he has captured while she was dancing over his sleeping body, 'Knew thow not weill I wes baith lord and king / Off beistis all?' (1430–1), and she acknowledges that she does know this now that she sees him awake, and addresses him as 'thy kinglie royalite' (1433). This identification is confirmed by Aesop himself in the opening lines of the *moralitas*:

> As I suppois, this mychtie gay lyoun
> May signifie ane prince or empriour,
> Ane potestate, or yit ane king with croun. (1573–5)

(By contrast, the *moralitas* to the only other fable in which the lion appears, the fifth, disqualifies him for the central position by identifying him as the world.) Moreover, though Aesop stops short of drawing out the full implications of the story, doubtless because in fifteenth-century Scotland it might have been dangerous to write in too much detail about the revenge taken by the oppressed poor against their rulers, he makes it clear that his teaching is not only about a king, but is addressed to 'king and lord' (1613). He ends by urging Henryson and all men to pray

> That tressoun of this cuntrie be exyld,
> And justice regne, and lordis keip thair fay
> Unto thair soverane lord baith nycht and day. (1617–19)

The story of the lion and the mouse, however, is not one which straightforwardly celebrates 'kinglie royaltie', nor one in which we see 'justice regne'. The lion sleeps, and his regal status is not recognized by the mice, who even suppose him to be dead. When he wakes, he threatens the captured mouse with death, until she persuades him that 'Without mercie, justice is crueltie' (1470). Then, when he in turn is in trouble, ignominiously 'hankit fute and heid' (1522) in a net laid for him by a band of hunters, the mouse on whom he had mercy hears his lamentations, and persuades her fellow-mice to set him free by biting through the net:

> Now is the lyoun fre off all danger,
> Lows and delyverit to his libertie
> Be lytill beistis off ane small power,
> As ye have hard, because he had pietie.   (1566–9)

Sovereignty here becomes problematic: we are made aware of its negligence, of the potential cruelty of its 'justice', and of its ultimate dependence on the goodwill of the least of its subjects. There is an obvious analogy with the *descriptio* of the gods in the *Testament*, where Apollo is placed in the centre as king, yet proves not to exercise the kingly function of justice in the trial of Cresseid. Yet sovereignty thus qualified and diminished can appropriately hold central place in the world of the *Fables*, an imperfect world in which we see not things as they ought to be, but things as they are.

If we now examine the mid point of this middle fable, we shall find that it too is appropriately occupied. *The Taill of the Lyoun and the Mous*, including its prologue and *moralitas*, consists of 43 seven-line stanzas, and I shall need to quote the central group of three, stanzas 21 to 23, in order to indicate Henryson's purpose:

> A, mercie, lord, at thy gentrice I ase,
> As thow art king of beistis coronate,
> Sober thy wraith, and let thi yre overpas
> And mak thy mynd to mercy inclynate.
> I grant offence is done to thyne estate,   1465
> Quhair foir I worthie am to suffer deid
> Bot gif thy kinglie mercie reik remeid.

> In everie juge mercy and reuth suld be,
> As assessouris and collateral;
> Without mercie, justice is crueltie,   1470
> As said is in the lawis spirituall:
> Quhen rigour sittis in the tribunall,
> The equitie off law quha may sustene?
> Richt few or nane, but mercie gang betwene.

Alswa ye knaw the honour triumphall   1475
Off all victour upon the strenth dependis
Off his compair, quilk manlie in battell
Throw jeopardie of weir lang defendis:
Quhat pryce or loving, quhen the battell endis,
Is said off him that overcummis ane man   1480
Him to defend quhilk nouther may nor can?

These three stanzas form the opening of the captive mouse's attempt to persuade the lion to treat her with mercy rather than strict justice. The central stanza does not enthrone the lion as royal judge, as might at first be expected: instead it deprecates a situation in which 'rigour sittis in the tribunall' (1472) in favour of one in which mercy may be said to 'gang betwene' (1474), or mediate. And this stanza arguing in favour of mercy does indeed 'gang betwene' two stanzas containing the references to sovereignty and triumph that would normally be expected to hold the mid point of a poem. These two are fittingly displaced by the poem's central emphasis on the need for mercy, so that the preceding stanza addresses the lion as 'King off beistis coronate' (1462) and the succeeding one refers to the 'honour triumphall / Off all victour' (1475–6). The latter is particularly striking to a reader of Fowler's *Triumphal Forms* for, as we have seen in considering Cresseid's complaint, the triumph especially exemplifies organization about the sovereign mid point. Henryson's argument indicates that he is not using the term *triumphall* loosely, but with a clear understanding of the function of a classical triumph, in which the honour gained by the victorious triumphator depends on the prestige of the captives who are displayed in his procession.[52] The lion would gain no glory from a procession of captive mice. The classical knowledge implied here is certainly in keeping with the idea of Henryson as 'in some sense a humanist'. Such a man would doubtless have shared the Renaissance assumption that the central place was proper not only for a king but for a triumphator. If, as some scholars believe, the *Fables* are late enough to show influence from Caxton's *History of Renard the Fox*, published in 1481, then it would even have been possible for Henryson to have read Roberto Valturio's *De re militari* (Verona 1472), which Fowler describes as 'the most important early work' on the form of triumphs, and which places the triumphator approximately at the centre of his procession, with captives before him and freed captives behind him.[53]

In the *Moral Fables*, then, we find a tale concerning the 'king of beistis coronate' at the centre of the collection, with its centrality strongly marked by a symmetrical framing device; and at the centre of that tale we find an elegant displacement of sovereignty and triumph in favour of mercy. It seems inconceivable that an organization so ingenious in itself and so appropriate to the meaning of the central tale and of the whole series could have occurred by chance. Whether or not we think of Henryson as a Renaissance figure, we must recognize in him an artist of considerable architectonic power and sophistication.[54]

3. Dunbar

William Dunbar was probably a younger contemporary of Henryson's; some of his work can be more securely placed in a Renaissance context. Related to the earls of Dunbar and March, he was born about 1460, and the poet may have been the William Dunbar who took his B.A. in 1477 and his M.A. in 1479 at St Andrews University. In 1501 he visited England, probably on royal service in connection with negotiations for the marriage of King James IV of Scotland to Margaret Tudor, the daughter of Henry VII of England. Like Chaucer, then, Dunbar was a courtier and diplomat, but in the service of a monarch who gives more certain evidence than Richard II of possessing cultural and intellectual interests, including some degree of interest in vernacular poetry. The young James was an ideal Renaissance prince in the range of his enthusiasms, which included warfare and chivalry (he held famous tournaments) but also music and the arts, and education too – Erasmus was for a time his young son's tutor, and the concern with education was a crucial means by which the Renaissance established and perpetuated itself. James further took an interest in shipbuilding, medicine and alchemy, and he was reputed to know many languages. He possessed a smattering at least of virtually all his age's knowledge, and ruled over a court that was brilliant if somewhat corrupt. What may now seem like his attempt to drag his country into the new cultural age came to an abrupt end in 1513, when Scotland suffered a devastating defeat by England at Flodden, and James himself and many of his nobles were killed. Dunbar – to return to what is known of him – was awarded a royal pension of £10 from 1500, and this was raised to £20 by 1507 and as high as £80 (though they were only Scottish pounds) in 1510. By 1504 he had taken orders as a priest. What happened to him after 1513 is not known: in his poems he frequently begs to be given a benefice, and it is possible that he received one, but it is thought likely that he died in about 1514.[55]

Dunbar's poetry is extraordinarily varied, and I shall therefore not attempt to generalize about it. None of his poems is very long: the longest, *The Tretis of the Tua Mariit Wemen and the Wedo*, is only 530 lines, and most are very much shorter than that. He seems to have passed rapidly from one type of work to another: he was a superb craftsman, who could turn his hand to anything, from courtly dream-allegory to obscene flyting. If justification is sought for this constant change in his work, it may be found in his sense of the constant changeability of life in this world, as set out tersely in a short poem about writing poetry, *This Warld Unstabille*:

> I seik about this warld unstabille
> To find ane sentence convenabille,
> Bot I can nocht in all my wit
> Sa trew ane sentence fynd off it
> As say, it is dessaveabille.
>
> For yesterday I did declair
> Quhow that the seasoun soft and fair
> Com in als fresche as pako fedder;
> This day it stangis lyk ane edder,
> Concluding all in my contrair.
>
> Yisterday fair up sprang the flouris,
> This day thai ar all slane with schouris;
> And fowllis in forrest that sang cleir
> Now walkis with a drery cheir,
> Full caild ar baith thair beddis and bouris.
>
> So nixt to summer winter bein;
> Nixt eftir confort, cairis kein,
> Nixt dirk mednycht the mirthefull morrow,
> Nixt efter joy aye cumis sorrow;
> Sa is this warld, and ay hes bein. (Kinsley 58)

There is no single *sentence* to be stated that is *convenabille* to the world, no meaning or opinion that fully corresponds to the nature of experience; yesterday's poem is contradicted by today's weather. The only constancy is that seen by Boethius, the constancy of the divine law that establishes earthly mutability: 'It is certeyn and establissched by lawe perdurable that nothyng that is engendred nys stedfast ne stable' (*Boece* II metrum 3, 21–3). Inevitably, perhaps, from a body of poetry corresponding to such a view of life, we gain little sense of an individual personality, but this does not mean, as is often alleged, that Dunbar's poetry is superficial or unfeeling. The feeling is there, but it is detached from the personality; neither medieval nor Renaissance poets generally aimed at self-expression, and Hoccleve is a remarkable exception to this rule. The feeling is attached rather to ideals, and it often seems to be provoked by a sense of the gap between permanent ideals and shifting realities. One of the ideals which act as a focus of feeling in Dunbar's poetry is that of poetry itself; and this belongs to the most Renaissance side of his work.

I begin with a poem that illustrates this concern with poetry and with his own status as poet, *To the King* (Kinsley 44). It is a begging-poem, and one that compares interestingly with Hoccleve's *Male Regle* and with the poems by Chaucer and Lydgate that were mentioned in chapter 3 as illustrations of the tradition to which Hoccleve's poem belongs. In northern Europe, where the traditions of civic humanism and civic patronage that had arisen in Italy were still missing, the poet of the early sixteenth century remained dependent for his very living on noble or royal patrons. But Dunbar has passed beyond the abject humility of Hoccleve, Lydgate and Chaucer, whose jokes, like those of household fools, had to be at their own expense. Dunbar must still keep up at least the outward profession of humility, though in this poem it wears very thin, but he is prepared to set a high value on his claim to royal generosity. The reason for this is not primarily that he was a more arrogant man than these earlier poets, and had a higher opinion of his own desert; it is rather that he valued his art more highly – the art of poetry, which is now seen, in classical and Renaissance terms, as able to grant permanence to its subject-matter. The world may be unstable, but poetry can at least give lasting expression to its instability. In this poem, two different kinds of value, and still more of power, are claimed for poetry, one creative, the other destructive, and the second eventually turns the poem's plea into a half-comic threat. The poem confronts the king with a logical argument consisting of five sections or paragraphs, each of which can appropriately be punctuated as a single sentence. I shall take them one by one.

> Schir, ye have mony servitouris
> And officiars of dyvers curis:
> Kirkmen, courtmen and craftismen fyne,
> Doctouris in jure and medicyne,
> Divinours, rethoris and philosophouris,
> Astrologis, artistis and oratouris,

> Men of armes and vailyeand knychtis
> And mony uther gudlie wichtis;
> Musicianis, menstralis and mirrie singaris,
> Chevalouris, cawandaris and flingaris,
> Cunyouris, carvouris and carpentaris,
> Beildaris of barkis and ballingaris,
> Masounis lyand upon the land
> And schipwrichtis hewand upone the strand,
> Glasing wrichtis, goldsmythis and lapidaris,
> Pryntouris, payntouris and potingaris –
> And all of thair craft cunning
> And all at anis lawboring,
> Quhilk pleisand ar and honorable
> And to your hienes profitable
> And richt convenient for to be
> With your hie regale majestie,
> Deserving of your grace most ding
> Bayth thank, rewarde and cherissing.

This 24-line sentence is a virtuoso piece of rhetoric, listing the king's many 'honorable' servants – the many professionals and craftsmen required by the wide-ranging activities and interests of a youthful Renaissance prince, from alchemists to glassmakers, from theologians to practitioners of the craft of printing, newly introduced into Scotland in 1507. From it we get a fascinating glimpse of the multifarious bustle of activity at James IV's command, in and out of court. Poetry is not yet mentioned, and its absence becomes more conspicuous (at least in the eyes of Dunbar himself) the longer the catalogue of other crafts. It is at best no more than one craft among others, in competition evidently with all these: there is little evidence that it was valued highly in the courts of northern Europe, except insofar as it could serve the purposes of propaganda.

> And thocht that I amang the laif
> Unworthy be ane place to have
> Or in thair nummer to be tald,
> Als lang in mynd my work sall hald,
> Als haill in everie circumstance,
> In forme, in mater and substance,
> But wering or consumptioun,
> Roust, canker or corruptioun,
> As ony of thair werkis all –
> Suppois that my rewarde be small.

In this 10-line section, poetry's claim is at last made, with Dunbar as its representative practitioner. It is put with outward humility – he is not worthy to be mentioned among all the other experts who receive the king's favour – yet he asserts that his work will last as long as theirs, despite the smallness of his reward. 'As long as' – but this is finely controlled understatement, for the claim is actually that his work will last for ever, and it is reinforced by allusion to the Gospels and the classics. 'Roust, canker or corruptioun' are surely intended to evoke a famous passage from the Sermon on the Mount, contrasting the impermanence of earthly wealth with the everlastingness of heavenly:

Lay not up to yourselves treasures on earth; where the rust and moth consume and where thieves break through and steal.

But lay up to yourselves treasures in heaven, where neither the rust nor moth doth consume, and where thieves do not break through nor steal.

(Matthew 6: 19–20)

In Dunbar's lines, poetry is associated by implication with the incorruptibility of heavenly riches (though what he is requesting from the king is a modest share of the other kind of wealth). But Dunbar must also have in mind the claims made by classical poets for the everlastingness of their work. A well-known example which he is likely to have remembered is the passage with which Horace concluded his first collection of odes, the famous 'Exegi monumentum aere perennius':

I have finished a monument more lasting than bronze and loftier than the Pyramids' royal pile, one that no wasting rain, no furious north wind can destroy, or the countless chain of years and the ages' flight.[56]

Dunbar's may be the first such claim for poetry in English.[57] Certainly he goes far beyond what Chaucer asserts in the *House of Fame* proems or at the end of *Troilus and Criseyde*, and Dunbar's greater confidence in the lasting power of the art he practises gives the final 'Suppois that my rewarde be small' the effect of cutting sarcasm.

> Bot ye sa gracious ar and meik
> That on your hienes followis eik
> Ane uthir sort, more miserabill
> Thocht thai be nocht sa profitable:
> Fenyeouris, fleichouris and flatteraris,
> Cryaris, craikaris and clatteraris,
> Soukaris, groukaris, gledaris, gunnaris,
> Monsouris of France (gud clarat cunnaris),
> Inopportoun askaris of Yrland kynd,
> And meit revaris, lyk out of mynd,
> Scaffaris and scamleris in the nuke,

And hall huntaris of draik and duik,
Thrimlaris and thristaris as thai war woid,
Kokenis, and kennis na man of gude;
Schulderaris and schovaris that hes no schame,
And to no cunning that can clame,
And can non uthir craft nor curis
Bot to mak thrang, Schir, in your duris,
And rusche in quhair thay counsale heir
And will at na man nurtir leyr;
In quintiscence eik ingynouris joly
That far can multiplie in folie –
Fantastik fulis bayth fals and gredy,
Off toung untrew and hand evill diedie
(Few dar of all this last additioun
Cum in Tolbuyth without remission).

There follow 26 lines on the king's 'more miserabill' servants, whom he is flatteringly alleged to tolerate only because he is so 'gracious' and 'meik'. This is another virtuoso sentence of great length, full of rollicking contempt for the motley crew of French wine connoisseurs, begging Irishmen, flatterers, spongers, scroungers, jostlers for place, and false alchemists whose only 'multiplication' is of folly. They are evidently physically present at court, and the crowded lines evoke the way they elbow each other aside to gain the king's attention. With the new, more effectively centralized monarchies of this period, the royal court became a unique centre of power and patronage as well as fashion, and this development is reflected in the growing importance of satire against the corruption of court life, found, for example, in Skelton's *Bowge of Court*, Wyatt's *Satires*, and Barclay's *Eclogues*, as well as many of Dunbar's poems.

And thocht this nobill cunning sort
Quhom of befoir I did report
Rewardit be, it war bot ressoun
Thairat suld no man mak enchessoun;
Bot quhen the uther fulis nyce
That feistit at Cokelbeis gryce
Ar all rewardit, and nocht I,
Than on this fals warld I cry, Fy:
My hart neir bristis than for teyne,
Quhilk may nocht suffer nor sustene
So grit abusioun for to se
Daylie in court befoir myn e.

This fourth section parallels the second, similarly beginning 'And thocht ...' and setting the poet's own claim against that of his competitors. He can endure to see the 'nobill cunning sort' listed in the first section rewarded more highly than himself, but he cannot bear to see the 'uther fulis nyce' of the third section so rewarded. The anger which he now admits leads into the unexpected conclusion – unexpected, that is, for a begging poem.

> And yit more panence wald I have
> Had I rewarde amang the laif.
> It wald me sumthing satisfie
> And les of my malancolie,
> And gar me mony falt ourse
> That now is brayd befoir myn e;
> My mind so fer is set to flyt
> That of nocht ellis I can endyt,
> For owther man my hart to breik
> Or with my pen I man me wreik;
> And sen the tane most nedis be –
> In to malancolie to de
> Or lat the vennim ische all out –
> Be war anone, for it will spout
> Gif that the tryackill cum nocht tyt
> To swage the swalme of my dispyt.

The argument of the final section offers a choice: if Dunbar were rewarded it would enable him to overlook the faults he has summarized; if he is not rewarded, he will take vengeance with his pen. His critical view of the court, and the anger it arouses in him, is seen as a disease over which he has no control, a *malancolie* producing a kind of swelling or boil from which the poisonous pus of satire gushes out. Or, at least, it will gush out unless his sickness is soothed with a *tryackill* or remedy – in this case, money or preferment. We may be reminded of the use of sickness-imagery in Hoccleve's *Male Regle* or Lydgate's *Letter to Gloucester*, where gold, *aurum potabile*, was seen as the only remedy to heal the sickness of the poet's purse. But here the sickness is not poverty itself but the sense of injured merit, and Dunbar is not humbly begging for aid, but is threatening a satiric exposure, or at the very least a nasty mess. The claim for the power of poetry is now different, and less typical of the Renaissance than that in the second section: now it is the claim of the Celtic bard to be able to damage or destroy his enemy with mere words.[58] Yet at the same time this threat in effect involves Dunbar himself in the degradation of his second catalogue: he becomes one of the 'Thrimlaris and thristaris' who are at court only for what they can get. After nearly five hundred years, this poem still has the power to move as well as to entertain, and it is all the more moving because in it feeling is held in check by logic and by this cynical reflexive humour.

My next sample of Dunbar's work is an occasional poem of a kind that doubtless helped him to earn his royal pensions. *The Thrissill and the Rois* was written to celebrate the wedding of James IV to Margaret Tudor that Dunbar had earlier helped to negotiate.[59] The marriage took place by proxy early in 1502 and in person at Holyrood on 8 August 1503. The poem concludes by dating itself 'Off lusty May upone the nynte morrow' (Kinsley 50 189); the significance of this precise date is not known, but it seems likely to have been written in May 1503, amidst the preparations for the wedding, and in any case a Maytime setting is appropriate for the courtly poetry of love, the conventions of which Dunbar is here following. The poem is set in a dream, and, if written some months before the wedding, it could be interpreted as offering a prophetic vision of what was about to happen. Though *The Thrissill and the Rois* is a poem of celebratory splendour, it is quite brief, and its plot is minimal: Dunbar's words form a verbal fiction corresponding to heraldic pageantry. In many ways it is comparable with the court masques of a century later, and especially perhaps with Ben Jonson's *Hymenaei*, which was performed before the king's great-grandson, James VI of Scotland and I of England, in 1606, to celebrate the wedding of the Earl of Essex to the daughter of the Earl of Suffolk. Like *The Thrissill and the Rois*, *Hymenaei* uses allegory to link a marriage that has dynastic implications with ideas concerning the alliance of neighbouring kingdoms, Scotland and England, and also with ideas of natural order and heavenly harmony.[60] The masque presents a series of celebratory and symbolic actions, not only through the medium of the poet's words, but through those of music, dance, and spectacle; Dunbar's poem, by contrast, conveys its actions in words alone, but the words evoke spectacle and music to the reader's imagination. In both works the events are non-realistic, but that does not mean (as some have suggested of *The Thrissill and the Rois*) that they are escapist or merely decorative: they are packed with meaning, because they are the symbolic expressions of ideas. Similar symbolism can be found elsewhere in other media related to the wedding of 1503: thus, as part of the preparations for the reception of Princess Margaret in Edinburgh, new glass windows were inserted into the Great Chamber of Holyrood Palace, showing the arms of Scotland and England together, and with them a thistle and a rose interlaced through a crown; and a comparable decoration is inscribed in the margin of the document ratifying the marriage-contract.

The events of Dunbar's poem are easily summarized. As the poet lies sleeping in bed one morning, he dreams that Aurora, with a singing lark on her hand, 'In at the window lukit by the day' (10) – which means, when translated out of the symbolic language of dream, that he is woken by the light of dawn shining through his bedroom window and by the sound of the birds (or so it appears, for in fact he is still sleeping). Then May stands before his bed, 'In weid depaynt of many divers hew' (16), and

> 'Slugird,' scho said, 'Awalk annone for schame,
> And in my honour sum thing thow go wryt;
> The lork hes done the mirry day proclame
> To rais up luvaris with confort and delyt;
> Yit nocht incress thy curage to indyt,
> Quhois hairt sum tyme hes glaid and blisfull bene,
> Sangis to mak undir the levis grene.'   (22–8)

The poet protests that this May the weather is cold and windy, and that that has kept him indoors, but

> With that this lady sobirly did smyll
> And said, 'Uprys and do thy observance;
> Thow did promyt in Mayis lusty quhyle
> For to discryve the Ros of most plesance'.   (36–9)

This opening is clearly a late offshoot of the courtly tradition of love-allegory that goes back to the *Roman de la Rose*, and it incorporates specific recollections of the Chaucerian form in which that tradition made its strongest impact on Dunbar. His dream of being awoken by May is a coming-to-life, an amplifying dramatization, of a passage in *The Knight's Tale* describing how Emelye rises early to gather flowers 'party white and rede',

> For May wole have no slogardie a-nyght.
> The sesoun priketh every gentil herte,
> And maketh hym out of his slep to sterte,
> And seith, 'Arys, and do thyn observaunce'.   (I 1053, 1042–5)

Now, however, the rose, which in the *Roman de la Rose* symbolized the object of masculine desire in general, has been given a more specific historical significance; like Emelye's flowers, it is 'of cullour reid and quhyt' (142), but it is now the Tudor rose, combining the colours of York and Lancaster (from both of which houses Margaret was in fact descended), and symbolizing the Tudor princess herself.

The poet obediently follows May into a beautiful enclosed garden – the appropriate setting for the rose of love-allegory – and here the weather is as it should be. The sun is shining 'In orient, bricht as angell' (51), and the birds are singing like the heavenly host. Dame Nature issues orders that the weather is to remain fine in the garden, and then sends messengers to the beasts, the birds, and the flowers to tell them to assemble before her in all their varieties as they do each May. This idea of a parliament of all living things summoned by Nature is also a development out of the Chaucerian tradition. It has as one of its main sources Chaucer's *Parliament of Fowls*, a poem which contains, too, much of the fundamental complex of ideas around which *The Thrissill and the Rois* is organized – the association of Nature, love, alliance, and a harmony which is both the music of the cosmos, *musica mundana*, and the song of the birds.[61] Whereas an earlier imitator of *The Parliament of Fowls*, such as Clanvowe in his *Boke of Cupide*, seems to have seen it only as a poem about the courtly idealization of human love, Dunbar grasped and even elaborated its philosophical scope. On the other hand, *The Thrissill and the Rois* is a more explicit work than *The Parliament of Fowls*: Dunbar's meaning, though the allegory may need decoding, is totally under rational control, whereas Chaucer works through a series of suggestive juxtapositions which require the reader to play a larger part in the creation of meaning. This total control is Dunbar's strength and his limitation.

The creatures come, and the chief of the beasts is, of course, the lion. He appears in heraldic form –

> Reid of his cullour as is the ruby glance;
> On feild of gold he stude fully mychtely
> With flour delycis sirculit lustely   (96–8)

– and Nature herself raises him up with a gesture that at once conveys her friendliness towards him and lifts him into the rampant posture of the lion in the Scottish royal arms, transforming him into a heraldic device:

> This lady liftit up his cluvis cleir
> And leit him listly lene upone hir kne,
> And crownit him with dyademe full deir
> Of radyous stonis most ryall for to se.   (99–102)

Nature makes the lion king and protector of the other beasts. He is to make them live in harmony with each other and is to 'Exerce justice with mercy and conscience' (106) – the ideal of Henryson's central fable put into practice (and, appropriately enough, the central stanza of *The Thrissill and the Rois* (lines 92–8) consists of a description of the royal lion). The other animals show reverence to him, and he shows mercy to them:

> And he did thame ressaif with princely laitis,
> Quhois noble yre is *parcere prostratis*.   (118–19)

(The Latin quotation associates his conduct with the Scottish royal motto, *parcere prostratis scit nobilis ira leonis*, 'the wrath of the noble lion knows how to spare those who submit'.) Next Nature crowns the eagle king of the birds, and tells him to rule them in a just and orderly way. Last, she crowns the thistle, 'kepit with a busche of speiris' (130), king of the flowers, and urges him to keep the other plants in order, to value those 'of vertew and of odor sueit' (136) above wild weeds, and above all others to cherish the rose. Nature's final act is to crown the rose herself as queen of the flowers. The other flowers all rejoice, and the birds sing praises and blessings on her. Just as birdsong woke the poet into his dream at the beginning, so it wakes him from his dream at the end:

> Than all the birdis song with sic a schout
> That I annone awoilk quhair that I lay.   (183–4)

It is similarly 'with the shoutyng' of the birds that the poet wakes at the end of *The Parliament of Fowls* (693). Dunbar finds that the court of his dream has vanished, and he writes down what he has dreamed, thus keeping the promise of which May reminded him in the dream.

The general outline of the meaning of *The Thrissill and the Rois* is as easy to follow as its sequence of events. In Henryson's *Moral Fables*, as we have seen, the *moralitas* is separate from the narrative and is frequently arbitrary; here the *significacio* is conveyed along with the narrative, and is natural and manifest to those familiar with the tradition of thought to which it belongs, that of the Boethian Neoplatonism that was widespread in the Middle Ages. The meaning of the allegory is not concealed; on the contrary, allegory here may be considered in part as a means of rhetorical amplification, of finding ingeniously multiple and memorable ways of conveying familiar meanings, and in part as a way of integrating different levels of meaning into a single system.

The lion, the eagle, and the thistle are all three allegorical representations of James IV as king of Scotland. The lion rampant belongs to the royal arms, and allegorically represents royal mercy, *parcere prostratis*; the eagle is really an inhabitant of Scotland, and represents royal liberality; the thistle is another national emblem, first used as such shortly before this poem, and represents royal power and also fidelity. The rose, as we have seen, stands for Margaret as representative of the Tudor dynasty. This is the historical level of the allegory, which attaches the poem to its specific occasion; but behind these historical identities lies a larger, transhistorical system of ideas. Natural species are seen as ordered hierarchically to form part of the great chain of being, and this ordering provides correspondences, the effect of which is to ratify the hierarchy of human society as a manifestation of a natural order which is divinely ordained. One influential statement of this system is found in Book II metrum 8 of Boethius's *De consolatione philosophiae*. This passage was rewritten by Chaucer to produce Troilus's song in praise of universal love, 'Love, that of erthe and se hath governaunce', in Book III of *Troilus and Criseyde* (1744–71), but is quoted here in its original version from Chaucer's *Boece*:

That the world with stable feyth varieth accordable chaungynges; that the contrarious qualites of elementz holden among hemself allyaunce perdurable; that Phebus, the sonne, with his goldene chariet bryngeth forth the rosene day; that the moone hath comaundement over the nyghtes, which nyghtes Esperus, the eve-sterre, hath brought; that the see, gredy to flowen, constreyneth with a certein eende his floodes, so that it is nat leveful to strecche his brode termes or bowndes uppon the erthes (that is to seyn, to coveren al the erthe) – al this accordaunce of thynges is bounde with love, that governeth erthe and see, and hath also comandement to the hevene. And yif this love slakede the bridelis, alle thynges that now loven hem togidres wolden make batayle contynuely, and stryven to fordo the fassoun of this world, the which they now leden in accordable feith by fayre moevynges. This love halt togidres peples joyned with an holy boond, and knytteth sacrement of mariages of chaste loves; and love enditeth lawes to trewe felawes. O weleful were mankynde, yif thilke love that governeth hevene governede yowr corages.

Love rules the whole earth, and keeps each power and element within its proper bounds: this is the justification for Nature's command to Neptune and Aeolus 'Nocht to perturb the wattir nor the air' (66). And this same love which creates the universal 'accordaunce of thynges' also joins peoples in alliance and couples in matrimony. This system of ideas is what underlies the conjunction in the poem of individual marriage, national alliance, and an ideally temperate dream-landscape. In Christian terms, which go beyond but are compatible with what is explicitly stated in the *De consolatione*, this love is that of God himself, and there is a hint of this idea in *The Thrissill and the Rois* by means of allusions to the Song of Songs. This book of the Bible was always interpreted allegorically in the Middle Ages, as a love-song from God to his Bride, the Church or the Blessed Virgin or the individual soul. Since the *hortus conclusus* or 'garden enclosed' of the Song of Songs was identified with the Bride herself, there is always a tendency for a 'lusty gairding gent' (44) such as that of this poem to have at least a potential for religious meaning. More specifically, some lines addressed by Nature to the rose – 'But ony spot or macull ..., / Cum, blowme of joy, with jemis to be cround' (152–53) – recall some verses addressed to the Bride in the Song of Songs:

Thou art all fair, O my love, and there is not a spot (*macula*) in thee.

Come from Libanus, my spouse, come from Libanus, come: thou shalt be crowned.   (4: 7–8)

What these allusions suggest is that the wedding of James and Margaret is an earthly figure of that between Christ and the Church. Matrimony, in the Christian tradition, always signifies the mystical union of Christ and his Church, but this wedding is an especially 'full' figuration of it.[62]

Finally, the 'accordaunce of thynges' created by divine love is a kind of musical concord. One of its products, in this world-view, is literally the music of the heavenly spheres, revolving in their proper order, and it is inevitably symbolized by both human and natural music. The song of the birds in the dream is associated with 'the blisfull soune of cherarchy' (57) – the blessed sound of the nine orders of angels that form the heavenly hierarchy – and this angelic bird-song culminates in the harmony of the different voices of thrush, blackbird, lark, and nightingale, forming one 'commoun voce' (176) in praise of the rose. The bird chorus with which the dream culminates *means* the underlying harmony of all things, which in 1503 found fortunate expression in the marriage of James and Margaret and the treaty between their peoples.

Thus the dream in Dunbar's poem is no mere fantasy, but the expression of a universal system of ideas; yet it might properly be asked, what relation do these ideas, splendid as they are, bear to the realities of daily experience? The committed Platonist would say that it is the ideas that are real, and that our material world approaches true reality only insofar as it corresponds to them. Most of us, however, are not Platonists for most of the time, and we may feel impelled to question the dream, and ask how far it can be related to the life men live in historical time. Such questions have indeed been put by twentieth-century critics, who have often come up with highly unfavourable answers. Patrick Cruttwell, referring to Dunbar's 'aureate' style as much as to his content, claims that the 'fatal effect' of poems such as *The Thrissill and the Rois* is 'to reduce the natural to the artificial'.[63] John Speirs writes of such poems as 'purely "literary" or "poetical," rootless, without actuality'.[64] Tom Scott heartily agrees, writing of *The Thrissill and the Rois*,

> The thing is forced, contrived, unreal, unconvincing, spurious, and Dunbar would not have written it off his own bat. It is indicative of the values obtaining among the ruling-classes of his age that this sort of thing was demanded of him ... Dunbar does not tell us in this poem what the peasantry had to suffer in pillage of their meagre produce to support the revels of the marriage.[65]

Walter Scheps, more subtly, but in my view almost equally mistakenly, finds an irony intended in the contrast between the poem and its historical context:

> we see the 'awfull' (129) Scottish thistle, king of flowers and plants, taking under his protection the otherwise defenseless English rose. In the context of the political realities of the time, Dunbar's description is ironic indeed and verges on gallows humour.[66]

It is important to grasp both that Dunbar is not offering his poem as a total substitute for historical reality and that he is not using his audience's knowledge of historical reality to reject by ridicule the ideals conveyed in his poem or the conventions through which they are conveyed. *The Thrissill and the Rois* is not a deception or a burlesque, but a vision that acknowledges its own limits: it genuinely celebrates an ideal, while at the same time admitting, with poise and toughness, that reality often diverges from it.

The events of *The Thrissill and the Rois*, as we have seen, are set in a dream, and, whatever a dream may be, it is not a transcript of everyday reality. In the Middle Ages, dreams had an ambiguous status: they might be visions of truth or they might be misleading fantasies, and many medieval dream-poems exploit this ambiguity, to make the dream a way of conveying the ambiguous status of poetic fiction.[67] In *The Thrissill and the Rois* the dream-world of idealization is clearly marked off from the everyday world. When Aurora appears to the poet, it is not in glittering splendour but 'with visage paill and grene' (11),[68] suggesting the chilly reluctance of a Scottish spring dawn. And then when May summons him to write something in her honour, he initially rejects this call of the seasonal convention, bluntly introducing May as it often is in Scotland to contrast with May as literary tradition says it should be:

> 'Quhairto,' quod I, 'sall I uprys at morrow? –
> For in this May few birdis herd I sing.
> Thai haif moir caus to weip and plane thair sorrow:
> Thy air it is nocht holsum nor benyng;
> Lord Eolus dois in thy sessone ring;
> So busteous ar the blastis of his horne,
> Amang thy bewis to walk I haif forborne.' (29–35)

Only after this protest does he consent to follow the demands of a convention that has now been defined as *not* a mere reflection of the phenomenal world.

The dream is thus an enclosed world set apart from Scottish normality; and then within this enclosure is a further enclosure, the 'lusty gairding gent' (44) or 'garth' (47), within which the allegorical action takes place. This is in effect a garden of poetic artifice, whose flowers and colours are those of rhetoric. (This is an idea developed more fully and explicitly in Dunbar's other dream-allegory, *The Goldyn Targe*.) There, if not outside the poet's window, the sun is shining and the birds are singing. Moreover, by a striking paradox, within this garden the 'natural order' – the state of affairs which is commanded by Dame Nature – is presented as something distinct from everyday reality. In the real Scottish May, Aeolus, god of the winds, is king, but in this dream-world

> Dame Nature gaif ane inhibitioun thair
> To fers Neptunus and Eolus the bawld
> Nocht to perturb the wattir nor the air,
> And that no schouris scharp nor blastis cawld
> Effray suld flouris nor fowlis on the fold;
> Scho bad eik Juno, goddes of the sky,
> That scho the hevin suld keip amene and dry. (64–70)

The implication is that 'Dame Nature' is the personification of an idea or ideal: we grasp what 'Nature' means not by plunging into the world of immediate experience, but by standing back from it in order to formulate an abstract idea. The allegorical dream represents a mode of abstract thought expressed in concrete symbols; and one of its lessons for us should be that the very concept of the natural, by which we may seek to criticise it, does not come naturally to us.

As for the poem's relation to its historical occasion, it is true that it says nothing about the suffering peasantry (but then it may be doubted whether such reference is an adequate criterion of poetic authenticity); however, it clearly implies a knowledge of the ways in which the real James IV did *not* conform to the ideal with which he is fictionally identified. This emerges from Nature's warning to the thistle as she crowns him:

> And sen thow art a king, thow be discreit;
> Herb without vertew thow hald nocht of sic pryce
> As herb of vertew and of odor sueit;
> And lat no nettill vyle and full of vyce
> Hir fallow to the gudly flour delyce,
> Nor latt no wyld weid full of churlichenes
> Compair hir till the lilleis nobilnes:
>
> Nor hald non udir flour in sic denty
> As the fresche Ros of cullour reid and quhyt;
> For gife thow dois, hurt is thyne honesty,
> Conciddering that no flour is so perfyt,
> So full of vertew, plesans and delyt,
> So full of blisfull angeilik bewty,
> Imperiall birth, honour and dignite.   (134–47)

Allegorically, the nettles vile and wild weeds must be unworthy mistresses competing with the inexperienced bride – Margaret was not yet fourteen when James married her – for the king's affections. James IV was a notorious womaniser, and it is known that in the very summer of his marriage he had left the court in order to renew acquaintance with an old flame. The warning, then, was sharply pointed; and it says something for James's tolerance that Dunbar felt able to include it in his celebratory offering. *The Thrissill and the Rois* is far less 'forced, contrived, unreal, unconvincing' – even if these are felt to be suitable terms for judgment – than many of the court masques written for his Stuart descendants on the English throne.

Dunbar's vision of an ideal world comes quickly to an end, when the harmony of birds turns into mere noise that wakes the poet from his dream. He looks for it as he wakes, but it has completely disappeared:

> And with a braid I turnyt me about
> To se this court, bot all wer went away.   (185–6)

And here a Shakespearean comparison may be helpful. The masque in Act IV, scene I, of *The Tempest* is also a celebration of an ideal of marriage (though it lacks the larger philosophical and political implications of *The Thrissill and the Rois*), and it also suddenly disappears into nothing. When it does so, Prospero reminds the onlookers that,

> like the baseless fabric of this vision,
> The cloud-capped towers, the gorgeous palaces,
> The solemn temples, the great globe itself,
> Yea, all which it inherit, shall dissolve,
> And, like this insubstantial pageant faded,
> Leave not a rack behind. We are such stuff
> As dreams are made on . . .

Dunbar's insubstantial pageant is literally a dream; and it is prepared to acknowledge both the gorgeousness and the insubstantiality of the system of ideas that it symbolizes.

My last example of Dunbar's work is his longest and in many ways most exciting and disturbing poem, *The Tretis of the Tua Mariit Wemen and the Wedo*. It has an even simpler plot than *The Thrissill and the Rois*. The poet, on Midsummer's Eve, lies hidden in the hedge surrounding a 'plesand garding' (Kinsley 14 16) to see and hear what he can. He sees three ladies sitting and drinking wine. One, a widow, asks the other two how they like marriage. Each gives a scathing account of her experiences as a wife, and then the widow gives an equally scathing account of how she mastered her two husbands and enjoyed illicit affairs. By the time their discourse has finished, the night is over, and the poet creeps away to write an account of what they said. He ends by asking the 'auditors most honorable' (527), 'Quhilk wald ye waill to your wif, gif ye suld wed one?' (530). By those who dislike Dunbar's courtly poetry the *Tretis* has been eagerly praised, but I believe for the wrong reasons – as 'colloquial, natural, and Scottish' rather than 'ornate, artificial, and English'.[69] Mystic notions of the virtue of nationality tend to interfere with our literary judgments, and the truth is that the *Tretis* is as ornate and artificial as *The Thrissill and the Rois* even though it is composed in alliterative verse rather than in Chaucerian rhyme royal. The excitement it arouses comes not from its belonging to a quite separate category from the courtly poems, but from its bringing together in a single composition elements that in Dunbar's work are usually kept apart by firm generic boundaries. I wrote earlier of the extremes of his work as being represented by courtly dream-allegory and obscene flyting; the *Tretis* has elements of both, and the mixture is explosive. It is widely acknowledged to be a poem that owes something to Chaucer, but here again it seems to me to have been praised for the wrong reasons. Almost all who have written about it have said that it is, in effect, Dunbar's version of *The Wife of Bath's Prologue*; and it is true that Dunbar's lascivious and self-assertive women owe something to Chaucer's Alison of Bath. Dunbar's first wife, for example, says that, if only she were free again,

> I suld at fairis be found, new faceis to se,
> At playis and at preichingis and pilgrimages greit,
> To schaw my renone royaly quhair preis was of folk, (70–72)

which is strongly reminiscent of Alison's description of how, in order 'to be seye / Of lusty folk',

> ... I made my visitaciouns
> To vigilies and to processiouns,
> To prechyng eek, and to thise pilgrimages.
> (*Wife of Bath's Prologue* III 552–3, 555–7)

But on the whole such similarities do not go much beyond what can be accounted for by a long tradition of writing about women, and especially widows, who challenge orthodox notions of feminine submissiveness and propriety. A subtler recent account sees in the *Tretis* 'an ironic tension created by the juxtaposition of two conventional ways of writing about sexual relationships, the modes of courtly romance and of *fabliau*', which is paralleled not in the Wife's *Prologue* so much as in the relation between her *Prologue* and her *Tale*.[70] However, this juxtaposition and the resulting tension are found in Chaucer far more strikingly in *The Merchant's Tale*, and I believe that Dunbar's perceptive reading of this work is likely to have supplied the most important Chaucerian impetus for the *Tretis*.[71]

The Merchant's Tale is the only one of Chaucer's *fabliaux* which has as its leading characters a knight and a squire, members of the social class that usually peoples courtly romance. It is full, too, of passages of rhetorical elaboration – *descriptio, chronographia, exclamatio*, and so on – that seem appropriate to romance, yet it is driven by a fierce contempt and disillusion, associated with the unhappily married Merchant himself, that have the effect of exposing the ideals of romance as gross impositions or self-delusions. Even that exquisitely beautiful speech based on the Song of Songs –

Rys up, my wyf, my love, my lady free!
The turtles voys is herd, my dowve sweete;
The wynter is goon with alle his reynes weete.
Com forth now, with thyne eyen columbyn!   (IV 2138–41)

– which, taken by itself, is one of the loveliest lyrics of praise and
idealization in Middle English, is addressed by the blind old fool
Januarie to a wife who is about to cuckold him in his presence, and is
brushed aside by the narrator with a single line of sour dismissal:
'Swiche olde lewed wordes used he' (2149). *The Merchant's Tale* has
the effect of a take-over bid, an attempt by *fabliau* to absorb and
destroy the major medieval idealizing genres – not just courtly
romance, but moral allegory in the Justinus–Placebo debate and
mythological fantasy in the Pluto–Proserpina episode. Justinus and
Pluto, characteristically, turn out to be as unhappily married and as
meanly disillusioned by the experience as the Merchant himself. It
might seem scarcely possible to go further than this in the destruction of ideals about women and the exposure to contempt of the men
who hold such ideals; but Dunbar's *Tretis* does it.

Among specific parallels, the following may be noted. The
widow puts her opening questions to the wives in terms of a harshly
ironic account of the joys of marriage and this is like a compressed
version of the ironic eulogy of the 'yok of mariage' (1285), and
especially of its indissolubility, in the long *digressio* near the beginning of *The Merchant's Tale*.

Think ye it nocht ane blist band that bindis so fast
That none undo it a deill may bot the deith ane?   (47–8)

asks the widow; and the first wife's answer that it is 'bair of blis' (51)
repeats the phrasing of Justinus's warning that he finds marriage 'of
alle blisses bare' (1548). Dunbar develops further the traditional
image of marriage as a yoke: the first wife says that if only women
were free, like birds, to choose a new mate every year – an idea that
goes back to Jean de Meun, and behind him to Ovid's Myrrha in
Book x of the *Metamorphoses*, using the habits of birds and beasts as
an argument in favour of incest – she would choose one who was
'Yaip and ying, in the yok ane yeir for to draw' (78), and then when
he was worn out another 'forky fure, ay furthwart and forsy in
draucht' (85). The yoke is not simply one that links the partners
together, but one in which the man must heave like a drayhorse to
satisfy his partner's appetite. This is entirely in keeping with *The*

217

Merchant's Tale's general presentation of sexual activity less as pleasure than as work (for example, in lines 1832–3 and 1842). Perhaps the most horribly memorable passage in *The Merchant's Tale* is the description of Januarie taking his bride to bed:

> With thikke brustles of his berd unsofte,
> Lyk to the skyn of houndfyssh, sharp as brere –
> For he was shave al newe in his manere –
> He rubbeth hire aboute hir tendre face.　　　　　(1824–7)

Dunbar reproduces this, again further intensified, as part of the first wife's description of her old husband:

> Quhen schaiffyne is that ald schaik with a scharp rasour,
> He schowis one me his schevill mouth and schedis my lippis;
> And with his hard hurcheone scyne sa heklis he my chekis,
> That as a glemand gleyd glowis my chaftis.　　　　　(105–8)

It is a recurrent part of the *Tretis*'s technique of debasement to put the conventional tokens of courtliness or femininity in false contexts; thus in these lines the modest blush of the lady confronted with male desire is transformed into jaws glowing like a coal from the friction of her husband's hedgehog-like bristles. (Two other examples of the same technique may be mentioned here. One, comparatively mild, is the use of the romantic image of the new moon glimpsed through clouds to apply to the widow peeping through her weeds to leer at men in church:

> And, as the new mone all pale, oppressit with change,
> Kythis quhilis her cleir face through cluddis of sable,
> So keik I through my clokis, and castis kynd lukis
> To knychtis, and to cleirkis, and cortly personis.　　　　　(432–5)

The other, peculiarly disgusting, caressingly evokes the rich texture of silk, such as a courtly lady's dress might be made of, only to apply it to the flaccid penis of the first wife's husband: 'Bot soft and soupill as the silk is his sary lume' (96).)

To return to *The Merchant's Tale*: I quoted above in my discussion of Henryson the lines inviting us to imagine May's feelings at the sight of Januarie sitting up in bed once the marriage has been consummated:

> But God woot what that May thoughte in hir herte
> Whan she hym saugh up sittynge in his sherte . . .　　　　　(1851–2)

Dunbar's second wife comments similarly on her response to the deceptive outward vigour of that 'right lusty schadow' (191), her husband: 'Bot God wait quhat I think quhen he so thra spekis . . . '

(195). In *The Merchant's Tale* the narrator goes on to fill in the gap left
for May's feelings, in case we are unable to do so ourselves – 'She
preyseth nat his pleyyng worth a bene' (1854) – and Dunbar's first
wife uses the same phrase to convey her old husband's incapacity: he
'may nought beit worth a bene in bed of my mystirs' (128). Finally,
one of the most destructive of *The Merchant's Tale*'s assaults on
courtly values lies in its ironic application of the fundamental
doctrine of courtliness, that *gentillesse* shows itself in ready compassion, to May's readiness to allow herself to be seduced by her
husband's squire: 'Lo, pitee renneth soone in gentil herte!' (1986).
Precisely the same application is made of this doctrine by Dunbar's
widow in explaining her willingness to marry her second husband,
who was of low birth but 'myghti of gudis' (296):

> That page wes nevir of sic price for to presome anys
> Unto my persone to be peir, had pete nought grantit.
> Bot mercy in to womanheid is a mekle vertu,
> For nevir bot in a gentill hert is generit ony ruth.　　　　(313–16)

In order that courtly idealism may be effectively crushed, it must
first be expressed in such a way as to be momentarily convincing.
The destructive irony of the *Tretis*, like that of *The Merchant's Tale*, is
ultimately directed not against the characters within the fiction but
against the narrator himself, who is the foolish victim of such
momentary conviction. Thus in turn the irony attacks the audience –
the 'auditors most honorable' to whom Dunbar addresses his con-
temptuous *demande d'amour* at the end of the poem – who have been
taken in by their foolish or malicious guide. In *The Merchant's Tale*
the belief in idealism about woman and marriage is assigned to the
past, through the characterization of the Merchant as narrator. He
was once taken in, but now, though too late, his eyes (unlike
Januarie's) have been opened, and he gets his revenge on life by
allowing us to be taken in. In the *Tretis*, however, more horrifyingly, this belief belongs equally to the present and to the future. The
fundamental movement of the poem is a recurrent exposure of what
is secret, so as to reveal the fatuousness of the deceptions by which it
has been concealed, but now no end to this process can be envisaged,
because the concealment is seen as being rooted in a biologically
grounded *self*-deception by men about women.

The *Tretis* begins, then, in an idealizing mode, with the description of a *locus amoenus*, an enclosed garden surrounded by the
beauties of nature, and containing three ladies, dressed with sump-

tuous elegance, garlanded with flowers and themselves compared to flowers:

> All full of flurist fairheid, as flouris in June,
> Quhyt, seimlie, and soft, as the sweit lillies
> Now upspred upon spray, as new spynist rose.   (27–9)

It seems a *hortus conclusus* of idealizing fiction, like the dream-world of *The Thrissill and the Rois*; and fiction it rapidly proves to be, as these 'sweit lillies' disclose their true nature as 'wyld weid[s], full of churlichenes' (*The Thrissill and the Rois* 139). But from the very beginning, the position of the narrator strikes a discordant note; he is a solitary male voyeur, hiding furtively to conceal his eagerness to see and hear what women say when they are by themselves. It seems likely that his solitariness and his confinement to the role of spectator where women are concerned should be related to Dunbar's real-life status as a priestly celibate, obsessed by what is forbidden to him. What he hears is what women 'really' think about men and about marriage, and what this in turn discloses about women themselves: behind their flower-like courtly exterior is concealed a bestial insatiability of appetite. It ought to be enough to shrivel any male auditor's self-esteem to nothing, and to put him off women for life; but this narrator seems quite unaffected by it, and as fatuously given to idealization of women at the end as he was at the beginning.

Without attempting an analysis of the whole poem, I can illustrate the extreme form of what it has to say about the relations between men and women by considering the widow's account of her second marriage. Her second husband, as we have seen, was wealthy but (according to her) short, middle-aged, and below her in social rank. The story she tells is not strictly chronological and must be reconstructed from the fragments she supplies. Before they were married, she showed him goodwill (323–4), evidently for the sake of his wealth; afterwards, nothing but hostility. She constantly reminded him of his inferiority to her, claiming that it was only out of *pete, mercy, ruth*, and *grace* (314–17) that she accepted him – an interesting example of how courtly doctrine might be used as a weapon even after marriage. She taunted him with the unaristocratic means by which he acquired the wealth for which she married him, calling him pedlar (302) and shopkeeper (309). The more she domineered over him, the more he cringed:

> He durst not sit anys my summondis, for, or the secund charge,
> He wes ay redy for to ryn, so rad he wes for blame.   (319–20)

And yet, 'the mair he loutit for my luf, the les of him I rakit' (322). Since he lacked the charms that would make him a 'glaidsum gest for a gay lady' (359), she used him in the more appropriate role of banker, and he 'thoght my favoris to fynd through his feill giftis' (364). He gave her fine clothes, but instead of wearing them she saved them to make herself attractive for his successor. Indeed, while he was ruining himself to make her splendid, she cuckolded him, so that the result of his generosity was to make 'a stalwart staff to strik him selfe doune' (384). She refused sexual relations with him for a whole year, and when she finally let him have his way,

> Alse lang as he wes one loft, I lukit one him nevir,
> Na leit nevir enter in my thoght that he my thing persit,
> Bot ay in mynd ane othir man ymagynit that I haid.   (388–90)

The shamefully intimate detail, showing how she managed to commit adultery in mind even on the rare occasions when she was not doing so in body, is precisely what a woman might be supposed to reveal to another woman, but never to a man.

The degrading of the widow's second husband goes further yet. In gaining the mastery, she brings about a reversal of the orthodox sexual roles: 'I crew abone that craudone, as cok that wer victour' (326). His submission made him despicable to her –

> For as a best I broddit him to ally boyis laubour:
> I wald haif ridden him to Rome with raip in his heid,
> Wer not ruffill of my renoune and rumour of pepill   (330–2)

– yet at first she usually managed to conceal her hatred with feigning. But once she had managed to gain control of his property (as May did of Januarie's in *The Merchant's Tale*) and he was entirely at her mercy, there was no reason for further concealment. No longer was the husband in control of the wife as the rider of a steed; on the contrary, she feminized her husband, and urged her female friends to take note how she had transformed her restive stallion into an obedient cart-horse. The passage is worth quoting at some length:

> Bot quhen my billis and my bauchlis wes all braid selit
> I wald na langar beir on bridill, bot braid up my heid;
> Thar myght na molet mak me moy na hald my mouth in;
> I gert the renyeis rak and rif in to sondir;
> I maid that wif carll to werk all womenis werkis
> And laid all manly materis and mensk in this eird.
> Than said I to my cummaris in counsall about:
> 'Se how I cabeld yone cout with a kene brydill –
> The cappill that the crelis kest in the caf mydding

221

Sa curtasly the cart drawis and kennis na plungeing
He is nought skeich na yit sker na scippis nought one syd'.
And thus the scorne and the scaith scapit he nothir.   (347–58)

(But when my letters and documents were fully sealed, I would no longer endure
the bridle, but tossed up my head; no bit could make me submissive or control
my mouth; I forced the reins to stretch till they broke apart; I made that
effeminate fellow perform all women's tasks and set aside completely all
masculine affairs and honour. Then I said secretly to my gossips here and there,
'See how I brought that colt under control with a harsh bridle – the horse that
threw its baskets into the chaff midden-heap now pulls the cart so humbly,
without thought of plunging, it is not spirited or restive, and does not spring
aside.' And thus he did not escape either scorn or harm.)

The themes of this section can be paralleled elsewhere in medieval
literature and art,[72] but it is worth noting that they also belong to a
certain type of modern pornography, in which the superiority of the
female sex is asserted by devices such as the enforced feminization of
men and the harnessing of men as horses.[73] Such fictions seem likely
to appeal to masochistic men rather than to women; and it is surely
the case that the horrific story the widow tells is more an uncovering
of the perverse sexual fantasies of men than of any 'truth' about
women that might be supposed to be hidden behind the façade of
courtliness. The *Tretis* repeatedly exposes what is secret. The second
wife will not answer the widow's questions till she is assured that the
other women will not repeat what she says, and she takes it for
granted that 'ther is no spy neir' (161); and again the widow sets out
with rhetorical formality the contrast between what she seems and
what she is, between her sober weeds and the mind and body they
conceal:

I weip as I were woful, but wel is me for evir;
I busk as I wer bailfull, bot blith is my hert;
My mouth it makis murnyng, and my mynd lauchis;
My clokis thai ar caerfull in colour of sabill,
Bot courtly and ryght curyous my corse is ther undir.   (415–19)

Feminine honour itself is no more than the concealment of licen-
tiousness, and the characteristic feminine accomplishment is feigning: 'Fy one hir that can nought feyne her fame for to saif!' (461). But
what is ultimately revealed in this repeated exposure is a nasty truth
about men – or at least about the poem's representative masculine
consciousness, the narrator-poet.

The widow's second husband is deprived by her of material
possessions and male sexuality; and her parallel description of both

acts as forms of emasculation – 'Quhen I that grome geldit had of gudis and of natur' (392) – shows a penetrating insight into the economic basis of orthodox ideas about marital relations. The narrator, however, is emasculated from the beginning. He is no participant but only a voyeur, and what he sees and hears is an unmasking of the false idealization of women and at the same time a revelation of his own fantasies about women – the fantasies of a celibate cleric, which are equally likely to be false. The first wife, already making the connection between sex and money, has said of her husband,

> And thoght his pene purly me payis in bed,
> His purse pays richely in recompense efter.   (135–6)[74]

At the end of the poem the poet tells us that he 'with my pene did report ther pastance most mery' (526). For him, appropriately enough for one whose profession combines literacy with celibacy, one kind of pen is a substitute for another. But finally, whatever his writing reveals, about women or about men, it seems to leave the narrator quite unchanged. The women's conversation lasts all night, and then dawn comes, with a resumption of the idyllicism of the opening. Perhaps the narrator was a little disturbed by what he overheard, but if so it is quickly forgotten:

> The soft sowch of the swyr and soune of the stremys,
> The sueit savour of the sward, singing of foulis,
> Myght confort ony creatur of the kyn of Adam,
> And kindill agane his curage, thoght it wer cald sloknyt.   (519–22)

When one reflects on this cheerful ending, it comes to seem one of the most depressing things in the poem. As was implied by *This Warld Unstabille*, human sorrow and joy follow each other as automatically as midnight and morrow, and may indeed be no more than products of the succession of times and seasons.[75] The night may have brought an experience gruesome enough to quench any man's *curage* (and we have to remember that *curage* means not just 'spirits' in general but more specifically sexual desire and potency[76]); but morning comes, the birds sing, and 'the kyn of Adam' are mechanically restored to their former state of aspiring rampancy. It is precisely that irrational *curage* of men that makes them project false images on to women and that enables women to gain the mastery over men; and the *Tretis* holds out no hope at all that this situation will ever change. It is as true of the narrator of the *Tretis* as of Januarie in *The Merchant's Tale* that, while outwardly his eyes may have been opened, he remains as complacently blind within as ever.

6 · Skelton and Hawes

We now return to England to consider the work of two poets also closely associated with the Chaucerian tradition, in its final harvest or waning in the early Tudor period. John Skelton and Stephen Hawes were as closely connected with the early Tudor court as William Dunbar with that of James IV of Scotland, though, like him, they were no more than two among 'mony servitouris / And officiaris of divers curis' of monarchs who showed no great enthusiasm for Renaissance claims for the value of poetry. Little is known of the life of Hawes. Born of a Suffolk family, perhaps in the 1470s or 1480s, he may have been educated at Oxford. By 1503 he was Groom of the Chamber to Henry VII, and in 1506 he was paid ten shillings 'for a ballett that he gave to the kinges grace' – an unusually early example of royal reward for what was presumably a vernacular love poem.[1] He is said by Anthony à Wood to have been able to 'repeat by heart most of our English poets; esp. Jo. Lydgate, a monk of Bury, whom he made equal, in some respects, with Geff. Chaucer'. We may hope that there is some exaggeration in this statement, but Hawes is certainly the most Lydgatean of English Chaucerians. His surviving works include *The Pastime of Pleasure, The Example of Vertue*, and *The Conforte of Loveris*. He may have been the 'Stephen Hawys' who became rector of Withern in 1508 and who was dead by 1511.[2]

Far more information is available about Skelton, who justly achieved wider fame than Hawes as a poet and a scholar. He was born in the early 1460s, possibly of a Yorkshire family, and was educated first at Cambridge and then at Oxford, where about 1488 he was granted the title of 'laureate' – by now no more than a degree or diploma in rhetoric (but, as we shall see, taken by Skelton himself to retain its earlier, Petrarchan associations with publicly recognized inspiration). He was granted the same degree by Louvain University in 1492 and by Cambridge in 1493. His major poetic work of the 1490s was *The Bowge of Court* (1498), but he may also have written then an early version of *The Garland of Laurel*, a poem which was not published in its complete form until 1523. In 1488 Skelton entered the service of Henry VII, and from about 1496 to 1501 he was tutor to his second son, Prince Henry. In 1498 he became a priest. When Henry VII's elder son, Prince Arthur, died in 1502, Prince Henry, now heir to the throne, was given a new tutor, and Skelton was evidently given a golden handshake in the form of the rectorship of Diss in Norfolk. He lived mainly at Diss from 1503 to 1512, and his chief works while there were *Phyllyp Sparowe* and *Ware the Hauke*. In view of the fact that Hawes's appearances in court records coincide with Skelton's absence from them, it may be that the younger poet had temporarily 'supplanted' the older in royal favour.[3] Both wrote flattering poems on the coronation of Prince Henry as King Henry VIII in 1509; but at some time later than this (probably in 1513, after Hawes was dead) Skelton returned to court with the new title of *orator regius*. His enormously long morality play *Magnyfycence* dates from 1515–16, and in 1521–2 he wrote three satirical works directed against Henry VIII's chancellor, Cardinal Wolsey – *Speke Parott, Collyn Clout,* and *Why Come Ye Nat to Courte?* He lived in the precincts of Westminster Abbey, and at some stage he may have been obliged to protect himself against Wolsey's anger by taking sanctuary there. He was eventually reconciled with Wolsey, and lived long enough to write *A Replycacion* (1528) against the 'horryble heresy' (line 21) of Lutheranism. He died in 1529.

Most of this chapter will be concerned with Skelton, the greatest identifiable English poet to have been born in the fifteenth century; Hawes will appear mainly for comparison and contrast. Hawes is a poet of a relatively simple kind; Skelton's interest is partly a matter of the conflicting energies embodied in his work, which make it seem to belong at once to the Middle Ages and to the Renaissance. Even as this is said, it may be necessary to remind oneself that those two historical concepts would have had no meaning for him. He had read some works that would now be described as 'humanist', but he had not visited Italy, and he had if anything even less sense than Chaucer of a cultural rebirth. He must have been aware of living in troubled times, but we should not project into his work any formulation of a 'Tudor revolution in government', still less any ability to imagine England's religious future as Protestant. In most respects Skelton was attached to a past which he must have seen as natural and permanent, not as a stage in any process of necessary change. As a satirist, he sees himself as the Juvenal of his times, and this is his justification for taking on himself to attack Wolsey:

> Some men myght aske a question,
> By whose suggestyon
> I toke on hand this warke,
> Thus boldly for to barke?
> And men lyst to harke,
> And my wordes marke,
> I wyll answere lyke a clerke:
> For trewly and unfayned,
> I am forcebly constrayned
> At Juvynals request
> To wryght of this glorious gest,
> Of this vayne gloryous best,
> His fame to be encrest
> At every solempne feest
> *Quia difficile est*
> *Satiram non scribere.*[4]   (*Why Come Ye Nat* 1202–17)

To one who does ask this question, he adds, 'Blame Juvinall, and blame nat me.'[5] But his sense of the identity of his times with Juvenal's has evidently not had to overcome any perception of historical distance and difference.

1. Skelton and the medieval past

Most of Skelton's instincts seem to have been conservative and even reactionary. This is true of his social attitudes: he was deeply attached to the fixed social hierarchy of the Middle Ages, which was being undermined by the Tudor monarchy and its great servants, Wolsey and Thomas Cromwell. *The Garland of Laurel* indicates Skelton's devotion to the old aristocracy, in the person of the Countess of Surrey and her ladies, and his violent and persistent criticism of Wolsey is partly based on the humble origins from which the Cardinal rose to greatness. Wolsey began as the son of an Ipswich butcher, and now Skelton derides him as 'So bolde a braggyng bocher' and 'So fatte a magott, bred of a flesshe-flye' (*Speke Parott* 485, 609). Even when we allow for early Tudor assumptions about the naturalness of social gradation, and allow too for what must be seen as a general coarsening of English sensibility in this harsh and grasping period, Skelton's jeering tone stands out. Nowhere in his work do we find any notion that nobility might be detached from social rank, an idea which was so prominent in Chaucer's work and which can be found in Skelton's own time in the interlude *Fulgens and Lucres*. On the other hand, Skelton sees clearly enough how the traditional distinction between knight and clerk was precisely what made the nobility of his time vulnerable to the worldly learning of Wolsey:

> For lordes of noble bloode,
> Yf they well understode
> Howe connynge myght them avaunce,
> They wolde pype you another daunce.
> But noble men borne,
> To lerne they have scorne,
> But hunte and blowe an horne,
> Lepe over lakes and dykes,
> Set nothyng by polytykes.
> Therefore ye kepe them base,
> And mocke them to theyr face.   (*Collyn Clout* 615–25)

How could lords resist that mockery except by acquiring a 'connynge' that was no part of the traditional apparatus of chivalry?

More important for our purposes, Skelton was usually attached to the past in intellectual matters too. This may be illustrated from his attitudes in the so-called 'Grammarians' War' of 1519–21, a vociferous dispute about the best method of instructing boys in Latin. In it personal rivalries confused the intellectual issues, but broadly speaking the dispute was between those who assumed continuity with the medieval situation, in which Latin was a colloquially spoken, living and changing language, and who wished instruction to be based on colloquial phrases illustrative of grammatical rules, and their opponents, who took the 'Renaissance' view that post-classical developments in Latin were barbarous corruptions – 'rather . . . blotterature than literature,' as John Colet put it[6] – and who wished learning to take the form of literary imitation of great authors. Both parties can now be seen as participating in a reform of education which was dependent on the availability of printed texts and textbooks, and without which the Renaissance in England could not have reached the point of take-off; but the latter party was more clearly pointing to the literary future. It was the former that Skelton supported, and his position was evidently well known. One of its leaders saluted him in 1519 as a poet favoured by Apollo, while a leader of the innovators described him as 'neither learned nor a poet'.[7] In *Speke Parott* Skelton deplores an excessive concern for the 'eloquens' of literary imitation, while the substance of what should be learnt is disregarded:

> Plautus in his comedies a chyld shall now reherse,
> And medyll with Quintylyan in his *Declamacyons*,
> That *Pety Caton* can scantly construe a verse,
> With '*Aveto*' in *Greco* and such solempne salutacyons,
> Can skantly the tensis of his conjugacyons;
> Settyng theyr myndys so moche of eloquens,
> That of theyr scole maters lost is the hole sentens.   (176–82)

Skelton would probably have agreed with C. S. Lewis: 'The war between the humanists and the schoolmen was not a war between ideas: it was, on the humanists' side, a war against ideas. It is a manifestation of the humanistic tendency to make eloquence the sole test of learning.'[8] As these lines indicate, Skelton was also opposed to the introduction of Greek into the school and university curriculum, which was beginning in his time with Wolsey's active support. This second wave of the Renaissance revival of classical antiquity was to lead to a far fuller and more discriminating grasp of ancient civilization, but Skelton's fear was that it involved a separation of learning from everyday life:

> But our Grekis theyr Greke so well have applyed
> That they cannot say in Greke, rydynge by the way,
> 'How, hosteler, fetche my hors a botell of hay!'
> *(Speke Parott 145–7)*

In the longest run, Skelton was right: once the excited imaginative response to antiquity was formalized as the academic subject 'Classics', it was bound to become a specialist preserve and to die for all but the few.[9] We cannot rightly credit him with seeing centuries into the future, but it would be wrong to think his objections merely stupid or eccentric.

An associated innovation that Skelton opposed was retranslation of the Bible. For him, no doubt, the Vulgate was part of a seamless web of Latin culture, as wide as Western Christendom itself, but the new Greek learning was calling that too in question, and making it possible, as it seemed, to return to the true light of God's word behind the darkness of medieval corruption. In 1516 Erasmus published his *Novum instrumentum*, a version of the Greek New Testament with a new Latin translation. It was criticized by conservative English ecclesiastics, and has been described by a modern authority as 'mostly no better than the Vulgate, which he sometimes altered without sufficient reason'.[10] It must have been with Erasmus's work in mind that Skelton wrote,

> For ye scrape out good scrypture, and set in a gall:
> Ye go about to amende, and ye mare all.   (*Speke Parott* 153–4)

Erasmus, of course, was and remained a Catholic, but he was unknowingly making straight the way for Luther, who did indeed mar all so far as the unity of Christendom was concerned.

One last example of Skelton's resistance to new tendencies may be mentioned, this time in the artistic sphere; and it is associated, as so often, with Wolsey, whom he saw for many years as the embodiment of all that was most hateful and menacing in his age. In *Collyn Clout* he attacks the luxurious dwellings of modern ecclesiastics, impiously Babel-like in their aspirations –

> With turrettes and with towres,
> With halles and with boures,
> Stretchynge to the sterres.   (936–8)

He is undoubtedly glancing at Wolsey's splendid palaces of York Place and Hampton Court; and he goes on to comment on the inappropriateness of their tapestries decorated with mythological scenes in the Renaissance manner:

> With Dame Dyana naked;
> Howe lusty Venus quaked,
> And how Cupyde shaked
> His dart, and bent his bowe,   (944–7)

and with 'tryumphes' (956) showing

> Naked boyes strydynge,
> With wanton wenches wynkyng.   (967–8)

The tapestries Skelton describes have been convincingly identified with specific wall-hangings of Petrarch's *Trionfi* owned by Wolsey, some of which still survive; and Skelton's contempt for the Renaissance delight in the nude body and the world of the senses is clear. Well over a century earlier, in *The Parliament of Fowls*, Chaucer (as usual with Boccaccio's help) had conveyed something of the amoral sensuousness of classical paganism; Skelton's attitude is more, not less, medieval than Chaucer's. Almost nowhere in Skelton's work do we find any attempt at, or sympathy with, the imaginative reconstruction of pagan antiquity. Whatever was going on around him, he seems in all these ways thoroughly, and indeed combatively, a man of the medieval world.

In view of what *was* going on around him, this means that much of his most vigorous writing takes the form of satire, and especially of political satire. We may find this un-Chaucerian form at its most un-Chaucerian in *Collyn Clout*, a poem of the early 1520s in some 1265 of those short, irregularly rhyming lines known as 'Skeltonics'. The English tradition to which it belongs is not that of Chaucer and his followers so much as that of *Piers Plowman*; and here it may be helpful to look back for a moment. The contrast between Chaucer and Langland suggests a further reason why Chaucer's influence on his English followers, though so powerful, was in some ways so unfruitful. As we have seen, the works of Chaucer that the fifteenth-century poets most imitated were those such as the three classical romances – poems that focus on love and philosophy, private experience and the cosmic order, with the intermediate level between those extremes, that of politics, having comparatively small importance. It is notorious that Chaucer's work contains very little overt reference to contemporary political events, and Chaucer himself, if not exactly a fourteenth-century Vicar of Bray, was certainly a skilful survivor in a dangerous age, and one who apparently found no difficulty, at the very end of his life, in transferring his allegiance (and with it his pension) from Richard II to his usurper Henry IV. To say this is not to imply that Chaucer lacked principle, nor is it to criticize a poet who did so much for failing to do everything; but the English fifteenth century, with its great political upheavals, may be thought to have needed a literary model with a political dimension, and that was not to be found in Chaucer. There is no telling, of course, what the fifteenth century might have made of a more political Chaucer; but at any rate a political satire such as *Collyn Clout* was almost bound to rely on different models. *Collyn Clout* is un-Chaucerian in almost every way but one (which I shall discuss later), its use of a dramatic persona – and the persona Skelton adopts is itself quite different from any of Chaucer's. He explains at the beginning that

> . . . yf ye stande in doute
> Who brought this ryme aboute,
> My name is Collyn Cloute. (47–9)

Collyn Clout is the common man desirous of good and truth, a more passive version of that Piers the ploughman who first enters Langland's poem as God's loyal servant. His voice is that of the common people, repeating without apparent art the substance of what is commonly said throughout the land – the recorder of proverbs, catchphrases, graffiti. He apologizes indeed for his lack of artistic skill:

> For though my ryme be ragged,
> Tattered and jagged,
> Rudely rayne-beaten,
> Rusty and moth-eaten,
> Yf ye take well therwith
> It hath in it some pyth.   (53–8)

In the last chapter we saw Dunbar, in his poem *To the King* (Kinsley 44), alluding to the Sermon on the Mount to claim that his work was comparable to those treasures laid up in heaven 'where neither the rust nor moth doth consume'. Collyn's attitude towards his art is the very opposite: his rhyme is at best an earthly treasure, 'Rusty and moth-eaten'. But Collyn Clout is not Skelton, and the raggedness of his rhyme is carefully calculated; even its improvisatory breathlessness is deliberately created and skilfully exploited.

Like many of Skelton's poems in Skeltonics, *Collyn Clout* appears to be, and perhaps is, only loosely structured. It has a decisive beginning and a moving end, in which the gap between Collyn and Skelton is closed and the extended image of the poet's life and poem as a ship carries us away from the stormy seas of earthly life to the heavenly remedy for all that is 'amys' in England:

> Nowe to withdrawe my pen,
> And now a whyle to rest,
> Me semeth it for the best.
> The forecastell of my shyppe
> Shall glyde and smothely slyppe
> Out of the wawes wodde
> Of the stormy flodde,
> Shote anker, and lye at rode,
> And sayle nat farre abrode,
> Tyll the coost be clere
> That the lodesterre appere.
> My shyp nowe wyll I stere
> Towarde the porte salue
> Of our Savyoure Jesu,
> Suche grace that he us sende
> To rectyfye and amende
> Thynges that are amys,
> Whan that his pleasure is.   (1248–65)

The traditional nature of this cluster of images – the poetic enterprise as a ship, life in Fortune's realm as a dangerous sea, Christ as lodestar and safe harbour – helps to create the feeling of a safe resting-place. But between the two fixed points of beginning and end the poem moves somewhat randomly from one object of satire to another. Amidst the general diffuseness, again and again some specific situation comes suddenly into sharp focus, and it is at such moments that one is most strongly reminded of *Piers Plowman*. For example, when Skelton turns to 'Relygyous men' (374) and 'sely nonnes' (389) and how – so 'The lay fee people rayles' (401) – they are forsaking the cloistered life, he recalls the dissolution of minor nunneries which had recently taken place under Wolsey's auspices (a sinister anticipation, as it now seems, of the greater dissolution that was to be carried out a decade later, after both Skelton and Wolsey were dead). The results of political greed are presented with bare concreteness:

> No matyns at mydnyght,
> Boke and chalys gone quyte;
> Plucke away the leedes
> Over theyr heedes,
> And sell away theyr belles,
> And all that they have elles.
>
> So that theyr founders soules
> Have lost theyr bedde roules;
> The money for theyr masses
> Spent among wanton lasses;
> Theyr dyriges are forgotten,
> Theyr founders lye there rotten.   (406–11, 421–6)

The unflinching statement of actual consequences is reminiscent of Langland's denunciation of 'religious that han no routhe though hit reyne on hir auters' (B X 310); only in the harsher age of the early Tudors it is not individual dereliction but official policy that corrupts monastic ideals and deprives the souls of pious benefactors of the comfort of the prayers of the living.

Skelton makes his points most powerfully by laying two contrasting realities alongside each other – precisely the characteristic method of the alliterative poets – as in a passage shortly after this that juxtaposes Christ's sufferings with the luxurious lives, 'Drowned *in deliciis*' (442), of the prelates who in theory bear his person:

> Yet swete meate hath soure sauce,
> For after *gloria, laus*,
> Chryst by cruelte
> Was nayled upon a tre;

> He payed a bitter pencyon
> For mans redempcyon,
> He dranke eysell and gall
> To redeme us with all,
> But swete ypocras ye drynke.   (448–56)

These lines work through a series of contrasts, stated or implied: sweet meat against sour sauce; the *gloria, laus* of Christ's entry into Jerusalem against the pain and humiliation of his crucifixion; the rich payments received by prelates against Christ's 'bitter pencyon' of suffering; the vinegar and gall he was given to drink on the cross against the sweet wines on which those nominally dedicated to imitating his life glut themselves. The contrast is rammed home in the last line quoted with a pun on *ypocras* (spiced wine) and hypocrisy, and Collyn goes on to hint that after the 'swete meate' of their earthly lives the prelates will have to swallow the 'soure sauce' of a 'penalte / For your iniquite' (461–2) – perhaps an earthly fall such as Wolsey's, perhaps God's wrath in the life to come.

It will be enough to bring forward one more example of the way in which Skelton uses concrete detail to give edge to a satiric point. He sees Wolsey as having risen on the wheel of Fortune to a position above that of his superiors by birth, and he has Collyn address Wolsey thus:

> To you that over the whele
> Lordes must crouche and knele,
> And breke theyr hose at the kne,
> As dayly men may se,
> And to remembraunce call;
> Fortune so tourneth the ball
> And ruleth so over all
> That honoure hath a great fall.   (627–34)

Fortune's wheel is to those lords an instrument of torture on which they are broken, their fawning postures as distorted as that of a tortured body. They kneel so eagerly and so low that they 'breke theyr hose at the kne', and thus look like the abject beggars that they have in fact become. Meanwhile, disregarded by the Cardinal, Fortune's wheel inexorably turns the whole globe, and will eventually make him a beggar too. So indeed it did.

I have examined *Collyn Clout* sufficiently to illustrate one side of Skelton's achievement – the side of him which is furthest from Chaucer and most strongly attached to the medieval past. It is an important aspect of his work, which might be represented equally well by *Why Come Ye Nat to Courte?* or by flytings such as *Agaynst the Scottes* or *Agenst Garnesche*, or by most of *A Replycacion*. But Skelton is also a genuinely Chaucerian poet – one who understood central elements of Chaucer's achievement far better than imitators such as Lydgate, and who learned from Chaucer not just to imitate but to develop what Chaucer had done. As we have seen, the Renaissance elements in Chaucer do not feed into an English poetic Renaissance: English culture in general was not at a stage at which that would have been possible, and Chaucer's individual imitators were not capable of going beyond their master's achievement. Skelton is the only English poet not subject to these limitations; unlike Lydgate, he wants something more than to *be* Chaucer, and, though his work is in most ways not at all like Chaucer's, it could not have been written but for what Chaucer had done. I want now to examine some of the ways in which Skelton used Chaucer's achievement as a springboard for his own.

2. Skelton and Chaucer

Chaucer began writing in the 1360s in a tradition well established in French poetry – a courtly tradition in which it was taken for granted that the courtier was a lover and that the essential subject of poetry was an idealizing form of love. Within the mythology of this tradition, the lover was the servant of Cupid, and the poet, if not himself a lover, was the servant of Cupid's servants, whose supreme task was to praise noble ladies as the inspirers of intense yet refined feelings in their lovers. This is the role ostensibly adopted by Chaucer in *Troilus and Criseyde*, as 'I, that God of Loves servantz serve' (I 15); it is his role in the dream-poems in which dreams bring to the poet who lacks personal experience of love 'mater of to wryte' (*The Parliament of Fowls* 168) in the form of 'tydynges / Of Loves folk' (*The House of Fame* 644–5). Near the end of *Troilus and Criseyde* Chaucer apologizes to 'every lady bright of hewe / And every gentil womman' (v 1772–3) for having written of a lady who did not prove a worthy object of love, and in the *Prologue* to *The Legend of Good Women* he is rebuked by Cupid himself for having written the *Troilus* and 'translated the Romauns of the Rose' (G 255), works which question the courtly ideology and thus constitute a heresy against the religion of love. Yet from the very beginning Chaucer had set scepticism alongside idealization, so that even in *The Book of the*

Duchess, a poem that as a whole unquestionably endorses the courtly outlook, he suggests at one point a relativizing limit to the Black Knight's worship of his lady:

> I leve yow wel, that trewely
> *Yow thoghte* that she was the beste,
> And to beholde the alderfayreste,
> *Whoso had loked hir with your eyen.*　　　　(1048–51)

More important, Chaucer aims to set the idealizing love of the courtly tradition in larger, philosophical and religious contexts – the context of the natural order, of 'commune profyt' (*The Parliament of Fowls* 47), and of the love of

> hym, the which that right for love,
> Upon a crois, oure soules for to beye,
> First starf, and roos, and sit in hevene above.　　(*Troilus* v 1842–4)

Though Chaucer was deeply immersed in the courtly tradition, and benefited greatly from it, he had also to struggle against it to gain his freedom to be a poet of more comprehensive scope than it encouraged. The same tradition retained its power for many years after Chaucer's death, offering a familiar role into which the poet could easily slip, with a fixed repertoire of gestures and conventions by means of which a gifted writer could still produce work of great interest – witness the poems of Charles of Orleans and of many anonymous fifteenth-century lyricists. Skelton as court poet was capable of writing within the same limits, as may be seen in idealizing lyrics such as 'Knoledge, aquayntaunce, resort, favour, with grace' (*Dyvers Balettys* iii) or 'Go, pytyous hart, rasyd with dedly wo' –

> One ther is, and ever one shalbe,
> For whose sake my hart is sore dyseasyd;
> For whose love, welcom dysease to me!
> 　　　　　　　　　　　　　(*Dyvers Balettys* v 8–10)

These are early poems; but similar idealization appears in later work too, for example in the second part of *Phyllyp Sparowe*, in the 'Commendacions' of that Jane Scrope whose lament for her dead bird makes up the poem's first part –

> The Indy saphyre blew
> Her vaynes doth ennew;
> The orient perle so clere,
> The whytnesse of her lere;
> The lusty ruby ruddes
> Resemble the rose buddes;

> Her lyppes soft and mery
> Emblomed lyke the chery,
> It were an hevenly blysse
> Her sugred mouth to kysse   (1031–40)

– or in the exquisite lyrics in praise of the Countess of Surrey and her ladies that are inserted into *The Garland of Laurel*:

> With margerain jentyll,
> The flowre of goodlyhede,
> Enbrowdred the mantill
> Is of your maydenhede.
>
> Plainly, I can not glose,
> Ye be, as I devyne,
> The praty primrose,
> The goodly columbyne.   (906–13)

Had Skelton always written thus, Cupid would have had no cause to rebuke *him* for heresy. Much of his work is concerned with other themes – moral, political, satirical – yet in ways that are compatible with courtliness. The flyting *Agenst Garnesche* is chiefly concerned to find ingenious ways of abusing its victim, a gentleman usher of Henry VIII, but it appropriately addresses 'ladies of bryght colour, / Of bewte that beryth the flower' (III 148–9) to warn them of the need to protect themselves against Garnesche's stinking breath. Other poems of Skelton's offer a reverse image of the idealization of women, as in 'Womanhod, wanton, ye want!' (*Agaynste a Comely Coystrowne* IV) or, at far greater length, in *Elynour Rummynge*:

> Her lothely lere
> Is nothynge clere,
> But ugly of chere,
> Droupy and drowsy,
> Scurvy and lowsy;
> Her face all bowsy,
> Comely crynklyd,
> Woundersly wrynklyd,
> Lyke a rost pygges eare,
> Brystled with here.   (12–21)

But at a deep level such compositions pay tribute to the idealization they reverse, assuming that the 'womanhod' the wanton lacks is the virtuous norm, and that a lady's countenance might be expected to be 'clere' rather than 'ugly'. In any case, there had always been room within the courtly tradition for direct parody or reversal, as may be

seen in Chaucer's 'Madame, ye ben of al beaute shryne' or Hoccleve's 'Of my lady wel me rejoise I may.'

What was not acceptable to the God of Love, as Chaucer well
knew, was the ambiguity of Jean de Meun's *Roman de la Rose* or his
own *Troilus and Criseyde*, mingling idealizing love equivocally with
lust and deceptiveness. Just such ambiguity is to be found in Skelton's
Phyllyp Sparowe. The occasion, or purported occasion, of this poem
was the death of a pet sparrow belonging to Jane Scrope, a young
woman in her early twenties, the daughter of a noble family with
whom Skelton was friendly during his period at Diss. Jane lived as a
kind of boarder with the nuns of Carrow Abbey, near Norwich, and
Skelton's poem falls into two parts: the first spoken as if by Jane, in
the form of a burlesque application of the funeral service to the dead
bird, the second spoken by the poet in praise of Jane, in the form of a
burlesque of a private devotion called the Commendation of All
Souls.[11] The basic idea of an elegy on a girl's dead sparrow comes
from a poem by Catullus, and Skelton may also have made use of
other sources, classical and contemporary Burgundian. Catullus's
'Lugete, O Veneres Cupidinesque' is a miniature of only eighteen
lines; Skelton has achieved a triumph of early Tudor amplification
by expanding it in his version to nearly fourteen hundred lines of
Skeltonics, yet it still conveys a small-scale effect. In *Phyllyp Sparowe*
the themes of serious medieval poetry about death are prettily
miniaturized. Jane's voice has a naive vehemence, a childlike
emotionalism that justifies the mock-heroic and mock-devotional
treatment of a trivial incident. One of the most original aspects of the
poem, and one that would doubtless have made it displeasing to the
Cupid of courtly mythology, is precisely its equivocality. From
Catullus – read surely with deeper understanding than by any earlier
English poet – Skelton takes an erotic suggestiveness in the intimacy
and freedom of the bird's relationship with its mistress, and his poem
becomes an exploration of the shadowy no man's land of feeling
bordered by the pious, the avuncular, and the sexual:

> For it wold come and go,
> And fly so to and fro;
> And on me it wolde lepe
> Whan I was aslepe,
> And his fethers shake,
> Wherewith he wolde make
> Me often for to wake
> And for to take him in

> Upon my naked skyn.
> Got wot, we thought no syn –
> What though he crept so lowe?
> It was no hurt, I trowe.
> He dyd nothynge, perde,
> But syt upon my kne. (159–72)

In the second part of *Phyllyp Sparowe* Skelton displays himself worshipping Jane with the Latin phrases that would appropriately be applied to the Blessed Virgin:

> *Hac claritate gemina*
> *O gloriosa femina,*
> *Memor esto verbi tui servo tuo!*
> *Servus tuus sum ego.* (1027–30)

Such a strategy might seem admirably in keeping with the religion of love; but Skelton shows himself at the same time eagerly and lasciviously imagining those parts of Jane and her apparel to which he does not have access, though the sparrow did:

> Wherto shuld I disclose
> The garterynge of her hose?
> It is for to suppose
> How that she can were
> Gorgiously her gere. (1175–9)

Looking back now over the first part of the poem from this second part, we seem to recognize in it a *Lolita*-like prurience in his imaginative construction of Jane's innocence – a prurience of which the real Skelton is of course perfectly aware, however indignantly the 'Skelton' of the poem may deny it in the cause of freedom of 'mery thought':

> Her kyrtell so goodly lased,
> And under that is brased
> Such pleasures that I may
> Neyther wryte nor say;
> Yet though I wryte not with ynke,
> No man can let me thynke,
> For thought hath lyberte,
> Thought is franke and fre;
> To thynke a mery thought
> It cost me lytell nor nought. (1194–1203)

This may be the first poem in English to give direct expression to underwear-fetishism: Chaucer in *The Miller's Tale* had *implied* naughty thoughts about what might be underneath the delicious

238

Alisoun's elaborate clothing, but Skelton makes the thoughts much more explicit.

I have, I hope, done enough to show how effectively Skelton, like Chaucer though in a different way, struggles against the limits set by courtly idealization. And he was perfectly aware of what was at stake. In *The Garland of Laurel* he dreams that Dame Pallas commands the Queen of Fame to have his name registered in her court, but the Queen objects on the grounds that he is 'wonder slake' (69),

> And wyll not endevour hymselfe to purchase
> The favour of ladys with wordis electe. (75–6)

The Queen is a descendant of the goddess Fame in Chaucer's *House of Fame*, but she is also ruler over a court not unlike that of Henry VII or Henry VIII, and she speaks for the courtly tradition in assuming that the poet's function must be to gain the favour of ladies by his words. Skelton is here making more explicit than ever Chaucer did the narrowness of courtly standards and the need for the true poet to subvert or transcend them.[12]

A second way in which Skelton moves on from Chaucer has to do with the role of the poetic 'I'. Though Chaucer perhaps never totally and systematically fictionalizes the narrators of his poems, even in *The Canterbury Tales*, his works certainly include many moments at which a narrator is identifiable as someone other than the poet Chaucer. We have seen how Lydgate failed to grasp this aspect of Chaucer's technique, so that, for example, he adopts as his own in *The Siege of Thebes* the nervously anti-pagan attitude that Chaucer attributed to the Franklin. Skelton on the contrary goes even further than Chaucer in the direction of a total dramatization of the speakers of his poems. He adopts a wide variety of different roles, each with its own distinctive attitudes and voice. Thus in the first part of *Phyllyp Sparowe*, as I mentioned above, he adopts the role of Jane Scrope – 'a mayde, / Tymerous, halfe afrayde' (607–8) – naively devoted to her pet and childishly grief-stricken at its death at the paws of 'Gyb, our cat savage' (375). This persona, like others, is not merely a piece of self-justifying 'characterization' but has specific uses. When attributed to Jane, a medieval poetic convention such as the encyclopaedic catalogue –

> The bitter with his bumpe,
> The crane with his trumpe,
> The swan of Menander,
> The gose and the gander,
> The ducke and the drake ... (432–6)

– becomes a childish chant, and is at once justified and defined as
unsophisticated. More important, literary judgments which are in
fact dangerously radical can be passed off under the guise of girlish
inexperience. Jane prefaces her simple Latin epitaph on Phyllyp with
a lengthy apology for her lack of literary skill,

> That never yet asayde
> Of Elyconys well,
> Where the muses dwell,   (609–11)

though, as she says, she has read a good many works in English. First
in the list of these, and discussed at considerable length, stands
Chaucer's *Canterbury Tales*; then come a whole host of romances, of
which *Troilus and Criseyde* is considered most fully. Chaucer's
pre-eminence is thus tacitly established. Next, after various Latin
and Greek authors whom she mentions only to say that they are too
difficult for her, are some comments on the trio of poets who had
come to stand for the English literary tradition, Gower, Chaucer,
and Lydgate. Here, masked by the *naïveté* of a young girl's view of
literature, are some shrewd discriminations. Chaucer is praised, not
for the stylistic elevation for which he was generally admired, but for
being 'plesaunt, esy and playne; / Ne worde he wrote in vayne'
(800–1). For a contemporary such as Stephen Hawes, Lydgate had
usurped the place of Chaucer as father and model: in *The Pastime of
Pleasure* he laments that

> Nothynge I am experte in poetry
> As the monke of Bury, floure of eloquence,   (26–7)[13]

yet aims

> To folowe the trace and all the parfytenesse
> Of my mayster Lydgate with due exercyse.   (47–8)

Jane, in a passage I quoted in part in chapter 5 to illustrate the
growing interest in conciseness, innocently reports other views of
the Monk of Bury:

> Also Johnn Lydgate
> Wryteth after an hyer rate;
> It is dyffuse to fynde
> The sentence of his mynde,
> Yet wryteth he in his kynd,
> No man that can amend
> Those maters that he hath pende;
> Yet some men fynde a faute,
> And say he wryteth to haute.   (804–12)

Her dutiful admiration has its limits ('in his kynd'), and conspicuously fails to conceal Skelton's perception of Lydgate's frequent obscurity and pomposity.

Similarly, in *Collyn Clout* the poem's 'I' is not Skelton but a
spokesman of the common people, and thus sharp and repeated
criticisms of the Church in general and Wolsey in particular can be
attributed to the people's ignorance and malice. In *The Bowge of
Court*, the speaker is a nervously ambitious courtier, who has no
more sense than to follow the crowd in their pursuit of the 'royall
marchaundyse' (41) of court favour:

> But than I thoughte I wolde not dwelle behynde:
> Amonge all other I put myselfe in prece. (43–4)

But he soon learns that he has entered a world beyond his power to
control or understand, and it emerges that his name is 'Drede' (77):
unusually in a medieval dream-poem, the dreamer has a name other
than the poet's own, and thus becomes one personification among
others in the allegorical drama. In this way Skelton is able to reveal
the truth about court life in terms not of secure moral doctrine but of
fearfully insecure experience. To take one last example, and that
perhaps the most striking of all, in *Speke Parott* the speaker identifies
himself in the very first line: 'My name ys Parott, a byrde of Paradyse
. . .' Parott is no more than a speaking bird, one who can be supposed
not to understand the fragments of various languages that he has
been taught to say. Thus Skelton goes one further than Chaucer had
done in the *Prologue* to *The Legend of Good Women*, where Alcestis
suggests on his behalf that he was a mere uncomprehending translator of the works that have angered the God of Love:

> Therfore he wrot the Rose and ek Crisseyde
> Of innocence, and nyste what he seyde. (G 344–5)

In this way any criticism of Wolsey that may be implied by Skelton's
poem can be explained as a mere product of chance – who can blame
a parrot for repeating what it hears? Yet at the same time Parott is 'a
byrde of Paradyse', and on another level speaks by divine inspiration. The choice of this equivocal persona was a stroke of genius on
Skelton's part, and I will examine in more detail later the use to
which he puts it. Meanwhile one general point to be made is this: we
should not take Skelton's recurrent creation of poetic personae as a
sign that an interest in individual psychology featured at all centrally

in the motivation of his work. Stanley Fish has claimed that 'the locus of a Skelton poem is the narrator's mind; and since the drama is internal, it will reveal itself to a reading which attends to the psychology of the speaker and proceeds from there to a consideration of scene, which moves, in short, from the internal to the external.'[14] It seems to me, though, that the structure of a Skelton poem is combinatory rather than organic, and that the persona is one means among others of bringing together the various elements of which it is made up. To think of Parott, above all, as possessing a unitary 'mind' or 'psychology' is to obscure Skelton's purpose.

A third way in which Skelton takes a Chaucerian development further has to do with that sense of poetic history that we saw emerging at the end of *Troilus and Criseyde*. Chaucer was the first to conceive of an English poetry that would look back to the classical achievement of 'Virgile, Ovide, Omer, Lucan and Stace', and that would continue to exist in the future. In *The Garland of Laurel* Skelton summons up a 'great nowmber ... / Of poetis laureat of many dyverse nacyons' (323–4) who follow Orpheus and Apollo in pursuit of fame. Apollo's laurel coronet is traced back to the laurel into which Daphne was transformed when he attempted to seize her, and he proclaims that

> ... in remembraunce of Daphnes transformacyon,
> All famous poetis ensuynge after me
> Shall were a garlande of the laurell tre. (320–2)

In Skelton's allegory the myth seems to imply ambiguously that poetry does indeed derive from love, as the courtly tradition assumes, but also that laureate poetry does not merely celebrate love but is the product of its frustration – the pearl into which the oyster transforms the painful grain of sand. Among the crowd following Orpheus and Apollo are all five of 'Virgile, Ovide, Omer, Lucan and Stace'; many other classical poets and orators; Boccaccio, Petrarch, and 'Poggeus also, that famous Florentine' (372), representing the Italian Renaissance; and the usual English trio bringing up the rear, 'Togeder in armes, as brethern, enbrasid' (393). Taken together, these 'poetis laureat' form an embodiment of the idea of 'alle poesye' – the single tradition of writing of lasting dignity and value, of which English poetry forms only one part. Skelton genially suggests that their inspiration comes not directly from Apollo (as Chaucer had requested in the proem to Book III of *The House of Fame*) but from

Bacchus, the god of wine: he repeats eight times as a refrain in
slightly varying forms,

> But blessed Bacchus, the pleasant god of wyne,
> Of closters engrosyd with his ruddy flotis
> These orators and poetes refreshed there throtis. (334–6)

Here, as occasionally elsewhere in *The Garland of Laurel*, there is a
touch of the spacious Mediterranean sensuousness that was to
receive fuller expression in the high Renaissance of English poetry
later in the sixteenth century, to culminate in the deliquescent
sensuality of Shakespeare's Antony:

> Come, let's all take hands,
> Till that the conquering wine hath steep'd our sense
> In soft and delicate Lethe. (*Antony and Cleopatra* II vii 106–8)

Skelton had suggested a connection between wine and poetic inspiration in his own case at the beginning of the *Garland*, in mentioning
'humors superflue, that often wyll crepe / Into the brayne by
drynkyng over depe' (31–2) as a possible cause of the dream which
frames his poem.

Chaucer's attitude towards this poetic tradition was one of
extreme modesty: he wished no more than that his 'litel bok' should
kiss the footsteps of his predecessors. Skelton, however, goes much
further. For him, the poetic tradition which he evokes so fully seems
to exist for his sake, rather than he for its. He notes complacently of
his English predecessors that 'Thei wantid nothynge but the laurell'
(397), and it eventually emerges that they have entered his dream
only in order to congratulate him and present him to the Queen of
Fame, so that he may receive the laurel crown they lack. The poem
becomes an immense list of his own works, amounting to an
irresistible claim to laureate status. Last of all in the list is 'the laurell'
(1503) – both the garland made for him by the Countess of Surrey
and her ladies and the present poem which recounts their making it.
Thus Skelton's poem celebrates itself and himself: now the anxiety
of Chaucerian influence is overcome, and the tradition of poetry
exists in order that Skelton may be its latest and most glorious
representative. In *The Garland of Laurel* Skelton makes explicit what
was obscurely implicit in Chaucer's response to Dante and to the
classical past: that the literary tradition is necessary for the poet in
order that it may constitute the role of poet for him to occupy.

The conception of poetry as inspired points to a last way in which

Skelton understands Chaucer and outdoes him. We have seen how in the *House of Fame* proems Chaucer toys somewhat uneasily with the notion of the poet as divinely inspired. The prologues to the five books of *Troilus and Criseyde* also invoke the aid of forces outside the writer himself, furies, gods, muses, fates – and now with greater confidence. But Chaucer's final work, *The Canterbury Tales*, seems to have abandoned such claims to inspiration, and it ends with a deeply medieval subordination of literary values to those of religion. Skelton, however, began his career with a revival of the invocation of the muse, and throughout a long succession of his works he recurrently asserted, with little sign of irony, that he was the spokesman of a higher power. His earliest dateable poem is an elegy 'Upon the dolorus dethe ... of the mooste honorable erle of Northumberlande' – Henry Percy, the fourth earl, slain by rebels against Henry VII in 1489. The second stanza strikingly revives Chaucer's apostrophic manner:

> Of hevenly poems, O Clyo, calde by name
> In the college of musis goddes hystoriall,
> Adres the to me, whiche am bothe halt and lame,
> In elect uteraunce to make memoryall!
> To the for succour, to the for helpe I kall,
> Myne homely rudnes and drighness to expelle
> With the freshe waters of Elyconys welle.   (8–14)

Like Chaucer in the prologue to Book II of *Troilus and Criseyde*, Skelton invokes Clio, the muse of history, and he does so in a way that combines medieval modesty with the Renaissance claim to participate in the sublime: Skelton needs the waters of Helicon to refresh his provincial roughness and dryness, and needs the aid of the muse precisely because in himself he is halt and lame in literary skills. Yet he demonstrates the opposite by his mastery of an 'artificial' style in this very stanza, of which the first two lines in particular have the phrases in an order as unnatural as that of Virgil's verse. Later in the poem, after a series of *exclamationes* familiar from Chaucerian rhetoric – O dolorous chance, O cruel Mars, O dolorous Tuesday, and so on – Skelton once more refers to the Muse, but now from a different point of view. *His* muse is 'homely' (144), and his pen 'enkankerd all with rust' (142), but even if he were 'Enbrethed with the blast of influence dyvyne' (157) by 'the hole quere of the Musis nyne' (155), even if he were assisted by the eloquence of 'laureat Phebus' (160), it would be all too little to match his great subject.

Here the figures associated with inspiration are used as a means of flattery; but inspiration evidently remains a real possibility.

Skelton himself associated laureation with inspiration, and it would appear that from about the time of 'Upon the dolorus dethe' onwards he was notorious for his exalted claims for his poetic vocation. As early as 1490 Caxton wrote of him in his preface to the *Eneydos*, 'I suppose he hath dronken of Elycon's well',[15] and later in the 1490s no less a figure than Erasmus wrote him a flattering poem, associating him with Apollo, the muses, and the Castalian springs, and describing him as England's Homer and Virgil.[16] Skelton himself went on claiming to be inspired in poem after poem, sometimes (it would seem) jokingly, sometimes with the utmost seriousness. In *Phyllyp Sparowe*, though Jane has 'never yet asayde / Of Elyconys well, / Where the muses dwell' (609–11), 'Skelton' seeks the 'grace dyvyne / Of the Muses nyne' (857–8) and the aid of Arethusa and Apollo (860, 863) in singing her praises. In *Agaynst the Scottes* he elaborately invokes Melpomene, the tragic muse, to help him recount the death of James IV of Scotland at Flodden, and at the same time Thalia, the comic muse, to make the English rejoice at the fall of their enemy; the outcome of this double inspiration will be 'A medley ... of myrth with sadnes' (87). In *Agenst Garnesche* he rebukes his opponent for taking upon him to write 'Agenst a poyet lawreat' (v 90), and proudly claims that, as Henry VIII's former tutor, he passed on something of his inspiration to the princely pupil:

> I yave hym drynke of the sugryd welle
> Of Eliconys waters crystallyne,
> Aqueintyng hym with the Musys nyne.   (v 98–100)

(It cannot be said that the King's recorded compositions, pleasant but conventionally courtly, bear any signs of this acquaintance with the muses.)

In *The Garland of Laurel* this exalted conception of poetry is celebrated not just in passing, and not just in connection with Skelton's own laureation, but in a vision of a heavenly garden, a 'Paradyce ... of syngular pleasure' (717); in it grows a laurel tree 'Enverdurid with levis contynually grene' (666), on which the phoenix sits, fanning a fire with her wings. The reminder that laurel is an evergreen, and still more the figure of the phoenix, are allegorical statements of the everlastingness of poetry itself. Round the tree dance 'the nyne Muses, Pierides by name' (680), accompanied by Dryads and pastoral figures. 'Cintheus' (687) (i.e. Apollo) plays his harp, and Iopas delivers his 'poemis and storis auncient' (689). Iopas is the Carthaginian poet who sings before Aeneas at the court of Dido in Book 1 of the *Aeneid*; but the theme of his song is not love, as might be expected in the circumstances, but the origin and nature of the cosmic order:

> Of Athlas astrology, and many noble thyngis,
> Of wandryng of the mone, the course of the sun,
> Of men and of bestis, and whereof they begone,
>
> What thynge occasionyd the showris of rayne,
> Of fyre elementar in his supreme spere,
> And of that pole artike whiche doth remayne
> Behynde the taile of Ursa so clere;
> Of Pliades he prechid with ther drowsy chere,
> Immoysturid with mislyng and ay droppyng dry,
> And where the two Trions a man shold aspy,
>
> And of the winter days that hy them so fast,
> And of the wynter nyghtes that tary so longe,
> And of the somer days so longe that doth last,
> And of their shorte nyghtes; he browght in his songe
> How wronge was no ryght, and ryght was no wronge. (690–704)

It is Skelton who has added to Virgil the final line, which identifies moral with cosmic order. Iopas is the poet not just as courtly entertainer, but as inspired *vates*, privileged to disclose to men the fundamental truths of heaven and earth. Nowhere else in his work does Skelton offer so noble an image of what poetry might be; but in his latest dateable work, *A Replycacion*, attacking two Lutheran heretics, he makes his most extreme claim to personal inspiration as a laureate poet. 'Why fall ye at debate', he contemptuously asks them,

> With Skelton laureate,
> Reputyng hym unable
> To gainsay replycable
> Opinyons detestable
> Of heresy execrable?
> Ye saye that poetry
> Maye nat flye so hye ... (300–6)

But, he reminds them, King David is described by St Jerome as 'Poete of poetes all, / And prophete princypall' (321–2), and so there is no excuse for saying that 'poetes do but fayne' (353). Skelton goes on that, if they read 'the Boke / Of Good Advertysement' (360–1) (one of his own lost works),

With me ye must consent
And infallibly agre
Of necessyte,
Howe there is a spyrituall
And a mysteriall
And a mysticall
Effecte energiall,
As Grekes do it call,
Of suche an industry
And suche a pregnacy,
Of hevenly inspyracion
In laureate creacyon,
Of poetes commendacion,
That of divyne myseracion
God maketh his habytacion
In poetes whiche excelles,
And sojourns with them and dwelles;
By whose inflammacion
Of spyrituall instygacion
And divyne inspyracion
We are kyndled in suche facyon
With hete of the Holy Gost,
Which is God of myghtes most,
That he our penne dothe lede.   (362–85)

It would be hard to imagine a more comprehensive claim to divine inspiration. Latin sidenotes refer both to Ovid and to the Psalms; and it is clear that here Skelton has fused classical ideas of inspiration with those that belong to the Christian tradition. For the priest or preacher, inspiration by the Holy Ghost was no mere metaphor; it held a place, in the most literal sense, in the medieval art of preaching, the *ars praedicandi*, and it may well have been that in this transitional period ideas of the poetic sublime could most readily be absorbed by secular poets who were also in holy orders, such as William Dunbar and Gavin Douglas, as well as Skelton himself. Skelton, at any rate, is the first English poet to appropriate to his own practice the theory of poetic inspiration that was expounded by Boccaccio in his *De genealogia deorum gentilium*.

3. Medieval to Renaissance in allegory

It will be recalled that one part of Boccaccio's claim for poetry was that great poets 'veil the truth with fiction' and that their work thus requires an effort of interpretation to disclose a meaning which is not expressed literally.[17] The interpretation of poetic fiction as allegory is a central feature of Renaissance thought about poetry. It was by no means new with the fourteenth-century Italian humanists; Homer had been interpreted allegorically as early as the sixth century B.C., and it was a long-standing belief that the obscurity of some places in Scripture could be resolved only by allegorical interpretation. Such obscurity, as St Augustine explained, was necessitated by the Fall of man, which was, among other things, 'a fall from direct knowledge into indirect knowledge through signs.'[18] But the obscurity also had a positive purpose, in making men feel the true value of doctrines so darkly expressed. Augustine wrote in his *De doctrina Christiana* that

many and varied obscurities and ambiguities deceive those who read casually, understanding one thing instead of another; indeed, in certain places they do not find anything to interpret erroneously, so obscurely are certain sayings covered with a most dense mist. I do not doubt that this situation was provided by God to conquer pride by work and to combat disdain in our minds, to which those things which are easily discovered seem frequently to become worthless.

Augustine adds that 'in a strange way' pleasure is to be gained from allegorical expression and its interpretation.[19] Medieval interpretation of Scripture, or of Virgil, Ovid, and other classical poets, is frequently allegorical, and medieval literature is often created in the form of allegory; but in general, and especially in the vernacular languages, this created allegory is not so obscure as to require any great effort of interpretation. In a work such as the *Queste del Saint Graal*, which is a Christian allegorization of Arthurian romance, consciously using the same methods as had been devised for Scriptural exegesis, the interpretative process is part of the literal text: round every corner the knights encounter a hermit who authoritatively expounds the meaning of their most recent adventure. Elsewhere personification-allegory is extremely common, but this is a means of analysis and clarification, not a means of veiling the truth; it is no more than an elaboration and systematization of certain features of European languages (such as that abstract nouns may be the subjects and objects of verbs), and it proclaims its own interpretation on its outer surface. An allegorical poem such as *Winner and Waster* is the medieval equivalent to an economic theory that in our time would be expounded in technical prose, formulas, graphs, and diagrams, and its meaning is actually clearer to the layman than such specialized discourse would be likely to be. There are undoubtedly difficult allegorical works in English, such as *Piers Plowman*, which does indeed require of its readers,

You must read, you must persevere, you must sit up nights, you must enquire, and exert the utmost power of your mind.[20]

Here too, however, the interpretative activity is taking place within the poem – 'Mercy, madame, what may this be to mene?' (B I 11), asks the dreamer at an early stage – and if there is a residue of obscurity in scenes such as the tearing of the Pardon or the shaking of the Tree of Charity, it seems to be there not because Langland was deliberately veiling a clear truth in order 'to conquer pride by work and to combat disdain in our minds', but because the truth itself was to him obscure and uncertain. On the whole, medieval allegory, especially in the vernacular languages, does not aim at obscurity but at clarification.

In this respect a change comes with the Renaissance. The idea that great poets conceal their meanings with a veil of allegory was one aspect of that general elevation of the status of poetry that we have seen to be characteristic of the Renaissance: poets could now legitimately demand their readers' fullest attention. Moreover, as Trinkaus has claimed, a theory such as that of Coluccio Salutati about the allegorical nature of all pagan poetry

meant a movement towards a universalising, not only of literature – a conception of the possibility of a world literature where a Christian Dante could stand beside a pagan Homer – but towards a universalising of human experience, so that a Renaissance Christian might understand the experience of an ancient pagan and also find in it elements that were comparable to his own. Therefore the principle and practice of allegorical interpretation in the Renaissance was not a mere vestige and prolongation of the Middle Ages but an instrument of innovation.[21]

But when did this change begin to affect poetry in English? Not, certainly, as early as Chaucer. He was a writer of strongly literal and rational temperament, who showed little interest in allegory or allegorization; and so this aspect of the Italian Renaissance is not reflected in his work, even in those poetic dreams which were generally among the commonest vehicles for allegory. In *The Book of the Duchess*, the myth of Ceyx and Alcyone appears to have no allegorical significance, but is understood by the narrator as a literal *exemplum* concerning death, mourning, and dreams; and though in his dream the man in black and 'goode, faire White' (948) are allegorical figures we can reasonably assume that their concealed historical identities would already have been well known to the poem's original public. (That of the man is in any case disclosed by a group of puns at the end of the poem.) In *The Parliament of Fowls*,

Cupid in the dream-garden is surrounded by personifications who are for the most part mere names, and in some cases, improbable though it may seem, not even that:

> Foolhardynesse, Flaterye, and Desyr,
> Messagerye, and Meede, and other thre –
> Here names shul not here be told for me. (227–9)

Chaucer's lack of interest in personification-allegory is manifest. The function of the personifications is simply to name different aspects of the courtly cult of love; and the 'noble goddesse Nature' (303) means no more and no less than her name indicates.[22]

In the works of his that most closely imitate Chaucer's dream-poems, Lydgate likes to suggest that there is some hidden meaning remaining to be expounded. Thus he ends *The Temple of Glass* by begging the (possibly imaginary) lady to whom the poem is addressed

> This simple tretis forto take in gre
> Til I have leiser unto hir heigh renoun
> Forto expoune my foreseid visioun;
> And tel in plein the significaunce
> So as it cometh to my remembraunce,
> So that herafter my ladi may it loke. (1387–92)[23]

Yet it is difficult to believe that the dream actually has any further *significaunce*, apart from its possible relationship (like that of *The Book of the Duchess*) to a real-life situation. The most recent editor of the *Temple* has suggested, with some ingenuity, that there is a hidden meaning in the opening incident, when the dreamer is first dazzled by the sunlight reflected from the temple, but then, after a cloud has covered the sun, he is able to find his way inside it: 'The symbolism here, that a knowledge of the power and nature of love is obtainable through its frustration and negation, is derived from *Troilus* II 764–70, 781 and 862ff.'[24] This cannot, I think, be regarded as more than a possibility, and even if it is correct it covers only a small part of the poem. As a whole, *The Temple of Glass* is even less in need of interpretation than *The Parliament of Fowls*.

More important allegorical elements may be found in some of Lydgate's religious poems, which make use of the typological methods of Scriptural exegesis. An example is the short poem, *A Defence of Holy Church*, a work illustrating that fear of heresy which I mentioned earlier as a factor that discouraged Chaucer's successors from developing his own imaginative openness towards non-

Christian world-views.[25] The *Defence* was written to urge the young King Henry V to put down with severity the Lollard rising of 1413–14 led by Sir John Oldcastle,[26] but this historical moment is also seen as a *figura* of other moments in sacred history, both past and future. Thus the English Church of the early fifteenth century, of which the king is 'protectour and diffence' (5),[27] is identified with Jerusalem – both the New Jerusalem, the eternal Church, which is 'Cristis spouse' (7), seen by St John in the Apocalypse 'coming down out of heaven from God, prepared as a bride adorned for her husband' (Apocalypse 21:2), and the Old Jerusalem of Psalm 136, the earthly Church exiled 'on the floodis of fell Babiloun' (15). The Lollards wish to deprive the Church of 'hir riche paramentez' (130), which would include the elaborate musical settings of her services. Thus, writes Lydgate, the Church,

> ... wher as she was wonte to play and syng
> In prays and honour of hir eternall lorde,
> On instruments of musik in accorde,
>
> Constreyned was, and almost at the prikk
> T'a'lefft hir song of holy notis trewe.
> And on the salwys olde, foule, and thikk
> To hang hir orgnes that were entuned newe.   (19–25)

In terms of the Psalm, this is the church in her Babylonian captivity hanging her harps upon the willows (Psalm 136:2). As Norton-Smith points out, the harps (Vulgate *organa*, Douai 'instruments') were often interpreted allegorically (as by St Augustine in his *Enarratio* on this psalm) as God's words, and the willows as the fruitless trees of the earthly city of sensual delights. But at the same time, the music is literal church music, which is itself a figure of heavenly harmony: line 21 alludes to a passage in Chaucer's *Parliament of Fowls* which evokes just such harmony –

> Of instruments of strenges in acord
> Herde I so pleye a ravyshyng swetnesse,
> That God, that makere is of al and lord,
> Ne herde nevere beter, as I gesse.   (*Parliament* 197–200)

Lydgate also identifies the Church with Noah's ark (a very common allegory), which is steered by the king away from dangers till it comes to rest 'on the hyllys hy of Armonye' (56) – Armenia, the site of Mount Ararat, but also no doubt the 'harmony' of heavenly peace. Finally, the king is addressed as 'Goddis knyht' (26), and, in the light of the poem's apocalyptic perspective, this suggests that he is himself a figure of the knight 'called faithful and true' who appears from the heavens in Apocalypse 19:11, and who with the sharp sword coming from his mouth destroys God's enemies, thus fulfilling the prophecy at the end of Psalm 136 of the destruction of Babylon. Lydgate's apocalyptic interpretation of the history of his time is conveyed through an extraordinarily rich and allusive allegory, of which my account has mentioned only a few major features. In one sense it is highly medieval, borrowing the methods of sermons and Scriptural commentaries; but such borrowing by vernacular and secular poetry is a major factor in creating the consciously obscure allegory of Renaissance literature.

If we now move on to the early Tudor period, we can find Stephen Hawes taking with the utmost seriousness the idea that great poets, virtually by definition, write obscure allegory, and attributing the intention to write such allegory to the English poets of the past, and above all to his favourite Lydgate. The prologue to Hawes's longest work, *The Pastime of Pleasure*, illustrates these assumptions with convenient clarity. He dedicates his poem to Henry VII, begging him to accept it even though

> Nothynge I am experte in poetry,
> As the monke of Bury, floure of eloquence,
> Which was in tyme of grete excellence
>
> Of your predecessour, the .v. kynge Henry.   (26–9)

Lydgate's 'fatall [i.e. prophetic] fyccyons' (33) are of lasting importance, and 'He cloked the trouthe of all his scryptures' (35), whereas, Hawes declares,

> The lyght of trouthe I lacke connynge to cloke;
> To drawe a curtayne I dare not to presume,
> Nor hyde my mater with a mysty smoke,
> My rudenes connynge dothe so sore consume;
> Yet as I maye I shall blowe out a fume
> To hyde my mynde underneth a fable
> By convert colour well and probable.   (36–42)

The notions that the art of poetry is essentially that of producing allegorical smokescreens to conceal one's meaning and that a poet ought to feel worried about his inability sufficiently to hide what he has to say are pleasingly absurd, but there is no reason to doubt that these were really Hawes's views. He goes on to claim ancient authority in his support (and here we probably see a muddled version of the doctrines of Boccaccio and other early humanists):

> For under a colour a truthe maye aryse,
> As was the guyse in olde antyquyte
> Of the poetes olde, a tale to surmyse
> To cloke the truthe, of theyr infyrmyte.　　　　(50–3)

(The last line and a half may perhaps mean, 'to imagine in their [pagan] weakness a fiction that cloaked the truth'.) Later in the poem, in a lengthy account of rhetoric as one of the seven liberal arts (lines 652ff), Hawes gives some examples of how, in his view, the poets of antiquity concealed truth under fiction. They said that Atlas bore heaven on his shoulders because he was an expert astronomer; the myth of the centaurs concerns the origin of horsemanship; the myth of Pluto, king of hell, relates to a wicked race of people; Cerberus's three heads symbolize the three vices of pride, avarice, and rapine; and so on. Such rationalizing and moralizing interpretations are the commonplaces of medieval and Renaissance mythography. Later in the *Pastime* Hawes laments the death of Lydgate because his successors are so inferior, substituting courtly lyrics whose meanings are all too clear for such dark allegories:

> They fayne no fables pleasaunt and coverte,
> But spend theyr tyme in vaynfull vanyte,
> Makynge balades of fervent amyte,
> As gestes and tryfles without fruytfulnes.　　　　(1389–92)

In other poems Hawes frequently states the same doctrine; one instance may stand for all. In *The Example of Vertue*, the ancient poets and philosophers are set side by side: the philosophers established 'the seven scyences lyberall' (898),

> And also poetes that were fatall
> Craftely colored with clowdy fygures
> The true sentence of all theyr scryptures.　　　　(901–3)[28]

　　For all his belief in obscure allegory, Hawes did not usually succeed in composing poems that were obscurely allegorical. *The Pastime of Pleasure*, for example, is an allegory in the sense that it uses personifications and symbols to convey a general picture of life under the guise of feigned personal experience; but its meaning is nearly always perfectly clear, often indeed tediously so. In doctrine, if not in form, the *Pastime* does indeed illustrate the move from medieval to Renaissance. Its hero begins his journey through life by consciously choosing not the path to 'contemplacyon' (85) but that to 'actyfe lyfe' (94), which will lead him to 'Labell Pucell, the fayre lady excellent' (97), and it is never suggested that the other choice would have been better. It is true that beyond his eventual marriage to Labell Pucell lie Age, Death, Fame, Time, and Eternity; but he is evidently as well equipped as a man can be to meet these ultimate ideals by his training in *activa vita*. This would not of course have been the normal medieval view. A great part of the poem is concerned with the training itself: it is characteristic of the early Tudor period in its concern with the education of the gentleman or courtier. Moreover, that education has abandoned the medieval distinction between clerk and knight: first the hero has to pass through the seven liberal arts, and only after he has received his 'lycence' (2913) or university degree from the last of them, Dame Astronomy, is he fit to proceed to the Tower of Chivalry and the knightly adventures by which he wins his lady.

The Pastime of Pleasure is a poem of some charm, and though, at 5816 lines, it is far too long, its leisureliness is also part of its attraction. Hawes is at his best poetically not, as he would pre- sumably have liked to think, at his most allegorical, but at the moments of romantic picturesqueness which really are reminiscent of his admired Lydgate, and which occasionally anticipate the sensuousness of *The Faerie Queene*:

> Forthe than I rode at myne owne adventure
> Over the mountaynes and the craggy rockes;
> To beholde the countrees I had grete pleasure
> Where corall growed by ryght hye stockes,
> And the popyngayes in the tre toppes.
> Than as I rode I sawe me beforne
> Besyde a welle hange bothe a shelde and a horne.   (4277–83)[29]

It should be mentioned that among the hero's adventures is a lengthy encounter with a foolish dwarf called Godfrey Gobylyve, who speaks in Kentish dialect and in rhyming couplets in place of the poem's usual rhyme royal, and whose function is to set a coarse antifeminism alongside the courtly idealization that shapes the work as a whole. The idea is ingenious, but the execution lacks wit. A final point worth noting is that Hawes's belief in universal allegory, absurd as it may be, can at times make him seem an intelligent deallegorizer. Thus when Fortune claims to dominate all things, Mars (who has the advantage of being a planet as well as an idea) deftly reduces her, with a triumphant 'Aha!' (3193), to a mere allegorical invention of the poets:

> How hast thou power in ony maner of case
> In heven or erthe without a dwellynge place,
>
> But that poetes hath made a fygure
> Of the for the grete sygnyfycacyon,
> The chaunge of man so for to dyscure
> Accordynge to a moralyzacyon?
> And of the trouth to make relacyon,
> The man is fortune in the propre dede,
> And not thou that causeth hym to spede.   (3205–13)

In the light of this, it is possible that we can recognize occasional jokes on Hawes's part at the expense of his own allegory. When the hero and Labell Pucell have to part after she has accepted his love, Hawes comments,

> Never before, as I trowe and wene,
> Was such departynge true lovers betwene.   (2379–80)

The whole point of the allegorical framework, however, is to generalize: the hero (whose name is Graunde Amour) represents all young lovers, and Labell Pucell all the ladies with whom they fall in love. Their experience represents not what is unique and unprecedented, but what has often been before and will often be again; and I would like to think (though this may be to take too optimistic a view of Hawes) that he was gently poking fun at the contradiction between the form of personification-allegory and its content.

There is one exception to my generalization that Hawes's allegories lack the obscurity he desired. This is what appears to be his last poem, *The Conforte of Lovers*. Here he begins with a statement of his usual belief about poetry –

> The gentyll poetes under cloudy fygures
> Do touche a trouth and cloke it subtylly:
> Harde is to construe poetycall scryptures,
> They are so fayned and made sentencyously   (1–4)

– and his usual devotion to Lydgate: he comes forward 'As none hystoryagraffe nor poete laureate' (20) (that is, not vying with Bernard André, Henry VII's official historiographer, or with poets laureated like André himself and Skelton), 'But gladly wolde folowe the makynge of Lydgate' (21). Then he explains how in a dream he met 'a lady of goodly age' (76), and

> To me she sayd, 'Me thynke ye are not well:
> Ye have caught colde, and do lyve in care.
> Tell me your mynde now shortly, everydele:
> To layne the trouthe I charge you to beware.'   (78–81)[30]

He tells his questioner how several years ago he fell in love with a young lady of noble birth:

> I durst not speke unto her of my love,
> Yet under coloure I dyvers bokes dyde make
> Full pryvely to come to my above.   (92–4)

The implication is that his earlier works were allegories intended to conceal yet reveal his personal experience; yet they can scarcely have been so dark as the *Conforte* itself, for he continues, in lines that defy precise understanding,

> Thretened with sorowe of many paynes grete,
> Thre yeres ago my ryght hande I dyde bynde;
> Fro my browes for fere the dropes doune dyde sweet.
> God knoweth all, it was nothynge my mynde!
> Unto no persone I durst my herte untwynde,
> Yet, the trouthe knowynge, the good gretest P
> Maye me releace of all my p/p/p thre.   (134–40)[31]

He adds that not long ago 'Above .xx. woulves dyde me touse and rent' (163); he realized that 'My ladyes fader they dyde lytell love' (168), and so,

> Seynge theyr falshode and theyr subtylte,
> For fere of deth, where as I loved best
> I dyde dysprayse . . .   (169–71)

There were attempts to suppress his books, but nevertheless their real meaning is that 'For the reed and whyte they wryte full true' (189). The reason for obscurity here would appear to be political danger: Hawes is affirming his loyalty to 'the reed and whyte' (the Tudor dynasty) and explaining that if his works seem to suggest otherwise it is because he had to conceal his true meaning for fear of enemies. Whether any love affair is really involved is doubtful: as often happens with the poetry of the early Tudor court, the language of love may be a way of expressing political allegiance.

The dreamer's interlocutor now invites him into a sumptuously decorated palace and leaves him there. He laments that nature, having incited him to love, does not incite his lady to return his feelings – a somewhat enfeebled version of the reproaches addressed to God in Chaucer's *Complaint of Mars* and Lydgate's *Complaynt of a Loveres Lyfe* and *Temple of Glass*.[32] But, he adds,

> Two thynges me conforte ever in pryncypall:
> The fyrst be bokes made in antyquyte
> By Gower and Chaucer, poetes rethorycall,
> And Lydgate eke, by good auctoryte
> Makynge mencyon of the felycyte
> Of my lady and me, by Dame Fortunes chaunce
> To mete togyders by wonderfull ordynaunce;
>
> The seconde is, where Fortune dooth me brynge
> In many placys, I se by prophecy,
> As in the storyes of the olde buyldynge,
> Letters for my lady depeynted wonderly,
> And letters for me besyde her mervayllously,
> Agreynge well unto my bokes all –
> In dyvers placys I se it in generall.   (281–94)

From these peculiar stanzas, it appears how literally Hawes meant it when he spoke of poets as 'fatall' (prophetic). He really believed that the works of Gower, Chaucer and Lydgate contained, beneath the veil of allegory, prophetic statements about himself and his lady; and similarly he was persuaded that references to the two of them could be found in inscriptions on old buildings. In one sense, no doubt, the generalizing treatments of love in medieval courtly poetry could be understood as applying to any individuals, present or future; and indeed Guillaume de Lorris had begun the *Roman de la Rose* (quoted here from the Chaucerian translation that Hawes is likely to have known) by asserting that men

> ... dremen in her slep a-nyghtes
> Ful many thynges covertly
> That fallen after al openly,   (18–20)

and that there was nothing in the allegorical dream of which his poem consisted 'That it nys afterward befalle' (29). But there can have been few readers of Guillaume who saw his generalizing literary allegory as proleptic biography of themselves, and there is surely something mentally unbalanced, perhaps paranoiac, in Hawes's reading of his predecessors.

In the palace, the dreamer sees three mirrors, which together seem to constitute a kind of allegory of allegory, reflecting past, present, and future. (The elaborate details of this section of the narrative have a visionary wildness that once more defies interpretation.) In the second mirror he sees

> How Prevy Malyce his messengers had sent
> With subtyll engynes to lye in a wayte,
> Yf that they coude take me with a bayte. (404–6)

Nearby hang a sword and a shield which bears a specific and presumably symbolic but now unidentifiable coat of arms. The sword is held by 'A hand of stele wherin was wryten "Pryde"' (500), and an inscription explains that it was placed there by 'a grete lady hondred yeres ago' (503) to be seized by 'One persone, chosen by God indede, / Of this ladyes kyndred' (506–7). Hawes's account of the dreamer's seizure of the sword has a touch of imaginative realism – what would it really be like to undergo such impossible experiences? – of a kind that can be found scattered throughout his work:

> I felte the hande of the stele so fyne:
> Me thought it quaked; the fyngers gan to stretche;
> I thought by that I came than of the lyne
> Of the grete lady that fyrst the swerde dyde fetche.
> The swerdes pomell I began to ketche:
> The hande swerved, but yet never the lesse
> I helde them bothe by excellent prowes.
>
> And at the last I felte the hande departe ... (582–9)

The dreamer takes this as an omen of his future success with the lady. He apostrophizes her at length in a soliloquy, and is then surprised to find her present. He kneels and addresses her, and she answers in lines which (like those of the 'lady of goodly age' quoted above) remind one in their colloquial simplicity of style of Hoccleve rather than Lydgate:

> 'Ihesu!' sayd she than, 'who hadde wende to fynde
> Your selfe walkynge in this place all alone?
> Full lytell thought I: ye were not in my mynde. . .' (701–3)

There is a dialogue between them of alternating stanzas, which throws more light on that cloaking of the truth that Hawes thought necessary in poetry. The lover says that the cause of his grief is unrequited love; the lady comments that she cannot suppose that any lady, 'yf that she gentyll be' (758), would refuse him her favour; he assures her that there is one lady who does, and she answers,

> Me thynke ye speke now under parable!
> Do ye se her here whiche is cause of your grefe? (771–2)

The 'parable' to which she refers is what we would call allusion rather than allegory, and it seems likely that Hawes would have counted as allegory that allusive quality that belongs to much early Tudor verse (including, for example, many of Wyatt's lyrics) – verse that is a means of conducting the 'game of love' verbally,[33] at a time when the private feelings involved might also have dangerous political implications.

The conversation continues in the same manner. The lady remarks,

> Of late I sawe a boke of your makynge
> Called *The Pastyme of Pleasure*, whiche is wondrous,
> For I thynke and you had not ben in lovynge
> Ye coude never have made it so sentencyous. (785–8)

Evidently, then, even a poem so unpromisingly cumbrous as *The Pastime of Pleasure* might have been a counter in the game of love and politics. The lover answers that he wrote it 'But ygnorauntly' (794), yet

> Many a one doth wryte I knowe not what in dede,
> Yet the effecte dooth folowe, the trouthe for to spede. (797–8)

By now, it would seem, Hawes had come to believe (or at the very least to affect to believe) that his own poems too were 'fatall fyccyons', foretelling a future of which he knew nothing when he wrote them. The lady finally agrees to accept his service if he will be prudent and patient – that, she says, is what will most displease his enemies. This prompts a stanza on how he has been persecuted, once more of all but impenetrable obscurity:

> Surely, I thynke, I suffred well the phyppe;
> The nette also dydde teche me on the waye;
> But me to bere I trowe they lost a lyppe,
> For the lyfte hande extendyd my journaye,
> And not to call me for my sporte and playe;
> Wherfore by foly yf that they do synne,
> The Holy Goost maye well the batayle wynne. (890–6)

Some believe that 'the phyppe' alludes to Skelton's *Phyllyp Sparowe*, which is alleged to contain joking parodic allusions to *The Pastime of Pleasure*.[34] This seems possible, though by no means certain. Finally, the lover and the lady agree to submit their case to Venus, and the lover wakes from his dream and concludes the poem with an *envoi* dedicating his literary services 'To every lady' (933) – just what the

Queen of Fame complained in *The Garland of Laurel* that Skelton was not sufficiently diligent in doing. *The Conforte of Lovers* is an extremely odd poem. In the views it conveys about the nature of poetry itself, it is difficult to assess the proportions of sober belief, affectation, and mental disturbance, but it is exceptionally valuable in its illustration of the ways in which an early Tudor poet might think it desirable for poetry to be obscurely allegorical.

To return from Hawes to Skelton is to enter a different world in terms of both genius and judgment; but Skelton too sees obscure allegory as one of the options for a poet, and some of his major works are obscure allegories, albeit in a more controlled and less misty way than those of Hawes. In *The Garland of Laurel* Pallas defends Skelton against the Queen of Fame's objections by listing three kinds of writing and the objections to them that may be made by captious readers. First, 'if he gloryously pullishe[35] his matter, / Then men wyll say how he doth but flatter' (83–4); second, 'if so hym fortune to wryte true and plaine, / . . . There sum wyll say he hath but lyttil brayne' (85–7); and third, he may write satirically but under allegorical concealment, and even then some readers will guess at his meaning;

> In generrall words, I say not gretely nay,
> A poete somtyme may for his pleasure taunt,
> Spekyng in paroblis, how the fox, the grey,
> The gander, the gose, and the hudge oliphaunt,
> Went with the pecok ageyne the fesaunt;
> The lesarde came lepyng, and sayd that he must,
> With helpe of the ram, ley all in the dust.
>
> Yet dyverse ther be, industryous of reason,
> Sum what wolde gadder in there conjecture
> Of suche an endarkid chapiter sum season.   (99–108)

Moreover, the broad Renaissance conception of allegory might well have led Skelton to class as allegorical any of his poems that were written in the person of a fictitious narrator. Thus in *Phyllyp Sparowe* the simple Latin of Jane's epitaph for the bird incorporates a statement that the real composer of the words is not Jane but Skelton:

> Per me laurigerum
> Britanum Skeltonida vatem
> Hec cecinisse licet
> Ficta sub imagine texta.   (834–7)

(Through me, Skelton, the laureate poet of Britain, it was possible for these [lines] to be sung under a feigned likeness.)

In *Collyn Clout* and elsewhere, Skelton also adopts voices other than his own and speaks truth 'Ficta sub imagine texta'. For him, as for Boccaccio, it is likely that any fiction designed to convey a truth counted as allegory.

4. Two Skeltonian allegories

I shall conclude, though, by examining two of Skelton's works which are allegorical in a more specific sense than this, and in which the obscurity of allegory also has a more specific purpose. The first is *The Bowge of Court*. This begins with a prologue in which Skelton expresses precisely the view of poetry as allegorical concealment that we have found in Hawes's work:

> I, callynge to mynde the great auctoryte
> Of poetes olde, whyche, full craftely,
> Under as coverte termes as coude be,
> Can touche a troughte and cloke it subtylly . . .,
> . . . was sore moved to aforce the same.   (8–11, 17)

He feels doubt as to his ability to follow their example, but fortunately his indecision wearies him, he falls asleep, and he has a dream. Thus his unconscious mind supplies him with the subtly cloaked truth that he feared his conscious mind was unable to devise. The events of the dream form a very simple story. He finds himself on the quayside at Harwich, where 'a shyppe, goodly of sayle' (36) and full of 'royall marchaundyse' (41) has just moored. Merchants flock aboard her to see her cargo and the great lady, 'Dame Saunce-Pere' (51), who owns her, and the dreamer follows them. He learns that the ship is called 'The Bowge of Courte' (49) (i.e. court rations), and he has a conversation with the lady's gentlewoman, Daunger (i.e. haughtiness), who discourages him, and with another gentlewoman, Desyre, who encourages him, in his wish to buy some of the cargo, which is Favour. Desyre urges him to make friends with the ship's steerswoman, Fortune. The ship sets sail, and the dreamer, whose name turns out to be not Skelton but Drede, has a series of baffling, frustrating, and somewhat frightening conversations with 'Full subtyll persones, in nombre foure and thre' (133), whose names are 'Favell, full of flatery' (134), 'Suspecte (136) alias 'Suspycyon' (181), 'Harvy Hafter that well coude picke a male' (138), and 'Dysdayne, Ryotte, Dyssymuler, Subtylte' (140). By the end of his conversations with these seven persons, Drede is so nervous that he thinks he sees men coming to slay him, and tries to leap overboard; but with this Skelton wakes, commenting that 'oftyme suche dremes be founde trewe' (538).

The names of the characters indicate that this dream is an allegory, but it is one of an unexpectedly complex kind. The ship tossing on stormy waves is a familiar emblem of the life of man in the world; such a life is lived at the mercy of Fortune, that entirely unreliable goddess of the ups and downs of life, who in this case is steerswoman of the ship. In Boethian–Christian terms, suicidal despair is a natural culmination of such a life for the man who dedicates himself to Fortune as this dreamer does, voluntarily leaving solid ground for a realm in which there are no fixed values to rely on. Skelton, however, puts no emphasis on winds or waves: his concern is with the experience of life on board the ship, which has uncertainties enough of its own. On one level, the dreamer's motivation is that of the traditional allegory of love, in the line going back to the *Roman de la Rose*. The ship's owner is a lady without equal,

> Whoos beaute, honoure, goodly porte,
> I have to lytyll connynge to reporte. (62–3)

The two gentlewomen, Daunger and Desyre, belong to the same realm, and all those who eagerly board the ship seek the lady's favour. But the allegory of love is also an allegory of trade, and it is difficult at first to determine the relationship between these two sets of meanings. Those who seek her favour are merchants (men whose way of life puts them especially at the mercy of Fortune[36]), and the favour they seek is 'royall marchaundyse' (41), 'royall chaffre' (54), 'ware' (79) which is dear to buy. The implication might be that merchants are like lovers, or that lovers are like merchants; but then, if we remember the title of the poem and the name of the ship, it emerges that the central meaning of the allegory is of yet another kind. The poem takes life at court as its special case of life at the mercy of Fortune; it is one of many works of this period (including, for example, Barclay's *Eclogues* and Wyatt's *Satires*) that give a satirical account of court life under the more powerful and ostentatious rule of the Tudor dynasty. Favour at court is appropriately personified as a lady named only 'Saunce-Pere' and never seen directly because she sits enthroned 'behynde a traves of sylke fyne / Of golde of tessew the fynest that myghte be' (58–9). Those who seek such favour are like lovers in their blind passion and like merchants in their acquisitory greed, and what they seek they can never have any certainty of possessing. Such a life is like a nightmare; and yet, alas, 'oftyme suche dremes be founde trewe'.

The seven 'subtyll persones' with whom Drede meets allegorize the general nature of life at court, dominated by flattery, suspicion, cheating, and the other disagreeable qualities indicated by their names. This personification-allegory, however, is very simple: there seem to be no significant relationships or activities linking the personifications, and the whole poem after the ship sets sail (at line 127) functions chiefly as a literal evocation of what it is like to live among courtiers. As such it is shrewd and horrifyingly convincing. Meaning is conveyed by Drede's descriptions of his fellow-voyagers, whose appearance is sometimes symbolic – Favell's 'cloke / That lyned was with doubtfull doublenes' (177–8), Suspycyon's rolling eyes and shaking hands, Hervy's fox-furred gown – and also by descriptions of his reactions to them: his purse is 'half aferde' (238) when Hervy gazes at him, he feels shame at Ryotte's licentious prattle. But the most important source of meaning is what the characters say, and this is hatefully lifelike in its insinuation, its veiled threats, its knowingness, its stale and unamusing wit, above all in the sense it conveys of intolerable tedium without itself ever being tedious. No quotation can do justice to the overall effect created by the dialogue, that one is at an appallingly long, appallingly noisy cocktail party, full of shallow, disagreeable, often vulgar people, all of whom know each other and many of whom know more about oneself than they ought, and of whom the most intrusively friendly are the least sincere and the most dangerous. What is especially striking is the constant allusiveness to things of which Drede knows nothing, so that it is as though events have a secret meaning from which he is excluded. Favell assures him, concerning Fortune, that

> I herde her speke of you within shorte space,
> Whan there were dyverse that sore dyde you manace,   (158–9)

but he adds, concerning these mysterious enemies of Drede's,

> Thyse lewde cok wattes shall nevermore prevayle
> Ageynste you hardely; therefore be not afrayde.   (173–4)

At once Drede overhears Suspycyon asking Favell what he (Drede) said about him, and Favell conspiratorially answering, 'What, lete us holde him up, man, for a whyle' (188). But now Suspycyon warns

Drede against Favell, as one who 'wyll begyle you and speke fayre to your face' (200), and then offers to reveal to him 'thynges that may not be disclosed' (217). Since Drede has promised secrecy, all he can tell us of Suspycyon's conversation is, '"By God," quod he, "this and thus it is"' (225), and so this time it is we who are left feeling dangerously excluded. Hervy assures Drede that he is in great favour, but then Drede overhears Hervy plotting with Disdayne to throw him overboard. Disdayne himself approaches Drede with the threatening question,

> Remembrest thou what thou sayd yesternyght?
> Wylt thou abyde by the wordes agayne?   (323–4)

– and thus another mystery is hinted without being explained. Dyssymulation's conversation, as we might expect from his name, consists almost entirely of baffling allusions:

> Ryghte now I spake with one, I trowe, I see –
> But, what, a strawe! I maye not tell all thynge.
> By God, I saye, there is a grete herte-brennynge
> Betwene the persone ye wote of, you –   (458–61)

> Iwys I coude tell – but humlery, home,
> I dare not speke, we be so layde awayte . . .   (467–8)

But for utter incomprehensibility the biscuit is taken by Disceyte:

> But by that Lorde that is one, two and thre,
> I have an errande to rounde in your ere.
> He tolde me so, by God, ye maye truste me.
> Parde, remembre whan ye were there,
> There I wynked on you – wote ye not where?
> In A *loco*, I mene *juxta* B:
> Woo is hym that is blynde and maye not see!   (512–18)

What emerges from all this, I think, is the very opposite of the clarification of meaning that is aimed at and achieved by most medieval allegories. It is a sense that there may well be layers beyond layers of meaning, wheels within courtly wheels, but that there is not the least hope that either Drede or we could ever understand them, even if our lives depended on it – as Drede's apparently does. Life at court is like living inside an obscure allegory, and the ancient poets were mere novices at cloaking truth subtly by comparison with Tudor courtiers. In *The Bowge of Court*, the obscurity of Renaissance allegory has a calculated expressive purpose: it does not conceal the poet's meaning, rather it enables him to evoke the concealment of meaning. Yet the question remains, is there any real meaning to be concealed, or is it the very process of concealment that creates the deceptive and ultimately destructive illusion of hidden meaning? Is meaning the peerless lady allegedly hidden behind the Boccaccian veil 'Of golde of tessew the fynest that myghte be' (59), but whom no-one ever actually sees?

> Than sholde ye see there pressynge in a pace
> Of one and other that wolde his lady see   (56–7)

– but what we see is the pressing of the merchants, not the lady they want to see. Indeed the very fact that she is 'his lady' to each of them may imply that she exists only as a projection of the desires of each of her admirers. One incident in the prologue certainly suggests that Skelton is aware of the potential deceptiveness of allegory itself, its tendency to turn ideas and wishes into fictive realities. Drede tells Desyre that he has 'but smal substaunce' (94) with which to purchase favour, and Desyre comfortingly says that she will lend him 'A precyous jewell, no rycher in this londe' (97). But this land is that of allegory, which contains only allegorical jewels – in this case, one called '*Bone aventure*'. '*Bone aventure* have here now in your honde!' (98) exclaims Desyre, with hearty benevolence; but '*Bone aventure*' means simply 'good luck', and the line itself is no more than the verbal equivalent of 'a good-luck handshake'.[37] All that has happened is that Drede has been informed that he will need good luck to obtain Fortune's favour – and that is a mere tautology. It is at least possible that Skelton's point was that, in both allegory and the court, behind all the obscure whisperings there is no stable reality at all, only one illusion veiling another.

My other example of Skeltonian allegory, *Speke Parott*, is undoubtedly the most difficult of all his works; in my view it is also the best. It is of approximately the same degree of difficulty as *The Waste Land*, and, indeed, with its polyglot style and its structure of juxtaposed fragments, its difficulty is often of much the same kind. Of it might be said what Petrarch wrote of his own allegorical eclogues (an early example of the obscure allegory of the Renaissance):

The nature of this kind of poetry is such that, unless it is expounded by the same man who composed it, the meaning can perhaps be guessed but it is impossible to understand it all.[38]

Skelton did not expound his own poem; he is probably the author of the Latin marginal glosses which survive for part of it, but these have something of the equivocal status of Eliot's notes on *The Waste Land* – 'not more of a skit than some things in the poem itself', as Eliot ambiguously put it.[39] Certainly the darkness is not much lightened when 'Cryste save Kyng Herry the viiith, owur royalle kyng!' (34) is glossed 'Policronitudo Basileos'. One begins to suspect that Skelton, pushing a little further Chaucer's intermittent fictionalization of himself in *Troilus and Criseyde* as pedantic historian, has created a sixteenth-century equivalent to Nabokov's *Pale Fire*, in which the pretentious irrelevance or mistakenness of the editor's notes is precisely their point.

Though *Speke Parott* is a poem of only just over five hundred lines, a complete study of it would need to be at least the length of this book – and even then it could not be truly complete, for 'it is impossible to understand it all'. Relying heavily on the investigations and speculations of others,[40] I can attempt only a sketch, in the hope of conveying the fascination of the work and of justifying Skelton's allegorical obscurity. I must begin by explaining that *Speke Parott* as we have it was put together by Skelton's first scholarly editor, Alexander Dyce, from two different sources: the printed text of Lant's *Certayne Bokes* (c. 1545), which contains only lines 1–237, and the manuscript notebook of John Colyns (c. 1525–35), a London mercer, which contains only lines 1–57 and 225 to the end. The Colyns manuscript includes the marginal glosses, mainly in Latin, mentioned above.[41] If the poem has been correctly put together, it was probably written in successive sections in the autumn of 1521, in direct response to current events as news of them reached Skelton. The Emperor Charles V and the French King Francis I were at war, and Wolsey was attempting to mediate between them in a summit conference held at Calais, then an English possession. In Skelton's view, Wolsey's greatest concern was not to bring about a settlement that would be favourable for England and for his master, Henry VIII, but to gain the emperor's support in his own bid to become Pope. Some modern historians suggest that Wolsey really was aiming at peace, though by somewhat devious means, and that it was the idea of Henry (at that time still a fervent papal supporter) rather than himself that he should be a candidate for the papacy; but the truth of the matter, if indeed it is attainable, need not concern us. As in *The Bowge of Court*, the political life of the time gives the

impression of being an obscure allegory of indeterminable meaning.
At the end of 1521, Pope Leo X died, and it was presumably then that
Skelton wrote of the hasty departure of 'owur clerke Cleros' and
'passe-a-Pase' (412–13), Thomas Clark and Richard Pace (Wolsey's
messengers to Italy on Leo's death), and of how 'Hyt ys to fere leste
he wolde were the garland on hys pate' (435); but in fact – evidently
after *Speke Parott* was completed – Wolsey's bid for supreme ecclesiastical power was unsuccessful.

In its composite form, the poem can be divided into four parts. In
Part I (lines 1–40) the speaker introduces himself as 'Parott', a talking
bird caged as a pet for ladies, praises the King and Queen, and attacks
under various names a person evidently intended to represent
Wolsey. In Part II (lines 141–232) Parott's chief concern is to attack
the new interest in Greek studies and the new ways of teaching Latin,
but he also tells us more about himself. Part III (lines 233–77) is a
mixture of English and Latin, arranged around a lyric spoken or sung
by Parott at the request of a lady called Galathea. This is in a different
metre from the rhyme royal stanzas in which most of the rest of the
poem is written, and it consists of a version of a contemporary love-
song, 'Come over the burne, Besse'. Part IV, the remainder of the
poem, is made up of four successive 'envoys' or farewells, followed
by a magnificently rhetorical general 'complaint' about the state of
England under Wolsey, all spoken, once more, by Parott.

Investigation of the allegory of this complex poem must begin
with its central figure, the speaker, who abruptly introduces himself
in the first stanza:

> My name ys Parott, a byrde of Paradyse,
> By Nature devysed of a wonderowus kynde,
> Deyntely dyetyd with dyvers delycate spyce,
> Tyll Eufrates, that flodde, dryvythe me into Ynde,
> Where men of that contre by fortune me fynde,
> And send me to greate ladyes of estate;
> Then Parot moste have an almon or a date. (1–7)

Parott's function, as the title suggests, is to speak: either to entertain
at the request of 'maydens' (11) –

> ... 'Speke, Parott, I pray yow,' full curteslye they sey,
> 'Parott ys a goodlye byrde and a pratye popagay' (13–14)

– or to speak freely, as he himself begs – 'I pray you, let Parrot have
lyberte to speke' (210) – or to speak out plainly, as Galathea requests
before he delivers his final complaint on the condition of England:

> Nowe, Parott, my swete byrde, speke owte yet ons agayn,
> Sette asyde alle sophysms, and speke now trew and playne. (447–8)

When Parott does 'speke owte' in these concluding stanzas, there
cease to be any references to him as a bird, and his voice becomes
indistinguishable from that of Skelton the poet. This final merging
confirms that Parott is a figure of the poet and of Skelton as poet.
(Birds have been a favourite metaphor for poets from the white crow
of Apollo in *The Manciple's Tale*, turned black and deprived of
speech for telling the truth, down to Shelley's conception of the
poet as a nightingale which 'sings to cheer its own solitude'.[42]) It is
because Parott, unlike other personae of Skelton such as Collyn
Clout, Jane Scrope, or Drede, is a poet that he tells us that his beak
was burnished by the muse Melpomene (209), who, as Skelton says
in his translation of Diodorus Siculus, represents the power of
poetry to produce in its listeners, 'of devyne influence', a kind of
mystical experience.[43]

Parott the poet's origin, then, was in paradise, and in saying this in
his first line Skelton is no doubt alluding to the Renaissance conception of poetry as divinely inspired, which we have found so often
elsewhere in his work. But subsequently some kind of literary Fall
has occurred, and Parott has been driven out of paradise, captured by
men, and given as a pet to 'great ladyes of estate', to be fed not on
'dyvers delycate spyce' but, more mundanely, on 'an almon or a
date'. The consequence is described in the second and third stanzas:

> A cage curyowsly carven, with sylver pynne,
> Properly payntyd to be my coverture;
> A myrrour of glasse, that I may tote therin;
> These maydens full meryly with many a dyvers flowur
> Fresshely they dresse and make swete my bowur,
> With, 'Speke, Parott, I pray yow,' full curteslye they sey,
> 'Parott ys a goodlye byrde and a pratye popagay.'
>
> Wythe my beke bente, and my lytell wanton iye,
> My fethyrs fresshe as ys the emerawde grene,
> Abowte my necke a cerculett lyke the ryche rubye,
> My lytell legges, my fete bothe fete and clene,
> I am a mynyon to wayte apon a quene;
> 'My propyr Parott, my lytell pratye fole.'
> With ladyes I lerne and goe with them to scole. (8–21)

The poet has declined from an inspired bard to the mere plaything of
ladies, speaking at their command, to amuse them: he has become
the poet of the courtly tradition, whose role is assumed to be 'to

purchase / The favour of ladys with wordis electe' (*Garland of Laurel* 75–6). He may serve a queen, but his role is only that of 'mynyon'; his cage may be 'curyowsly carven' and 'Properly payntyd', but it is still a cage, restricting his liberty, and its door is pinned shut, even though the pin is made of silver. In one direction, this layer of allegory points towards an insight commonly offered in early Tudor poetry, that favour at court is a glorious imprisonment. As a short poem (which may be by Wyatt) from *Tottel's Miscellany* puts it,

> ... who so joyes such kinde of life to holde,
> In prison joyes, fettred with cheines of gold.[44]

Parott's feathery 'cerculett lyke the ryche rubye' might be compared with the collar 'graven with diamondes' about the neck of the hind in Wyatt's 'Who so list to hounte' (MT VII), which is inscribed 'Cesars I ame'. Another poem attributed to Wyatt sees death as the alternative to such imprisonment:

> Like as the byrde in the cage enclosed
> The dore unsparred and the hawke without,
> Twixte deth and prison piteously oppressed,
> Whether for to chose standith in dowt:
> Certes, so do I ...   (MT CCXLVI 1–5)

And indeed, insofar as Parott represents not just the poet in general but Skelton as poet, he may have felt himself to be in a similar situation. He was not in favour, at least with Wolsey, when *Speke Parott* was written, and for him the cage may possibly represent the confinement but safety of the sanctuary of Westminster, within the precincts of which he was residing from 1518 onwards. He comments later on Wolsey's unsuccessful attempt in 1519 to get the law concerning sanctuary changed,

> And *assilum*, whilom *refugium miserorum*,
> Non *phanum, sed prophanum*, standyth in lytyll sted.   (124–5)

(And asylum, formerly the refuge of the wretched, not sanctuary but secular, is of little use.)

It is more certain that the cage, and the mirror too, have allegorical meanings on a different level, which are made more explicit in two stanzas from Part II:

> The mirrour that I tote in, *quasi diaphonum*,
> *Vel quasi speculum, in enigmate,*
> *Elencticum*, or ells *enthimematicum*,
> For logicions to loke on, somwhat *sophistice*;

Retoricyons and oratours in freshe humanyte,
Support Parrot, I pray you, with your suffrage ornate,
Of *confuse tantum* avoydynge the chekmate.

But of that supposicyon that callyd is arte,
Confuse distrybutyve, as Parrot hath devysed,
Let every man after his merit take his parte;
For in this processe, Parrot nothing hath surmysed,
No matter pretendyd, nor nothyng enterprysed,
But that *metaphora, alegoria* withall
Shall be his protectyon, his pavys and his wall.   (190–203)

Here a rough and hesitant attempt at translation of Skelton's deliberate obscurity may be in order:

The mirror in which I peep is as it were transparent, or as if 'through a glass, in a
dark manner' [I Corinthians 13:12], in the form of a refutation or an argument
based on probability [*elenchus* and *enthymeme* being technical terms in logic], for
logicians to regard somewhat quibblingly; you rhetoricians and orators, full of
the new Latin learning, I pray you to support Parott with your elegant prayers of
intercession, avoiding the defeat of utter confusion. But so far as that postulate
called learning is concerned, as Parott has contrived it in ordered confusion, let
every man, according to his merit, take his own part [i.e. apply it as he sees fit?],
for in this discourse Parott has supposed nothing, claimed nothing, and ventured
nothing, save that metaphor and indeed allegory should be his protection,
defence, and wall.

The quotation from St Paul indicates that Parott's mirror stands for
the obscure vision that man on earth has of the higher reality which
in heaven he will see 'face to face'. The poet is an inspired visionary
or prophet, but on earth his prophecy is obscure and can be conveyed
only 'in part' (1 Corinthians 13:9); to the strict logician it may seem
mere confusion but, given sufficient faith and a sufficiently perceptive exegesis, the order within the confusion will become apparent.
The outward confusion is not just a consequence of the Fall, but is
necessary as a form of protection: enclosed within his cage of
allegory, Parott can safely declare that *he* is not making dangerous
political comments – the danger, if any, lies in the intelligent
application of his nonsense by those who hear it. Parott's vision, in
this poem, is chiefly political; he is concerned to convey the truth,
under whatever disguise may be necessary, about the danger to
which England is exposed by Wolsey's lust for power. But there is
also a more general and timeless meaning, implied by Parott's
paradisal origin, of which the poem's political message is only one
facet. Man too, not just the poet, had his origin in Paradise, and
though, as a result of his Fall, his body has now entered the world of

time and death, his soul retains its paradisal immortality. It is of this
that we are reminded in the closing stanzas of Part II;

> Parrot is a fayre byrd for a lady;
> God of his goodnes him framed and wrought;
> When Parrot is ded, he dothe not putrefy;
> Ye, all thyng mortall shall torne unto nought
> Except mannes soule, that Chryst so dere bought;
> That never may dye, nor never dye shall:
> Make moche of Parrot, the popegay ryall.
>
> For that pereles prynce that Parrot dyd create,
> He made you of nothynge by his magistye;
> Poynt well this probleme that Parrot doth prate,
> And remembre amonge how Parrot and ye
> Shall lepe from this lyfe, as mery as we be.
> Pompe, pryde, honour, ryches and worldly lust,
> Parrot sayth playnly, shall tourne all to dust.   (211–24)

Parott here stands not only for the poet, but for man's soul, and at
the same time for the poet's power to remind man of his true nature,
origin, and end. Parott gazes in his mirror, and sees himself – but
himself as he really is, immortal, not only in the sense that the poet
gains undying fame by his works, but in the sense that all men have
immortal souls. In medieval birdlore, it was not parrots but pea-
cocks that were said not to putrefy;[45] Skelton is creating his own
myth (as Chaucer did in the *Prologue* to *The Legend of Good Women*,
with his story of the transformation of Alcestis into a daisy) and
'Parrot is a fayre byrd for a lady' is surely an ironic understatement.
As in *The Garland of Laurel* 'the laurel' is the poem itself as well as the
poem's central symbol, so here 'Parott' is the poem, the 'litelle
quayre namyd the Popagay' (278),[46] as well as its speaker. Thus in
Part IV Skelton sends his work out into the world:

> Goe, lytyll quayre, pray them that yow beholde,
> In there remembraunce ye may be inrolde.
>
> Yet some folys say ye arre furnysshyd with knakkes,
> That hang togedyr as fethyrs in the wynde;
> But lewdlye ar they lettyrd that your lernyng lackys ...   (290–4)

It is the bird as much as the book which might be accused by
imperceptive readers of being no more than 'fethyrs in the wynde';
and similarly it is the book as much as the bird which might be seen
by such readers, at least before Parott is persuded to 'speke owte', as
suitable for ladies.

If Parott is a symbol of man and his immortality, this helps to explain why in Part III he is called on by Galathea to declare 'Whate mone he made when Pamphylus loste hys make' (234). The marginal gloss at this point – 'Hic occurrat emorie Phamphilus de Amore Galathee' (Here let *Pamphilus de Amore Galatheae* come to memory) – calls attention to a widely read twelfth-century Latin poem in the Ovidian manner, an 'art of love' built on the framework of Pamphilus's pursuit and loss of Galathea. What follows is in fact an English lyric in which the speaker addresses his 'loste … make' as 'Besse', promises her 'ferme and stabyll' love (246), and begs her to return to him. But it has been pointed out that 'Pamphilus' means 'All-Lover', and suggested that he might be interpreted allegorically as Christ, lamenting the loss of his 'make' or spouse, mankind, as a result of the Fall.[47] In this case Galathea would stand for mankind, or more specifically for the human sinfulness represented by Eve; and this seems to be confirmed by another marginal gloss, opposite the following lines:

> Alas, I am dysdayned,
> And as a man halfe-maymed,
> My harte is so sore payned,
> I pray the, Besse, unfayned,
> Yet com agayne to me! (252–6)

The gloss quotes Virgil, *Eclogues* III 64–5: 'Malo me Galathea petit, lasciva puella, Et fugit ad salices, & c.' (With an apple Galathea entices me, lascivious girl, and flees to the willows). In a Christian context, enticement by an apple inevitably suggests the Fall, and it is in this way that God is 'dysdayned' and then, when the Fall has led to the Incarnation, 'halfe-maymed'. The *lasciva puella*, then, is Galathea–Eve, and it is at least possible that the willows are those by the rivers of Babylon of Psalm 137, the 'salwys olde, foule, and thikk' as Lydgate put it in the *Defence of Holy Church*, which were seen as symbolizing the corrupt pleasures of the senses. Corresponding to the allegorization of Pamphilus and Galathea is an allegorization of the English lyric 'Come over the burne, Besse'. In Skelton's time this already existed in a number of moralized versions, such as that in Ritson's MS, which explains that 'Besse ys mankynde' to whom 'Christ stondes and clepys'.[48] In Skelton's version, too, the speaker is evidently Christ, suffering for the love of mankind, 'as a man halfe-maymed', and begging it to turn back to him. In this allegorized form, the lyric is surprisingly touching; and one effect of this section of *Speke Parott* is to suggest the possibility not only of the redemption of mankind but of the redemption of the poet from his fallen role as courtly entertainer. By means of allegory, even a simple lyric of secular love can be shifted on to a higher plane of significance; and Parott, the pet of ladies, can speak of immortality and salvation. Perhaps too Galathea may be thought of as having a higher role. She is the courtly lady who begs the poet for a love-poem, and then within that poem's allegorical fiction she becomes Eve and her offspring; but, in her exterior role here and subsequently, as the one who calls on Parott to 'speke' (233, 416), and then to 'Sette asyde all sophysms, and speke now trew and playne' (448), Galathea may be seen as the poet's Muse, the power which inspires his utterance. In Chaucer's *Prologue* to *The Legend of Good Women* there was a similar elevation of the daisy (who is also Alcestis) from the object of courtly devotion to 'The maistresse of my wit' (F 88). The evident serious-ness of Skelton's belief in inspiration makes this at least possible.

One other aspect of Parott that must be mentioned is his ability to speak many languages. On the literal level, this is of course a matter of his imitating whatever he hears, even animal noises – 'Lyke owur pus-catt, Parott can mewte and crye' (24) – and thus providing amusement for ladies. Not unlike Collyn Clout, he is a mere reporter of the words of others, and thus cannot be held personally responsible if they offend or shock. But he claims too that this imitative skill is a degenerate form of the paradisal insight he once possessed:

> My lady mastres, Dame Phylology,
> Gave me a gyfte in my neste when I lay,
> To lerne all langage and hyt to speke aptlye.   (43–5)

Now, however, in the fallen world of Wolsey's England, the pursuit of excess has turned insight into madness:

> Now *pandes mory*, wax frantycke som men sey;
> Phronessys for frenessys may not holde her way.   (46–7)

(*Pandes mory* is French for 'go mad' or 'wax frantycke', and Phronesis or prudence is the mother of Philologia in Martianus Capella's *De nuptiis Philologiae et Mercurii*.) The outward appearance of much of *Speke Parott* is certainly of frenzy rather than prudence – a kind of multilingual madness, as the lines under discussion illustrate. The poem has more scraps of Latin than anything else, but it also contains French, Greek, German, Welsh, Flemish, Spanish, 'Affryc tongue'

(80), a phrase in an unidentifiable *lingua franca*, and imitations of Scottish and Irish accents. Like allegory, the poem's multilingualism is partly a form of self-protective obscurity, especially since many of the phrases Parott repeats are quotations from or allusions to literary texts which themselves contain the point he wants to make. The reader has to be unusually quick and well informed to grasp what meaning of Skelton's is hidden behind Parott's rapidly chattered nonsense, and he can never be quite sure that he has succeeded in grasping it fully (or in some cases at all). But Parott's multilingualism also has a special aptness to the two major fields on which the poem's satire plays – international affairs and reforms in education, with the domineering part played by Wolsey in both. I mentioned earlier Skelton's opposition to new teaching methods for Latin and his taking the part of the 'Trojans' against the Greeks; I shall say no more about these except that they are the major themes of Part II of *Speke Parott*, and they are appropriately expressed with the help of Greek and Latin quotations. Current affairs are dominated by the Calais conference, and the modern languages Parott explicitly claims to speak are those of the parties to the conference:

> Dowche Frenshe of Paris Parot can lerne,
> Pronownsyng my purpose after my properte,
> With, '*Parlez byen, Parott, ow parles ryen*'.
> With Dowche, with Spaynyshe, my tonge can agree;
> In Englysshe to God Parott can supple:
> 'Cryste save Kyng Herry the viiith, owur royall kyng,
> The red rose in honour to flowrysshe and sprynge!'   (29–35)

French 'of Paris' (rather than the antiquated Norman French still used by English lawyers) is the language of Francis I; German and Spanish are those of Charles V's dominions; and English that of Wolsey, though Skelton uses it (as throughout the poem) to emphasize his own loyalty to Henry VIII however harsh his attacks on his chief minister. In *Collyn Clout* one effect of the many reports of popular sayings, as C. S. Lewis put it, is 'that of listening to the voice of the people itself. A vast muttering and growling of rumours fills our ears';[49] similarly in *Speke Parott* the 'shredis of sentence' (92) in many languages build up a sense of the immense complication of European affairs, with, as ground-bass, the perennial wisdom of the Bible and the Roman poets.

I have considered the allegory in which Parott himself is involved, but a word must be said, finally, of the political allegory contained in what he says, in which the central figure is Wolsey. It would take impossibly long to disentangle this completely, because Wolsey designedly appears under many different names, among them '*Vitulus* in Oreb' (59), Moloch (60), possibly Jethro (115), Sihon (121), 'Og, that fat hog of Basan' (122), Lyacon (289, 400), Zadok (304), and 'Syr Sydrake' (326). This too is part of the deliberate obscurity with which Skelton protects himself; it also helps to suggest the ubiquity of Wolsey's power (he is the reality behind all these names); but above all, given that most of the names have Scriptural contexts, we can see that Skelton, like Lydgate in the *Defence of Holy Church*, is reading the history of his own time in typological terms.[50] Antichrist appears in many guises throughout history, and Wolsey is the chief guise in which Skelton sees him in his own England. Antichrist is inevitably associated with apocalypse, and there is a strong sense in *Speke Parott*, again as in Lydgate's *Defence*, that only a clear-sighted and decisive monarch can save England from apocalyptic destruction. Skelton is not optimistic that Henry VIII has the will or even the power to drive away the gathering clouds:

> The skye is clowdy, the coste is nothyng clere;
> Tytan hath truste up hys tressys of fyne golde;
> Jupyter for Saturne darre make no royall chere;
> Lyacon lawghyth thereatt and berythe hym more bolde;
> Racell, rulye ragged, she is like to cache colde;
> Moloc, that mawmett, there darre no man withsay;
> The reste of suche reconyng may make a fowle fraye.   (397–403)

Saturn may gain the upper hand over Jupiter; but, however threatening the situation, Parott is not terrified, and continues to speak out to the end.

> ... trowthe in parabyll ye wantonlye pronounce,
> Langagys divers; yet undyr that dothe reste
> Maters more precious than the ryche jacounce,
> Diamounde, or rubye, or balas of the beste,
> Or eyndye sapher with oryente perlys dreste.   (364–8)

So Skelton claims, applying to Parott's teaching the imagery of sapphire, pearl and ruby that he had applied in courtly compliment to Jane Scrope;[51] but if the precious truth is to be discovered beneath the 'parabyll' and the 'Langagys divers', the poem must have readers who are prepared to participate actively in the creation of its meaning. *Speke Parott* is manifestly not one of those works that can be passively absorbed by their readers as a consumer-product: the reader must be constantly alert, willing not just to read but to interpret. 'Som sey they cannot my parables expresse' (386), laments Parott, but that is because they are not ready to 'postyll' his discourse, to comment on it as men were used to comment on Scripture:

> O causeles cowardes, O hartles hardynes,
> O manles manhod, enfayntyd all with fere,
> O connyng clergye, where ys your redynes
> To practise or postyll thys prosses here and there? (390–3)

Before Parott's opening words, Skelton sets a Latin sentence followed by a verse couplet:

> *Lectoribus auctor recipit opusculy huius auxesim*
>
> *Crescet in immensum me vivo pagina presens;*
> *Hinc mea dicetur Skeltonidis aurea fama.*

(From his readers the author receives an amplification of his little work. This present book will grow boundlessly while I am living; thence will the golden fame of Skelton be proclaimed.)

This epigraph makes the Renaissance claim that poetry confers undying fame on its author, carrying his name down to posterity, but it perhaps also goes beyond that in suggesting that this very growth of fame through readership adds new meaning to the work itself. As Parott puts it later,

> Thus myche Parott hath opynlye expreste;
> Let se who dare make up the reste. (381–2)

It is we who must 'make up' the work's meaning by the intelligence and imagination of our response to it. This response cannot be simply a matter of digging up specific treasures which the author has concealed; it must also involve a willingness to participate in a boundless play of language and of languages. Not infrequently, Skelton's obscure allusions produce lines of bizarre, surrealistic beauty, whose sound and meaning echo far beyond the historical events to which they allude. For example:

> Go, litelle quayre, namyd the Popagay,
> Home to resorte Jerobesethe perswade;
> For the cliffes of Scaloppe they rore wellaway,
> And the sandes of Cefas begyn to waste and fade,
> For replicacion restles that he of late ther made;
> Now Neptune and Eolus ar agreed of lyclyhod,
> For Tytus at Dover abydythe in the rode.

Lucina she wadythe among the watry floddes,
And the cokkes begyn to crowe agayne the day;
Le tonsan de Jason is lodgid among the shrowdes . . .   (278–87)

The roaring lamentation of the cliffs, the wasting and fading of the
sands, the wading of the moon-goddess amidst the floods, the
crowing of the cocks – these strange sounds and sights have a
resonance that escapes from the realm of politics, and that confirms
Parott's inspired creativeness. But the reader too must do his part: he
must be willing to share in this creativeness, and interpretation of the
poem must correspondingly be prepared to admit its own subjectivity and provisionality.

7 · Wyatt and Surrey

Sir Thomas Wyatt was born about 1503, of a father who had been a loyal supporter of Henry Tudor both before and after he came to the throne as Henry VII, and who held high office under both of the earliest Tudor kings. In 1516 the son entered St John's College, Cambridge, and in the same year he is first recorded at court. He held office as Clerk of the King's Jewels and as a royal esquire, took part in a tournament in which Henry VIII himself also participated, married Lord Cobham's daughter and later separated from her. He was High Marshal of Calais, and he took part in a series of important diplomatic missions, to France, to Italy, to Flanders, and to the court of the Emperor in Spain, where he remained as ambassador for two years. Such a career as courtier and diplomat under Henry VIII brought risks as well as rewards: Wyatt was accused of having been a lover of Anne Boleyn, was imprisoned, and only narrowly escaped execution; and he was imprisoned again when charged with alleged treason while ambassador to the Emperor. He was pardoned again, and, after this crowded life, died while on diplomatic service in England in 1542.

1. Wyatt's poetic role

From this sketch of his career, it is already possible to judge that Wyatt was a poet of a quite different kind from any previously discussed in this book. Many of the poets we have considered wrote within the ambit of a courtly tradition and were themselves courtiers, but the term courtier can have a variety of meanings. A distinction should be drawn, it has been suggested, 'between the gentlemen-poets and the household poets ... John Skelton had celebrated Flodden Field, and John Leland wrote ditties for Anne [Boleyn]'s coronation. Both were respected as royal servants, but neither ranks with the gentlemen-poets, whose work was for private, not public, occasions.'[1] Wyatt is the first gentleman-poet we have had to consider and perhaps only the third of any significance who can be identified as having written in English; the first two being King James I of Scotland and Charles, Duke of Orleans, both foreigners who, it may be supposed, would not have become English poets but for the accident of a long period of enforced residence in England as prisoners. Of the poets whose work we have examined, Hoccleve was a middling civil servant and scribe, Lydgate was a monk, and the Wakefield Master (probably), Henryson (possibly), and Dunbar, Skelton, and Hawes (certainly) were priests. All were clearly on the 'clerkly' side of the medieval division between clerks and knights. Only Chaucer's status is (characteristically) uncertain: he came from the prosperous bourgeoisie, but he seems to have associated freely with those of higher rank; his son was knighted, and his granddaughter married an earl and eventually became a duchess. But even Chaucer when he writes of love, the quintessential courtly subject, generally does so in the role of an outsider, a servant of Cupid's servants rather than an intimate of Cupid's chamber; and he is certainly not above writing a *Complaint to his Purse* as an acknowledgement of his dependence on his social superiors for material support. We have glanced at similar pleas for funds by Hoccleve, Lydgate, and Dunbar.

It is impossible to imagine such a plea by Wyatt, and indeed the whole corpus of his work forms a configuration quite different from that of any earlier poet in English, with the possible exception of Charles of Orleans. None of Wyatt's poems is a public contribution to a public occasion: there are poems marking events such as the fall of Thomas Cromwell (MT CCXXXVI: 'The piller pearisht is whearto I lent') and the execution of those alleged to have had adulterous relations with Anne Boleyn (MT CLXXVI and CXLVI: 'Who lyst his welthe and eas retayne' and 'In mornyng wyse syns daylye I increas'[2]), but the responses they record are essentially private. The only work of Wyatt's to be published during his lifetime was the prose translation from Plutarch, *The Quyete of Mynde*, written for Katherine of Aragon;[3] his poems circulated only in manuscript collections among a small circle of friends of his own social class. He is the first English poet whose work takes the form which since the Renaissance has come to seem normal – that of a large collection of short secular poems purporting to record isolated moments of personal emotional experience. (I do not mean to imply that Wyatt's poems can be read as autobiography without the intervention of fiction, literary source, or literary and social convention, only that

that is the impression they aim to give.) He is also the first whose life and work represent the breakdown of the medieval separation of clerk from knight. Like the hero of Hawes's *Pastime of Pleasure*, Wyatt went to university before embarking on the career of service appropriate to a knight (he was actually knighted in 1535). The service in question is not merely that of a lady; it is public service in the Renaissance manner, service of 'My kyng, my contry, alone for whome I lyve' (MT XCIX 7). His work includes translations from Latin, French and Italian, and he commends the teaching of Seneca and Epictetus in a letter to his son and that of Seneca and Plato in one of his sonnets; but except for the strange and unfinished *Iopas' Song* (MT CIV), none of his unquestionably authentic writing is ostentatiously clerkly. There is no Chaucerian name-dropping,[4] no Lydgatean moralizing, no Skeltonian bandying of quotations and technical terms, no scholasticism, no encyclopaedism, no informativeness, little classical mythology, no sustained allegory, almost no personification,[5] no elevated diction, no amplification. In many ways, considered against the background of this book's earlier chapters, Wyatt's work looks like a marked repudiation of the tradition of English poetry begun by Chaucer – a tradition that, as I have argued, can be seen in Chaucer's own work as a reaching out towards some central characteristics of the fourteenth-century Italian Renaissance, but that then, in the work of his followers, generally becomes more medieval. This book's perspective is to some extent a misleading one for Wyatt, for it has paid no attention to the many short fifteenth-century poems of love, mostly anonymous, to certain of which his poems bear certain similarities; on the other hand, in his own century Wyatt was already recognized by Puttenham as part of a new phenomenon, a 'new company of courtly makers' that 'sprong up' in the latter part of Henry VIII's reign.[6]

If we consider those 'Renaissance' elements of Chaucer's own achievement that did survive or get revived in the Chaucerian tradition – aspects of style, some of which help to convey an unmedieval *idea* of poetry – they too are conspicuously absent from Wyatt's work. In his poems there are no Muses (except the homely Kentish Muses of the first *Satire* [MT CV 101]), no appeals to Apollo, no apostrophic prologues, above all no sense that the poem is ratified by its place in the literary tradition that its words evoke. This last point can be illustreated from a sonnet of Wyatt's that is unusual in the literary allusiveness of its language:

> You that in love finde lucke and habundance
> And live in lust and joyful jolitie,
> Arrise for shame, do away your sluggardie,
> Arise, I say, do May some observance!
> Let me in bed lye dreming in mischaunce,
> Let me remembre the happs most unhappy
> That me betide in May most commonly,
> As oon whome love list litil to avaunce.
> Sephame saide true that my nativitie
> Mischaunced was with the ruler of the May.
> He gest, I prove of that the veritie:
> In May my welth and eke my liff, I say,
> Have stoude so oft in such perplexitie.
> Rejoyse! let me dreme of your felicitie.   (MT XCII)

Wyatt's language here incorporates recollections of Chaucer, which the reader is surely expected to recognize. Lines 2 and 3 recall the passage in *The Knight's Tale* in which Emelye goes a-Maying and thus unwittingly provokes Palamon and Arcite to fall in love with her:

> For May wole have no slogardie a-nyght.
> The sesoun priketh every gentil herte,
> And maketh hym out of his slep to sterte,
> And seith, 'Arys, and do thyn observaunce!'   (I 1042–5)

There is an overlapping recollection of Pandarus's urging of Criseyde to 'don to May som observaunce' (*Troilus and Criseyde* II 112), while line 8 recalls Troilus's fear that if his love for Criseyde becomes known he will be mocked by lovers as one 'Of hem that Love list febly for to avaunce' (*ibid.*, I 518). There is a striking similarity between this poem of Wyatt's and the moment in Dunbar's *The Thrissill and the Rois* when May stands before the poet's bed and urges him to rise, with allusions to the very same passage from *The Knight's Tale*.[7] In both cases, the idealism of the courtly literary tradition is defined by Chaucerian recollection only to be rejected as inapplicable to the poet's actual circumstances. In *The Thrissill and the Rois*, however, the rejection is only temporary: it is a way of establishing that the idealizing allegory of love is a consciously chosen artifice rather than a mere reflection of nature; after that, Dunbar continues with the artifice appropriate for a public occasion. But in Wyatt's sonnet, the rejection of all the Chaucerian lines evoke is permanent and is grounded in private experience. Others may joyfully perform the old courtly rites, but for Wyatt

himself they represent a mere dream of felicity, harshly incon-
gruent with the 'perplexitie' and danger that have belonged to May
in his own life. As so often in Wyatt, the only 'proof', the only
source of judgment, whether of poetic tradition or astrological
prediction, lies in what he has actually experienced for himself. The
Chaucerian tradition, well though he obviously knows it, is no
longer valid.

There is no equivalent in Wyatt to the claim to poetic inspiration
that we saw entering English poetry in *The House of Fame* and
pervading the work of Skelton in Wyatt's own youth. The absence
of any such claim is a feature not just of his short lyrical poems, but
equally of his few longer works, the *Satires* and the *Penitential Psalms*.
It is true that at one point in the latter David recognizes a power
greater than himself at work in his song –

> . . . he knew he hath alone exprest
> Thes grete thinges that greter spryte compilde,
> As shalme or pype letes out the sownd inprest,
> By musikes art forgid tofore and fyld   (MT CVIII 634–7)

– but it is striking that the 'grete thinges' consist of the doctrine of the
Psalms rather than their art, the 'diepe secretes . . ./Off mercy, off
fayth, off frailte, off grace, / Off Goddes goodnes, and off justyfy-
ing' (509–11). Unlike Skelton in his *Replycacion*, Wyatt implies no
analogy between David as musician and himself as poet.

We saw how in the *Prologue* to *The Legend of Good Women* Chaucer
addressed the daisy, later personified as Alcestis, the preserver from
death, as 'The maistresse of my wit' (F 88); and, in this last of his
claims to poetic inspiration, he continued:

> My word, my werk, ys knyt so in youre bond
> That, as an harpe obeieth to the hond,
> And maketh it soune after his fyngerynge,
> Ryght so mowe ye oute of myn herte bringe
> Swich vois, ryght as yow lyst, to laughe or pleyne.   (F 89–93)

Although Wyatt, in many of his lyrics, characterizes himself as a
lutanist, no such notion can be found in them of the poet as an
instrument inspired to music by a lady who is the poet's muse.
Wyatt's different conception of the nature of poetry emerges clearly
from one such poem, 'Blame not my lute' (MT CCV). This, like many
of the lyrics, is addressed to the lady herself, and the situation it

reveals (whether actual or fictional) is that she has blamed the poet's lute and broken its strings for disclosing her infidelity. The poet argues that the lute is not to blame;

> My lutte, alas, doth not ofend
> Tho that perfors he must agre
> To sownd such teunes as I entend
> To sing to them that hereth me. (8–11)

The poet, then, is no instrument of higher power; on the contrary he is the master of an instrument that has no choice but to do his will. The poem's argument does not stop here, however; Wyatt goes on to argue that the lady must blame no-one but herself:

> Blame but thy selffe that hast mysdown
> And well desarvid to have blame;
> Change thou thy way so evyll bygown
> And then my lute shall sownd that same. (29–32)

It is never suggested, though, that the reason for this is that it is she who directly inspires the poet's song, but rather that 'Of right' (25) the poet must record the truth about the lady. The 'spight' of his song is 'rightfull' (20) because it corresponds to the spite she has shown towards him: if the song causes her discomfort, it is only 'By thy desartt' (34). The repeated claim of this poem, and of many others, is simply that, in accordance with the poet's will, it tells the truth about the lady.

In Wyatt, as within the medieval courtly system, to be a poet and to be a lover are still virtually the same thing, but neither love nor poetry is now seen as inspired by a superior being. Lover and lady confront each other as equals, partners and rivals in negotiation, autonomous beings of whom aggression and moral responsibility can equally be expected,[8] and the relations between them are to be governed not by grace on the one side and self-abasement on the other, but by justice.

> Yf it be yea, I shalbe fayne;
> If it be nay, frendes as before;
> Ye shall an othre man obtain,
> And I myn owne and yours no more. (MT XXXIV 9–12)

We may suspect that the very bluntness is calculated, a pose adopted for its persuasive force; but certainly the absence of any doctrine of poetic inspiration from Wyatt's poetry corresponds to a changed conception of the nature of love.

It must be added, parenthetically, that the equalizing of lover and lady is frequently conceived in terms that now seem so materialistic as to preclude any possibility of romantic love. The lover is, as before, his lady's 'servant', but the relationship between them is seen by the lover as one in which his 'service' deserves and ought to receive its 'reward':

> If fansy would favour
> As my deserving shall,
> My love, my paramour,
> Should love me best of all.
>
> But if I cannot attain
> The grace that I desire,
> Then may I well complain
> My service and my hiere.   (MT XLIII 1–8)

There is a fundamental contradiction here between the traditional conception of the lady's 'grace', which, like God's grace, is given freely and cannot be earned, and the speaker's notion that his service should receive its appropriate 'hire'. The courtly conception of love was based, among other things, on an imaginative feudalization of the love-relationship; Wyatt, more realistically, seems to envisage a relationship analogous to the 'bastard feudalism'[9] of the late Middle Ages, in which lordship and service derived from payment at market rates rather than from customary tenurial bonds.

The Chaucerian sublime, which, as we have seen, has its origins in Chaucer's Italian reading, was appropriately discarded by Wyatt, though it was to return as a fruitful influence in the poetry of following generations, and especially in that of Spenser. Chaucer had derived much from Italy; his followers derived much from him, but they read the Italian Renaissance secondhand, through him, and thus in ways that often involved dilution and distortion. Wyatt went back directly to Italian sources – sometimes to the same sources as Chaucer – and this led to a further burst of innovation in English poetry, a fresh beginning, a century and a half later, on the creation of an English poetic Renaissance. I will consider Wyatt's translations later, but here I want to emphasize that his rejection of the Chaucerian elevated style is nevertheless accompanied by a renewal of interest in the forms and techniques of poetry, comparable with Chaucer's own. Even on the level of metrical forms, English poetry had been living for a century and a half on those introduced by Chaucer, mainly from Italian, and especially on rhyme royal and pentameter couplets. Wyatt went back once more to Italian to find other possibilities of lasting importance: the sonnet, terza rima, ottava rima. The nature of his technical interests can be illustrated from a specimen sonnet which is not a translation:

> If waker care, if sodayne pale coulour,
> If many sighes, with litle speche to playne,
> Now joy, now woo, if they my chere distayne,
> For hope of smalle, if muche to fere therfore,
> To hast, to slak my pase lesse or more
> Be signe of love, then do I love agayne.
> If thow aske whome, sure sins I did refrayne
> Brunet that set my welth in such a rore,
> Th'unfayned chere of Phillis hath the place
> That Brunet had: she hath and ever shal.
> She from my self now hath me in her grace;
> She hath in hand my witt, my will, and all.
> My hert alone well worthie she doth staye,
> Without whose helpe skant do I live a daye.   (MT XCVII)

Here the octave plus sestet of the Italian sonnet's normal rhyme-scheme is counterpointed against a sestet plus octave in its argument: a single sentence of six lines, followed by two semantic units each of four lines. (Similar counterpointing effects are found in Petrarch's own sonnets, and Wyatt was clearly sensitive to them: thus in 'Ever myn happe is slack and slo in commyng' (MT XXX) he exactly reproduces the 4 + 7 + 3 sentence-structure of Petrarch's 'Mie venture al venir son tarde et pigre' (*Rime* 57), playing it against the 4 + 4 / 3 + 3 of the rhyme-scheme.) Lines 1–6 are concerned with the outward 'signe(s) of love', and the main verb of the sentence they form is deferred until the second half of line 6 by a series of *If* ... clauses, themselves interestingly various in their length and their relation to the metrical pattern. Line 7 opens with another *If* ... clause, and lines 7–10 present in a single sentence the transition from 'Brunet', the old love, to 'Phillis', the new. Finally, lines 11–14 consist of a series of parallel statements about 'Phillis', each with 'She' as its subject, the first two simple in structure and occupying one line each, the last complex in structure, inverted in word-order, and occupying two lines. This last quatrain implies an analogy between 'Phillis' and a Protestant conception of God, and the sonnet as a whole moves from the symptoms of love, indicating change-ability, to the assured stability of the new faith that underlies them. It would be difficult to discover this degree of small-scale technical accomplishment and refinement in any English poetry between

Chaucer and Wyatt. Nor is it simply a matter of aesthetically pleasing patterns of sound and rhythm: the new forms give a new shape, a differently and more finely organized dynamic, to poetic *thought*.

2. Wyatt as courtly lyricist

In general, I believe that Wyatt's most interesting poems are his translations. He shows little sign of being a powerful or original thinker, and he was dependent on the use of sources and models for density and continuity of discourse. It is in his translations that he comes closest to the idea of literature as work of intrinsic and lasting value as we saw it developed in English for the first time by Chaucer. In the short lyrical poems without sources that make up, quantitatively, the great bulk of Wyatt's work, any such ambition is in abeyance. Indeed, it has been denied that these lyrics can properly be thought of as literature at all. John Stevens has written that 'much of what we today call the "literature" of medieval England, is a *symptom* of a certain kind of social activity. Of no "literature" is this more true than of the literature of courtly love.' Just as most of the shorter medieval religious poems are best considered as reflections of 'the religious activity of a community', so secular poems such as Wyatt's are reflections, and not necessarily anything more, of the 'attitude and behaviour, words and actions' of the court as it played 'the game of love'.[10] The implication of this is that we should not, as readers, expect too much of such merely symptomatic writings. Certainly they were not intended to demand the kind of perseverance, nocturnal study, and exertion of intellectual power that Boccaccio specified as necessary for the interpretation of poetry.

This is not to say that the poems are without difficulties. Wyatt begins one lyric (MT CCX) by alleging that in the past his lyrics have been misunderstood:

> My songes ware to defuse;
> Theye made folke to muse.　　　　　　　　　　(6–7)

He therefore determines, for once, to write 'more plaine' (9), and ends by saying:

> Yf this be undre miste,
> And not well playnlye wyste,
> Undrestonde me who lyste,
> For I reke not a bene;
> I wott what I doo meane.　　　　　　　　　　(41–5)

But the difficulty to which he refers is not intrinsic to his poems, nor is the 'miste' that of allegory: it has to do with their relation to the 'social activity' which is their matrix. The poem has its full meaning only for the individual (usually a woman) to whom it is addressed, and for those few in the know who are able to identify her – 'ye that be here', as he puts it in one rondeau (MT XVII 2), perhaps consciously recalling Chaucer's address in *Troilus and Criseyde* to 'ye loveres that ben here' (II 1751). Yet this meaning is not conveyed explicitly in the poem's words, which remain on a level of generality that will stimulate guesswork – perhaps malicious guesswork – by others.

Writing in the role, usually, of unhappy lover, Wyatt represents himself as being in the position of the squire Aurelius in *The Franklin's Tale* when he falls in love with Arveragus's wife:

> He was despeyred; no thyng dorste he seye,
> Save in his songes somwhat wolde he wreye
> His wo, as in a general compleynyng;
> He seyde he lovede, and was biloved no thyng.
> Of swich matere made he manye layes,
> Songes, compleintes, roundels, virelayes,
> How that he dorste nat his sorwe telle. (V 943–9)

Aurelius *dared* say nothing of his love except in general terms – the word *dorste* occurs five times in the whole passage[11] – for reasons that had to do with his own feelings; his love for Dorigen was intensely idealizing, a quasi-religious reverence, and he feared the inner wound he would suffer if she rebuffed him. Such fear was part of a centuries-old tradition of courtly feeling; but by Wyatt's time, in the court of Henry VIII, there were also external reasons for fear and concealment, as Wyatt himself had cause to know.

> Syns that in love the paynes ben dedly,
> Me thinck it best that reddely
> I do retorne to my first adresse;
> For at this tyme to great is the prese,
> And perilles appere to abundauntely
> For to love her. (MT XV 10–15)

The politics of amatory relations under Henry VIII might make love's pains deadly indeed, its perils all too abundant: in 1536 five men accused of sexual relations with Anne Boleyn were executed, and so was she, and Wyatt seems only narrowly to have escaped execution himself. Indeed, in this real-life setting, much of the age-old metaphorical material of courtly poetry – love as suffering, love as imprisonment, love as death – became capable of a terrifying reliteralization. In the ballade 'Like as the byrde in the cage enclosed' (MT CCXLVI) Wyatt compares himself to a caged bird uncertain whether to prefer imprisonment or death at the claws of the waiting hawk, and he ends with a *demande d'amour* closely resembling that at the end of Part I of *The Knight's Tale*:

> This birde to deliver, youe that here her playne,
> Your advise, yowe lovers, wyche shalbe best:
> In cage thraldome, or by the hauke to be opprest,
> And which for to chuse? (24–7)

The question, like Chaucer's, is addressed to 'you lovers', but it is impossible to be certain from the poem whether the imprisonment is metaphorical or literal. Many of Wyatt's poems raise similar doubts: they imply a situation in which love was politicized and politics were eroticized. (We should not disregard the erotic charge of the play of power and submission conveyed by many of the poems: 'Who so list to hounte' (MT VII) and 'They fle from me' (MT XXXVII) are especially striking examples.) For one who might be literally 'Twixte deth and prison piteously oppressed' (MT CCXLVI 3), there was the most urgent reason for the love lyric to remain obscure because vague and general.

The 'you' addressed in Wyatt's lyrics, or the 'She unto whome I sue for grace' (MT CLXXXIII 18) to whom they refer, remains unidentified: 'she hathe no name' (MT CCXIX 31). The language is usually bare, plain, unspecific, traditional, and the particular situation and emotions concerned (which in *The Franklin's Tale* or *The Knight's Tale* were spelt out in a lengthy narrative) are often indicated only in the vaguest terms as 'Suche happe as I ame happed in' (MT XXXVI 1) or 'The thing that I require' (MT XXXIX 2). The identity of the recipient may be conveyed only by a meaning glance from the poet or a blush from one lady among a little group of listeners. 'Blame not my lute' ends by pointing outside itself to just such a blush:

> And yf perchance this folysh ryme
> Do make the blush at any tyme,
> Blame nott my lutte. (MT CCV 40–2)

The poem's meaning is completed not by its words but by the blush they provoke, and by the eagerness of other listeners to detect it. The world of such poems is an amatory version of one already familiar to us from Skelton's *Bowge of Court*, a world drably or frighteningly lacking in specificity:

> He tolde me so, by God, ye maye truste me.
> Parde, remembre whan ye were there,
> There I wynked on you – wote ye not where?
> In A *loco*, I mene *juxta* B:
> Woo is hym that is blynde and maye not see!   (514–18)

Skelton is concerned to define such a world; the lyrics of Wyatt and other poets of the early Tudor court may appear simply to be its products.

What might seem to be implied by all this is that the strictly literary achievement of Wyatt's lyrics cannot be expected to be very high. John Stevens writes: 'Nothing strikes a reader who is making his first acquaintance with the courtly lyric so forcibly as its drab lifelessness. (I speak of the great bulk of lyrics, not of a few anthology pieces.)'[12] The adverse criticism had been made in a more extreme form by H. A. Mason: 'I would assert that most of Wyatt's "lyrics" are not poems at all ... By a little application we could compose a dictionary of conventional phrases which would show that many of these poems of Wyatt's are simply strung together from these phrases into set forms. There is not the slightest trace of poetic activity.'[13] Before accepting this criticism we should bear in mind that Mason is saying about Wyatt what scholars have come to say about traditional poetry of a quite different kind – the epic with its stylistic origin in oral composition, as in Homer or the twentieth-century South Slav examples discussed by A. B. Lord.[14] Mason is declaring that Wyatt's lyrics are formulaic; but to say this is not necessarily to imply that there is no 'poetic activity' at work in them. There may be 'poetic activity', but it will be found elsewhere than in the invention of original phrases. I shall return to this point shortly.

I do not deny that many of the lyrics attributed to Wyatt, and especially those from the Devonshire Manuscript, are of little merit or intrinsic interest. It is true, too, that to read through the whole of Wyatt's collected poems is a dispiriting task (and one, to be sure, that Wyatt himself can never have envisaged imposing on any reader).[15] It is dispiriting partly because of the monotony of the subject-matter.

> At moost myschief
> I suffre greif,
> For of relief
> Syns I have none

My lute and I
Continuelly
Shall us apply
To sigh and mone.   (MT LI 1-8)

'Continuelly' indeed; poem after poem is a demand for attention to the speaker's self-enclosed misery. An extreme example is 'Lyke as the swanne towardis her dethe' (MT LXX), in which a single pair of rhymes (*dethe / note / brethe / note*) is dolefully repeated five times, as is the refrain, 'I dy! I dy! and you regarde yt note' (though with a telling change in the final line). We come to feel stifled by the narrowness of focus, which excludes everything but the speaker and his unhappiness, and it is striking that a rare instance such as 'Resound my voyse, ye woodes that here me plain' (MT XXII), where the speaker is set in an open landscape, brings a sense of relief even though the woods, hills and rivers are present only to echo his grief.

A more important cause of the narrowness of scope of Wyatt's lyrics is his abandonment of the philosophical ambitions of the Chaucerian tradition. The world of Wyatt's lyrics is in essence the world ruled by Fortune defined by Boethius in Book II of the *De consolatione philosophiae*, and Wyatt's familiarity with Boethian thought, gained, in all probability, through his reading of Chaucer's *Boece*, is confirmed by a poem such as 'If thou wilt mighty be' (MT CCLXI). This ballade, preserved only in *Tottel's Miscellany* but bearing all the marks of authenticity, has as its formal model short philosophical poems by Chaucer such as *Truth* and *Gentilesse*, and takes the material for its three stanzas from *metra* 5, 6 and 3 of Book III of the *De consolatione*. It urges the reader, for example,

If to be noble and high thy minde be meved,
Consider well thy grounde and thy beginnyng:
For He that hath eche starre in heaven fixed,
And geves the moone her hornes and her eclipsyng,
Alike hath made the noble in his workyng.   (8-12)

But this connection of human actions with a divinely governed cosmic order is extremely rare in Wyatt's poetry, and a more typical example of Wyatt's use of Boethius is to be found in 'Most wretchid hart, most myserable' (MT XCI), a dialogue between the self and the heart which removes the dimension of cosmic order and leaves only man in a meaninglessly hostile world. The heart's refrain-line, in answer to the self's 'Most wretchid harte, why arte thou nott ded?', is 'he is wretchid that wens hym so', and this is derived from

Chaucer's ballade-sequence *Fortune* (also a dialogue-poem): 'No man is wrecched, but himself it wene' (25). In Chaucer this line is spoken by Fortune herself, and is to be interpreted as part of a Boethian philosophical scheme which she also expounds:

> Lo, th'execucion of the majestee
> That al purveyeth of his rightwysnesse,
> That same thing 'Fortune' clepen ye,
> Ye blinde bestes, ful of lewednesse! (65–8)

Wyatt attributes the heart's refrain to one 'that knoweth what is what' (31) (meaning presumably either Chaucer or Boethius), but the heart can rely only on Stoic self-possession or self-assertion as the basis for its confidence.[16] For it, there is no philosophically conceived Fortune that executes God's will, but only 'happe' (46) – a favourite word of Wyatt's – and 'heven' means no more than stellar influences, which may intend to 'worke me woo' (21–2). The heart's integrity is guaranteed only from within, by a strenuous self-assertion which has neither objective grounding nor any means of self-criticism. And even in Wyatt's religious poetry, the relation to God seems to be possible only through an equally precarious, equally strenuously asserted faith, not, as for Chaucer, through a universal order in which divine meanings are written. Wyatt (or the speaker of his poems) is in a situation almost as desperate as that of Chaucer's pagans – indeed more desperate in some ways, for they have a chance of salvation by 'doing what is in them', without the need to strain for personal faith.

The speakers of Wyatt's secular lyrics are constantly subjected to unpredictable and inexplicable changes of situation. The force that brings about these changes is sometimes personified as Fortune in the traditional way: 'Ons, as me thought, Fortune me kyst' (MT LXV 1), or

> For she hath turned so her whele
> That I, unhappy man,
> May waile the time that I did fele
> Wherwith she fedde me than. (MT CCXLIX 25–8)

But Wyatt generally has nothing to say about Fortune, because he has no larger scheme of thought to fit her into. Even when Fortune's malice unexpectedly produces beneficial results, he can say no more than that 'Spite of thy hap, hap hath well hapt' (MT XXIII 7). There is nothing to carry his speakers beyond the narrow limits of their own subjective experience. The ground of value and the source of liberation from misery are to be found only in personal integrity, which the speaker often asserts in himself but rarely finds in others. Wyatt's lyrics echo with the demand for *trouth*, his name for this integrity or fidelity; but, like Wyatt's Fortune and unlike Chaucer's *trouthe*, Wyatt's *trouth* has no explicit connection with any structures of philosophical or religious thought that might help to place individual experience intelligibly in relation to God, the world, and history. The conclusion is inevitably pessimistic:

> What vaileth trouth, or by it to take payn,
> To stryve by stedfastnes for to attayne
> To be juste and true and fle from dowblenes,
> Sythens all alike, where rueleth craftines,
> Rewarded is boeth fals and plain?
> Sonest he spedeth that moost can fain;
> True meanyng hert is had in disdayn.
> Against deceipte and dowblenes
>   What vaileth trouth?
>
> Decyved is he by crafty trayn
> That meaneth no gile and doeth remayn
> Within the trapp withoute redresse,
> But for to love, lo, suche a maisteres
> Whose crueltie nothing can refrayn,
>   What vaileth trouth?   (MT II)

Chaucer's Troilus was driven to ask just such questions as this when confronted with incontrovertible proof of Criseyde's infidelity –

> 'O God,' quod he, 'that oughtest taken heede
> To fortheren trouthe, and wronges to punyce,
> Whi nyltow don a vengeaunce of this vice?' (*Troilus* v 1706–8)[17]

– and, whatever may be thought of the answers that belong to a Christian faith outside Troilus's experience, the questions have an intellectual context large enough to make them, at the very least, interesting to think about. Such sources of interest are lacking in Wyatt's lyrics.

In a more general sense, the egoism of Wyatt's lyric poetry can seem oppressive. It is the egoism of a strong mind, but one that quite lacks the relativism or negative capability that characterizes Chaucer's work, and, as one reads, one seems to be imprisoned inside its powerful walls. It would not be correct to describe the speaker of the lyrics as a solipsist, for one never doubts the real existence of the lady addressed or referred to. 'It was no dreme: I lay brode waking' (MT XXXVII 15): the lady is certainly something more than a lover's fantasy, and there is nothing in Wyatt's poetry that corresponds to the element of reverie or vision in Petrarch's. But the lady appears to exist for the sole purpose of affecting the lover in some way – usually to provoke cynicism or despair by her cruelty. On the rare occasions when the speaker imagines the lady's thoughts and feelings, the effect is quite unlike Chaucer's entering into the inner life of Criseyde or the Wife of Bath or even May. Sometimes the assumption is that her thoughts and feelings have to do solely with the speaker, as in the following admirably hard-edged epigram:

> Who hath herd of suche crueltye before,
> That, when my plaint remembred her my woo
> That caused it, she, cruell more and more,
> Wisshed eche stitche, as she did sit and soo,
> Had prykt myn hert for to encrese my sore!
> And, as I thinck, she thought it had ben so,
> For as she thought, 'This is his hert in dede,'
> She pricked herd and made her self to blede.   (MT XLII)

Might she not simply have been thinking of some difficulty in her needlework, and might not that have caused her to prick herself? For the speaker of the lyric, such possibilities clearly do not arise. Very occasionally, a reversal of the normal situation is imagined, as in the unusually tender lyric, 'There was never nothing more me payned' (MT XXXVIII). Here it is the speaker who has lacked *trouth*, and the lady who laments that she ever loved him, and nostalgically regrets the 'restfull nyghtes and joyfull daies' (16) she possessed in that distant past. And yet her grief is framed within his. The poem begins –

> There was never nothing more me payned
> Nor nothing more me moved
> As when my swete hert her complayned
> That ever she me loved,
>   Alas the while!   (1–5)

– and it ends:

> Her paynes tormented me so sore
> That comfort had I none
> But cursed my fortune more and more
> To se her sobbe and grone,
>   Alas the while!   (26–30)

The speaker's empathy is striking yet limited: ultimately the lady's sorrow matters because of the sorrow it causes him to feel. The most powerful token of sorrow is her tears, and they have a material existence that makes them no mere symbols:

> She wept and wrong her handes withall;
> The teres fell in my nekke. (21–2)

But it is his neck that is made wet with her tears.

The rarity of even such limited capacity for 'Feelynge his similitude in peynes smerte' (*Squire's Tale* v 480) in Wyatt's poetry is closely related to the sense of imprisonment mentioned above. Not only the reader but the speaker seems to be imprisoned by 'armed sighes . . . , / Twixt hope and drede locking my libertie' (MT LVI 7–8). Constraint, constriction, frustration, being clogged and fettered, these are the characteristic experiences, and much of the imagery is of futile action – striving against the stream (MT XCI 27 and LVIII 5–6), climbing rotten boughs (MT XIII 14), holding the wind in a net (MT VII 8). Once more, Chaucer offers an appropriate yardstick. What emerges from *The Franklin's Tale* is that the *libertee* which Dorigen and Arveragus seek is to be found not in contractual bonds but as the result of a *franchise* that abrogates bonds. It is because Aurelius is capable of empathizing with them and of feeling *compassioun* and *routhe* for their inward sufferings (v 1515, 1520) that the outcome can be one of release, with the question 'Which was the mooste fre, as thynketh yow?' (1622). Wyatt's poetry is rarely touched with such generosity.

A last reason why it can be dispiriting to read through the complete collection of Wyatt's lyrics is the plainness and bareness of their style; and this returns us to the topic raised earlier by the criticisms of Stevens and Mason. Though egoistic, this poetry is, paradoxically, anonymous. The speaker, though insistently and unmistakeably present as 'I', is as vaguely characterized as the 'you' or 'she', and his language is such as to elude or defeat the attention he seeks. One reason for this, though, is that we are not accustomed to pay attention to poetic language so unobtrusive, and we are therefore not very perceptive in discriminating between more and less skilful uses of it. A few examples may help to suggest the kind of effects to be looked for in the sober and subdued style of these poems: they have to do not with graphic imagery or surprising juxtapositions of words, but with the assured syntactical and metrical ordering of conventional phrases and the release of their hidden semantic power.

I begin with two stanzas from 'Where shall I have at myn owne wil' (MT LIII):

> I speke not now to move your hert
> That you should rue upon my pain;
> The sentence geven may not revert;
> I know such labour were but vayn.
>
> But syns that I for you, my dere,
> Have lost that thing that was my best,
> A right small losse it must appere
> To lese thes wordes and all the rest.   (13–20)

In theme this poem as a whole is yet another expression of grief at his rejection by a lady who had once shown him favour. (We had better not speculate, perhaps, about the advice Wyatt might have received to question his own behaviour and attitudes if he had been able to seek the counsel of an 'agony aunt' about the multiple rejections and betrayals suffered by the speakers of his poems. We cannot assume that the lyrics are autobiographical, or, even if they were, that failures in human relations would be identical with literary faults.) In diction 'Where shall I have' is notably plain, with a very high proportion of monosyllabic words; there are few metaphors, and of those only the jesting words that 'sparkill in the wynde' (21) are at all unusual. In the stanzas quoted only six words out of 59 are not monosyllables, and one of those six (*geven*) may be elided to a monosyllable; there are no metaphors at all, I think, or at least none that are not part of a courtly idiom so familiar as to seem entirely literal. What is distinctive about these two stanzas is their firm exclusion of the emotions that such lyrics commonly express with great freedom, an exclusion that is made syntactically explicit by negation: 'I speke *not* now', 'The sentence geven may *not* revert' (and 'but vayn' has a similar effect). The intensity of the speaker's feelings is measured by the strength of the barriers required to keep them out (and earlier in the poem too we find 'my plaint shall have *none* end', 'My teres can*not* suffice my woo', 'have I *no* frend', 'Comfort . . . have I *none*', '*Nought* moveth you'). The feeling is then all the more convincing when it evades these multiple barriers, to creep in parenthetically with 'my dere'. And within this subdued style a figure of words such as *adnominatio* (polyptoton), in the play on 'lost . . . losse . . . lese', is far more noticeable than it would be in a more graphic style; and the very vagueness of 'and all the rest' once more gives the impression of fending off emotions that it would be too painful to detail.

A second example, in which the stanzaic structure now plays a more important part, is the following single stanza from 'Sins you will nedes that I shall sing' (MT CCIX):

> A brokin lute, untunid stringes,
> With such a song maye well bere parte,
> That nether pleasith him that singes
> Nor theim that here, but her alone
> That with her herte wold straine my herte
>   To here yt grone.   (19–24)

Once more the poem as a whole expresses the familiar 'depe dispaire and dedlye payne' (4) of the rejected lover, this time intensified by the assumed social obligation of the courtier to 'sing'. As often, the lyric creates its own sense of a circle of listeners, among whom 'in this place' (15) is the lady who has rejected him. She, in her cruelty, rejoices at the speaker's woe; the other listeners are grieved by its expression in his song; what 'plesaunt game' (27) then, he asks, must he suffer himself? Once more the language is simple, largely mono-syllabic, and lacking in any imagery except the enclosing fiction of the poet as lutanist.[18] The stanza quoted, like each of the poem's five stanzas, consists of a single sentence. The sentence extends itself by a series of subordinate clauses, all relative except for the last, which is consecutive: '*That* nether pleasith', '*that* singes', '*that* here', '*That* . . . wold straine', '*To* here yt grone'. The sense given is of strain and approaching exhaustion, as the sentence strives to match the fixed length of the stanza, like a singer forced unwillingly to sing; this sense is reinforced by the throbbing repetition of *herte* in the penulti-mate line (supported by the similar sounds of *here* and *her*); until sentence and stanza expire together in the short last line.

Many of Wyatt's lyrics have refrains, and these provide interesting examples of how simple and conventional language can be made to yield meanings that are not simple and conventional. One such lyric is the following:

> *In eternum* I was ons determed
> For to have lovid, and my mynde affermed,
> That with my herte it should be confermed
>   *In eternum.*
>
> Forthwith I founde the thing that I myght like,
> And sought with love to warme her hert alike,

For as me thought I shuld not se the like
  In eternum.

To trase this daunse I put my self in prese;
Vayne hope ded lede and bad I should not cese
To serve, to suffer, and still to hold my pease
  In eternum.

With this furst rule I fordred me apase
That, as me thought, my trowghthe had taken place
With full assurans to stond in her grace
  In eternum.

It was not long er I by proofe had found
That feble bilding is on feble grounde,
For in her herte this worde did never sounde:
  In eternum.

In eternum then from my herte I keste
That I had furst determind for the best;
Now in the place another thought doeth rest
  In eternum.

(MT LXXI)

As we have come to expect, the vocabulary is plain and familiar, with a great preponderance of monosyllables and several entirely monosyllabic lines (7, 10, 17). Such figurative elements as can be found in the language are so conventional as not to call attention to themselves: the heart as the locus of thought and feeling, 'to warme her hert', the dance of love, the Scriptural-proverbial 'That feble bilding is on feble grounde.' There is the ghost of a personification in 'Vayne hope ded lede', strengthened by the proximity of 'this daunse'. In this case the syntax too lacks complexity. There is a slight narrative element, but what is recounted is entirely familiar in Wyatt's work: the speaker sought stability and fidelity in a love-relationship, was disappointed by the lady's failure to reciprocate, and renounced his quest. The refrain is unvarying, the Latin phrase (meaning 'for ever') being repeated at the end of each stanza and also at the beginning of the first and the last. But interesting things happen to this refrain in the different contexts supplied for it by each stanza. It would be tedious to attempt to define the precise shade of meaning in each case (and would in any event encroach on the reader's freedom of response), but it may at least be noted that there is a gradual process of detachment of the phrase from its original place in the language as a mere tag. By the penultimate stanza it has become a quotation; and in the final stanza it is first undermined by being used to contradict its use in the first (he determines for ever to reject what he had once affirmed for ever) and then the very undermining is the means by which its fullest meaning is disclosed: 'another thought' rests in the place of the thought that was once undertaken for ever, but that other thought, it is implied, is of eternity. The speaker has grasped that the characteristic 'for ever' of love-poetry has a literal meaning only in terms of heavenly values, not of earthly values. The very process of spelling this out so far, I am aware, runs the risk of damaging the poem: its purpose is not at all to make us pause, analyse, interpret, but to disclose in an instant the fulness of meaning in a phrase that has begun by being used trivially.

A second example will illustrate what is more distinctive of Wyatt, the use of the variable refrain, in a justly well-known poem:

> My lute, awake! perfourme the last
> Labour that thou and I shall wast
> And end that I have now begon;
> For when this song is sung and past,
> My lute, be still, for I have done.
>
> As to be herd where ere is none,
> As lede to grave in marbill stone,
> My song may perse her hert as sone;
> Should we then sigh or syng or mone?
> No, no, my lute, for I have done.
>
> The rokkes do not so cruelly
> Repulse the waves continuelly
> As she my suyte and affection,
> So that I ame past remedy,
> Whereby my lute and I have done.
>
> Prowd of the spoyll that thou hast gott
> Of simple hertes thorough Loves shot,
> By whome, unkynd, thou hast theim wone,
> Thinck not he haith his bow forgot,
> All tho my lute and I have done.
>
> Vengeaunce shall fall on thy disdain
> That makest but game on ernest pain;
> Thinck not alone under the sonne
> Unquyt to cause thy lovers plain,
> All tho my lute and I have done.
>
> Perchaunce the lye wethered and old,
> The wynter nyghtes that are so cold,
> Playnyng in vain unto the mone;
> Thy wisshes then dare not be told;
> Care then who lyst, for I have done.

And then may chaunce the to repent
The tyme that thou hast lost and spent
To cause thy lovers sigh and swoune;
Then shalt thou knowe beaultie but lent,
And wisshe and want as I have done.

Now cesse, my lute; this is the last
Labour that thou and I shall wast,
And ended is that we begon;
Now is this song boeth sung and past;
My lute, be still, for I have done.

(MT LXVI)

In this poem the invariable refrain-phrase 'I have done' is extremely simple in itself, but is given a variety of meanings by its contexts: 'I have finished', 'I have done all I can', 'I do not care', 'I have previously done'. Alastair Fowler has noted that the variation in the refrain-line is not random: it is the same in the first and last stanzas, which also have the same rhyme-words and other similarities in wording; and it is the same in stanzas 4 and 5. Reading or hearing the poem in sequence, one notes that stanza 4 contains the lady's triumph, in which the spoils displayed are the hearts of her lovers; one expects that to form the poem's centre, only to discover that her triumph is converted in the following stanza into Cupid's vengeance, and that the poem has an even number of stanzas and a double centre.[19] The syntax of the first three stanzas is relatively simple, and in the third the rhythm has a rocking monotony that in retrospect seems almost to parody the paralysis of the lover's grief. In stanza 4 a great change comes: the poet turns from the lute, which he has addressed in stanzas 1 and 2, to the lady, who now becomes not 'she' but 'thou'. The syntax of this stanza is complex and concise, and it serves to explain a new relationship and disclose a new weapon: it is 'Loves shot' (that is, sexual attraction) that has gained the lady her easy victories, and Cupid's bow remains a dangerous weapon even though the poet's lute may lack power. Self-regarding melancholy has been galvanized into thoughts of revenge, and stanza 5, still moving quickly through close-packed grammatical elements, reminds the lady that she has no reason to expect to be invulnerable. Gloatingly the poet goes on to imagine the future in which Cupid will take revenge on his behalf: she will grow old, but her 'wisshes' (for sexual satisfaction) will not lessen, only then they 'dare not be told'. The moon, contrasting with the prosperous sun of stanza 5, is present not only to evoke the coldness of the winter night, but as Diana, goddess of chastity – here a chastity which is quite involuntary. Then she will know what it is to suffer the frustration she has imposed on the poet; and added to that will be the gall of recognizing that her exercise of power in the past was 'tyme . . . lost and spent' – in frustrating her lover she also frustrated herself. With these pleasing thoughts the poet can return for the last time to intimacy with his lute, and the song, like the love-affair, can be brought to an end. 'My lute, awake' is one of the most satisfyingly complete of Wyatt's lyrics: the symmetry of its external patterning is not merely decorative, but is the outward expression of a crisp and energetic argument.

3. Wyatt at Petrarchan translator

A high proportion of Wyatt's most successful poems are translations, and a high proportion of those are translations from Petrarch. I intend, however, to write about his translations from Petrarch more briefly than about his lyrics, partly because the lyrics seem to me in greater need of explanation and discrimination, and partly because the Petrarchan versions have been discussed with enviable subtlety by several recent scholars.[20] There remain things to be said about Wyatt as translator; and the first question to be asked is, what did Wyatt gain from Petrarch? It is easy for the modern reader who is not an Italian specialist to confuse Petrarch with Petrarchism, and to think of him as a writer bound by the conventions to which he gave currency among his many imitators, rather than as a great original poet. It is perhaps worth saying, then, that Petrarch is unquestionably a greater poet than Wyatt (as it could not be said that Boccaccio is a greater poet than Chaucer). There was an active cult of Petrarch in Italy and elsewhere in Europe in Wyatt's lifetime; he was a 'modern classic', whose work was published in annotated editions, of which Wyatt probably made use. But Wyatt was not merely a follower of fashion: Petrarch provided him with qualities he desperately needed, and that he could not have gained from any English models. The earliest English translation from Petrarch, as we have seen, is by Chaucer. Chaucer, Petrarch's younger contemporary, admired him as a 'lauriat poete' (*Clerk's Prologue*, IV 41), but his only identified use of his vernacular poetry is his translation of one sonnet, 'S' amor non è' (*Rime sparse* 132), to form Troilus's song in Book I of *Troilus and Criseyde* (lines 400–20). The sonnet is a definition of the symptoms of love in terms of those paradoxes – sweet torment, living death, delightful harm, shivering at midsummer, burning in winter – that were to become the most easily recognizable conventions of Petrarchism, but that had in fact already long been part of the language of courtly poetry. Chaucer's translation is relatively free and ample: turning the sonnet into three rhyme-royal stanzas, it does not aim to reproduce the sonnet form itself in English, but it does show clear understanding of that form by putting the octave into two stanzas and the sestet into one. In the English courtly poetry of the Chaucerian tradition we can find in a diluted state many of the same images and paradoxes as characterize Petrarch's poetry, but we do not find any translation of Petrarch close enough to suggest his incomparably subtle, concise, mellifluous and closely argued style. The first English sonnets are Wyatt's own, some sixteen of them translated from Petrarch; and, as Patricia Thomson has put it of one of them, 'Quite simply, there is much more *in* the fourteen lines of "The longe love" than in any comparable English poem of the fourteenth or fifteenth centuries.'[21] Only one of the Petrarch sonnets that Wyatt chose to translate can be regarded as an example of standard Petrarchism: this is 'Pace non trovo et non ò da far guerra' (*Rime* 134), the progenitor of an unending line of presentations of 'love's contraries' throughout Europe. Here Wyatt's extremely close, line by line translation can no doubt be regarded as a stylistic exercise, in which he eventually nerves himself to add one paradox more, replacing Petrarch's final line, 'In questo stato son, Donna, per vui' (In this state am I, lady, on account of you), with 'And my delite is causer of this stryff' (MT XXVI 14). Such an exercise was no doubt of great value for Wyatt himself, but it is unlikely to be of comparable interest to readers of subsequent centuries. But Wyatt's relation to his Petrarchan sources was rarely of this straightforward kind, and indeed it varies widely in different cases. Occasionally he responds to Petrarch in a medieval spirit, borrowing an idea or sequence of thought without any attempt at stylistic imitation. Thus in 'O goodely hand' (MT LXXXVI) he begins by translating quite closely the first quatrain of a sonnet (*Rime* 199), though turning it into a six-line lyrical stanza, but then gradually diverges from his source (while retaining occasional phrases), finally substituting for a sad generalization about life – 'O inconstanzia de l'umane cose!' – an urgent prayer to the lady to relieve his sufferings. When translating Petrarch as much as when translating Boethius, Wyatt tends to reduce philosophical generalization to individual experience: his world is one of 'hap' or 'chance', about which no significant generalization is possible. A somewhat similar case is 'Perdy, I sayd hytt nott' (MT CLVIII), which borrows its general argument and certain images from Petrarch's 'S' i' 'l dissi mai' (*Rime* 206), but with drastic simplification of Petrarch's intricate and difficult stanza-scheme.

More often, Wyatt translates in the spirit of the Renaissance, attracted at the very least by specific patterns in the relation of sense and sound, and aiming to find some equivalent to them in English. An interesting example is 'The piller pearisht is whearto I lent' (MT CCXXXVI). This derives from Petrarch's 'Rotta è l'alta colonna' (*Rime* 269), a double commemoration of the death of Laura, the lady of his love-poems, and of that of his patron, Cardinal Giovanni Colonna. Wyatt adapts the sonnet to a different purpose of his own, for 'The piller pearisht is' probably laments the execution of Thomas Cromwell. Thus Petrarch's puns on *colonna* and *lauro* disappear completely, and there are many other fundamental changes: not death but 'happe' (5) is said to have deprived the poet of what he values, and, as in 'O goodely hand', a plangent generalization about the transience of earthly happiness gives way to a conclusion that looks inward at the poet's self-destructive grief – 'And I my self my self alwayes to hate' (13). Nevertheless, the first half of Wyatt's sestet is plainly an attempt to reproduce in English the thought and movement of the corresponding lines in the Italian:

> But syns that thus it is by destenye,
> What can I more but have a wofull hart,
> My penne in playnt, my voyce in wofull crye . . . ?

> Ma se consentimento è di destino,
> che posso io più se no aver l'alma trista,
> umidi gli occhi sempre, e 'l viso chino?

But, since this is the intent of destiny, what can I do except have my soul sad, my eyes always wet, and my face bent down?

Wyatt's unusual substitution of *destenye* in his ninth line for the *unhappe* and *happe* of his fifth line is clearly due to his wish to imitate the musicality and philosophical grandeur of the corresponding Petrarchan line. (There is an exactly similar case in Wyatt's 'Som fowles there be that have so perfaict sight' (MT XXIV), where the word *destyne* occurs as part of an almost word for word imitation of the final three lines of Petrarch's *Rime* 19, with 'My destyne to behold her doeth me lede' (13) translating 'mio destino a vederla mi conduce'.)

'The piller pearisht is' is typical of Wyatt's translations from Petrarch, in that the poet's attitude towards his source derives from the coexistence of two conflicting tendencies, both of which may be associated with the Renaissance – imitation and individualism. Wyatt is finely sensitive to the formal and stylistic features of Petrarch's verse, and shows at times extraordinary skill in finding English equivalents to them, yet at the same time his attitude towards Petrarch reveals an egoism comparable to that which pervades his own lyric poetry – a determination to appropriate, even to devour, Petrarch's work so that it will serve his own purposes. There is something predatory in Wyatt's attitude towards Petrarch, and his adaptation is at times brutal. A familiar example is 'Who so list to hounte' (MT VII), in which he seizes on Petrarch's 'Una candida cerva' (*Rime* 190) and wrenches its dreamlike allegory and serene sadness into an expression of inner torment and frustration, uneasily balanced between secular and religious – '*Noli me tangere*, for Cesars I ame' (13) – and hinting at obscure depths which it never fully explores. Petrarch's poem creates and completes the limpid vision of a single event; Wyatt's exists as an unstable balance of opposing impulses, complete as a poem but smokily incomplete as an experience. It is Wyatt who introduces the image of hunting into the poem, admitting the predatory nature of the speaker's attitude towards women; and there is a telling parallel between this predatoriness, implied by so many of Wyatt's original poems, and the literary predatoriness of Wyatt's attitude towards Petrarch. He is determined to seize the Italian source and force it to his own purpose – as it were, to ravish it. But Petrarch, for all the smoothness, elegance, and apparent vulnerability of his style (at least to the English ear) is in fact a poet of formidable intellectual and emotional strength, and is fully capable of resisting Wyatt's rough design. He exists for Wyatt with the irreducible reality of the 'you' or 'she' of the lyrics. And this is precisely what Wyatt needs – a source that will both provoke and resist the attempt at appropriation. Wyatt's translations from Petrarch generally lack the perfection of their originals, and the perfection that Wyatt himself achieved in some of his lyrics, but they have something no less fascinating than perfection to offer: an inner conflict that demands the reader's participation, and that seems to resolve itself differently on each reading.

I conclude this brief consideration of Wyatt as translator of Petrarch with a discussion not of one of the most obviously success-

ful of his translations – for there already exist enough appreciations of
'The longe love that in my thought doeth harbar' (MT IV) or 'My galy
charged with forgetfulnes' (MT XXVIII) – but of an intriguingly
imperfect sonnet which provides a better illustration of the opposing
forces at work within Wyatt's Petrarch:

> Though I my self be bridilled of my mynde,
> Retorning me backewerd by force expresse,
> If thou seke honour to kepe thy promes,
> Who may the hold, my hert, but thou thy self unbynd?
> Sigh then no more, syns no way man may fynde
> Thy vertue to let, though that frowerdnes
> Of Fortune me holdeth; and yet, as I may gesse,
> Though othre be present, thou art not all behinde.
> Suffice it then that thou be redy there
> At all howres, still under the defence
> Of tyme, trouth, and love to save the from offence,
> Cryeng, 'I burne in a lovely desire
> With my dere maisteres that may not followe,
> Whereby his absence torneth him to sorrowe.'   (MT XXVII)

As it stands, this is a poem of exceptional obscurity, even for Wyatt,
and its purpose and argument do not begin to emerge clearly until it
is compared with its Petrarchan source, which was only recently
identified[22] (earlier editors manifestly failed to make sense of it):

> Orso, al vostro destrier si po ben porre
> un fren che di suo corso indietro il volga,
> ma 'l cor chi legherà che non si sciolga
> se brama onore e 'l suo contrario aborre?
> Non sospirate: a lui non si po torre
> suo pregio perch' a voi l'andar si tolga,
> ché come fama publica divolga
> egli è già là che null'altro il precorre.
> Basti che si ritrove in mezzo 'l campo
> al destinato dì sotto quell'arme
> che gli dà il tempo, amor, vertute e 'l sangue,
> gridando, 'D'un gentil desire avampo
> col signor mio, che non po seguitarme
> et del non esser qui se strugge et langue'.   (*Rime* 98)

Orso, on your charger can be put a rein that will turn him back from his course,
but who can bind your heart so that it cannot get loose, if it desires honor and
abhors the contrary? Do not sigh: no one can take away his worth even though
you are prevented from going, for, as public fame makes known, your heart is
already there, no other can precede him. Let it suffice that he will be in the field
on the appointed day, under the arms he has from time, love, valor, and birth,
crying, 'One with my lord, I burn with a noble desire, but he cannot follow me
and suffers and is sick that he is not here'.

Petrarch's poem is addressed to Orso dell'Anguillara, a Roman nobleman who had evidently been prevented against his will from taking part in some social occasion, represented in the poem as a tournament: Petrarch argues that, though Orso's horse and himself may be absent, his heart will be present, and thus he will lose no honour. This charming but trivial conceit was interpreted by six-teenth-century commentators on Petrarch as a love-poem, with Orso's *destrier* representing his desire, and this is the key to the adaptation by Wyatt, who must have read Petrarch in an annotated edition.[23] With his characteristic self-obsession and subjectivism, Wyatt turns the poem into an address to his own heart, distin-guishing 'my hert' (4) from 'I my self' (1). He follows exactly the stages of Petrarch's argument, coinciding as they do with the sonnet's formal divisions, with 'Sigh then no more' corresponding to 'Non sospirate', 'Suffice it' to 'Basti', and 'Cryeng' to 'gridando'. But the chivalric language, which in Petrarch is either to be taken literally (if the poem really does allude to a tournament) or is part of a systematic fiction, now becomes metaphorical and suggestive rather than systematic. Now it is not the horse that is bridled but 'my self': if *mynde* has its modern sense, then 'bridilled of my mynde' conveys that the speaker recognizes rational considerations that speak against the pursuit of his lady, but if, as is possible, *mynde* here means 'desire', the phrase must signify 'bridled in respect of my desire'. (Such uncertainties of interpretation are so common in Wyatt's poems that he can reasonably be thought to have intended to create tensions between alternative meanings.) *Honour* in line 3 is also quasi-metaphorical: it seems too strong a word to name what is sought and gained merely by keeping promises (though honour may certainly be lost by breaking them), and the line may perhaps be glossed, 'If you seek that everyday equivalent to chivalric honour that is to be gained by keeping your promise.' The precise sense of this line, and indeed of the poem as a whole, can be assessed only if we read it alongside the Italian and recognize how Wyatt is trans-forming chivalric fiction into metaphor. Similarly in lines 7 and 8, Petrarch's 'fama publica' is omitted as having no bearing on Wyatt's exploration of inwardness, and 'Though othre be present, thou art not all behinde' converts a boast of public pre-eminence into an assurance that the speaker's heart is not always in the rear of the lady's thoughts. The scene of the sestet is not 'in mezzo 'l campo' but still in the thoughts of the lady, and, once we read Petrarch in the

light of his commentators, we see that 'still under the defence / Of
tyme, trouth, and love to save the from offence', otherwise almost
unintelligible, is another metaphorization of chivalric terminology,
meaning something like 'bearing the arms that you derive from your
long service, your fidelity, and your love, which will protect you
from your lady's anger'. Finally, Petrarch's 'gentil desire' becomes 'a
lovely [i.e. loving] desire', and we can see, in the light of the Italian,
that 'With my dere maisteres' must mean 'corresponding to that of
my dear master'.

Wyatt's closing lines seem to me comparatively weak in sense and
movement, especially by contrast with the beautiful singing quality
of 'Who may the hold, my hert, but thou thy self unbynd? / Sigh
then no more . . . ' Even more than the rest of the poem, the close
demands our awareness of the source being adapted, and thus of the
ingenuity of the adaptation. What Wyatt has written here is, in
effect, another and more radical gloss on Petrarch's sonnet, to add to
those of the Italian commentators, and there is a sense in which the
power of 'Though I my self' lies less in the poem itself than in the
space between it and its source, a space criss-crossed with currents of
attraction and repulsion. Wyatt, characteristically, has wrenched
Petrarch to his own purpose, a purpose that centres in his own inner
life; but at the same time, and equally characteristically, he has been
unable to resist Petrarch's argumentative structure, and has found in
his chivalric fiction a more varied and interesting means than he
could have invented for himself of articulating the world of his own
mind.

4. Wyatt as satirist

Before leaving Wyatt, I want to look at one more poem which is not
a translation (though it probably owes something to Horace, *Satires*
II 5). This is the third of Wyatt's three satires in the form of letters
or addresses, works which are of a more sustained and serious kind
than his lyrics or sonnets, and which (along with his *Penitential
Psalms*) must have been what led Tottel to refer later in the sixteenth
century to 'the weightinesse of the depewitted sir Thomas Wyat the
elders verse'.[24] *Satire III* is addressed to Sir Francis Brian, another
courtier, diplomat and poet. The fact that Brian had a low moral
reputation and that Wyatt made a disparaging reference to him in a
letter of 1539 has led some to suppose that the Brian in the poem is

treated critically; but the poem itself offers no support for this view, and we can easily suppose that it was written in the middle 1530s, when Wyatt was still on good terms with Brian. In *Satire III* Brian is presented as a man of integrity, eager to serve his king and country, and horrified at the cynical advice the speaker gives him on how to gain material prosperity as a courtier. The poem takes the form of a dialogue, with lines 18–27, 30a, and 80–4 spoken by Brian and the remainder by Wyatt. It is crucial to recognize the sustained irony of Wyatt's part, especially in lines 32–79, where he counsels Brian how to make a success of his career. Let him avoid telling the truth, and instead make friends by flattery; never lend except for profit, like the social-climbing merchant Kitson; fawn on a rich old man in the hope of becoming his heir, and, if that fails to work, marry his ugly and decrepit widow; act as a bawd to the womenfolk in his own family (but let him take care not to be so foolish as Chaucer's Pandarus, who did not accept money for it); above all, 'Be next thy self' (MT CVII 78) – be your own best friend, look after number one. I doubt whether such a sustained and controlled passage of irony can be found in any English poet between Chaucer and Wyatt himself. Its existence implies not just confidence and self-control on the poet's part but also an audience (probably only very small) that could be relied on to recognize irony and to relish the suppression of any overt moral condemnation on the speaker's part.

Satire on the corruption, venality and wretchedness of court life already had a long history in European literature by Wyatt's time, going back at least as far as satires directed against the papal *curia* at the time of the Investiture Contest.[25] It received new impetus in the Renaissance, however, with the spread of absolute rulers who made their courts centres of power as well as of taste and fashion, a type represented in England by Henry VIII. In English, from the late fifteenth century onwards, anti-court satire becomes an important genre: we have seen it in some of Skelton's poems (especially *The Bowge of Court*), and it can be found further in works by Barclay, Surrey, Spenser, and others as well as Wyatt. In the example before us, the power of the satire lies not just in the daring irony but (somewhat as in Skelton's anti-Wolsey satires) in the concise con- creteness with which the behaviour held up to implied ridicule and condemnation is described. Kitson in his 'long white cote' – the garb of a menial, perhaps – 'From under the stall ... Hath lept into the shopp' (47–9) in a single aspiring jump; Brian is advised to 'tred owte' (55) the disgusting spittle of the coughing dotard whom he is supporting by the arm; the rich widow married for her money may have 'A ryveld skyn, a stynking breth', but at least her 'tothles mowth' will not bite him when he feels obliged to kiss her (61–2). This world of violent energy and assaults on the senses is as memorable as that of Ben Jonson's comedies, of which at times it seems a remarkable anticipation. An important contribution to its power is Wyatt's imitation of the rhythms of laconic speech. In the writing of, say, Lydgate, certain metrical 'licences', such as the omission of an unstressed syllable at the caesura, are found again and again, to no apparent purpose. Wyatt's metrical resources are the same as those of his fifteenth-century predecessors (there is no necessity to devise elaborate theoretical justification for the rhythm of his lines), but he uses these resources with far greater expressive skill: thus in line 72 the pause at the caesura, lengthened by that 'missing' syllable, underlines the irony of 'It's *only* love' – 'It is but love – turne it to a lawghter.'

It is important to grasp the values on which Wyatt's satire is based. In part, these are the traditional, hard wisdom of proverbs. *Satire III* begins with the application to the busy life of the courtier of two proverbial statements of truth that seem callous because they have nothing to do with moral ideals, but that have survived simply because they correspond to the facts of human experience:

> 'A spending hand that alway powreth owte
> Hade nede to have a bringer-in as fast'
> And 'on the stone that still doeth tourne abowte
> There groweth no mosse' – these proverbes yet do last;
> Reason hath set theim in so sure a place
> That lenght of yeres their force can never wast.   (1–6)

And the satire ends with another proverb, offering no comfort, no moral idealism, but simply a cold truth: *if* you persist in leading this life of busy duty, and *if* you are unwilling to adopt the means described to make it profitable, then all you can expect is 'coyne to kepe as water in a syve' (91). The pebble-like concreteness of proverbs, worn smooth and hard by repeated human experience, gives the poem a firm framework; but it is also concerned with moral ideals and the clash of opposing moral systems. As we have seen, in the Middle Ages true virtue was not to be found in life in the world, but in renunciation, asceticism, withdrawal from earthly ambitions and responsibilities. However imperfect an individual religious might be in failing to live up to the ideals of his or her order, the monastic life was still seen as that which was best for the soul. As Langland put it,

> For if hevene be on this erthe, and ese to any soule,
> It is in cloistre or in scole, by manye skiles I fynde.
>
> (*Piers Plowman* B X 297–8)

The Renaissance, as we have also seen, involves a turning away from that ideal to one of civic or public virtue, while the Reformation brings an often violent rejection of monastic institutions. Indeed, antimonasticism often precedes the doctrinal severance from Catholicism: Henry VIII dissolved the English monasteries while rejecting the teachings of Luther, and certainly not considering himself a Protestant. In *Satire III*, the division between good and evil for Wyatt is not, as it was in the Middle Ages, between the otherworldly and the worldly, but between two different ways of living a life in the world. Why, Wyatt asks Brian, does he live a life of such restless anxiety, as one who 'trottes still up and downe' (11) and wears his 'body to the bones' (14), when he could sleep comfortably, drink good ale and amass wealth? Brian's answer is a violent repudiation of such a life of ease as one of bestial oblivion of true values, as bad indeed as that of the monks, whom he describes as 'sackes of durt . . . filled up in the cloyster' (22) and as worth less than 'fatted swyne' (23) which, whatever their lack of spiritual perception, are at least good to eat. (It is worth commenting on the brutality of Wyatt's writing here, a brutality characteristic not only of himself but of the whole age. Such coarsely destructive contempt and rejection can be found in More's anti-Lutheranism as much as in Wyatt's antimonasticism. Wyatt indeed was among the more generous spirits of a strikingly ungenerous age.)

The ideal opposed to this ignoble ease is that of royal service: 'Yet woll I serve my prynce, my lord and thyn' (25), Brian declares. Next comes Wyatt's satirical account of what one must do to make such a life of service profitable; and Brian's response is still not to choose the ideal of retirement:

> Wouldest thou I should, for any losse or gayne,
> Chaunge that for gold that I have tan for best,
> Next godly thinges – to have an honest name?
> Should I leve that? then take me for a best!   (81–4)

Such pursuit of material wealth is as bestial as the cloistered life would be, and Brian asserts that his highest value – 'Next godly thinges' – is to possess an honourable reputation. There is no suggestion that a concern for 'name' might be incompatible with the salvation of one's soul. Service of the prince, then, has become a high value; but when the prince in question was Henry VIII, and the writer was a man as intelligent and serious as Wyatt, it could not be the highest, even setting aside 'godly thinges'. Wyatt's highest ideal here seems to be named in the word that we found echoing through his lyrics – *trouth*. At the beginning of the ironic advice, *trouth* is repeated several times, as the definition of what Brian will have to give up if he is to make a profit out of court life:

> Thou knowest well, first, who so can seke to plese
> Shall pourchase frendes where *trowght* shall but offend.
> Fle therefore *trueth* – it is boeth welth and ese –
> For tho that *trouth* of every man hath prayse,
> Full nere that wynd goeth *trouth* in great misese.　　　　(32–6)

Here *trouth* means 'telling the truth' (as opposed to flattering), but also acting with integrity in general. And at the end of the satire *trouth* is mentioned again, once more with both the restricted and the more general meaning: it is the value that Brian will not abandon and that will therefore ensure that his life is not one of earthly prosperity –

> Nay then, farewell, and if you care for shame,
> Content the then with honest povertie,
> With fre tong, what the myslikes, to blame,
> And, for thy *trouth*, sumtyme adversitie.　　　　(85–8)

I suggested that in Wyatt's lyrics it often seems a weakness that *trouth* is a purely subjective value, attached to no larger philosophical scheme. In this satire, however, its meaning has to do with behaviour in public life, and it is assumed that there is a public opinion capable of bringing *shame* to the man whose behaviour lacks integrity. The effect of the sustained irony, which demands our active participation if we are to interpret it correctly, is to force us to become part of (indeed, in a sense, to constitute) the small but select public that gives *name* and *shame* a living force. If we are to grasp the full weight of the lyrics, we need perhaps to read them as part of the same body of work as the satires, and to recognize that for Wyatt private and public life are different faces of the same experience.

5. Surrey

Henry Howard was born in 1517, and became Earl of Surrey in 1524, when his father was made Duke of Norfolk. From 1530 he was brought up at Windsor as a companion to Henry VIII's bastard son, Henry Fitzroy. His life, like Wyatt's, and like that of many others in prominent positions under Henry VIII, was one of violent changes of fortune; but Surrey was unusually hot-tempered and imprudent, and must have done something to bring such changes upon himself. In 1537 he was imprisoned for striking another courtier within the precincts of the court (much the same offence as that for which Theseus in *The Knight's Tale* threatened Palamon and Arcite with death). In 1541 he was made a Knight of the Garter, but in 1542 he witnessed the execution of his cousin, Catherine Howard, Henry VIII's fifth queen, and he was again imprisoned for challenging a courtier. In 1543 he was imprisoned once more, this time for riotous behaviour in London and for eating meat in Lent – no doubt a demonstration of his Protestant sympathies, which were more clear-cut than Wyatt's. He saw military service in the north of England, against the Pilgrimage of Grace; in Scotland; and in France, with the Emperor Charles V. In 1545 he was put in charge of Boulogne, temporarily an English possession, and his aggressive leadership there, against his father's wishes, encouraged the king in his war policy. In 1546 he was recalled and, along with his father, who had been Henry VIII's loyal counsellor throughout his reign, was arrested on charges of treason. This was at the very end of Henry VIII's life, when the leading members of the Council, Hertford and Dudley, were sometimes acting in his name, and the motives for the arrest are uncertain. (Once more one has the sense that the political realities of the early Tudor court constitute a dark allegory, susceptible of varying interpretations, and with its true meaning buried beyond recovery.) Surrey's religious sympathies were strongly Protestant: among his last works were verse translations of Ecclesiastes and of some of the Psalms, which lay a sharp emphasis on the Protestant doctrine of salvation by faith alone. The charges against him, however, were political rather than doctrinal, and, for whatever reason, he was beheaded in January 1547, before his thirtieth birthday; his father was fortunate to be saved by the king's death. His collected poems form a correspondingly slim volume.

For a long time Surrey's poetry was valued more highly than that of his older contemporary Wyatt, for reasons indicated in the critical language of the late eighteenth century by Thomas Warton. Wyatt, he writes, 'is confessedly inferior to Surrey in harmony of numbers, perspicuity of expression, and facility of phraseology. Nor is he equal to Surrey in elegance of sentiment, in nature and sensibility.'[26] In this century, however, the position has been reversed and a widespread taste (among intellectuals) for difficulty, ambiguity and the irregular rhythms of speech has led Wyatt to be preferred to Surrey. I share this preference; on the other hand it seems clear that, despite superficial resemblances, Surrey's achievement is of a different kind from Wyatt's, and there is little to be gained by using either as a stick to beat the other. The nature of Surrey's achievement has been defined in an admirable essay by Emrys Jones, forming the introduction to his edition of Surrey, and to this I am much indebted, as all modern readers of the poet must be.[27] Jones notes that Warton described Surrey as 'the first English classical poet', and in the context of the present book it is especially useful to recognize Surrey as the earliest English poet in whom the classicism of the Renaissance is established and dominant, and whose work has links at least as important with Augustan neoclassicism as it has with the medieval past.

Surrey's classicism is most noticeable on the level of style, and especially in his style as a translator. We saw in the last chapter how Skelton was opposed to the early-sixteenth-century reforms in education which emphasized the close stylistic imitation of classical authors. One of the earliest English expressions of the new ideals was John Colet's version of William Lily's *Rudimenta*, and the final sentence of Colet's addition neatly sums up their goal: 'For reading of good books, diligent information of taught masters, studious advertance and taking heed of learners, hearing eloquent men speak, and, finally, easy imitation with tongue and pen more availeth shortly to get the true eloquent speech than all the traditions, rules, and precepts of masters.'[28] Surrey is the first English poet to put this ideal fully into effect in his own work. His longest work is a translation of Books II and IV of Virgil's *Aeneid*, for which he invented blank verse. In the 1530s and 1540s, unless some alliterative verse that has not survived was still being written, all English verse was rhymed. Gavin Douglas's splendid translation of the whole *Aeneid*, completed in 1513 and demonstrably known to Surrey, is in pentameter couplets, and Wyatt's *Iopas' Song* (MT CIV), derived from a passage in Book I, uses 'poulter's measure' (alternating six- and seven-stress lines, rhyming in couplets) as a rhymed equivalent to Virgil's hexameters. There were experiments in unrhymed vernacular verse in early-sixteenth-century Italy, of which Surrey may have known, but his blank verse (unrhymed pentameters) was the first in English. Inevitably, perhaps, in establishing this radically new form, Surrey sometimes fell into rhythmic monotony, but the lack of rhyme also made possible finer, subtler, less emphatic effects in the patterning of sound and syntax, often in direct imitation of Virgil. Such imitation includes Latin constructions and word-order (now modelled directly on Latin, rather than through the intermediary of Italian, as in Chaucer); and in an uninflected language this can sometimes lead to obscurity. Surrey gives far closer attention than had been usual in English to the exact details of phrasing, and Jones notes how he will place adjectives before or after their nouns to produce local auditory music and overall variation, or again will deliberately vary the two English forms of the genitive, inflected in –s and uninflected with *of*, to produce lines such as 'Upsprang the crye of men and trompettes blast' (II 399) or 'In Priams ayd and rescue of his town' (II 439). I do not intend to offer any detailed analysis of Surrey's blank verse; but, although in chapter 3 I noted the emergence earlier in the Chaucerian tradition of individual lines in which every word was chosen to produce beauty of sound and meaning, Surrey's is perhaps the first verse in English where one can be sure that every line has been tested for elegance of auditory and syntactical pattern.

A second aspect of Surrey's classicism is to be found in his historical sense. The imitation of Virgilian style is itself an example of that sense of the difference and distance of the past, accompanied by the attempt to reconstruct a past culture imaginatively from within, that marks the Renaissance. But in a number of Surrey's original poems too we find an impressive mastery of temporal context and temporal relation:[29] the recognition of the past's distance paradoxically makes it more available for comparison and contrast with the present. A simple example, in which this relating of imagined past to experienced present forms the basis of a whole poem is 'When ragyng love with extreme payne' (Jones 1). Here the argument of the first four stanzas may be summarized as follows: 'When I suffer the pains of love, I think of the immense efforts the Greeks made in their ten-year siege of Troy before they recaptured

Helen; this encourages me to continue to suffer for the sake of a lady who is worthier than Helen.' The four stanzas form a single, admirably controlled and shaped sentence:

> When ragyng love with extreme payne
> Most cruelly distrains my hart;
> When that my teares, as floudes of rayne,
> Beare witnes of my wofull smart;
> When sighes have wasted so my breath
> That I lye at the poynte of death:
>
> I call to minde the navye greate
> That the Grekes brought to Troye towne,
> And how the boysteous windes did beate
> Their shyps, and rente their sayles adowne,
> Till Agamemnons daughters bloode
> Appeasde the goddes that them withstode;
>
> And how that in those ten yeres warre
> Full manye a bloudye dede was done,
> And manye a lord, that came full farre,
> There caught his bane, alas, to sone,
> And many a good knight overronne,
> Before the Grekes had Helene wonne;
>
> Then thinke I thus: sithe suche repayre,
> So longe time warre of valiant men,
> Was all to winne a ladye fayre,
> Shall I not learne to suffer then,
> And thinke my life well spent to be
> Servyng a worthier wight than she?

Then the fifth and final stanza repeats the same pattern in a more compressed form: 'Thus, just as spring comes after winter, so may joy succeed my grief':

> Therfore I never will repent,
> But paynes contented stil endure:
> For like as when, rough winter spent,
> The pleasant spring straight draweth in ure,
> So after ragyng stormes of care
> Joyful at length may be my fare.

One experience is compared with another: first one from classical history (a story repeated, of course, in Book II of the *Aeneid*) is compared with that of the lover in the present; then, more briefly and conventionally, that of the seasons with that of the lover. The historical comparison gives more force to the seasonal comparison; both are governed by an ability to separate the things being compared, rather different from the typical medieval habit of running them together (so that love and spring are felt to be not so much comparable as the same).

The relativism which underlies the historical sense, in Surrey as in Chaucer, also manifests itself in an ability to enter into the mind of the opposite sex. Wyatt's lyrics, as we have seen, are almost entirely written from within his own, masculine situation, and a rare exception such as 'There was never nothing more me payned' serves only to prove the rule, by framing the lady's grief within that of the lover. Several of Surrey's comparatively small body of poems are written in the person of a woman. Two of these – 'O happy dames, that may embrace' and 'Good ladies, you that have your pleasure in exyle' (Jones 23 and 24) – form a pair, in which a woman lamenting the absence of her husband overseas, evidently on military service, asks the sympathy of other women, first those who are luckier than she, then those who share her situation. The second is a particularly touching poem, in which the wife dreams that her husband has returned to play 'with T. his lytle sonne' (22) and to ask her, 'My deare, how is it now that you have all this payne?' (28); but then she wakes, to 'fynde it but a dreame' (31) and to be more unhappy than before. Surrey really did have a son called Thomas, and in the last year of his life he greatly annoyed Henry VIII by asking that his wife should be allowed to join him at Boulogne (to which the king's uncharming reply was that the warlike situation there made it 'unmeet for women's imbecilities'[30]). It may well be, then, that the sympathetic entry into the wife's situation in these poems is the product of genuine husbandly affection. An even more striking instance of a relativistic adoption of a woman's role can be found in another pair of poems (Jones 21 and 22), the first written as by a man, the second as by a woman. The first, 'Wrapt in my carelesse cloke', makes all the traditional male accusations of how women are irresistible yet unscrupulously deceptive. It clearly implies the antifeminism which so often underlies the courtly idolization of women; and this implication is turned into an explicit exposure by the woman's reply, which begins

> Gyrtt in my giltlesse gowne, as I sytt heare and sowe,
> I see that thinges are not in dead as to the owtward showe.

The reply discloses that the speaker of the first poem once attempted, 'wrapt in a craftye cloke' (15) (not the 'carelesse cloke' of Stoic detachment to which he lays claim), to seduce her, without success. She compares her situation to that of Susanna and the elders: it is precisely her virtue that has provoked his unjustified accusations. It is probably true to say that Surrey, on his small scale, more effectively expresses sympathy with women than any other English poet since Chaucer – more effectively, because his sympathy, like Chaucer's, is based on a shrewd understanding of the motives and interests of men as well as women.[31]

A third and last aspect of Surrey's classicism is a quality found in virtually all his original poems: a concern for simplicity and consistency of overall effect.[32] There had been a movement towards this in Chaucer, for example in his rejection of the polyphonic narrative of French courtly romance in favour of the simpler plot-patterns of Boccaccian narrative, which he then simplified still further. But, as Lydgate's *Siege of Thebes* showed, Chaucer's fifteenth-century followers tended to revert to more complex and rambling narratives; and there was an equivalent reversion in lyrical and other shorter poems. Even major poets such as Dunbar and Skelton continue to aim at a 'Gothic' variety and at the juxtaposition of incompatible perspectives. Surrey, however, seems to have had simplicity and consistency as his conscious goals, even at the expense of the emotional complexity and unpredictability that we find in many of Wyatt's poems. Each of Surrey's poems gives the impression of being fully planned in advance, often on the basis of some familiar pre-existing scheme of ideas. Like Wyatt, Surrey probably possessed little power of creating narrative or argument: 'His powers of invention and of forming independent structures were small,' as Jones puts it.[33] Thus he often relies on catalogues to provide the framework of substantial parts of his poems – of places in and near Windsor in 'So crewell prison' (Jones 27), or parts of the body in 'W. resteth here' (Jones 28), or the names of places and persons in 'Norfolk sprang thee' (Jones 35), or the seven deadly sins in 'London, hast thow accused me' (Jones 33). Taking some such simple scheme as these as his basis, he will present it in terms of elegant variation, so that it will become something more interesting and pleasing than a bald list – and often more moving too. Each poem 'hangs together', has a satisfying coherence and completeness, with few obtrusive elements. This means, perhaps, that Surrey was not capable of greatness as a poet, even apart from the small scale and bulk of his work, for greatness demands a greater willingness to take

risks and to include material and feelings that resist subordination to
a simple pattern. But Surrey did possess qualities that English poetry
needed in the early sixteenth century, and greater poets than he, who
constitute the full flowering of the English poetic Renaissance –
Spenser, Sidney, even Shakespeare – owe more to him than they do
to Wyatt, even though Wyatt's work now seems of higher intrinsic
interest.

In considering a few specific poems, I propose to concentrate on
some of Surrey's elegies, which would be generally agreed to be
among his most successful works. I begin with 'So crewell prison'
(Jones 27), his epitaph on Henry Fitzroy, Duke of Richmond, his
boyhood companion at Windsor, who had married Surrey's sister,
Lady Mary Howard, before his death from consumption at the age
of only seventeen. The poem presumably dates from 1536/7, the
year of Richmond's death, when Surrey was temporarily
imprisoned at Windsor.

> So crewell prison howe could betyde, alas,
> As prowde Wyndsour, where I in lust and joye
> With a kinges soon my childishe yeres did passe,
> In greater feast then Priams sonnes of Troye;
>
> Where eche swete place retournes a tast full sowre: 5
> The large grene courtes, where we were wont to hove,
> With eyes cast upp unto the maydens towre,
> And easye syghes, such as folke drawe in love;
>
> The statelye sales; the ladyes bright of hewe;
> The daunces short, long tales of great delight,   10
> With wordes and lookes that tygers could but rewe,
> Where eche of us did plead the others right;
>
> The palme playe, where, dispoyled for the game,
> With dased eyes oft we by gleames of love
> Have mist the ball and got sight of our dame   15
> To bayte her eyes which kept the leddes above;
>
> The graveld ground, with sleves tyed on the helme,
> On fomynge horse, with swordes and frendlye hertes,
> With chere as thoughe the one should overwhelme,
> Where we have fought and chased oft with dartes;   20
>
> With sylver dropps the meades yet spredd for rewthe,
> In active games of nymbleness and strengthe
> Where we dyd strayne, trayled by swarmes of youthe,
> Our tender lymes, that yet shott upp in lengthe:
>
> The secret groves, which ofte we made resound   25
> Of pleasaunt playnt and of our ladyes prayes,
> Recording soft what grace eche one had found,
> What hope of spede, what dred of long delayes;

The wyld forest, the clothed holtes with grene,
With raynes avald and swift ybrethed horse,   30
With crye of houndes and mery blastes bitwen,
Where we did chase the fearfull hart a force;

The voyd walles eke, that harbourd us eche night;
Wherwith, alas, revive within my brest
The swete accord, such slepes as yet delight,   35
The pleasaunt dreames, the quyet bedd of rest,

The secret thoughtes imparted with such trust,
The wanton talke, the dyvers chaung of playe,
The frendshipp sworne, eche promyse kept so just,
Wherwith we past the winter nightes awaye.   40

And with this thought the blood forsakes my face,
The teares berayne my cheke of dedlye hewe;
The which, as sone as sobbing sighes, alas,
Upsupped have, thus I my playnt renew:

'O place of blisse, renewer of my woos,   45
Geve me accompt wher is my noble fere,
Whome in thy walles thou didest eche night enclose,
To other lief, but unto me most dere.'

Eache stone, alas, that dothe my sorowe rewe,
Retournes therto a hollowe sound of playnt.   50
Thus I alone, where all my fredome grew,
In pryson pyne with bondage and restraynt,

And with remembraunce of the greater greif,
To bannishe the lesse I fynde my chief releif.

The main structure of this poem is provided by an enumeration of places, a rhetorical division or *partitio* of Windsor itself, introduced by the phrase 'eche swete place' in line 5. A single place is mentioned in each stanza from the second to the ninth, along with the activities associated with it, activities which generally have some connection with the 'game of love' as played by the two youths. Stanza 2 mentions 'The large grene courtes', where the activities are lingering, looking up, and sighing 'easye sighes' (which recall the 'esy sykes' of the lover in *Troilus and Criseyde* III 1363). Stanza 3 is concerned with 'statelye sales', where dances and conversations about love take place. Stanza 4 moves to the court where 'palme playe' (a kind of cross between tennis and fives) takes place, along with flirtatious looks. In stanza 5 the place is 'The graveld ground' where the young men joust, wearing tokens of their ladies on their helmets. In stanza 6 various 'active games' are held in the meadows outside the castle. Stanza 7 moves further off to 'The secret groves' of Windsor Forest, where they speak of success and failure in love. Stanza 8 is set deeper in this 'wyld forest' by which Windsor is surrounded; there the appropriate activity is hunting, but hunting 'the fearfull hart' strongly suggests the traditional metaphor of the hunt of love. Finally, stanza 9 returns to the 'voyd walles' of the castle, to which the youths come back at night, and which are the scene of private talk of love and friendship and other indoor activities; this more varied and partly summarizing item in the list spills over into stanza 10.

The 'secret thoughtes' (37) recalled from the past here lead back to 'thought' (41) in the present, and thence to lamentation or 'playnt' (44), echoed by the castle walls (50), walls which in the past were protective but which now form a prison. Thus the poem's sequence of thought, apparently randomly associative but in fact carefully organized, concludes with a paradox: in the very place where Surrey's 'fredome' grew up (51) – the term, as in *The Franklin's Tale*, means both liberty and generosity or nobility – he now pines in prison. This paradox repeats that of the first stanza, in which Windsor, once the scene of 'lust and joye' (2), is now a 'crewell prison' (1), and all the crueller because of its former happy associations. The final couplet gives a summary of the poem's purpose for its speaker: two causes of grief (Richmond's death and his own imprisonment), both linked with the same place, compete for his attention, and he uses the first and greater to banish the smaller, his imprisonment, from his mind.

The poem offers an admirable evocation of the castle and its boyhood associations, youthful experience now being seen with nostalgia and affectionate superiority, as in the mock-heroic 'wordes and lookes that tygers could but rewe' (11) and 'With chere as thoughe the one should overwhelme' (19). The frame, as has been explained, is a list of places, moving from 'eche swete place' (5) to 'O place of blisse' (45); and these are real, topographical places, but they are also the 'places' of memory. As Frances Yates shows in *The Art of Memory*, mnemonic techniques were of great importance in the culture of antiquity and the Middle Ages, and remained important in the Renaissance even after the spread of printing and literacy had made them less indispensable.[34] A basic technique of the art of memory was the association of things or ideas to be remembered with a series of 'places', often parts of a real or imagined building. A sixteenth-century commentator on Dante even suggested that the *Inferno* could be used as a memory-system for memorizing the sins and their punishments.[35] 'So crewell prison' is a poem *about* memory and its paradoxes – 'eche swete place retournes a tast full sowre' – in which the speaker deliberately uses the memory-traces of a series of places in order to fill his mind with images that will blot out his present miseries. Places have attached to them not just activity but emotion, and, since there seems to be a recollection of *Troilus and Criseyde* in line 8, it is possible that behind the memories of personal experience lies a literary memory of the passage in Book v of Chaucer's poem, in which Troilus, now abandoned, rides round Troy 'forby places of the town' (v 563) in order to stir up memories of the events and emotions that occurred at each before Criseyde's departure. The techniques of Chaucer and of Surrey are at least similar; but they are also natural, and they help to make 'So crewel prison' a poem that moves us, not just a pre-electronic memory system.

Surrey's description of noble youth in a past devoted to love and chivalry is appropriately embodied in the language of medieval and Petrarchan courtliness, with a recurrent use of antithesis, paradox, and oxymoron, in phrases such as 'daunces short, long tales' (10) (a chiastic construction), 'with swordes and frendlye hertes' (18), 'pleasaunt playnt' (26), 'What hope of spede, what dred of long delayes' (28). And since the poem's argument turns on a larger contrast, between the former pleasant associations of places in and about Windsor and the opposite feelings that they now arouse, antithesis is an especially pervasive figure, in passages such as 'Where eche swete place retournes a tast full sowre' (5) (based on a highly disagreeable implied image of heartburn caused by over-rich food), 'O place of blisse, renewer of my woos' (45), 'Thus I alone, where all my fredome grew, / In pryson pyne' (51–2). On the level of style, Surrey's present situation, as prisoner and mourner of a friend of whom he is bereft, is presented as comparable to that of the lover of literary convention (Troilus, for example), tormented by contrary feelings. In literary convention the lover is a prisoner and the loss of love is death, and thus in this poem, as in so many of Wyatt's, courtly metaphor is reliteralized: the metaphorical prison of hopeless love has become a literal prison, and the beloved friend is really dead. The general elegance of the poem's style is worth notice. If the subject-matter demands antithesis, this is sometimes further varied by the

ABBA patterns of chiasmus: 'Where eche swete place retournes a tast full sowre' (5) (adjective–noun/noun–adjective) or 'The daunces short, long tales' (10) (noun–adjective/adjective–noun). Chiastic organization is also found independently of antithesis, as in 'The statelye sales; the ladyes bright of hewe' (9) (adjective–noun/noun–adjective) or 'With raynes avald and swift ybrethed horse' (30) (noun–participial adjective/participial adjective-noun). Throughout the poem, the relationship of sense-units to verse-units is shifted by means of syntactical variations. Sometimes the central catalogue is presented paratactically, with two brief items per line in juxta-position (e.g. lines 9–10, 29–31, 35–6, 38–9); sometimes hypotaxis strings out a single complex sentence across a whole stanza (e.g. lines 1–4, 21–4); relative clauses are frequent, and in view of the depend-ence of the poem on places, these are especially likely to be clauses of place beginning 'where ...'. The poem demands and repays the closest possible attention as a structure of words; but this is not merely a matter of 'verbal music', pleasing auditory effects, but of what might be called 'semantic music' – that is, the attention required is to meaning as well as to sound.

A second example is 'W. resteth here' (Jones 28), an epitaph on Wyatt. Wyatt died in 1542, aged thirty-eight, and it may be for this reason that the poem has 38 lines.[36] Surrey's formal, dignified eulogy is perhaps more fully a poem of the Renaissance than any of Wyatt's own. Wyatt is seen in it as corresponding to the Renaissance idea of *homo universalis*, a familiar definition of which is found in Ophelia's praise of Hamlet:

> The courtier's, soldier's, scholar's, eye, tongue, sword,
> Th'expectancy and rose of the fair state,
> The glass of fashion and the mould of form,
> Th'observed of all observers ... [37]

> W. resteth here, that quick could never rest;
> Whose heavenly giftes encreased by disdayn
> And vertue sank the deper in his brest:
> Such profit he by envy could obtain.

> A hed, where wisdom misteries did frame;
> Whose hammers bet styll in that lively brayn
> As on a stithe, where that some work of fame
> Was dayly wrought to turne to Britaines gayn.

> A visage stern and myld; where bothe did grow
> Vice to contemne, in vertue to rejoyce;
> Amid great stormes whom grace assured so
> To lyve upright and smile at Fortunes choyce.

5

10

A hand that taught what might be sayd in ryme;
That reft Chaucer the glory of his wit;
A mark the which, unparfited for time,   15
Some may approche, but never none shall hit.

A toung that served in forein realmes his king;
Whose courteous talke to vertue did enflame
Eche noble hart; a worthy guide to bring
Our English youth by travail unto fame.   20

An eye, whose judgement none affect could blinde,
Frendes to allure, and foes to reconcile;
Whose persing loke did represent a mynde
With vertue fraught, reposed, voyd of gyle.

A hart, where drede was never so imprest   25
To hyde the thought that might the trouth avance;
In neyther fortune loft nor yet represt,
To swell in wealth, or yeld unto mischance.

A valiant corps, where force and beawty met;
Happy, alas, to happy, but for foes;   30
Lived and ran the race that Nature set;
Of manhodes shape, where she the molde did lose.

But to the heavens that simple soule is fled,
Which left with such as covet Christ to know
Witnesse of faith that never shall be ded;   35
Sent for our helth, but not received so.

Thus, for our gilte, this jewel have we lost.
The earth his bones, the heavens possesse his gost.

Wyatt's qualities include wisdom, poetic skill, diplomacy,
beauty, strength, and courage; he is, for Surrey, the very embodiment of a Renaissance concept of virtue (a word repeated in lines 3,
10, 18, and 24) as the classical *virtus* – a perfection attainable in the
active life, not in contemplation or monastic withdrawal from the
world. In this respect the Renaissance idea is strengthened by the
Reformation, and this is clearly a Protestant poem, with its emphasis
on 'grace' (11) and its references to religion as 'knowing Christ' (34)
(without the mediation of priesthood or other ecclesiastical institutions) and to Wyatt's *Penitential Psalms* as 'Witnesse of faith' (35). The
poem's nationalism and concern for national reputation – 'Britaines
gayn' (8) and 'Our English youth' (20) – also align it with the
Renaissance, as does its promise of 'fame' as the earthly reward for
worthily guided 'travail' (19–20). As in many of the poets we have
been considering, there is a sense of an English literary tradition

going back to Chaucer; but this is the earliest poem I know in which a more recent poet is said to have improved on Chaucer. Even Skelton claimed no more than to be his equal. The idea of progress in the arts is central to the Renaissance, and here again it is associated with personal fame: Wyatt has 'reft Chaucer the *glory* of his wit' (14). Finally, as in Wyatt's *Satire III*, the highest earthly ideal is seen as that of royal service; and the king is centrally placed in the first line of the poem's middle quatrain (17).[38]

The form of this poem is once more based on a simple catalogue, a list of the parts of Wyatt's body – the head, the face, the hand, the tongue, the eye, the heart, the body as a whole ('A valiant corps' in line 29), and last the soul – each, with its appropriate activity, given a single stanza. (The 'eye, tongue, sword' of Ophelia's speech similarly praises by division and metonymy.) The subject-matter which is divided by *partitio* might be referred to in rhetoric as *corpus materiae*, the body of the material; here it is a literal *corps*, not a metaphorical body, that is divided to provide the framework of the poem. The epitaph begins at the graveside – 'W. resteth *here* . . . ' – and then at the end the word 'corps' (meaning both the living body and the corpse in its modern sense) takes us back to the graveside, where only the bones remain;[39] but both Wyatt's works and his soul live on elsewhere. As in 'So crewell prison', the style of this poem is full of parallelism, antithesis, and paradox, from the first line, with its contrast between the repose of the dead and the restlessness of the living man, to the last, which has the form of a condensed sentence, with the verb *possesse*, the hinge of both statements, held back to the second, so that we can only take in the line as a whole. This poem of objective statement (rather than the personal emotion of 'So crewell prison') has an especially Augustan feel: a line such as 'Frendes to allure, and foes to reconcile' (22), in which a balanced antithesis is underlined by alliteration and other auditory patterns, could almost be by Pope. It is a poem appropriately written by a man who built for himself what was probably the first great house in England in a classical style of architecture; the house has utterly disappeared, but the classical plan and finish of the poem remain.

My last example of Surrey's work is another epitaph on Wyatt; it is also unquestionably Surrey's most difficult poem. 'In the rude age when science was not so rife' (Jones 30) is a sonnet, of a brevity and compression appropriate for inscription on a tombstone, where much is to be said but space is strictly limited. Jones gives it up as a 'tangle', perhaps requiring emendation;[40] subsequent attempts at interpretation come closer to following it as it stands, but still, in my view, fail to trace out Surrey's intricate argument in every detail.[41] I am bold enough to think that I understand it, but, whether or not I am right, the important thing is to grasp the nature of its difficulty, which tells us something about the kind of poet Surrey is. Passages in Lydgate or Hawes are sometimes difficult because those poets aim at a stylistic elevation that is beyond their control. Skelton is sometimes difficult because he wished to conceal politically dangerous meanings beneath layers of allegory and allusion. Some of Wyatt's poems are difficult because they present ambiguities, alternative possibilities of meaning, which the reader cannot resolve, so that he is left, as Wyatt must have intended, uneasily suspended between different attitudes. The difficulty of a poem such as 'In the rude age' is a product of the extraordinary yet perfectly controlled involution and complexity of its syntax. The poem is in the nature of a problem, testingly hard, yet capable of being solved correctly and unambiguously, given sufficient logical power and patience in the reader. (Here it is unquestionably a reader that we must think of, not a listener; Surrey belongs to the literary world that is familiar to us, in which the essential activity is that of the private reader making his way carefully through a stable written text.)

> In the rude age when science was not so rife,
> If Jove in Crete and other where they taught
> Artes to reverte to profyte of our lyfe
> Wan after deathe to have their temples sought;
> If vertue yet in no unthankfull tyme   5
> Fayled of some to blast her endles fame –
> A goodlie meane bothe to deter from cryme
> And to her steppes our sequell to enflame;
> In dayes of treuthe if Wyattes frendes then waile
> (The only debte that ded of quycke may clayme)   10
> That rare wit spent, employed to our avayle
> Where Christe is tought, deserve they monnis blame?
> His livelie face thy brest how did it freate,
> Whose cynders yet with envye doo the eate!

In order to interpret this poem, we need to begin by grasping two basic ideas. The first is that the octave and sestet of the sonnet present a contrast between two epochs: 'the rude age when science [i.e. true knowledge] was not so rife' as it is now, and the 'dayes of treuthe' in which Wyatt and his friends live. The contrast, that is, is between pagan and Christian times, and it is seen with the aid of a Renaissance historical sense, which interprets the pagan gods euhemeristically, as human teachers revered and deified for their wisdom. It is a more complicated version of the contrast and parallel in 'When ragyng love' between the Greeks and the poet. The second idea is that 'In the rude age' is about the fame brought to virtue by commemoration, and in that sense it is a poem in defence of itself. The active virtue attributed to Wyatt and the reward of fame are, as we have seen, both Renaissance themes; and this is also a poem of the Reformation, in asserting that commemorative lamentation and praise are 'The *only* debte that ded of quycke may clayme' – prayer for the souls of the dead, the debt that Guenevere's mother came to beg her to fulfil in *The Awntyrs off Arthure*, is no longer regarded as valid. (We may suspect, in the light of this, that the poem's explicit contrast between pagan and Christian is intended to suggest an analogy to that between Catholic and Protestant.)

The whole poem except for its final couplet comprises a single complex sentence of great intricacy, in the form of an *interrogatio* or rhetorical question, dependent upon three parallel conditional clauses: 'If Jove ... and other ...', 'If vertue ...', and 'if Wyattes frendes ...' These three *Ifs* introduce the sonnet's three quatrains; and its final couplet then, by contrast, is a sharply pointed, though still complex, exclamation, addressed to a real or imagined enemy of Wyatt, in implicit response to the question. The poem may be paraphrased as follows:

If, in the uncultivated age when true knowledge was less widespread than now, Jove in Crete, and other teachers in the places where they taught doctrines that would recall men to gain true profit from their lives, succeeded in attracting followers to their temples after their deaths;

If indeed virtue in any age, however thankless, never lacked some men to broadcast its undying fame – an excellent means both of deterring people from evil actions and of encouraging our descendants to follow in virtue's footsteps;

If then, in these days of true knowledge, Wyatt's friends pay the only debt that the dead may claim of the living, by lamenting that fine intelligence that was worn out for our advantage in the world where Christianity is taught, do they deserve to be blamed for it?

You who so blame us, how his living face must have tormented your hearts, when his ashes still consume you with envy!

Thus the poem combines eulogy of Wyatt, as a man who sacrificed himself for the benefit of his fellow-Christians, with a defence of eulogy against the malice of Wyatt's enemies. It might appropriately be called a 'satiric elegy',[42] ending as it does not with consolation but with anger, harshly expressed in a metaphor which turns Wyatt's ashes into corrosive cinders. If one follows the argument of 'In the rude age' through all its intricate turns, one ends the poem exhausted yet satisfied, as the complicated rhetorical and semantic pattern finally overcomes every obstacle and reaches its aggressive conclusion. No such poem had ever been written in English before.

Epilogue: The Shepheardes Calender

In his four epitaphs or elegies on Wyatt – 'W. resteth here', 'In the rude age', 'Dyvers thy death', and 'The great Macedon' – Surrey in effect re-creates his admired contemporary in such a way as to make him correspond to the Renaissance idea of what a great English poet should be. This ideal Wyatt is a poet in the tradition of Chaucer, who yet outdid his great progenitor and established a model for later poets to emulate:

> A hand that taught what might be sayd in ryme;
> That reft Chaucer the glory of his wit.   (Jones 28 13–14)

He is a faithful servant of the English crown – 'A toung that served in forein realmes his king' (Jones 28 17) – yet one in whose work

> ... rewlers may se in a myrrour clere
> The bitter frewte of false concupiscense.   (Jones 31 10–11)

His work brings glory to himself and also to his nation, for he was 'a worthy guide to bring / Our English youth by travail unto fame', and one in whose head 'some work of fame / Was dayly wrought to turne to Britaines gayn' (Jones 28 19–20, 7–8). He was a wise teacher of the true (that is, the reformed) faith, 'the lyvely faythe and pure, / The stedfast hope, the swete returne to grace' (31 7–8). He was indeed a modern, Christian Homer (this is the argument of 'The great Macedon'); yet, in the imperfect world in which he lived, his very virtues aroused envious malice among his contemporaries, who 'Weape envyous teares to here thy fame so good' (Jones 29 8):

> His livelie face thy brest how did it freate,
> Whose cynders yet with envye doo the eate!   (Jones 30 13–14)

As a picture of Wyatt's poetic achievement, this is seriously distorted, in particular through its omission of his large body of lyrical love-poetry. It is possible to imagine how Wyatt's whole poetic career might have been presented in terms of the most serious Renaissance expectations, if Surrey had chosen to do so: the love-poetry might have been seen as early and immature, along perhaps

with the pastoral of *Satire II*; then this phase could have been supposed brought to an end with the sonnet 'Farewell Love and all thy
lawes for ever' (MT XIII), to yield place to the serious religious poetry
of the *Penitential Psalms*. But Surrey did not choose to do this,
largely, I think, because he saw poetry as only one of many fields in
which Wyatt served king and country, achieved excellence, and won
fame. The *literary* career did not exist, or need to make sense, as an
autonomous whole. For Surrey himself, too, poetry was but one
product of the life of a nobleman: it is significant that he concludes
the poem which, according to his son, was the last he wrote, while
awaiting execution, with an allusion not to his poetry but to his cou-
rageous soldiership, 'that blood that hath so oft bene shed / For Bri-
tannes sake' (Jones 38 16–17). The first English poet to design for
himself an entire career *as poet* on the Renaissance model was
Edmund Spenser. He served queen and country in other ways too,
but for him all other kinds of ambition were subordinate to his aspiration to poetic achievement, for he saw poetry as 'a profession that
might justifiably claim a man's life and not merely the idleness or
excess of his youth.'[1] Spenser saw himself not as a gentleman whose
poetry was only one of his accomplishments, but as a poet whose
poetry might have the power to shape gentlemen. I cannot hope to
survey Spenser's whole career, but this book can appropriately end
with a brief consideration of the work in which Spenser first presented himself to the world as a poet, *The Shepheardes Calender*.

The *Shepheardes Calender* was published in 1579, and it came
before the public anonymously but accompanied by a preface and
glosses by his 'verie special and singuler good frend E. K.'.[2] Skelton
had written some glosses for his own poetry, but this was the first
time a contemporary English poet had appeared in a systematically
glossed edition in such a way as to claim for him the status of a
'modern classic'.[3] In Italy, Boccaccio had written allegorizing
glosses on his own *Teseida*, and both Dante and Petrarch were
available in annotated editions, while in France Ronsard had collabo-
rated in the production of an edition of his early works, glossed and
commented on by Antoine Muret; in England, by contrast, even
Chaucer's work was not published with explanatory notes until
Speght's edition of 1598. With *The Shepheardes Calender* the novelty
and the classic status go together: the preface begins by setting
alongside each other 'the olde famous poete Chaucer' (7–8) and 'this
our new poete' (19), and E. K. later explains,

Herunto have I added a certain glosse or scholion for th'exposition of old wordes
and harder phrases: which maner of glosing and commenting, well I wote, wil
seeme straunge and rare in our tongue: yet for somuch as I knew many excellent
and proper devises both in wordes and matter would passe in the speedy course
of reading, either as unknowen, or as not marked, and that in this kind, as in
other, we might be equal to the learned of other nations, I thought good to take
the paines upon me, the rather for that by meanes of some familiar acquaintaunce
I was made privie to his counsell and secret meaning in them.   (183–93)

As E. K. says, the glosses are concerned with 'matter' as well as
'wordes': he calls attention not only to archaic expressions but to
parallels in classical poetry and to the allegory by which, for
example, 'Colin' stands for Spenser and 'Tityrus' for Chaucer (who
is thereby paralleled to 'the worthines of the Roman Tityrus, Virgile'
[*Preface* 15]). Though it is not so spectacularly obscure as Skelton's
Speke Parott, *The Shepheardes Calender* is truly a work of the Renaissance in being a dark allegory – Milton indeed, in the next century,
read it as prophetic, 'not without some presage of these reforming
times'.[4] Many of Spenser's allusions to contemporary political and
religious affairs are still matter for scholarly controversy; but this is
not territory that I propose to enter. My concern is with Spenser's
conception and treatment of poetic history.

In this book as a whole I have been recurrently concerned with
two elements in the growth of English poetic history. One is the way
in which Chaucer's sense of history and of literary history enabled
him to establish a new relationship with the classical past and
classical poetry, and thus to achieve a new conception of poetry
itself. My other concern has been with the ways in which subsequent
English poets drew on Chaucer's historical sense to establish their
relationship to the classical past and to Chaucer himself. In an
important way, *The Shepheardes Calender* marks the final culmination of these processes. On the one hand, it presents an English
poet who moulds his career on a classical model, beginning with
pastoral eclogues, and thus 'following the example of the best and
most auncient poetes' (*Preface* 158–9) from Virgil to Marot. On the
other hand, it firmly establishes Chaucer as a poet of the past –
admirable and worthy of imitation, but no longer threatening in his
superiority. He is now an archaic poet, and, especially within the
pastoral mode, there is a connection between archaism and a patroni-
zable rusticity. Sidney, while affirming that 'The *Shepherd's Calendar*
hath much poetry in his eclogues', referred disapprovingly to Spenser's 'framing of his style to an old rustic language':[5] 'old' and 'rustic'

evidently went naturally together. Skelton had noted that
Chaucer's language was becoming old-fashioned, and Wyatt, in his
nearest approach to pastoral, in *Satire II*, had characterized the
simple language of 'My mothers maydes when they did sowe and
spynne' (MT CVI I) with what may be touches of archaism;[6] but
Spenser is the first English poet to imitate, consciously and fairly
systematically, the forms and vocabulary of Middle English to create
an archaizing poetic style.

Thus, while the lament for Chaucer's death and the consequent
loss of his skill can be repeated as in fifteenth-century poetry, its
placing as archaic and rustic now prevents us from taking it too
seriously. Chaucer's work is now no more than 'mery tales', and the
anxiety of the late-comer is merely part of the overall pastoral
fiction:

> The God of shepheards, *Tityrus*, is dead,
> Who taught me homely, as I can, to make.
> He, whilst he lived, was the soveraigne head
> Of shepheards all that bene with love ytake:
> Well couth he wayle his woes, and lightly slake
> The flames which love within his heart had bredd,
> And tell us mery tales, to keepe us wake,
> The while our sheepe about us safely fedde.
>
> Nowe dead he is, and lyeth wrapt in lead
> (O why should death on hym such outrage showe?)
> And all hys passing skil with him is fledde,
> The fame whereof doth dayly greater growe.
> But if on me some little drops would flowe
> Of that the spring was in his learned hedde,
> I soone would learne these woods to wayle my woe,
> And teache the trees their trickling teares to shedde.   (*June* 81–96)

(It is worth noting that this account of Chaucer misses his normal
stance as outsider in relation to love, and assimilates him to the
pattern of those courtly poets such as Wyatt and Surrey who express
their own 'woes' and 'flames' in their writings.) For the first time,
Spenser has managed to make Chaucer part of a *usable* history of
English poetry. In one aspect, Tityrus may be Chaucer considered as
the English Virgil, but in another he is no more than a 'good old
man', 'Keeping his sheepe on the hils of Kent' (*Februarie* 96, 93), and
a general representative of the native tradition of poetry. There is
little specific quotation from or allusion to Chaucer in the *Calender*;
the fable of the oak and the briar attributed to Tityrus in the February
eclogue is not by Chaucer and, as E. K. notes, 'is cleane in another

kind, and rather like to Æsopes fables' (*Februarie* 287). Chaucer himself had been able to become a Renaissance poet (to the limited extent that he did) only by rejecting and parodying the English tradition of popular poetry, even though it continued to provide the staple of much of his verse; but for Spenser, by one of time's ironies, the merging of the archaic and the rustic in pastoral deprived Chaucer of his power to intimidate by making him seem a popular as well as a learned poet.

The twelve eclogues that make up *The Shepheardes Calender* offer a variety of different conceptions of and attitudes towards poetry. Within the learned tradition of pastoral, 'The term "shepherd" had come to mean "poet"',[7] and that this was so even in England before Spenser Alexander Barclay's *Eclogue IV* bears witness. But Spenser went further, and what has been written of his June eclogue is true to some extent of the whole *Calender*: 'Spenser has really shifted the grounds for the pastoral complaint. There is a good deal more about poetry here than about love.'[8] The treatment of poetry in *October* is perhaps the most elevated and most complex. Cuddie, 'the perfecte paterne of a poete', as E. K. announces (*October*: Argument), insists that poetry is inspired, but also that it depends on generous patronage to support it and on worthy deeds to form its subject-matter:

> Indeede the Romish *Tityrus*, I heare,
> Through his *Mecœnas* left his oaten reede,
> Whereon he earst had taught his flocks to feede,
> And laboured lands to yield the timely eare,
> And eft did sing of warres and deadly drede,
> So as the heavens did quake his verse to here.
>
> But ah, *Mecœnas* is yclad in claye,
> And great *Augustus* long ygoe is dead;
> And all the worthies liggen wrapt in leade
> That matter made for poets on to play;
> For ever, who in derring doe were dreade,
> The loftie verse of hem was loved aye.
>
> But after vertue gan for age to stoupe
> And mighty manhode brought a bedde of ease,
> The vaunting poets found nought worth a pease
> To put in preace emong the learned troupe.
> Tho gan the streames of flowing wittes to cease,
> And sonnebright honour pend in shamefull coupe.   (*October* 55–72)

Even in the present age of iron, Colin might be capable of creating poetry by flying on wings of 'aspyring wit' (83) to the heavens, but he is bound to the earth by Cupid's tyranny. Cuddie concludes by proposing the connection between poetic fervour and intoxication, Apollo and Bacchus, that Skelton had celebrated in *The Garland of Laurel*; but he adds, 'my corage cooles ere it be warme' (115). Like Chaucer in *The House of Fame*, but with more confidence, Spenser is transforming an existing literary kind (love-vision in Chaucer's case, pastoral eclogue in Spenser's) whilst trying out a number of different roles for the English poet.

The Shepheardes Calender concludes with a two-stanza epilogue which brings together the two extremes of pride and humility in Spenser's attitude to poetry. The first stanza claims nothing short of permanence for the work he has completed (and E. K. duly notes the precedents in Horace and Ovid):

> Loe, I have made a Calender for every yeare,
> That steele in strength and time in durance shall outweare;
> And if I marked well the starres revolution,
> It shall continewe till the worlds dissolution,
> To teach the ruder shepheard how to feede his sheepe,
> And from the falsers fraud his folded flocke to kepe.
>
> (*December* 235–40)

The very form of this epilogue seems to enact the claim to everlastingness, for, like the heavenly city described in Apocalypse, chapter 21, it stands squarely measuring twelve times twelve (twelve lines, each of twelve syllables).[9] But the second stanza takes us back almost to our starting-point, to the 'Go, litel bok . . .' passage near the end of *Troilus and Criseyde* (v 1786ff). There, as we saw, Chaucer more obliquely asserted that his work would last, even if in miswritten or mismetred form, and he urged it to kiss the footsteps of its classical predecessors, 'Virgile, Ovide, Omer, Lucan, and Stace' (v 1792). Spenser similarly urges his 'lyttle Calender' to 'adore' the footsteps of its forerunners, but the idea of literary history that Chaucer began for English poetry has now reached fruition, and the predecessors are not the classical poets, but those of the medieval English past, Chaucer himself and Langland:[10]

> Goe, lyttle Calender, thou hast a free passeporte,
> Goe but a lowly gate emongste the meaner sorte.
> Dare not to match thy pype with Tityrus his style,
> Nor with the Pilgrim that the Ploughman playde a whyle:
> But followe them farre off, and their high steppes adore;
> The better please, the worse despise, I aske nomore.
>
> (*December* 241–6)

After two centuries, the English literary history created by Chaucer and his admiring descendents has at last come of age.

Notes

1 Renaissance and medieval

1 Among the works to which I am most indebted I must mention Peter Burke, *The Renaissance Sense of the Past* (London 1969); Wallace K. Ferguson, *The Renaissance in Historical Thought* (Cambridge, Mass., 1948); Denys Hay, *The Italian Renaissance in its Historical Background*, 2nd edn (Cambridge 1977); Erwin Panofsky, *Renaissance and Renascences in Western Art* (London 1960).

2 Herbert Weisinger, 'The Self-Awareness of the Renaissance as a Criterion of the Renaissance', *Papers of the Michigan Academy of Science, Arts and Letters* 29 (1943), 561–7; pp. 562, 567.

3 Jules Michelet uses the phrase in the preface to his *Histoire de France*, vol. VII (Paris 1855), and it was borrowed by Jacob Burckhardt as the title of Part IV of his *Die Kultur der Renaissance in Italien* (Basel 1860).

4 Charles Trinkaus, *In Our Image and Likeness* (London 1970), pp. 181–2.

5 See Heiko A. Oberman, 'Some Notes on the Theology of Nominalism with Attention to Its Relation to the Renaissance', *Harvard Theological Review* 53 (1960), 47–76, and William J. Courtenay, 'Nominalism and Late Medieval Religion', in *The Pursuit of Holiness*, ed. Charles Trinkaus with Heiko A. Oberman (Leiden 1974), pp. 26–59.

6 *Prologue* to *The Legend of Good Women* G 414–15.

7 See A. C. Spearing, *The Gawain-Poet* (Cambridge 1970), pp. 30–2, 79–90.

8 *Patience*, lines 524–7, from *The Poems of the Pearl Manuscript*, ed. Malcolm Andrew and Ronald Waldron (London 1978).

9 Panofsky, *Renaissance and Renascences in Western Art*, p. 29.

10 Quoted from the translation of Thomas Twyne (1579), as cited by E. H. Wilkins, *Life of Petrarch* (Chicago 1961), p. 139.

11 Trinkaus, *In Our Image and Likeness*, p. 192.

12 Trans. P. O. Kristeller, in *The Renaissance Philosophy of Man*, ed. E. Cassirer, P. O. Kristeller and J. H. Randall (Chicago 1948), pp. 227, 224–5.

13 *Ibid.*, p. 227.

14 Luke 10:42.

15 *Familiarium rerum libri* XXIV 3; for a translation see *Letters from Petrarch*, trans. Morris Bishop (Bloomington 1966), pp. 206–7.

16 *De sui ipsius et multorum ignorantia*, trans. Hans Nachod, in *The Renaissance Philosophy of Man*, p. 103.

17 E. H. Wilkins, 'The Coronation of Petrarch', *Speculum* 18 (1943), 155–97.

18 J. B. Trapp, 'The Owl's Ivy and the Poet's Bays', *Journal of the Warburg and Courtauld Institute* 21 (1958), 227–55, p. 239; and Wilkins, 'The Coronation of Petrarch', p. 174.

19 I quote the *De genealogia* from *Boccaccio on Poetry*, trans. C. G. Osgood (Princeton 1930), pp. 17, 39, 26, 54, 60, 62. The quotation from the *Life of Dante* is cited by Osgood, p. xxiii, n. 25. Many of the ideas expressed in these

quotations had already been put forward by Petrarch in his coronation oration, in the *Africa*, the *Invectivae contra medicum*, and elsewhere.

20 The crucial nature of the importance of printing for this development is exaggerated by Elizabeth L. Eisenstein, *The Printing Press as an Agent of Change* (Cambridge 1979), e.g. p. 121. All the essential features of the literary Renaissance antedate the printing press.

21 *Apologia contra cuiusdam anonymi Galli calumnias*, quoted by T. E. Mommsen, 'Petrarch's Conception of the "Dark Ages"', *Speculum* 17 (1942), 226–42, p. 227.

22 *Africa* IX 453–7, as translated by Panofsky, *Renaissance and Renascences*, p. 10, a livelier version than in *Petrarch's Africa*, trans. Thomas G. Bergin and Alice S. Wilson (New Haven 1977).

23 John 3:3. Cf. Panofsky, *Renaissance and Renascences*, pp. 36–8.

24 *Decameron* VI 5, trans. G. H. McWilliam (Harmondsworth 1972), p. 494.

25 (London 1952), p. 41: '... the thousand years that intervened between the decline of the antique and the birth, in [Giotto's] person, of modern painting.'

26 See Ferguson, *The Renaissance in Historical Thought*, pp. 19–20.

27 Cited by Hay, *The Italian Renaissance in its Historical Background*, p. 12, from Palmieri's *Della vita civile* as translated in W. H. Woodward, *Studies in Education during the Age of the Renaissance* (Cambridge 1906), p. 67.

28 Louis Althusser, *For Marx*, trans. Ben Brewster (London 1977), p. 227. I am indebted to my colleague Iain Wright for directing me to this essay.

29 Catherine Belsey, *Critical Practice* (London 1980), p. 131.

30 R. R. Bolgar, *The Classical Heritage* (Cambridge 1954), p. 263.

31 *Renaissance and Renascences in Western Art*, p. 4.

32 *De vulgari eloquentia*, translated by Sally Purcell as *Literature in the Vernacular* (Manchester 1981), I i.

33 *Ibid.*, II iv, vi.

34 *Inferno*, I 71–2, 79–87. This and subsequent quotations from the *Commedia*, in Italian and in translation, are taken from *The Divine Comedy of Dante Alighieri*, ed. and trans. John D. Sinclair (London 1939–46).

2 Chaucer

1 For fuller discussion of comparative social conditions and their cultural reflections, see Denys Hay, 'England and the Humanities in the Fifteenth Century', in *Itinerarium Italicum*, ed. Heiko A. Oberman with Thomas A. Brady (Leiden 1975), pp. 305–67.

2 I quote Chaucer here and subsequently from *The Works of Geoffrey Chaucer*, ed. F. N. Robinson, 2nd edn (London 1957).

3 Cf. Jill Mann, *Chaucer and Medieval Estates Satire* (Cambridge 1973), especially chapters 1 and 9.

4 Quentin Skinner, *The Foundations of Modern Political Thought* (Cambridge 1978), vol. I, p. 90. Evidence in favour of the literacy and literary interests of late-medieval English noblemen is gathered in an important chapter in K. B. McFarlane, *The Nobility of Later Medieval England* (Oxford 1973), pp. 228–47, but this does not affect the difference of ideals.

5 *Troy Book*, ed. H. Bergen, EETS ES 97, 103, 106, 126 (London 1906–20), III 4241, 4245, 4258.

6 Quoted from *Chaucer: The Critical Heritage*, ed. D. S. Brewer (London 1978), vol. I, p. 88.

7 *Ibid.*, p. 104.

8 *An Apology for Poetry*, ed. Geoffrey Shepherd (London 1965), pp. 96f, 133. John Leland had earlier suggested that Chaucer was spurred by the example of Petrarch, who 'flourished with fame in Italy, and by his labors the common speech of that land was brought to such a point of refinement that it vied with Latin itself for the palm of eloquence' (*Chaucer: The Critical Heritage*, pp. 92–3, quoting T. R. Lounsbury's translation of Leland's Latin account of Chaucer, c. 1540).

9 *Chaucer: The Critical Heritage*, p. 240. Godwin is still much influenced by Renaissance historiography, however, and mentions Giotto and Dante as Chaucer's predecessors.

10 See John Larner, 'Chaucer's Italy', in *Chaucer and the Italian Trecento*, ed. Piero Boitani (Cambridge 1983), pp. 7–32; pp. 18–19.

11 See Howard Schless, 'Transformations: Chaucer's Use of Italian', in *Geoffrey Chaucer*, ed. Derek Brewer (London 1974), pp. 184–223; pp. 190–7.

12 I now feel less certain of this than when I wrote *The Gawain-Poet*, pp. 17–18; but for a recent argument in favour of this poet's acquaintance with Italian see John Finlayson, '*Pearl*, Petrarch's *Trionfo Della Morte*, and Boccaccio's *Olympia*', *English Studies in Canada* 9 (1983), 1–13.

13 *The Springs of Helicon* (London 1909), pp. 10–11.

14 'Chaucer and the Renaissance', in his *Form and Style in Poetry* (London 1928), p. 73. It should be noted that Ker goes on to say that 'the Renaissance element in his work is not very large,' and that he is as much concerned to delimit as to affirm the view that 'Chaucer belongs to the Renaissance.'

15 Thus in a recent article Beverly Boyd writes 'It is not usual to speak of the Renaissance in Chaucer's time, but the influence is unquestionably there' ('Whatever Happened to Chaucer's Renaissance?', *Fifteenth Century Studies* 1 (1978), 15–21; p. 20). The article is valuable for reminding us that the question posed by its title is important, but is too slight to make much progress in suggesting possible answers.

16 First published in *Essays and Studies* 19 (1932), and reprinted in his *Selected Literary Essays* (Cambridge 1969), pp. 27–44; page-citations from the latter. An earlier and more judicious study of Chaucer's treatment of Italian poetry was Mario Praz, 'Chaucer and the Great Italian Writers of the Trecento', *The Monthly Criterion* (1927), 18–39, 131–57, 238–42, reprinted (with considerable revision) in his *The Flaming Heart* (New York 1958), pp. 29–89. It would be interesting to know whether Lewis had read Praz, and also whether he had read J. S. P. Tatlock's admirable article, 'The Epilog of Chaucer's *Troilus*', *Modern Philology* 18 (1920–1), 625–59. If he had read the latter, then, in presenting Chaucer as a medievalizer, Lewis must have been consciously reversing Tatlock's view that 'Whether deliberately or not, so far as he could, Chaucer precisely undid the medievalizing introduced into the Troy story by Benoit de S. Maure' (p. 642).

17 *A Preface to Chaucer* (Princeton 1963), p. 51.

18 The inserted phrase has been discussed by Praz, *The Flaming Heart*, p. 50, and by John M. Fyler, *Chaucer and Ovid* (New Haven 1979), pp. 33–4. Praz aptly remarks that 'It is Virgil interpreted by a mediaeval minstrel; but Chaucer was himself also a mediaeval minstrel', while Fyler sees the phrase as implying 'the uncertain ability of art to be true to the facts.'

19 *Paradiso* I 63, a line which follows closely after a passage that Chaucer will adapt in the proem to his second book.

20 Cf. John H. Fisher, *John Gower* (New York 1964), p. 210: 'The depiction of the temple of Venus . . . as merely a hallway leading to a sterile wasteland would appear to be an . . . explicit judgment upon erotic love as the stuff of literature.'

21 I have written about it more fully, and from a somewhat different point of view, in my *Medieval Dream-Poetry* (Cambridge 1976), pp. 73–89. The present discussion of the proems was written before I had the advantage of reading Piero Boitani's valuable essay, 'What Dante Meant to Chaucer', in *Chaucer and the Italian Trecento*, pp. 115–39.

22 *Dantis Alagherii Epistolae*, ed. Paget Toynbee, 2nd edn (London 1966), p. 203.

23 Jonathan Culler, *The Pursuit of Signs* (London 1981), pp. 139, 142, 143.

24 The latter instances are noted by J. A. Burrow, *Medieval Writers and their Work* (Oxford 1982), p. 18.

25 *Poetria nova*, l. 176, in *Les arts poétiques du XIIe et du XIIIe siècle*, ed. Edmond Faral (Paris 1926), p. 205.

26 Dante, *La Vita Nuova*, trans. Barbara Reynolds (Harmondsworth 1969), pp. 73–4. *Dic mihi, Musa, virum* translates the opening of the *Odyssey*.

27 There are probably other recollections of Dante in Chaucer's proems, as suggested, for example, by J. A. W. Bennett, *Chaucer's Book of Fame* (Oxford 1968), pp. 53–5, but to avoid confusion I disregard them.

28 I do not share Bennett's view (*ibid.*, p. 56) that the enjambements in these lines produce 'an effect of eager expectancy'; they seem to me rather to convey the difficulty appropriate to stylistic elevation.

29 In an interesting commentary on this proem, J. A. Burrow states that 'the difficulty is not marked, for the diction remains simple (except in the phrase "tresorye . . . of my brayn") . . .' (*Ricardian Poetry* (London 1971), p. 22); but the difficulty of other elements beside this phrase seems sufficiently attested by the failures of modern scholars to understand them (e.g. James Winny, *Chaucer's Dream-Poems* (London 1973), pp. 33–4). It should be added that the notion of there being a 'treasury' of recollections in the brain was not new in scientific writings: John Trevisa, in his translation of the *De proprietatibus rerum* of Bartholomeus Anglicus, writes of '*memorativa*, the vertu of mynde' which 'holdith and kepith in the tresour of mynde thingis that beth apprehendid and iknowe bi the ymaginatif and *racio*' (*On the Properties of Things*, ed. M. C. Seymour (Oxford 1975), vol. I, p. 98). See further A. J. Minnis, 'Langland's Imaginatif and late-medieval theories of imagination', *Comparative Criticism* 3 (1981), 71–103.

30 Later in *The House of Fame* Chaucer includes among the poets in Fame's hall 'Marcia that loste her skyn' (1229). He must have supposed Dante's *Marsia* to be a feminine form, and have had no other information about the myth.

31 *Rime sparse* 40, lines 5–6. This and subsequent quotations from Petrarch, in the original and in translation, are taken from *Petrarch's Lyric Poems*, trans. and ed. Robert M. Durling (Cambridge, Mass., 1976). It is uncertain to which of his works Petrarch was referring in this sonnet.

32 Thus P. M. Kean aptly comments on two stanzas from *The Second Nun's Prologue* (VIII 36–49): 'The fact that Chaucer had read Dante and had understood and could reproduce his special blend of the unswerving line of purely intellectual argument with imagery precisely and vividly realized, separates much of his religious poetry from all other English writing of this kind, both

before and immediately after him.' (*Chaucer and the Making of English Poetry* (London 1972), vol. II, p. 197.)

33 For examples of such study, see Praz, 'Chaucer and the Great Italian Writers of the Trecento'; Piero Boitani, *Chaucer and Boccaccio* (Oxford 1977); N. R. Havely, *Chaucer's Boccaccio* (Cambridge 1980).

34 Burke, *The Renaissance Sense of the Past*, p. 19; see also Carlo Cipolla, *Clocks and Culture 1300–1700* (London 1967); Jean Gimpel, *The Medieval Machine* (London 1977), chapter 7; Jacques le Goff, *Time, Work and Culture in the Middle Ages* (Chicago 1980), pp. 29–52.

35 'Chaucer's Sense of History', in his *Essays and Explorations* (Cambridge, Mass., 1970), pp. 12–26; pp. 23, 17.

36 *Ars poetica* 60–2, in *Ancient Literary Criticism*, ed. D. A. Russell and M. Winterbottom (Oxford 1972), p. 281.

37 Trans. Purcell, I ix. There is another Dantean parallel to Chaucer's thought in a vernacular work, the *Convivio*, I v 55–66; see J. L. Lowes, 'Chaucer and Dante', *Modern Philology* 14 (1916–17), 129–59.

38 *Teseida* XII, stanzas 84–5. One undoubted classical source for both Boccaccio and Chaucer is Statius's conclusion to his *Thebaid*, where he urges his book to honour the footprints of Virgil's *Aeneid* (XII 816–17).

39 Cf. Tatlock, 'The Epilog of Chaucer's *Troilus*', p. 630, n. 8; this pioneer discussion has been cloudily reconsidered by Alice S. Miskimin, *The Renaissance Chaucer* (New Haven 1975), pp. 271–88, and expanded and made more precise by Glending Olson, 'Making and Poetry in the Age of Chaucer', *Comparative Literature* 31 (1979), 272–90. Tatlock points out that Dante and Petrarch are the only two post-classical writers to whom Chaucer applies the term 'poet'. Dante, in the chapter of the *Vita nuova* quoted above (pp. 25–6), defends the use of 'poet' to refer to vernacular writers.

40 *Inferno* IV 102. Tatlock however points out (p. 630, n. 8) that 'his list of ancient writers is pretty much the common one.'

41 Terry Eagleton, *Literary Theory: An Introduction* (Oxford 1983), pp. 11, 204, 217. Chaucer was undoubtedly an élitist, but his aim (following Boethius, Jean de Meun, Dante, and others) seems to have been to transform a social into a moral élite: 'he is gentil that dooth gentil dedis' (*The Wife of Bath's Tale*, III 1170). He would have seen that aim not as a Christian or 'bourgeois' innovation, but as the outcome of a perennial moral wisdom having its roots in the thought of virtuous pagans.

42 Cf. the 'lytel laste bok' of *The House of Fame* 1093. Tatlock (pp. 628–30) traces the diminutive form back to classical and medieval sources, including Boccaccio's *Fiammetta*, *Corbaccio* and *Filocolo*, but notes that 'Nowhere before Boccaccio do I find the "little book" conceit at the end of a long work' (p. 630).

43 Thomas Hoccleve, *The Regement of Princes*, 1961, in *Works*, ed. F. J. Furnivall, vol. III, EETS ES 72 (London 1897).

44 'Preface to Fables Ancient and Modern', in John Dryden, *Of Dramatic Poesy and Other Critical Essays*, ed. George Watson (London 1962), vol. II, p. 280.

45 E. H. Gombrich, *Norm and Form* (London 1966), p. 10.

46 Kean, *Chaucer and the Making of English Poetry*, vol. I, p. 5.

47 'The Relationship of Chaucer to the English and European Traditions', in *Chaucer and Chaucerians*, ed. D. S. Brewer (London 1966), pp. 1–38.

48 See, for example, the discussion of *Canterbury Tales* I 4292–312 in *The Reeve's Prologue and Tale*, ed. A. C. and J. E. Spearing (Cambridge 1979), pp. 64–5,

and the further comments by Gregory Roscow, *Syntax and Style in Chaucer's Poetry* (Cambridge 1981), pp. 124–7.

49 Brewer, 'The Relationship of Chaucer', p. 4.

50 *The Testament of Love* III iv, in *Chaucerian and Other Pieces*, ed. W. W. Skeat (Oxford 1897), p. 123.

51 *The Works of Geoffrey Chaucer*, ed. F. N. Robinson, p. 717.

52 *Il Penseroso*, line 109.

53 *Renaissance and Renascences*, pp. 19, 29–30.

54 Evidence in favour of the influence of the *Filocolo* on Chaucer has recently been marshalled by David Wallace, 'Chaucer and Boccaccio's Early Works,' in *Chaucer and the Italian Trecento*, pp. 141–62.

55 On this process of classicization, see J. S. P. Tatlock, *The Scene of the Franklin's Tale Visited* (London 1914). Tatlock notes that 'Chaucer took much pains to put the story back in Roman times, and in doing so showed an historical imagination rare in the Middle Ages outside Italy' (p. 20).

56 Morton W. Bloomfield, 'Distance and Predestination in *Troilus and Criseyde*', in his *Essays and Explorations*, pp. 200–16; see p. 207 (and n. 7 for the apparent exception of III 1165).

57 There is disagreement as to whether Chaucer knew Boccaccio's commentary on the *Teseida*. Boitani, *Chaucer and Boccaccio*, offers evidence suggesting that he did.

58 See *The Knight's Tale*, ed. J. A. W. Bennett, 2nd edn (London 1958), p. 136.

59 Cf. A. J. Minnis, *Chaucer and Pagan Antiquity* (Cambridge 1982), pp. 16–21.

60 It is for this reason that one must reject readings such as that of Douglas Brooks and Alastair Fowler, 'The Meaning of Chaucer's *Knight's Tale*', *Medium Ævum* 29 (1970), 123–46, a brilliantly elaborate allegorization constituting the kind of commentary on the tale that might have been written by a learned Renaissance mythographer; and that of John P. McCall, *Chaucer among the Gods* (University Park 1979), pp. 63–86. These are by no means the only modern examples of misplaced scholarship in the reading of Chaucer – attempts to supply precisely those interpretations that Chaucer refrained from employing.

61 *Chaucerian and Other Pieces*, p. 123. Caxton too was later to refer to Chaucer as 'that noble and grete philosopher' (*Caxton's Own Prose*, ed. N. F. Blake (London 1973), p. 61).

62 *Selected Literary Essays*, p. 33.

63 C. S. Lewis, *The Discarded Image* (Cambridge 1964), p. 78. (The Visigoths were not Catholics but Arians.)

64 P. 11.

65 *Ibid.*, p. 47.

66 For surveys of controversy on such issues, see, in addition to Minnis's book, Heiko A. Oberman, *The Harvest of Medieval Theology* (Cambridge, Mass., 1963) and 'Fourteenth-Century Religious Thought: A Premature Profile', *Speculum* 53 (1978), 80–93; Janet Coleman, *Piers Plowman and the "Moderni"* (Rome 1981), chapters 1 and 4; William J. Courtenay, 'Nominalism and Late Medieval Religion'. I am indebted to Professor Thomas G. Hahn, of the University of Rochester, for helpful discussion of this topic, and for letting me read his unpublished paper, 'Indulgence for Good Pagans in Fourteenth-Century England'.

67 Cited by Charles Trinkaus, *The Poet as Philosopher* (New Haven 1979), p. 99.
68 *Boccaccio on Poetry*, p. 98.
69 Cited by Trinkaus, *In Our Image and Likeness*, p. 700.
70 *The Renaissance Philosophy of Man*, pp. 115, 80, 83.
71 Cf. Trinkaus, *The Poet as Philosopher*, pp. 53–4: 'Recent scholarship has emphasized the significant parallels between the rise of Renaissance humanism and the scholastic *via moderna* of the *nominales* of the fourteenth and fifteenth centuries.'
72 Cf. Robert B. Burlin, *Chaucerian Fiction* (Princeton 1977), p. 99: 'The pagan world . . . provided an ideal setting in which to explore the mind's grasp of fundamental metaphysical issues, suspending for the nonce some of the central tenets of Christian faith.'
73 *Chaucer and Pagan Antiquity*, pp. 132, 133.
74 The contrast Minnis draws between Emelye and 'the heroine of *Le Roman de la Rose* who exercises supreme power over her lover, and has the sole responsibility for deciding the outcome of his suit' (*ibid.*, p. 133) is also misleading. The heroine of *Le Roman de la Rose* is shown to be dominated by two kinds of supreme power: that of the gods who represent the passions by which she is moved (in this she resembles the characters of *The Knight's Tale*); and that of the unnamed men on whose behalf she is being defended against Amant. My assumption is that Chaucer understood this better than most modern interpreters of the *Roman* have done.
75 *Ibid.*, p. 122. Minnis draws apt parallels with the pagan judge of *Saint Erkenwald* and with Trajan himself, one of the test cases as to the possibility of salvation for virtuous pagans. The notion that Chaucer intended Theseus to be seen as 'a typical Italian tyrant' and 'a sordid political schemer', recently revived by Terry Jones (*Chaucer's Knight* (London 1980), pp. 192, 195), seems to be based on a misunderstanding of the inevitable imperfection even of well-intentioned rule in a world dominated by Saturn. On the contrast between Creon, who is repeatedly described as a tyrant, and Theseus as his antithesis, see further J. D. Burnley, *Chaucer's Language and the Philosophers' Tradition* (Cambridge 1979), pp. 25–8.
76 In this Theseus does no more than was permitted by the medieval law of war when a city refused to surrender and was taken by assault.
77 Cf. p. 46 above.
78 See Philippe's *Letter to King Richard II*, ed. G. W. Coopland (New York 1976), pp. 127–9.
79 *Purgatorio* VI 118–19.
80 The analogy with Genesis is implied by Dale Underwood, 'The First of *The Canterbury Tales*', *English Literary History* 26 (1959), 455–69; p. 459.
81 *Chaucer and Pagan Antiquity*, p. 135. A more balanced view is offered by Elizabeth Salter in a brilliant posthumously published essay: 'the incomplete transposition of materials into a "classical" format guarantees that the problems are not sealed off as parts of a historically distanced narrative' (*Fourteenth-Century English Poetry: Contexts and Readings* (Oxford 1983), p. 153). A similarly balanced view of the paganism of *Troilus and Criseyde*, and of its relation to the Renaissance, is to be found in Donald R. Howard, 'The Philosophies in Chaucer's *Troilus*', in *The Wisdom of Poetry*, ed. Larry D. Benson and Siegfried Wenzel (Kalamazoo 1982), pp. 151–75.
82 For the compatibility of scepticism with faith, cf. Sheila Delany, *Chaucer's House of Fame: The Poetics of Skeptical Fideism* (Chicago 1972), chapter 2.

3 The Chaucerian tradition

1 *The Anxiety of Influence* (New York 1973), p. 5. In this chapter Bloom's ideas will often be in the background. For a proposal as to the applicability of his theory to Boccaccio's influence on Chaucer, see Donald R. Howard, 'Fiction and Religion in Boccaccio and Chaucer', *Journal of the American Academy of Religion* 47/2 Supplement (June 1979), 307–28.

2 *The English Language in Medieval Literature* (London 1977), pp. 14–15 and chapter 1 *passim*. Blake's argument is of great interest, but in my view he seriously underestimates the differences that mark the fifteenth century off from earlier periods of English writing. See also Burrow, *Medieval Writers and their Work*, chapter 5.

3 V. J. Scattergood, 'The Authorship of *The Boke of Cupide*', *Anglia* 82 (1964), 37–49.

4 *Confessio Amantis*, ed. G. C. Macaulay (Oxford 1901), VIII 2945.

5 *The Regement of Princes*, 1961–4.

6 *Troy Book* III 553 and II 4697–700.

7 *Epistolae rerum senilium* V 2, trans. Bishop, *Letters from Petrarch*, p. 244.

8 Ed. John Norton-Smith (Oxford 1971), 1373–9.

9 This and subsequent quotations from Dunbar are taken from *The Poems of William Dunbar*, ed. James Kinsley (Oxford 1979). Poems are identified by their numbers in this edition.

10 See the collections in *Five Hundred Years of Chaucer Criticism and Allusion*, ed. Caroline F. E. Spurgeon (London 1925) and *Chaucer: The Critical Heritage*, ed. Brewer, vol. I. For discussion, see D. S. Brewer, Derek Pearsall and Denton Fox in *Chaucer and Chaucerians*, pp. 164–270, and Denton Fox, 'Chaucer's Influence on Fifteenth-Century Poetry', in *Companion to Chaucer Studies*, ed. Beryl Rowland (Toronto 1968), pp. 358–402.

11 *The Proloug of the First Buke of Eneados*, 339–43, in *Virgil's Aeneid*, ed. David F. C. Coldwell, vol. II (Edinburgh 1957).

12 *Boccaccio on Poetry*, p. 79.

13 For a more precise analysis of Chaucer's immediate reading public and its disintegration after his death, see the penetrating article by Paul Strohm, 'Chaucer's Fifteenth-Century Audience and the Narrowing of the "Chaucer Tradition"', *Studies in the Age of Chaucer* 4 (1982), 3–32.

14 It has rightly been pointed out by Kean (*Chaucer and the Making of English Poetry*, vol. II, pp. 210–11) that 'Chaucer's plainer ways of writing' were also imitated by some fifteenth-century poets; but it remains true that it was his rhetorical high style that was most widely and greatly admired.

15 *The Serpent of Division*, ed. H. N. MacCracken (London 1911), p. 65.

16 Compare the admirable remarks of C. S. Lewis:
> Often a single line such as
>> Singest with vois memorial in the shade
> seems to contain within itself the germ of the whole central tradition of high poetical language in England. It is not so much poetical as 'English poetry' itself – or what Englishmen most easily recognize as poetry; and the diction of the Chaucerians in the century that followed is a blundering witness to the fact. (*The Allegory of Love* (Oxford 1936), p. 201)

17 *Ricardian Poetry*, p. 43.

18 *The Fall of Princes*, ed. H. Bergen, EETS ES 121–4 (London 1918–19), III 2201–2.

19 *La Male Regle*, 112. This and subsequent quotations from works of Hoccleve other than *The Regement of Princes* are taken, unless otherwise stated, from *Hoccleve's Works: The Minor Poems*, ed. F. J. Furnivall and I. Gollancz, rev. Jerome Mitchell and A. I. Doyle, EETS ES 61 and 73 (London 1970).

20 Epilogue to his edition of Chaucer's *House of Fame*, in *Caxton's Own Prose*, ed. Blake, p. 103. Caxton writes about Chaucer in similar terms in the prologue to his edition of *The Canterbury Tales*. Cf. *General Prologue* 304–6.

21 It has been generally assumed that, in the words of Derek Pearsall, 'He had no patron for this work, which gives it an added importance since it encourages us to assume that he wrote it because he chose to'. (*John Lydgate* (London 1970), p. 151; cf. *The Siege of Thebes*, ed. Axel Erdmann and Eilert Ekwall, EETS ES 108, 125 [London 1911, 1930], vol. II, p. 111, and Alain Renoir, *The Poetry of John Lydgate* (London 1967), p. 111) More recently it has been argued that 'No fifteenth-century English poet wrote at such length without a patron in mind', and Gloucester has been proposed as a likely patron for the *Siege* (*Selections from Hoccleve*, ed. M. C. Seymour (Oxford 1981), p. xxx, n. 20).

22 *The Anxiety of Influence*, p. 66.

23 Line 48. *The Siege of Thebes* is quoted here and subsequently from the edition cited in note 21. The references to Chaucer in the notes to this edition are helpful but by no means exhaustive; wherever possible, I have taken my material from parallels not noted by Erdmann and Ekwall. Because the specific redaction of the *Roman de Thèbes* used by Lydgate has not yet been identified, I do not attempt to relate the *Siege* systematically to its source; but if the normal assumption is correct, that the source was closely similar to the 1491 *Ystoire de Thèbes*, then most of the passages I discuss are Lydgate's own additions.

24 N. F. Blake would presumably argue that he was imitating an earlier imitation that formed part of *The Canterbury Tales* as it came down to him: see 'The Relationship between the Hengwrt and the Ellesmere Manuscripts of the *Canterbury Tales*,' *Essays and Studies* n. s. 32 (1979), 1–18.

25 It is interesting that Derek Pearsall (*John Lydgate*, p. 66) should class this line among the 'touches of revealing description and observation' in the prologue. Like many such touches in Lydgate (and in Chaucer too, of course,) its 'observation' is of earlier literature.

26 Eleanor P. Hammond in her edition of *English Verse Between Chaucer and Surrey* (Durham, North Carolina, 1927), p. 42, notes the specific parallel between *Siege* 76 and *Canon's Yeoman's Prologue* VIII 566–7, but without suggesting any more general similarity in the two scenes.

27 *Troy Book* v 2927–31. This is noted by Renoir, *The Poetry of John Lydgate*, p. 113. We might suppose, too, that Lydgate had in mind to supply the 'geste / Of the siege of Thebes' read to Criseyde and her ladies at *Troilus* II 81–4.

28 Cf. *Troilus* v 1849–55. Pearsall, *John Lydgate*, p. 53, notes that Lydgate frequently echoes this particular sequence, and quotes an example from *Troy Book* III 4224–6.

29 'Medieval History, Moral Purpose, and the Structure of Lydgate's *Siege of Thebes*', *Publications of the Modern Language Association of America* 73 (1958), 463–74; pp. 463, 468. I regret that the discussion of *The Siege of Thebes* in John N. Ganim, *Style and Consciousness in Middle English Narrative* (Princeton 1983), was not available in time to be considered here.

30 *The English Language in Medieval Literature*, p. 32.

31 *John Lydgate*, p. 52.

32 E.g. J. C. Mendenhall, *Aureate Terms* (Philadelphia 1919); Elfriede Tilgner, *Die 'Aureate Terms' als Stilelement bei Lydgate* (Berlin 1936); *John Lydgate: Poems*, ed. John Norton-Smith (Oxford 1966), pp. 192–5.

33 Pearsall, *John Lydgate*, pp. 50–1.

34 E.g. *Astrolabe* pro. 9. *Orizonte* also occurs poetically in *Merchant's Tale* IV 1797, alongside *ark diurne, latitude*, and *hemysperie*. Possibly there, and probably in *Franklin's Tale*, there is an element of parody.

35 E.g. *Astrolabe* II 39 7.

36 *The Discarded Image*, p. 195.

37 The ambitious clumsiness of this sentence has been discussed, e.g. by Hammond, *English Verse Between Chaucer and Surrey*, p. 415, and Pearsall, *John Lydgate*, p. 59.

38 In this book I deliberately omit consideration of the complicated problems posed by the metre of Chaucer and his successors. My own opinion, to put it briefly and dogmatically, is that Chaucer was an innovator in metre as in style, and that in his decasyllabic verse (derived from French and especially Italian models, and the first such verse in English) he was struggling to overcome the strong tendency of the native English line to fall into a pattern of two two-stress phrases separated by a pause. In Chaucer's own work, the result is a delicate but increasingly confident and successful compromise between the syllabic and the accentual, but most of his English disciples, including Lydgate, while able to compose individual lines of a Chaucerian type, fail to grasp the principles of compromise and allow the native English pattern to reassert itself. In this as in other respects, what Chaucer strove to do single-handed had to be re-done in the early sixteenth century, and was not securely achieved until then.

39 The substance of this passage may be influenced, as Erdmann and Ekwall suggest, by *Anelida and Arcite* 50–3, but its rhetorical form parallels Arcite's 'O crueel goddes' (*Knight's Tale* I 1303).

40 For *digressio ad aliam partem materiae* see Geoffroi de Vinsauf, *Documentum*, in *Les arts poétiques*, ed. Faral, pp. 274–5, discussed in *The Works of Sir Thomas Malory*, ed. Eugene Vinaver (Oxford 1947), vol. I, pp. li-lii. Lydgate appears to have misunderstood Chaucer's use of *sentement* to mean 'personal, inner experience' (e.g. *Troilus* II 13); here, and in *Siege* 1903 quoted above, as Erdmann and Ekwall explain in their glossary, he uses it to mean 'substance'.

41 The source here is probably the *Roman de Edipus*, quoted by Erdmann and Ekwall, vol. II, p. 109.

42 E.g. *Le Livre du Cueur d'Amours Espris* of René d'Anjou, ff. 2, 12v, 47v, 55 (ed. F. Unterkircher (London 1975)), or the *Grandes Heures* of Anne of Brittany, f. 68v (in *Books of Hours*, ed. John Harthan (London 1977)).

43 The point is made by Dorothy Everett, *Essays on Middle English Literature* (Oxford 1956), p. 7, quoting Ker's remark from his *Epic and Romance* (London 1908), p. 321.

44 Cf. Spearing, *Medieval Dream-Poetry*, p. 173. A different view is taken by Judith Davidoff, 'The Audience Illuminated or New Light Shed on the Dream Frame of Lydgate's *Temple of Glass*', *Studies in the Age of Chaucer* 5 (1983), 103–25.

45 Cf. *Legend of Good Women* 875: 'How with his blod hirselve gan she peynt.'

46 1 *Tamburlaine* I i 80.

47 *John Lydgate*, p. 66.

48 'Medieval History, Moral Purpose', p. 467.

49 *A Map of Misreading* (New York 1975), p. 3. But I see no reason to suppose,
   with Lois Ebin, 'Chaucer, Lydgate, and the "Myrie Tale",' *Chaucer Review*
   13 (1978–9), 316–36, that Lydgate's misreading was a reinterpretation of
   Chaucer's conception of a "myrie tale" and thus 'an effort to deal with a
   problem Chaucer raises and resolves in one way in the *Canterbury Tales*'
   (p. 333).
50 Amphiorax too denounces
        The wooful wrath and contrariousté
        Of felle Mars in his cruelté.   (2398–9)
51 Ayers writes ('Medieval History, Moral Purpose', p. 465) that 'The moral
   and philosophical framework outlined by Lydgate in the almost countless
   moral passages of the poem appears to be essentially Boethian in character.'
   This may be so if one generalizes sufficiently, but I find nothing specifically
   reminiscent of Boethius in *The Siege of Thebes*.
52 Cf. the discussion of Lydgate's knowledge and appreciation of antiquity in
   C. David Benson, 'The Ancient World in John Lydgate's *Troy Book*',
   American Benedictine Review 24 (1973), 299–312.
53 Renoir's argument that in this passage among others Lydgate 'presents
   classical antiquity in a much more appealing light' than in his source (*The
   Poetry of John Lydgate*, pp. 119, 121–3) seems to me quite unconvincing, even
   if we could be sure that his source was identical with the extant *Roman de
   Edipus*. For similar denunciation by Lydgate of pagan superstition, see *Troy
   Book* I 909–11 (cited by Pearsall, *John Lydgate*, p. 131).
54 E. Talbot Donaldson, 'The Ending of *Troilus*', in his *Speaking of Chaucer*
   (London 1970), p. 99.
55 My emphasis is quite different from that of Renoir, who finds in the *Siege* and
   other later works of Lydgate 'a somewhat unmediaeval attitude towards
   classical antiquity', an attitude which approaches that of 'Renaissance
   humanism' (*The Poetry of John Lydgate*, p. 126). He even sums up the *Siege* as a
   'French mediaeval romance translated into an English Renaissance epic'
   (*ibid.*, p. 135). Renoir, in my view, sees the *Siege* in a false perspective
   through not considering the nature of its relationship to Chaucer's work.
   Kean similarly declares that 'We can certainly see, in Lydgate's praise of
   Classical heroes, a continuation of the attitude, and even the phrasing, of
   Chaucer in the *Knight's Tale* and the *Troilus*' (*Chaucer and the Making of English
   Poetry*, vol. II, p. 214); but this view too seems to me to derive from a failure
   to take account of the distinctive Renaissance elements in Chaucer's attitude.
   The views of Stephan Kohl, 'The *Kingis Quair* and Lydgate's *Siege of Thebes*
   as Imitations of Chaucer's "Knight's Tale"', *Fifteenth Century Studies* 2
   (1979), 119–34, are based on a reduction of *The Knight's Tale* to Boethian
   asceticism and an insufficiently close reading of *The Siege of Thebes*.
56 *The Springs of Helicon*, p. 17.
57 Margaret Aston notes that, so far as fifteenth-century learning in general is
   concerned, 'The earliest indigenous exponents of learning in the north were
   those who ... had experienced Italian culture firsthand' ('The Northern
   Renaissance', in *The Meaning of the Renaissance and the Reformation*, ed.
   Richard L. DeMolen (Boston 1974), pp. 71–129; p. 75).
58 See K. B. Mcfarlane, *Lancastrian Kings and Lollard Knights* (Oxford 1972),
   pp. 137–226.
59 *Documents of the Christian Church*, ed. Henry Bettenson, 2nd edn (Oxford
   1963), p. 182.

Notes to pages 90–107

60 *John Lydgate: Poems*, ed. Norton-Smith; lines 269–72. Cf. *Troilus and Criseyde* v 1706–8.

61 Ed. Norton-Smith, lines 226–8, 234–9.

62 *Selections from Hoccleve*, ed. Seymour, lines 1–4. The opening six stanzas of this poem are omitted from Huntington MS HM 111 and therefore from the edition cited in note 19 above.

63 Ed. Norton-Smith, lines 92–5, 103–5.

64 Ed. Furnivall, lines 379–85, 4982–3, 5006–8.

65 *Hoccleve's Works: The Minor Poems*, pp. 40, 41.

66 *Ibid.*, p. 18.

67 *De rerum natura* III 9; Horace, *Epistles* I xix; Propertius III iii 6; *De oratore* II 10; *De legibus* I 5. I am much indebted to Dr James Diggle for supplying me with these references.

68 As cited in chapter 2, note 44; p. 270.

69 *Chaucer and his World* (London 1978), p. 43.

70 'Parents and Children in the *Canterbury Tales*', in *Literature in Fourteenth-Century England*, ed. Piero Boitani and Anna Torti (Tübingen 1983), pp. 165–83.

71 Macrobius, *Commentary on the Dream of Scipio*, trans. William H. Stahl (New York 1952), p. 90.

72 *Medieval Dream-Poetry*, p. 11.

73 For an excellent study of this aspect of *The Parson's Tale*, see Lee W. Patterson, 'The "Parson's Tale" and the Quitting of the "Canterbury Tales"', *Traditio* 34 (1978), 331–80.

74 'Parents and Children in the *Canterbury Tales*', pp. 169–70, quoting *Man of Law's Tale* II 295.

75 Cf. chapter 2, note 41.

76 For a valuable study of the medieval conceptions of *auctoritas* which form the background to Chaucer's attitude, see M.-D. Chenu, *Introduction à l'étude de saint Thomas d'Aquin* (Montreal and Paris 1950), chapter 4.

77 *Inferno* I 82; *Purgatorio* XXII 67–9.

78 For more detailed discussion see my *Criticism and Medieval Poetry*, 2nd edn (London 1972), chapter 4.

79 Boccaccio was born in 1313, John Chaucer between 1310 and 1312.

80 *The Works of Geoffrey Chaucer*, p. 854.

81 Roland Barthes, *Image–Music–Text*, trans. Stephen Heath (London 1977), pp. 160, 161, 145, 146, 161.

82 *Ibid.*, p. 146.

83 *The Regement of Princes*, lines 1961–6.

84 Henry Scogan also recalls this theme from Chaucer's *Gentilesse* in his *Moral Balade*, in *Chaucerian and Other Pieces*, ed. Skeat, lines 65–104.

85 *Regement* 2084–5.

86 *Of Dramatic Poesy and other Essays*, ed. Watson, vol. I, p. 85.

87 *Caxton's Book of Curtesye*, ed. F. J. Furnivall, EETS ES 3 (London 1868), lines 330, 324, 400–6.

88 F 73–7.

89 *Fall of Princes*, ed. Bergen, II 999–1000.

90 *Troy Book* II 4715–19.

91 *Chaucerian and Other Pieces*, lines 239–40.

92 II 33–6, in *English Verse Between Chaucer and Surrey*, ed. Hammond, p. 42.

93 *The Anxiety of Influence*, p. 11. I note with interest, however, that in more

344

recent work Bloom announces that he has changed his mind and now acknowledges that 'the anxiety of influence ... is crucial in Euripides confronting Aeschylus or in Petrarch dreaming about Dante' (*The Breaking of the Vessels* (Chicago 1982), p. 15)

94 *Familiarium rerum libri* XXXII 19, trans. Bishop, *Letters from Petrarch*, pp. 198–9. The distinction Petrarch draws here is itself imitated from a classical author, the younger Seneca, to whom indeed he refers immediately after the passage quoted. Seneca writes:

> Even if there shall appear in you a likeness to him who, by reason of your admiration, has left a deep impress upon you, I would have you resemble him as a child resembles his father, and not as a picture resembles its original; for a picture is a lifeless thing. (*Epistulae Morales*, ed. and trans. R. N. Gumere (Cambridge, Mass., 1970), no. 84)

95 *The Anxiety of Influence*, p. 6.

96 *The Letters of D. H. Lawrence*, vol. I, ed. James T. Boulton (Cambridge 1979), p. 509.

97 *Troy Book* V 3519–26.

98 *Testament of Cresseid*, lines 41, 64. This and subsequent quotations from Henryson are taken from *The Works of Robert Henryson*, ed. Denton Fox (Oxford 1981).

99 *The Proloug of the First Buke of Eneados*, ed. Coldwell, lines 407, 418.

100 See J. A. Burrow, 'Autobiographical Poetry in the Middle Ages: the Case of Thomas Hoccleve', *Proceedings of the British Academy* 58 (1982), 389–412; p. 395, note 1.

101 *Regement of Princes* 2077–9.

102 On this general question, see Richard F. Green, *Poets and Princepleasers* (Toronto 1980). Green observes that 'the first English record of a specific payment for literary services is that made by John Wethamptstead, abbot of Saint Albans, to Lydgate, "for his translation of the life of Saint Alban into our language"' (p. 157).

103 *Letter to Gloucester*, ed. Norton-Smith. We have to imagine a medieval purse, a leather bag which would be stomach-shaped and could be turned inside-out when empty.

104 Cf. E. A. Thornley, 'The Middle English Penitential Lyric and Hoccleve's Autobiographical Poetry,' *Neuphilologische Mitteilungen* 68 (1967), 295–321. Burrow, in 'Autobiographical Poetry in the Middle Ages' (pp. 407–11), points out that petitions of a different kind were the main business of the Privy Seal office, and that Lord Fournival 'could be trusted to appreciate' Hoccleve's ingenious variant form of petition.

105 Cf. *OED*, 'token', senses 4 and 5, and Chaucer, *Shipman's Tale* VII 390; *by redy token* = 'in ready money'. There is a similar pun on the word earlier in *Shipman's Tale* VII 359.

106 Cf. Anne Middleton, 'Narration and the Invention of Experience: Episodic Form in *Piers Plowman*,' in *The Wisdom of Poetry*, ed. Benson and Wenzel pp. 91–122.

107 A parallel in this respect between Hoccleve and Margery Kempe is noted by Stephen Medcalf, in *The Later Middle Ages*, ed. Stephen Medcalf (London 1981), pp. 108ff.

108 Donald Davie, *The Poet in the Imaginary Museum* (Manchester 1977), p. 264.

109 *Selections from Hoccleve*, ed. Seymour, p. 106.

110 *Merchant's Tale* IV 1793; *Male Regle* 260.

111 Cf. Arthur B. Ferguson, *The Articulate Citizen and the English Renaissance* (Durham, N. C., 1965), chapter 3. Ferguson notes that Hoccleve's *Regement of Princes* belongs to the same tradition, but does not mention *La Male Regle*.

112 *Regement of Princes* 1975–7.

113 Cf. p. 258 below.

114 Cf. Pearsall, *John Lydgate*, p. 1: 'The history of English poetry, and of much Scottish poetry too, in the fifteenth century is as much the record of Lydgate's influence as of Chaucer's.' For this case as applied to Dunbar, see P. H. Nichols, 'Dunbar as a Scottish Lydgatian', *Publications of the Modern Language Association of America* 46 (1931), 214–24, and R. D. S. Jack, 'Dunbar and Lydgate,' *Studies in Scottish Literature* 8 (1970–1), 215–27.

4 Outside the Chaucerian tradition

1 For date see Thorlac Turville-Petre, *The Alliterative Revival* (Cambridge 1977), p. 124 and n. 28.

2 Cf. Kenneth Clark, *The Gothic Revival*, rev. edn (London 1962), chapter 1.

3 *The Awntyrs off Arthure*, ed. Ralph Hanna (Manchester 1974), p. 1. I quote the text of the *Awntyrs* from this edition.

4 In one of the most recent studies of alliterative poetry, *Middle English Alliterative Poetry and Its Literary Background*, ed. David A. Lawton (Cambridge 1982), it is attributed to the late fourteenth century by the editor (p. 12) and to the fifteenth by one of his contributors (p. 38).

5 *Awntyrs*, ed. Hanna, p. 52; A. I. Doyle, in *Middle English Alliterative Poetry*, ed. Lawton, p. 96. An early fifteenth-century date also seems to be implied by Thorlac Turville-Petre's study of the 'school' of poets using the thirteen-line stanza: '"Summer Sunday", "De Tribus Regibus Mortuis" and "The Awntyrs off Arthure": Three Poems in the Thirteen-Line Stanza', *Review of English Studies* n. s. 25 (1974), 1–14.

6 *A Literary History of England*, 2nd edn (London 1967), vol. 1, p. 190, n. 22.

7 'The English Alliterative Romances,' in *Arthurian Literature in the Middle Ages*, ed. R. S. Loomis (Oxford 1959), p. 527.

8 *Middle English Literature* (London 1951), pp. 52–3.

9 *Medieval English Poetry: the Non-Chaucerian Tradition* (London 1957), p. 252.

10 In his edition of the *Awntyrs* and '*The Awntyrs off Arthure*: An Interpretation,' *Modern Language Quarterly* 31 (1970), 275–97. Other discussion of the poem's structure is to be found in S. O. Andrew, 'Huchown's Works', *Review of English Studies* 5 (1929), 17, and David N. Klausner, 'Exempla and *The Awntyrs off Arthure*', *Mediaeval Studies* 34 (1972), 307–25.

11 '*The Aunters of Arthur at the Tern-Wathelan, Teil* I: Handschriften, Metrik, Verfasser' (Dissertation, Berlin 1883).

12 Cf. Philippa Tristram, *Figures of Life and Death in Medieval English Literature* (London 1976), pp. 162–7.

13 *Awntyrs*, p. 24.

14 The distinction between 'cohesion' and 'organic unity' is proposed by Derek Brewer, in connection with Malory's work, in *Essays on Malory*, ed. J. A. W. Bennett (Oxford 1963), p. 42 and n. 1.

15 *Triumphal Forms: Structural Patterns in Elizabethan Poetry*, (Cambridge 1970).

16 *Ibid.*, p. 21.

17 *Ibid.*, p. 23.

18 *Ibid.*, pp. 24–5.

19 *Ibid.*, p. 97, n. 1.
20 *Ibid.*, pp. 65, 97. It is perhaps worth noting that III 1271 is the central line of *Troilus and Criseyde* only in texts such as that of Robinson. A text based on one of those manuscript versions that omit Troilus's Book IV soliloquy or the stanzas describing the ascent of his soul through the heavenly spheres would have a different centre. This may have some bearing on the relationship of the different manuscript versions, for example in confirming the argument of B. A. Windeatt ('The Text of the *Troilus*', in *Essays on Troilus and Criseyde*, ed. Mary Salu (Cambridge 1979), pp. 1–22) that the shorter manuscripts do not represent an earlier Chaucerian plan.
21 See my article, 'Central and Displaced Sovereignty in Three Medieval Poems', *Review of English Studies*, n. s. 33 (1982), 247–61, pp. 257ff, and *Awntyrs*, ed. Hanna, pp. 44–7.
22 I am assuming, with Hanna and other editors, that the omission from the manuscripts of a line required by the pattern of rhyme and metre in the fourth stanza is the result of scribal error in the archetype.
23 This near-symmetry is obscured in Hanna's edition by the fact that he presents the final stanza as a separate unit, headed 'The Concluding Stanza' and seen as belonging to the first episode, and attaches the penultimate stanza to the second episode despite its having a different location.
24 *Awntyrs*, pp. 46–7.
25 For discussion of the general idea of diptych structure in medieval narrative, see William W. Ryding, *Structure in Medieval Narrative* (The Hague 1971), pp. 25–7, 40, and *passim*.
26 Serge Eisenstein, *The Film Sense* (London 1943), p. 14.
27 *Ibid.*, p. 19.
28 Written in 1929 about the situation of 1926; published in Serge Eisenstein, *Film Form* (London 1951), pp. 37–8. I am much indebted to Dr Stephen Heath for directing me to this passage, and for disentangling the chronology of Eisenstein's thought.
29 Larry D. Benson, *Art and Tradition in Sir Gawain and the Green Knight* (New Brunswick, 1965), p. 163.
30 *Scottish Alliterative Poems in Rhyming Stanzas*, ed. F. J. Amours, STS series 1, 27 and 38 (Edinburgh 1892, 1897).
31 *Awntyrs* 8, *Gawain* 1156.
32 *Sir Gawain and the Green Knight: A Stylistic and Metrical Study* (New Haven 1962), Part I, *passim*.
33 *Medieval English Poetry*, p. 257.
34 E.g. 'The failure of Guinevere to recognise the danger of her regal posturing is matched by Gawain's parallel failure to see that neither warfare nor courage provides a viable mode of existence' ('*The Awntyrs off Arthure*: An Interpretation', p. 291).
35 *The Alliterative Morte Arthure*, ed. Valerie Krishna (New York 1976), lines 515–53.
36 Rosalind Field, 'The Anglo-Norman Background to Alliterative Romance', in *Middle English Alliterative Poetry*, ed. Lawton, pp. 54–69; p. 66.
37 M. H. Keen, *England in the Later Middle Ages* (London 1973), p. 81.
38 More work remains to be done on the political context and implications of the *Awntyrs*. Further investigation might help to make its date more certain, though the very openness of interpretation associated with the diptych struc-

ture would require tactful handling and might still leave matters in
uncertainty.

39 A. C. Cawley *et al., Medieval Drama* (London 1983).
40 Derek Pearsall, *Old English and Middle English Poetry* (London 1977),
p. 252.
41 See for example the account of Stanley J. Kahrl, *Traditions of Medieval English
Drama* (London 1974), pp. 114–19, which notes how successfully *Mankind*
has been performed by students in pubs.
42 *English Drama from Early Times to the Elizabethans* (London 1950), p. 75.
43 This point is made by M. C. Bradbrook, *The Rise of the Common Player*
(London 1962), p. 32.
44 The argument against an evolutionary interpretation of the history of
medieval drama has been put in a distinguished essay by O. B. Hardison,
which appears as chapter 1 of his book, *Christian Rite and Christian Drama in
the Middle Ages* (Baltimore 1965).
45 A. C. Cawley notes, as evidence of this growing prosperity, that 'towards
the middle of the fifteenth century a start was made on rebuilding the Parish
Church, which by about 1470 was completely transformed into the Perpen-
dicular style' (ed. *The Wakefield Pageants in the Towneley Cycle* (Manchester
1958), p. xvii, n. 3).
46 E.g. Rossiter, *English Drama from Early Times to the Elizabethans*, chapter
4.
47 This and subsequent quotations from the Wakefield Master are taken from
the edition cited in note 45.
48 Richard Axton, however, has suggested that, in a performance lasting two
days, 'the *Prima Pastorum* concluded the first day's playing and the *Secunda
Pastorum* began the second day' (*European Drama of the Early Middle Ages*
(London 1974), p. 190).
49 Suggested by Rosemary Woolf, *The English Mystery Plays* (London 1972),
p. 192.
50 (Stanford 1966). Chapter 4 in particular expounds the structure of the cycles
and the meaning of that structure. Like almost everyone who writes
about the Mystery cycles, I am much indebted to Kolve's book in what
follows.
51 See Erich Auerbach, 'Figura', in his *Scenes from the Drama of European
Literature* (New York 1959), pp. 11–76. To this too I owe an obvious debt in
what follows.
52 I quote here and subsequently from *The York Plays*, ed. Richard Beadle
(London 1982).
53 *De diversis quaestionibus* II, qu. 2, n. 2, cited by Auerbach, 'Figura', p. 43.
54 Book V, pr. 6.
55 Cf. Burke, *The Renaissance Sense of the Past*, p. 27, and J. G. Mann, 'Instances
of Antiquarian Feeling in Medieval and Renaissance Art', *Archaeological
Journal* 89 (1932), 254–74.
56 Cf. p. 41.
57 Cf. K. B. Mcfarlane, 'Bastard Feudalism', *Bulletin of the Institute of Historical
Research* 20 (1943–5), 161–80.
58 It seems to be first found in the *Rhetorica ad Herennium* IV 8 (ed. and trans.
Harry Caplan (London 1954), pp. 252ff).
59 Ed. G. Mari, *Romanische Forschungen* 13 (1902), 920.
60 *Mimesis*, trans. W. Trask (Princeton 1953), p. 134.

61 I quote *Piers Plowman* here and subsequently from *The Vision of Piers Plowman*, ed. A. V. C. Schmidt (London 1978).

62 The notion of a general analogy between the culinary and rhetorical arts is implied, for example, in an extended metaphor used by Geoffroi de Vinsauf. Listing the various *morae* by which amplification may be achieved, he comes to apostrophe:

> Take delight in apostrophe; without it the feast would be ample enough, but with it the courses of an excellent cuisine are multiplied. The splendour of dishes arriving in rich profusion and the leisured delay at the table are festive signs. With a variety of courses we feed the ear for a longer time and more lavishly. Here is food indeed for the ear when it arrives delicious and fragrant and costly (*Poetria Nova of Geoffrey of Vinsauf*, trans. Margaret F. Nims (Toronto 1967), lines 266–71).

In this passage there is the most direct parallel between rhetorical *morae* and *mora mensae / Tardior* as the marker (*signum*) of a festive occasion. In the next passage quoted from the *Prima pastorum* it might not be too fanciful to see an analogy between the 'Good sawse' of the imaginary feast and the 'sawes swete' of eloquence by means of which Lydgate says that Chaucer preserves what he writes about (cf. p. 69 above), or between the 'chekyns endorde' (i.e. glazed with yolk of egg, but literally 'gilded', from OF *endoré*) and the 'aureate' terms of the high style.

63 Cf. discussion of *poesye* on p. 33 above.

64 *European Drama of the Early Middle Ages*, p. 192.

65 Cf. *Manciple's Tale* IX 203–22.

66 Cf. *Pardoner's Tale* VI 946–55.

67 Cf. chapter 3, note 38, above.

68 Woolf, *The English Mystery Plays*, p. 188, notes that this tale was also 'the subject of a lost French farce.'

69 It might be compared with the examples given by Barbara M. H. Strang, *A History of English* (London 1970), pp. 66–9, from the work of a twentieth-century popular novelist, Anne Blaisdell, to illustrate 'accurate observation of colloquial structures' (p. 66). The similarities are striking.

70 VI 1267–392.

71 2 388–96.

72 See especially Erwin Panofsky, *Early Netherlandish Painting* (Cambridge, Mass., 1953), vol. I, chapter 5.

73 Cf. *ibid.*, p. 144.

74 The following suggestions are among those proposed by Eugene B. Cantelupe and Richard Griffith, 'The Gifts of the Shepherds in the Wakefield "Secunda Pastorum": An Iconographical Interpretation', *Medieval Studies* 28 (1961), 328–35. I would not wish to follow the authors in the further refinements of their interpretation.

75 Studied by Robert C. Cosbey, 'The Mak Story and its Folklore Analogues', *Speculum* 20 (1945), 310–17.

76 Edgar Schell, 'Seeing Through a Glass Darkly: The Action Imitated by the *Secunda Pastorum*', *Modern Language Quarterly* 37 (1976), 3–14; p. 6

77 Claude Chidamian, 'Mak and the Tossing in the Blanket', *Speculum* 22 (1947), 186–90.

78 *Purity* 1088, from the edition cited in chapter 1, note 8.

79 I argued the case for this in *The Pardoner's Prologue and Tale*, ed. A. C. Spearing (Cambridge 1965), pp. 41–5.

5 Henryson and Dunbar

1 That little is set out and assessed by Douglas Gray, *Robert Henryson* (Leiden 1979), chapter 1, and Matthew P. McDiarmid, *Robert Henryson* (Edinburgh 1981), chapter 1.
2 Kinsley 62, lines 81–2.
3 John MacQueen, *Robert Henryson* (Oxford 1967), p. 22; see also chapter 1, *passim*.
4 Gray, *Robert Henryson*, p. 25. One aspect of the sceptical case has been rigorously argued by R. J. Lyall, 'Henryson and Boccaccio: A Problem in the Study of Sources', *Anglia* 99 (1981), 38–59.
5 It has been suggested that Henryson was consciously repeating Chaucer's 'elaborate literary joke' of a fictional source (Gregory Kratzmann, *Anglo-Scottish Literary Relations 1430–1550* (Cambridge 1980), p. 85). This is possible, though we cannot be sure that Henryson saw Lollius as a joke.
6 MacQueen, *Robert Henryson*, p. 55.
7 *Poems of Robert Henryson*, ed. Fox, notes on lines 478 and 518.
8 *Caxton's Book of Curtesye*, ed. Furnivall, lines 337–43.
9 Page 66.
10 This and subsequent quotations from Skelton are from *John Skelton: The Complete English Poems*, ed. John Scattergood (Harmondsworth 1983).
11 Lib. I, col. 5, in *Opera omnia* (Leiden 1703–6), vol. I.
12 J. L. Vives, *Opera omnia* (Valencia 1782–90), vol. II, p. 113.
13 Cited by Elizabeth Sweeting, *Early Tudor Criticism* (Oxford 1940), p. 110.
14 I set out the argument more fully in *Criticism and Medieval Poetry*, 2nd edn (London 1972), pp. 163–72.
15 See *Poems of Robert Henryson*, ed. Fox, p. 350.
16 Gray, *Robert Henryson*, p. 181.
17 An interesting further piece of evidence that this was a normal medieval view is found in Le Roy Ladurie, *Montaillou*, trans. Barbara Bray (New York 1978), p. 145: Arnaud de Verniolles testifies that, having relations with a prostitute 'At the time when they were burning the lepers', and then getting a swollen face, 'I was terrified and thought I had caught leprosy.'
18 A different view is taken by Ralph Hanna, 'Cresseid's Dream and Henryson's *Testament*', in *Chaucer and Middle English Studies*, ed. Beryl Rowland (London 1974), pp. 228–97. Hanna argues that Cresseid's vision is actually a self-deceptive dream, and 'thus has to be taken with a certain degree of ironic detachment' (p. 295); though I find this view attractive, it is not what the poem's narrator thinks, nor can I see any indication that it is what Henryson meant.
19 Kratzmann, *Anglo-Scottish Literary Relations*, p. 66.
20 *Poems of Robert Henryson*, ed. Fox, p. lxxxvii.
21 R. Klibansky, E. Panofsky and F. Saxl, *Saturn and Melancholy* (London 1964), pp. 203–4, cited in *ibid.*, p. 351.
22 *Ibid.*, p. lxxxviii.
23 Frank Kermode, *Essays on Fiction 1971–82* (London 1983), p. 43.
24 Gretchen Mieszkowski, 'The Reputation of Criseyde 1155–1500', *Transactions of the Connecticut Academy of Arts and Sciences* 43 (1971), 71–153.
25 *Filostrato* VIII 29, trans. Havely, *Chaucer's Boccaccio*, p. 101.
26 *The Prolog of the First Buk of Eneados*, ed. Coldwell, line 449.
27 This is the refrain of a popular fifteenth-century lyric in ironic praise of

women; see *Secular Lyrics of the Fourteenth and Fifteenth Centuries*, ed. R. H. Robbins (Oxford 1952), no. 38.

28 Mieszkowski, 'The Reputation of Criseyde', p. 121.

29 So *The Testament of Cresseid*, ed. Denton Fox (London 1968), p. 23.

30 *Triumphal Forms*, chapter 2.

31 Lee W. Patterson, 'Christian and Pagan in *The Testament of Cresseid*', *Philological Quarterly* 52 (1973), 696–714; p. 709.

32 *Ibid.*, pp. 707–8.

33 This is the refrain-line of Chaucer's balade, *Truth* (translating, of course, John 8:32).

34 This does not, however, imply that she has risen above Troilus, as is suggested by C. David Benson, 'Troilus and Cresseid in Henryson's *Testament*', *Chaucer Review* 13 (1978–79), 263–71: 'Although she seems to be in an inferior position to Troilus throughout the poem, Cresseid's response to her lot finally makes her morally a more admirable figure' (p. 268). Troilus's moral status is never questioned or even discussed in the *Testament*.

35 Gray, *Robert Henryson*, p. 33. Chapters 2–4 of Gray's book form an excellent general account of Henryson's fables.

36 M. H. Abrams, *The Mirror and the Lamp* (New York 1953), p. 272, citing Landino's *Commentary on Dante* (1481). The corresponding idea that God is an artist is not uncommon in the Middle Ages, especially in commentaries on the beginning of Genesis, but, as Panofsky has pointed out, even Leonardo in the sixteenth century avoids applying the terms *creare* and *creazione* to the artist (*Renaissance and Renascences*, p. 188, n. 3).

37 *Apology for Poetry*, ed. Shepherd, p. 100.

38 I am much indebted to the detailed annotation in *Poems of Robert Henryson*, ed. Fox.

39 The doubt is noted by I. W. A. Jamieson, '"To preue thare prechyng be a poesye": some thoughts on Henryson's poetics', *Parergon* 8 (April 1974), 24–36; p. 28.

40 Cf. William Kerrigan, 'The Articulation of the Ego in the English Renaissance', in *The Literary Freud: Mechanisms of Defense and the Poetic Will*, ed. Joseph H. Smith (New Haven 1980), pp. 261–308, for this view of Latin.

41 Fox cites a stanza from the Prologue to *The Fall of Princes* (435–41); for the *abbreviatio/amplificatio* theme see also *A Complaynt of a Loveres Lyfe*, 201–3.

42 This point is made by I. W. A. Jamieson, 'The Beast Tale in Middle Scots', *Parergon* 2 (April 1972), 28–36; p. 29.

43 *Poems of Robert Henryson*, ed. Fox, p. 196, n. 1. Lydgate's version is in his *Minor Poems*, vol. II, pp. 568–74.

44 E.g. Ferdinand de Saussure, *Course in General Linguistics*, trans. Wade Baskin (London 1974), p. 113.

45 *The Prison-House of Language* (Princeton 1972), pp. 143–4.

46 *Eruditionis Didascalicae Libri Septem*, Lib. VII, cap. iv, *Patrologia Latina* 176, col. 814.

47 Cf. Emile Mâle, *The Gothic Image* (London 1961), pp. 194–5.

48 This view has recently been reaffirmed by McDiarmid, *Robert Henryson*, p. 19: 'a collection of separate tales' which Henryson 'abandoned rather than completed.'

49 Noted by H. H. Roerecke in an unpublished dissertation cited in *Poems of Robert Henryson*, ed. Fox, p. lxxvii.

50 E.g. in *The Preiching of the Swallow* he writes,

> I tuke my staff, quhen this wes said and done,
> And walkit hame, for it drew neir the none.   (1823–4)

51 I discuss these in *Medieval Dream-Poetry*, pp. 187–90.

52 Fox substitutes *compair* (line 1477) from the Charteris print and the Bannatyne MS for the Bassandyne and Harleian reading *conqueist*, retained in *Poems and Fables of Robert Henryson*, ed. H. Harvey Wood, 2nd edn (Edinburgh 1958) and in *Robert Henryson: Poems*, ed. Charles Elliott, 2nd edn (Oxford 1974). Wood offers no explanation of *conqueist*; Elliott appears to misunderstand it, explaining (p. 156) that '*conqueist*, from the rest of the stanza, seems to mean "conquered one".' An instructive parallel to Henryson's use of the word to mean captives displayed in triumph can be found in a passage from Shakespeare quoted by *OED* to illustrate the term:

> What conquest brings he home?
> What tributaries follow him to Rome,
> To grace with captive bonds his chariot wheels?

(*Julius Caesar* I i 37–9)

Conqueist in this sense is an appropriate accompaniment to *honour triumphall*, and this is an argument in favour of retaining the Bassandyne and Harleian reading. It may be added that *tribunall* (line 1472) also appears to be used in its precise classical sense, and that this is an earlier instance of the word than any recorded in *OED*.

53 *Triumphal Forms*, p. 30.

54 If my argument concerning the symmetrical structure of the *Fables* is accepted, then it strongly suggests that the Bassandyne print, rather than the Bannatyne MS with its ten fables arranged in a different order, which is favoured by MacQueen, represents Henryson's own plan for the complete work. I discuss this question in more detail in 'Central and Displaced Sovereignty in Three Medieval Poems', pp. 256–7.

55 For further information on Dunbar and James IV see J. W. Baxter, *William Dunbar: A Biographical Study* (Edinburgh 1952); R. L. Mackie, *King James IV of Scotland* (Edinburgh 1958); Ian Simpson Ross, *William Dunbar* (Leiden 1981), Part I.

56 *Odes* III 30, lines 1–5, in *Horace: the Odes and Epodes*, trans. C. E. Bennett, (London 1914).

57 A comparable passage, slightly later in date, is in the *Conclusio* to Douglas's translation of the *Aeneid*; this too has a classical source, being translated from Ovid, *Metamorphoses* XV 871–9.

58 'If a *fili* [bard] was slighted, if the hospitality extended to him fell short of his often exorbitant demands, he instantly retaliated with a savage invective. It was popularly believed that such invective could literally raise blisters, and since nobody willingly had contact with those cursed by the bards, it could actually ruin its victim, his kith and kin' (Kurt Wittig, *The Scottish Tradition in Literature* (Edinburgh 1958), p. 70).

59 Information about the historical background to *The Thrissill and the Rois* is taken, without detailed acknowledgment, from the works listed in note 55 above and from Kinsley's annotations. I have written about the poem from a different point of view in *Medieval Dream-Poetry*, pp. 192–6, and also more briefly in 'Dream-Poems', in *Medieval Literature: Chaucer and the Alliterative Tradition*, ed. Boris Ford (Harmondsworth 1982), pp. 235–48; pp. 238–9.

60 For the interpretation of *Hymenaei* see the classic study by D. J. Gordon,

'*Hymenaei*: Ben Jonson's Masque of Union', in his *The Renaissance Imagination* (Berkeley 1975), pp. 157–84.

61 On this aspect of *The Parliament of Fowls* see David Chamberlain, 'The Music of the Spheres and *The Parliament of Fowls*', *Chaucer Review* 5 (1970–1), 32–56.

62 Here too there is a parallel with Jonson's *Hymenaei*, in which the marriage of Essex and Frances Howard is related to the desire of James VI and I to be the 'husband' to the 'whole isle' of Britain of which he was now king – another kind of mystical union (see Gordon, *The Renaissance Imagination*, pp. 168–74).

63 'Two Scots Poets: Dunbar and Henryson', in *Medieval Literature*, ed. Ford, pp. 318–30; p. 319.

64 *The Scots Literary Tradition*, 2nd edn (London 1962), p. 55.

65 *Dunbar: A Critical Exposition* (Edinburgh 1966), pp. 48, 52.

66 '*The Goldyn Targe*: Dunbar's Comic Psychomachia', *Papers on Language and Literature* 11 (1975), 339–56; p. 354.

67 I have argued this case in *Medieval Dream-Poetry*, *passim*.

68 Ross, *William Dunbar*, p. 242, suggests that the pale and green visage belongs to Dunbar himself 'as a typical Ovidian lover'; but nothing in the poem defines the poet as a lover at all. His role is that frequently adopted by Chaucer, as the observer and servant of lovers, not of love, and he is summoned not to love but to compose a poem. Compare too the opening line of Gavin Douglas's *Palice of Honour* (*The Shorter Poems of Gavin Douglas*, ed. P. J. Bawcutt (Edinburgh 1967)), which Dunbar may have been imitating: 'Quhen paill Aurora with face lamentabill . . . '

69 So Cruttwell, 'Two Scots Poets', pp. 318–19.

70 Kratzmann, *Anglo-Scottish Literary Relations*, p. 132.

71 This is not meant to deny the possibility of other influences, such as that of the sub-genre of French poem defined as the *jugement* by Roy J. Pearcy, 'The Genre of William Dunbar's *Tretis of the Tua Mariit Wemen and the Wedo*', *Speculum* 55 (1980), 58–74. I believe, however, that it is mistaken to suppose, as Pearcy evidently does, that the disturbing effect of the *Tretis* can be disposed of by relating it to this sub-genre and thus defining it as an 'entertainment' or '*jeu d'esprit*' (pp. 72–4).

72 Some evidence is given by Ross, *William Dunbar*, pp. 221ff.

73 See Gillian Freeman, *The Undergrowth of Literature* (London 1967), chapters 7 and 8.

74 There are complicated puns here on *payis*, meaning 'pleases' as well as 'pays', and on *purse*, meaning 'scrotum' as well as 'purse'.

75 As in *Meditatioun in Wyntir* (Kinsley 69).

76 As in lines 67, 188, 203, 215 and 485 of the *Tretis*. Ross (*William Dunbar*, p. 220) notes that '*Curage* in the sense of sexual vigour and inclination is a key term in the poem.' In the light of this it may be noted how neatly the phrase 'curage to indyt' (*The Thrissill and the Rois*, line 26, quoted on page 207 above) links sexual potency with writing: the May morning 'raises up' lovers but fails to arouse Dunbar's potency as a writer.

6 Skelton and Hawes

1 See Green, *Poets and Princepleasers*, p. 127.

2 The information about Hawes is conveniently collected in *Stephen Hawes: The Minor Poems*, ed. Florence W. Gluck and Alice B. Morgan, EETS OS 271 (London 1974), pp. xi–xiv.

3 This is the suggestion of Maurice Pollet, *John Skelton, Poet of Tudor England* (London 1971), p. 59.

4 The Latin is from Juvenal, *Satire* I, line 30: 'For it is difficult *not* to write satire.'

5 Line 8 of a supplement to *Why Come Ye Nat*, headed '*Contra quendam doctorem / Suum calumpniatorem*'.

6 *Statutes of Paul's School*, from *The Thought and Culture of the English Renaissance*, ed. Elizabeth M. Nugent (Cambridge 1956), p. 41.

7 Robert Whittinton, *In clarissimi Scheltonis Lovaniensis poeta*, and William Lily, epigram translated by Thomas Fuller; both cited from *Skelton: The Critical Heritage*, ed. Anthony S. G. Edwards (London 1981), pp. 49–53 and 48.

8 *English Literature in the Sixteenth Century* (Oxford 1954), p. 30.

9 Cf. *ibid.*, pp. 20ff.

10 Owen Chadwick, *The Reformation*, rev. edn (Harmondsworth 1968), p. 38.

11 See F. W. Brownlow, '*The book of Phyllyp Sparowe* and the Liturgy', *English Literary Renaissance* 9 (1979), 5–20.

12 For detailed comment on this incident from a somewhat different point of view, see Stanley E. Fish, *John Skelton's Poetry* (New Haven 1965), pp. 226–30.

13 I quote *The Pastime of Pleasure*, here and subsequently, from the edition of W. E. Mead, EETS OS 173 (London 1928).

14 *John Skelton's Poetry*, pp. 29–30. A salutary objection to Fish's approach is put by David A. Lawton in an important article, 'Skelton's Use of *Persona*', *Essays in Criticism* 30 (1980), 9–28: 'A literary *persona* is more likely to be a means than an end – a means, that is, of focusing our attention on various aspects of the text and the issues it raises. It is less likely that the primary function of a *persona* is to attract attention to itself for its own sake.' (p. 9).

15 *Caxton's Own Prose*, ed. Blake, p. 81.

16 *Carmen extemporale*, cited from *Skelton: The Critical Heritage*, ed. Edwards, pp. 44–5.

17 Cf. page 7 above.

18 Peter Brown, *Augustine of Hippo* (London 1967), p. 261, referring to *De Genesi contra Manichaeos* II 32.

19 *On Christian Doctrine*, II vi 7, trans. D. W. Robertson (Indianapolis 1958), p. 37.

20 Boccaccio, quoted on page 7 above.

21 *In Our Image and Likeness*, p. 703.

22 One tendency in discussion of these poems, of which Bernard F. Huppé and D. W. Robertson, *Fruyt and Chaf* (Princeton 1963), may stand as a representative example, has indeed read them as allegories requiring interpretation. The justification for doing so is based on a general view of medieval culture which seems to me fundamentally erroneous.

23 I quote the *Temple* from *John Lydgate: Poems*, ed. Norton-Smith.

24 *Ibid.*, p. 177.

25 See pp. 89–92 above.

26 This date for the *Defence*, accepted by Norton-Smith and Pearsall, seems more likely than the suggestion of W. F. Schirmer (*John Lydgate: A Study in the Culture of the Fifteenth Century* (London 1961), p. 134) that the poem belongs to 1431.

27 I quote the *Defence* from *John Lydgate: Poems*, ed. Norton-Smith.

28 I quote poems of Hawes other than the *Pastime* from the edition cited in note 2 above.

29 The finely appreciative account of the *Pastime* by C. S. Lewis (*The Allegory of Love*, pp. 278–85) does justice to this aspect of Hawes's achievement.

30 In line 81 I have restored *layne* (= 'conceal'), the reading of the Wynkyn de Worde text, in place of Gluck and Morgan's inexplicable emendation to *sayne*.

31 'P' may mean God the Father (*Pater*) and 'p/p/p' pains or sins (*peccata*). See Gluck and Morgan's note on this passage.

32 Cf. pp. 56–7, 90, above.

33 Cf. John Stevens, *Music and Poetry in the Early Tudor Court* (London 1961), chapter 9.

34 See the lengthy note by Gluck and Morgan on pp. 160–2 of their edition.

35 Scattergood follows the Fakes print in reading *publisshe*. In view of the argument of the passage quoted and of such phrases later in the poem as 'pullisshyd eloquence' (421) and 'Ornately pullysshid' (816), I think it better to follow the reading of the Cotton Vitellius MS.

36 See Scattergood, note on line 120.

37 So Paul D. Psilos, '"Dulle" Drede and the Limits of Prudential Knowledge in Skelton's *Bowge of Court*', *Journal of Medieval and Renaissance Studies* 6 (1976), 297–317; p. 312.

38 *Epistolae de Rebus Familiaribus et Variae*, ed. Joseph Fracassetti, vol. III (Florence 1863), pp. 410–11, Epist. Var. XLII; trans. and quoted by Helen Cooper, *Pastoral* (Cambridge 1977), p. 36.

39 Cited by Hugh Kenner, *The Invisible Poet* (New York 1959), p. 181, without reference.

40 I am especially indebted to the annotations in *John Skelton: Poems*, ed. Robert S. Kinsman (Oxford 1969), and to the discussions of Fish, *John Skelton's Poetry*, and F. W. Brownlow, '*Speke, Parrot*: Skelton's Allegorical Denunciation of Cardinal Wolsey', *Studies in Philology* 65 (1968), 124–39, and 'The Boke Compiled by Maister Skelton, Poete Laureate, Called Speake Parrot', *English Literary Renaissance* 1 (1971), 3–26.

41 Scattergood omits these, and I therefore quote them from *John Skelton: Poems*, ed. Kinsman.

42 *English Critical Essays (Nineteenth Century)*, ed. Edmund D. Jones (Oxford 1947), p. 110

43 Noted by Brownlow, 'The Boke Compiled', p. 8, n. 16.

44 This and subsequent quotations from poems by or attributed to Wyatt are from *Collected Poems of Sir Thomas Wyatt*, ed. Kenneth Muir and Patricia Thomson (Liverpool 1969), the poems being identified by 'MT' followed by their numbers in this edition; but for emendation, punctuation and interpretation I am often indebted to *Sir Thomas Wyatt: The Complete Poems*, ed. R. A. Rebholz (Harmondsworth 1978). The poem quoted here is MT CCLIX.

45 Brownlow, 'The Boke Compiled', p. 11.

46 The second, third and fourth Envoys all begin by addressing the book simply as 'Parott' (301, 324, 357).

47 H. L. R. Edwards, *Skelton: The Life and Times of an Early Tudor Poet* (London 1949), p. 193.

48 Text from John Stevens, *Music and Poetry*, p. 348.

49 *English Literature in the Sixteenth Century*, p. 139.

50 For a convincing statement of this interpretation, see Brownlow, '*Speke, Parrot*: Skelton's Allegorical Denunciation'.
51 See page 235 above.

7 Wyatt and Surrey

1 Patricia Thomson, *Sir Thomas Wyatt and his Background* (London 1964), p. 32.
2 If indeed the latter is by Wyatt; the unctuousness with which it concedes the failings of those it purports to mourn makes me hope that it is not. There are serious problems in establishing the canon of Wyatt's work. 'In mornyng wyse' is found in the Blage MS, where it is not attributed to him.
3 The poem 'Dryvyn to desyre, a drad also to dare' (MT CXXIX) was published in the late 1530s. I see not the smallest reason to suppose that it is by Wyatt.
4 An apparent exception is 'Payne of all payne' (MT CCXIII), which has a stanza beginning 'Recorde of Therence in his commedis poeticall' (24). It also includes references to 'Cupido' (10) and to 'Lucrese' (31) and 'Tarquinus' (33) and an invocation, 'O Venus, ladye, of love the goddess' (45). It clearly belongs to a quite different literary tradition, and there is neither evidence that it is by Wyatt nor reason to attribute it to him. It is a very bad poem.
5 Among the rare exceptions is 'jalous Dispite', who starts suddenly aside in dismay in MT XLVI. This poem may well be a translation, though no source has been identified. Love and Fortune are not infrequently given active roles, but they had perhaps come to feel more like mythological figures than personifications.
6 George Puttenham, *The Arte of English Poesie* (1589), ed. G. D. Willcock and A. Walker (Cambridge 1936), p. 60. See John Stevens, *Music and Poetry*, pp. 147ff, for an admirable account of the background to Wyatt's 'balets' in the life of the medieval courts, to which I am much indebted. It remains the case that, with the exception of Charles of Orleans, we have no identifiable courtier-poet the morphology of whose work is at all comparable with Wyatt's. The situation might, of course, be different if a large body of lyrics by, say, the Duke of Suffolk had happened to survive.
7 See p. 207 above.
8 For a fine account of the sexual politics of Wyatt's love-poetry, see Stephen Greenblatt, *Renaissance Self-Fashioning* (Chicago 1980), chapter 3.
9 Cf. chapter 4, note 57.
10 *Music and Poetry*, p. 151. My whole acount of Wyatt as courtly lyricist owes much to Stevens's classic reconstruction of the 'game of love'; he also uses (p. 216) as one of his illustrations the passage from *The Franklin's Tale* that I go on to quote.
11 Lines 941, 943, 949, 952, 954.
12 *Music and Poetry*, p. 212.
13 *Humanism and Poetry in the Early Tudor Period* (London 1959), pp. 168, 171.
14 *The Singer of Tales* (Cambridge, Mass., 1960).
15 Cf. C. S. Lewis, *English Literature in the Sixteenth Century*, p. 230.
16 Cf. John Kerrigan, 'Wyatt's Selfish Style', *Essays and Studies* n. s. 34 (1981), 1–18: 'Chaucer, Lydgate and those early Tudor poets who followed Lydgate in the *De casibus* tradition were fascinated by fortune because of her power over the destiny of all mankind. Wyatt was interested in her only in so far as she threatened the integrity of the particular self' (p. 1). For a substantial and perceptive general comparison with Chaucer, see Helen Cooper, 'Wyatt and Chaucer: A Re-appraisal', *Leeds Studies in English* 13 (1982), 104–23.

17 Chaucer's repetition of *trouthe* in this part of Book v is striking: see lines 1670, 1676, 1679, 1681 (*trowe*), 1687, 1707, 1712 (*trewe*).

18 The 'hammers' that work in his head (7) and 'tune the tempre to my song' (10) are of course metaphorical, but deeply conventional.

19 I summarize Fowler's acount from *Triumphal Forms*, pp. 99–101. I do not share his view that stanza 5 can be seen as showing 'God's retribution' or that the reference to the sun in that stanza is meant to suggest *Sol Justitiae*. The poem in my opinion remains within the limits of courtly mythology, and vengeance is taken not by God but by Cupid. 'Behold, Love, thy power how she dispisith' (MT 1) turns on a similar idea, derived from its Petrarchan source.

20 I would mention especially Thomson, *Sir Thomas Wyatt and his Background*; D. L. Guss, 'Wyatt's Petrarchism: An Instance of Creative Imitation in the Renaissance', *Huntington Library Quarterly* 29 (1965), 1–15; Greenblatt, *Renaissance Self-Fashioning*, chapter 3; Thomas M. Greene, *The Light in Troy* (New Haven 1982), chapter 12.

21 *Sir Thomas Wyatt and his Background*, pp. 172–3.

22 By Sergio Baldi, 'Sir Thomas Wyatt and Vellutello', *English Studies Today* 4 (Rome 1966), 121–7. Baldi, following Thomson, believes that Wyatt read Petrarch with Vellutello's commentary, newly published when he visited Italy in 1527.

23 I rely on Muir and Thomson's edition for information about the early commentaries on *Rime sparse* 98.

24 From the preface to the first edition of *Tottel's Miscellany* (*Songes and Sonettes*, 1557), quoted from *Wyatt: The Critical Heritage*, ed. Patricia Thomson (London 1974), p. 32.

25 See John A. Yunck, *The Lineage of Lady Meed* (Notre Dame 1963), chapters 2 and 3.

26 *The History of English Poetry* (1781), cited from *Wyatt: The Critical Heritage*, ed. Thomson, p. 41.

27 *Henry Howard Earl of Surrey: Poems* (Oxford 1964). I quote Surrey from this edition, identifying the poems by the numbers Jones gives them.

28 *The Thought and Culture of the English Renaissance*, p. 121.

29 Cf. Walter R. Davis, 'Contexts in Surrey's Poetry', *English Literary Renaissance* 4 (1974), 40–55.

30 J. J. Scarisbrick, *Henry VIII* (London 1976), p. 621.

31 It might be added that Surrey's relativism also enables him to enter imaginatively into other situations: thus 'Laid in my quyett bed' (Jones 25) is written as if by a man far older than Surrey lived to be.

32 This too is discussed by Davis, 'Contexts in Surrey's Poetry'.

33 *Henry Howard Earl of Surrey: Poems*, p. xxiii.

34 (London 1966).

35 Yates, *ibid.*, p. 104.

36 Noted by Fowler, *Triumphal Forms*, p. 102. Elsewhere Fowler points out that Petrarch wrote a 38-line panegyric on his mother, who also died aged 38; see *Conceitful Thought* (Edinburgh 1975), p. 30.

37 *Hamlet* III i 153–56.

38 Fowler, *Triumphal Forms*, p. 70. Fowler also notes (pp. 101–1) that the quatrains are arranged symmetrically about the sovereign mid point, with Fortune in stanzas 3 and 7 and 'manufacturing imagery' (*stithe* and *molde*) in stanzas 2 and 8. It might be added that the references to heaven in the first and last quatrains enclose those to Fortune; she in her mutability is ruler of the

earthly world, but is defeated by Wyatt's constancy of mind, given him from above. I am not convinced by Fowler's suggestion that the Seven Gifts of the Holy Spirit, listed in an unusual order, form an underlying scheme for the poem (*Conceitful Thought*, pp. 25–30).

39 Cf. C. W. Jentoft, 'Surrey's Five Elegies: Rhetoric, Structure, and the Poetry of Praise', *Publications of the Modern Language Association of America* 91 (1976), 23–32; p. 26. I am generally indebted to this article, and also to another by Jentoft, 'Surrey's Four "Orations" and the Influence of Rhetoric on Dramatic Effect', *Papers on Language and Literature* 9 (1973), 250–62.

40 *Henry Howard Earl of Surrey: Poems*, p. 125.

41 E.g. Jentoft, 'Surrey's Five Elegies', p. 29, with letter by Anthony Low and Jentoft's reply, *Publications of the Modern Language Association of America* 91 (1976), 914–15.

42 Jentoft, 'Surrey's Five Elegies', p. 27.

Epilogue: *The Shepheardes Calender*

1 Richard Helgerson, *Self-Crowned Laureates* (Berkeley 1983), p. 60. Helgerson's book, published after most of mine was written, offers insights of great importance into the developing system of authorial roles in the English Renaissance.

2 I quote *The Shepheardes Calender* from *Spenser's Minor Poems*, ed. Ernest de Sélincourt (Oxford 1910), with his line numbers for both prose and verse. The phrase quoted here is from the heading to the preface.

3 In my view, E. K.'s commentary, unlike Skelton's eccentric glosses on *Speke Parott*, is intended with entire seriousness, and it is only a current fashion for ironic readings that makes a recent critic write as follows: 'E. K.'s commentary may be a kind of academic in-joke. E. K. represents one way of confronting a literary text: detached, analytical, aware of precedents, full of schemes, but curiously aloof from the emotional force of the poetry. His commentary figures as a parody of a certain kind of overly zealous reader.' (Bruce R. King, 'On Reading *The Shepheardes Calender*', *Spenser Studies* 1 (1980), 69–93; p. 89).

4 *Animadversions upon the Remonstrants Defence* (1641), cited in *Spenser: The Critical Heritage*, ed. R. M. Cummings (London 1971), p. 163.

5 *An Apology for Poetry*, ed. Shepherd, p. 133.

6 Cf. Mason, *Humanism and Poetry*, pp. 229–30.

7 W. L. Renwick, *Edmund Spenser: An Essay on Renaissance Poetry* (London 1925), p. 39.

8 Hallett Smith, *Elizabethan Poetry* (Cambridge, Mass., 1952), p. 38.

9 King, 'On Reading *The Shepheardes Calender*', p. 90, notes the 12 × 12 form but not the connection with the New Jerusalem.

10 I assume that Spenser's Protestantism might have led him to read *Piers Plowman* in its sixteenth-century printed form; but the allusion may be to the pseudo-Chaucerian *Plowman's Tale*.

Index

Index

Index

Index

Index

Spearing, A. C. 3 n7, 23 n21, 35 n48, 81 n44, 94 n72, 101 n78, 127 n21, 163 n79, 169 n14, 196 n51, 199 n54, 206 n59, 212 n67
Spearing, J. E. 35 n48
Speght, Thomas 328
Speirs, John 124, 134, 212
Spenser, Edmund 64, 92, 284, 307, 317, 328–32
  Faerie Queene 38, 254
  Shepheardes Calender 328–32
Spurgeon, Caroline F. E. 62 n10
Statius 33, 100, 242, 332
  Thebaid 32 n38, 42
Stevens, John 259 n33, 272 n48, 280 n6, 286 and n10, 289, 294
Stopes, Marie 21
Strang, Barbara M. H. 157 n69
Strode, Ralph 44
Strohm, Paul 63 n13
Surrey, Countess of 226, 236, 243
Surrey, Henry Howard Earl of 307, 311–26, 327–8, 330
Sweeting, Elizabeth 169 n13
Szarmach, Paul E. viii

Tatlock, J. S. P. 20 n16, 33 nn39, 40 and 42, 40 n55
Tennyson, Alfred Lord 64
Theodoric 44
Thomson, Patricia 269 n44, 278 n1, 300 n20, 301, 304 n22, 305 n23, 306 n24
Thornley, E. A. 112 n104
Thynne, William 17, 166
Tilgner, Elfriede 72 n32
Torti, Anna viii, 93 n70
Tottel's Miscellany 269, 290, 306
Toynbee, Paget 24 n22
Trajan 52 n75
Trapp, J. B. 6 n18
Trental of St Gregory 124, 125
Trevisa, John 27 n29
Trinkaus, Charles 2 n4, 4 n11, 45 n67, 46 nn69 and 71, 249
Tristram, Philippa 125 n12

Tudor, Margaret 199, 206, 208, 210, 211, 214
Tuke, Sir Brian 17
Turville-Petre, Thorlac 122 n1, 123 n5
Twyne, Thomas 3 n10

Underwood, Dale 55 n80
Usk, Thomas, *Testament of Love* 35, 39, 43, 60

Valturio, Roberto, *De re militari* 198
Van Eyck, Hubert and Jan 159
Vellutello, Alessandro 304 n22
Venus 23 n20, 24, 26, 27, 47, 48, 50, 113, 166, 169, 172–3, 174, 175, 176, 229, 259, 280 n4
Villani, Filippo, *Liber de civitatis Florentiae famosis civibus* 10
Vinaver, Eugene 78 n40
Vincent of Beauvais 45
Vinci, Leonardo da 187 n36
Virgil 12, 13, 14, 22 and n18, 23, 24, 33, 38, 45, 100–2, 108, 110, 147, 152–3, 242, 244, 245, 248, 312–13, 329–30, 332
  Aeneid 9, 13, 22, 32 n38, 76, 110, 122, 153, 180, 196, 203 n57, 246, 312, 314
  Eclogues 147, 153, 272
  Georgics 153
Visconti, Bernabò 18
Vives, Juan Luis 169–71

Wakefield Master 143–63, 279
  Coliphizacio 144
  Mactatio Abel 144
  Magnus Herodes 144
  Prima pastorum 144, 146–7, 148–9, 151–3, 152 n62, 155
  Processus Noe 144, 158
  Secunda pastorum 144, 146, 147, 149, 151, 153–4, 157–8, 159–62
Waldron, Ronald 3 n8
Wallace, David 38 n54
Walton, John 107
Wars of Alexander 122

368